Finding a Voice at Work?

Finding a Voice at Work?

New Perspectives on Employment Relations

Edited by

Stewart Johnstone

Peter Ackers

OXFORD
UNIVERSITY PRESS

UNIVERSITY PRESS

Great Clarendon Street, Oxford, OX2 6DP,
United Kingdom

Oxford University Press is a department of the University of Oxford.
It furthers the University's objective of excellence in research, scholarship,
and education by publishing worldwide. Oxford is a registered trade mark of
Oxford University Press in the UK and in certain other countries

© Oxford University Press 2015

The moral rights of the authors have been asserted

First Edition published in 2015
Impression: 2

Published in the United States of America by Oxford University Press
198 Madison Avenue, New York, NY 10016, United States of America

British Library Cataloguing in Publication Data

Data available

Library of Congress Control Number: 2014945599

ISBN 978–0–19–966800–7 (Hbk.)
ISBN 978–0–19–966801–4 (Pbk.)

Printed and bound by
CPI Group (UK) Ltd, Croydon, CR0 4YY

Links to third party websites are provided by Oxford in good faith and
for information only. Oxford disclaims any responsibility for the materials
contained in any third party website referenced in this work.

To Jayshree
To Moira

FOREWORD

For all its ambiguities, voice can perhaps best be seen as the Holy Grail of employee relations; it is the promise of a harmonious and effective employment relationship built on trust, fairness, and respect. Historically, voice was viewed as a means for employees to influence their terms and conditions, or to express dissatisfaction with the employment relationship: 'voice or exit' (Hirschman 1970; Freeman and Medoff 1984). Voice in this sense had only limited appeal for many employers. Shifting attitudes occurred when employee voice was seen to be key to employee *involvement* in the workplace, and employers continue to search for more effective ways of releasing employee voice. Case-study research by Marchington et al. for the Chartered Institute of Personnel and Development (CIPD) in 2001 on *Management Choice and Employee Voice* found managers were in little doubt that voice had a positive impact on performance, particularly through the number of ideas that emerged from employee feedback. CIPD Employee Outlook Surveys also confirm a relationship between employee engagement and the quality of top-down and bottom-up communications, and highlight the need for organizations to further improve communication in both directions (CIPD 2013). Where they are persuaded that engagement is the objective, employers understandably want to know what practical steps they can take to deliver it. Seen in this context, voice is essentially an empirical question regarding what actions by management, employees, and/or trade unions are best geared to releasing or promoting voice. This will depend in part on organizational history and context.

While there is a significant element of continuity in management interest in employee voice in recent decades, organizations have certainly put more effort into getting messages out to employees. The major influence on the shape of voice mechanisms has been the changing institutional, industrial, technological, and demographic environment to which managers have had to adapt. Despite the decline in collective bargaining and statutory support for consultation on a range of issues from health and safety to collective redundancies, formal consultation processes have continued to be used, particularly in the public sector. However, there is also an irony in that the sector that pioneered and continues to make most use of collective consultation—the public sector—is also the sector where employees are least likely to feel that their voice is being heard, and least satisfied with the way they are managed. The overall balance has shifted towards more direct voice forms. Some kinds of voice initiative, including problem-solving groups, have declined in significance while others, including the use of employee surveys, have increased.

The development of the 'Engage for Success' movement also suggests that releasing authentic employee voice, in the sense of a two-way dialogue, is attracting increased interest by employers. Employee voice, whether expressed through direct or indirect means, was identified in the initial report by the employee engagement task force (MacLeod and Clarke 2009) as one of the four key drivers of employee engagement. Although it is the least well understood of the four engagement drivers identified, employee voice can be seen as the ingredient building on and reinforcing the other three drivers—leadership, integrity, and line management. In other words, it is the product of a workplace culture where people feel able to speak out with a degree of confidence that they will be heard and not penalized for doing so. For all the criticism that repeated use of employee engagement surveys may become mechanical and add little value, well-designed surveys have the merit of focusing attention on the bottom line for employee engagement. Indeed, as contributors to this book suggest, it is becoming increasingly difficult to distinguish between the concepts of employee voice and engagement (CIPD 2010).

However, the Workplace Employment Relations Studies (WERS) have continued to find no significant change in institutions for tapping into employee voice, with no expansion of workplace joint consultation machinery between 2004 and 2011 (Kersley et al. 2006; van Wanrooy et al. 2013). While anecdotal evidence suggests it is becoming increasingly difficult in many organizations to find people willing to serve as employee representatives on consultation bodies, there is evidence (e.g. Marchington and Kynighou 2012) that employer interest in promoting employee involvement and participation, including direct forms of employee voice, is increasing. The findings of the WERS 2011 survey also show a majority of employees believe that managers are either good or very good at seeking their views, though rather fewer believe that employers are good at responding to suggestions or allowing them to influence decisions (van Wanrooy et al. 2013). Possibly the least contested form of employee voice, and certainly less easy to monitor or measure than other forms of voice, is that identified by Marchington as 'informal' (Marchington and Suter 2013). This links closely with workplace culture and high performance working practices, and will reflect the degree to which line managers are willing to encourage feedback by employees and take action on their ideas. Informal voice will often rely on excellent working relationships between employees and front-line managers. These relationships do not typically rely on formal voice mechanisms and may be influenced as much by people with psychology or organization development backgrounds as by employee relations professionals.

Though research suggests it is the combination of direct and indirect forms of voice that has the most positive impact on employee attitudes, few British employers see collective forms of voice as critical to implementing strategies to increase employee engagement, preferring to focus on the exchange of information directly between managers and employees. Clearly, however, there can be a significant interaction between collective and individual forms of employee voice, which can be mutually reinforcing. An unswerving focus on individual attitudes may lead employers to underplay wider factors, such as restructuring or the design of pay systems, that can have a significant influence on attitudes across the workforce. In the absence of some form of employee representation, employees' opinions may come across to managers as little more than background noise. Interestingly, with notable exceptions (e.g. Johnstone et al. 2010; Charlwood and Angrave 2014), the role of non-union representatives on joint consultation bodies has been relatively neglected by mainstream academic research. In recent years a number of employers have set up new employee forums involving elected non-union representatives, and a CIPD survey of employee relations in 2011 found that more than a third of employers with representative arrangements for informing and consulting with employees made use of non-union employee representatives (only), while two in five consulted with both union and non-union representatives (CIPD 2011).

Early conferences in the CIPD/LSE annual series on *Voice and Value*, initiated in 2000, were dominated by discussions of the EU directive on employee information and consultation. A major focus of continuing public policy debate is whether *further* legislation is needed to drive increased take up of formal consultation, and there have been calls for the existing regulations to be strengthened, possibly by requiring a lower threshold of employee support for consultation machinery to be established. However, a study by Warwick researchers for the Department of Business and Industry confirmed there has been little trade union interest in making use of the legislation (Hall et al. 2010), so in light of trade union ambivalence about the value of consultation processes, it seems unlikely such calls will be influential. Given the long-term mistrust that trade unions in the UK have displayed of the consultation process, it must be doubtful how much impact amending the legislation would have on their behaviour. The Warwick study also shows that, in order to be effective, consultation needs to have positive support by the employer. If remodelling the existing regulations was seen mainly as a vehicle for reviving trade union influence in the workplace, this would do little to encourage employers to embrace it as a means of promoting improved business performance. But if voice is not simply about maintaining or increasing trade union influence in the workplace, what are its boundaries and how is it to be identified, measured, and supported?

For example, the treatment of whistleblowers offers an instructive test for the presence of employee voice. Do employees feel comfortable raising concerns about misbehaviour and wrongdoing in the workplace? Recent debate about whistleblowing has focused largely on seeking to strengthen the legal framework for protecting, or at least offering legal remedies to, whistleblowers. But much evidence suggests that such remedies are unlikely to be effective in those many cases where the whistleblower's action threatens the reputation of the organization or the jobs of colleagues. Whistleblowers may be reluctant to come forward unless they feel that senior management really wants to hear—and take action on—their message. Increased use of social media has also opened up a new front in the voice debate. There is no doubt that tools such as Yammer can give employees opportunities to engage in open discussion about a range of matters affecting their everyday working lives. What is currently less clear is how far social media has enhanced the quality of dialogue between managers and employees, and what greater influence employees may feel they have over management decisions. Employee engagement may be a flawed concept but it is not a passing fad. It inherits and builds on the legacy of past generations of academics and managers who have promoted good practice in managing the employment relationship. Employee voice may be equally hard to pin down but it represents a belief that how employees are treated matters. However, we need to learn to look at employee voice through a number of different lenses.

In many organizations, voice is not about trade unions or about collective consultation, but about changing the culture. Management development and coaching, and organization development techniques, can have a bigger part to play in improving the effectiveness of communication between colleagues at all levels. The behaviour of line managers and their ability to engage their team members, though identified as one of the four key drivers, is a chronically neglected area of practice, and an interesting area for further research is the scope for coaching line managers in how to conduct positive conversations with their teams. Partnership relations between employers and unions can be used to effect culture change but many employers are tackling culture change more directly, by encouraging employees to be more assertive in putting forward ideas and by training line managers to listen more intelligently. A report for CIPD in 2012 (*Where Has All the Trust Gone?*) emphasized the significance of communication for maintaining and repairing employee trust (Hope-Hailey et al. 2012). So voice can reinforce the key message that senior managers need to be open, transparent, and authentic if they wish to build workplace relationships that can be a basis for high levels of engagement and sustainable business performance.

Did the global financial crisis produce a shift in management thinking about voice? The crisis demonstrated that many employers were willing, and indeed anxious, to build on their relationships with trade unions to negotiate or reinforce support for negative changes in pay and/or conditions of employment in the interest of protecting jobs. Research suggests that changes following the crisis were rarely imposed without employee consultation of some kind (Marchington and Kynighou 2012). It has long been evident that formal practices for consulting employees can be crucial at times of crisis (the 'burning platform'). But the economic crisis probably said more about employer understanding of the risks involved in making major changes to employment conditions, combined with a welcome realism by trade unions, than about any significant long-term shift in employer attitudes. The concept of voice suffers from the malaise that has afflicted much thinking about employee relations since the decline of trade unions and collective bargaining has displaced many of the former certainties about its proper content and focus. Like other forms of democracy, there is no reason for thinking that workplace democracy should be easy to manage. Voice shares with 'mutuality' and 'partnership' the nature of an aspiration, and in order to be effective, voice needs to be underpinned by mutual trust, fairness, and respect. Employers need to pay attention to the quality and outcomes of voice within their organization, not just the process (Beaumont and Hunter 2003, 2005).

Mike Emmott
Chartered Institute of Personnel and Development

■ REFERENCES

Beaumont, P. and Hunter, L. C. (2003) *Information and Consultation: From Compliance to Performance.* London: Chartered Institute of Personnel and Development.

Beaumont, P. and Hunter, L. C. (2005) *Making Consultation Work: The Importance of Process.* London: Chartered Institute of Personnel and Development.

Charlwood, A. and Angrave, D. (2014) *Worker Representation in Great Britain 2004–2011: An Analysis Based on the Workplace Employment Relations Study.* London: ACAS.

CIPD (2010) *Voice and Engagement: How Does Collective Consultation Contribute?* London: CIPD. [Online.] Available at: <http://www.cipd.co.uk/hr-resources/research/voice-engagement-collective-consultation-contribution.aspx> [accessed 19 May 2014].

CIPD (2011) *Employment Relations 2011.* London: CIPD. [Online.] Available at: <http://www.cipd.co.uk/hr-resources/survey-reports/employment-relations-2011.aspx> [accessed 19 May 2014].

CIPD (2013) *Employee Outlook.* London: CIPD. [Online.] Available at: <http://www.cipd.co.uk/research/_employee-outlook> [accessed 19 May 2014].

Freeman, R. and Medoff, J. (1984) *What Do Unions Do?* New York: Basic Books.

Hall, M., Hutchinson, S., and Purcell, J. (2010) *Information and Consultation under the ICE Regulations: Evidence from Longitudinal Case Studies.* London: Department for Business, Innovation and Skills. [Online.] Available at: <https://www.gov.uk/government/uploads/system/uploads/attachment_data/file/32158/10-1380-information-consultation-ice-regulations.pdf> [accessed 19 May 2014].

Hirschman, A. (1970) *Exit, Voice and Loyalty: Responses to Decline in Firms, Organizations and States.* Cambridge, MA: Harvard University Press.

Hope-Hailey, V., Searle, R., and Dietz, G. (2012) *Where Has All the Trust Gone?* London: Chartered Institute of Personnel and Development. [Online.] Available at: <http://www.cipd.co.uk/hr-resources/research/where-trust-gone.aspx> [accessed 19 May 2014].

Johnstone, S., Ackers, P., and Wilkinson, A. (2010) Better than Nothing? Is Non-Union Partnership a Contradiction in Terms? *Journal of Industrial Relations*, 52(2), 151–68.

Kersley, B., Alpin, C., Forth, J., Bryson, A., Bewley, H., Dix, G., and Oxenbridge, S. (2006) *Inside the Workplace: Findings from the 2004 Workplace Employment Relations Survey.* Basingstoke: Routledge.

MacLeod, D. and Clarke, N. (2009) *Engaging for Success: Enhancing Performance through Employee Engagement.* London: Department for Business, Innovation and Skills. [Online.] Available at: <http://www.bis.gov.uk/files/file52215.pdf> [accessed 19 May 2014].

Marchington, M. and Kynighou, A. (2012) The Dynamics of Employee Involvement and Participation during Turbulent Times. *International Journal of Human Resource Management*, 23(16, September), 3336–54.

Marchington, M. and Suter, J. (2013) Where Informality Really Matters: Patterns of Employee Involvement and Participation in a Non-Union Firm. *Industrial Relations*, 52(S1, January), 284–313.

Marchington, M., Wilkinson, A. J., Ackers, P., and Dundon, T. (2001) *Management Choice and Employee Voice.* London: Chartered Institute of Personnel and Development.

van Wanrooy, B., Bewley, H., and Bryson, A. (2013) *The 2011 Workplace Employment Relations Study: First Findings.* London: Department for Business, Innovation and Skills in association with ACAS, ESRC, NIESR, and UKCES. [Online.] Available at: <http://www.gov.uk/government/publications/the-2011-workplace-employment-relations-study-wers> [accessed 19 May 2014].

■ CONTENTS

■ LIST OF FIGURES

▨ LIST OF TABLES

▓ LIST OF BOXES

■ LIST OF ABBREVIATIONS

ACAS	Advisory, Conciliation, and Arbitration Service
APF	Area Partnership Forum
ATTAC	*Association pour la Taxation des Transactions Financière et l'Aide aux Citoyens* (Association for the Taxation of Financial Transactions and Aid to Citizens)
AUT	Association of University Teachers
BAOT	British Association of Occupational Therapists
BIS	Department for Business, Innovation, and Skills
BLS	Bureau of Labour Statistics
BMA	British Medical Association
BME	Black and Minority Ethnic
BRIC	Brazil, Russia, India, and China
BUIRA	British Universities Industrial Relations Association
BUSWE	British Union of Social Work Employees
BVU	British Veterinary Union
CAC	Central Arbitration Committee
CBI	Confederation of British Industry
CDU	*Christlich Demokratishe Union Deutschlands* (Christian Democratic Union Confederation)
CEO	Chief Executive Officer
CF	Communication Forum
CHCC	College of Health Care Chaplains
CIA	Central Intelligence Agency
CIO	Congress of Industrial Organizations
CIPD	Chartered Institute of Personnel and Development
CME	Coordinated Market Economy
CMS	Critical Management Studies
CPHVA	Community Practitioners and Health Visitors Association
DBB	*Deutscher Beamtenbund* (National Union of Civil Servants)
DGB	*Deutsche Gewerkschaftsbund* (German Confederation of Trade Unions)
DWP	Department of Work and Pensions

EEF	formerly the Engineering Employer's Federation
EI	Employee Involvement
EIRO	European Industrial Relations Observatory
ELM	External Labour Market
ER	Employment Relations
ETUC	European Trade Union Confederation
EU27	All twenty-seven member countries of the European Union
EWC	European Works Council
FTSE	Financial Times Stock Exchange
GDR	German Democratic Republic
GMB	formerly General, Municipal, Boilermakers, and Allied Trade Union
GMBH	*Gesellschaft mit Beschränkter Haftung* (company with limited liability)
GMWU	General and Municipal Workers' Union
HCM	High Commitment Management
HPWS	High Performance Work System
HR	Human Resources
HRM	Human Resource Management
ICD	Information and Consultation Directive
ICE	Information and Consultation of Employees
ICT	Information and Communications Technology
IG BCE	*Industriegewerkschaft Bergbau, Chemie, Energie* (Mining, Chemical, and Energy Union)
IG Metall	*Industriegewerkschaft Metall* (Metalworking Union)
ILM	Internal Labour Market
ILO	International Labour Organisation
IPA	Involvement and Participation Association
IR	Industrial Relations
ISTC	Iron and Steel Trades Confederation
ITUC	International Trade Union Confederation
JCC	Joint Consultation Committee
JCNC	Joint Consultation and Negotiation Committee
KFAT	National Union of Knitwear, Footwear, and Apparel Trades
LE	Labour Economics
LGBT	Lesbian, Gay, Bisexual, and Transgender
LMA	League Managers Association

LO	*Landsorganisationen i Sverige* (Swedish Trade Union Confederation)
LR	Labour Relations
LSE	London School of Economics
MHNA	Mental Health Nurses Association
MPU	Medical Practitioners' Union
NACODS	National Association of Colliery Overmen, Deputies, and Shotfirers
NATFHE	National Association of Teachers in Further and Higher Education
NGG	*Gewerkschaft Nahrung-Genuss-Gaststätten* (Food, Beverages, and Catering Union)
NHS	National Health Service
NLBD	National League of the Blind and Disabled
NLRA	National Labor Relations Act
NUDAGO	National Union of Domestic Appliance and General Operatives
NULMW	National Union of Lock and Metal Workers
NUPIT	National Union of Professional Interpreters and Translators
ONS	Office of National Statistics
PHD	Doctor of Philosophy
PLCWTWU	Power Loom Carpet Weavers and Textile Workers Union
RCN	Royal College of Nursing
RMT	National Union of Rail, Maritime, and Transport Workers
ROI	Republic of Ireland
SE	*Societas Europaea* (a European public company)
SGHD	Scottish Government Health Department
SME	Small and Medium-Sized Enterprise
SPF	Scottish Partnership Forum
TGWU	Transport and General Workers Union
TQM	Total Quality Management
TUC	Trades Union Congress
UCJM	Unite Criminal Justice Managers of Probation Officers
UCU	University and College Union
UK	United Kingdom
US	United States
USA	United States of America
Usdaw	Union of Shop, Distributive, and Allied Workers
USSR	Union of Soviet Social Republics
UWES	Utrecht Work Engagement Scale

WERS	Workplace Employment Relations Study
WPF	Welsh Partnership Forum
WSI	*Wirtschafts- und Sozialwissenschaftliches Institut* (Institute of Economic and Social Research)
WZB	*Wissenschaftszentrum Berlin für Sozialforschung* (Berlin Social Science Centre)

NOTES ON CONTRIBUTORS

Peter Ackers is Professor of Industrial Relations and Labour History, School of Business and Economics, Loughborough University, UK.

Ingrid Artus is Professor of Sociology, Friedrich-Alexander-Universität Erlangen-Nürnberg, Germany.

Nick Bacon is Professor of Human Resource Management at the Cass Business School, City University, London, UK.

Tony Dobbins is Reader in Employment Studies, Bangor Business School, Bangor University, Wales.

Tony Dundon is Professor of Human Resource Management and Employment Relations at the School of Business and Economics, National University of Ireland Galway, Ireland.

Mike Emmott is Adviser on Public Policy at the Chartered Institute of Personnel and Development, UK.

Michael Gold is Professor of Comparative Employment Relations in the School of Management at Royal Holloway University of London, UK.

Anne-marie Greene is Professor of Employment Relations at Leicester Business School, De Montfort University, UK.

David E. Guest is Professor of Organizational Psychology and Human Resource Management at King's College, London, UK.

Edmund Heery is Professor of Employment Relations at Cardiff Business School, Cardiff University, Wales.

Richard Hyman is Emeritus Professor of Industrial Relations at the London School of Economics and Political Science, UK, and is Founding Editor of the *European Journal of Industrial Relations*.

Stewart Johnstone is Senior Lecturer in Human Resource Management at Newcastle University Business School, Newcastle University, UK.

Bruce E. Kaufman is Professor at the Department of Economics, Georgia State University, USA, and Senior Research Fellow, Centre for Work Organization and Wellbeing and Department of Employment Relations and Human Resources, Griffith University, Brisbane, Australia.

Peter Samuel[†] was Lecturer in Human Resource Management at Nottingham University Business School, UK, but sadly he passed away in 2013, during the writing of this book. Peter was a colleague and friend to many of the contributors of this volume and is much missed.

Melanie Simms is Professor of Work and Employment at the School of Management, University of Leicester, UK.

Andrew R. Timming is Reader in Management in the School of Management at University of St Andrews, Scotland.

Michael Whittall is Professor of Sociology, Technische Universität, Munich, Germany.

Introduction: Employee voice

The key question for contemporary employment relations

Stewart Johnstone and Peter Ackers

Why voice and what sort of voice?

How much 'say' should employees have in the running of business organiza-tions and what form should this 'voice' take? This is both the oldest and the latest question in employment relations. How we answer this question has a direct influence on just about every other aspect of human resource manage-ment (HRM) and employment relations: how rewards are distributed, how health and safety are managed, how secure people's jobs are, and so on. Such answers are likely to reflect our fundamental views regarding the employment relationship, or what Alan Fox (1966) labelled 'frames of reference'. Do we assume employers and workers are a team united by a common purpose and shared goals (unitarism), or do we believe some conflict is inevitable as a result of competing interests and tensions between the parties (pluralism)? And if we accept the inevitability of conflict within the employment relation-ship, can different interests be reconciled and mediated by strong workplace institutions as pluralism suggests, or is industrial conflict symptomatic of a more fundamental problem with capitalist work organizations predicated upon exploitation (a radical or critical perspective)? Thus, how we view the basic employment relationship will shape whether we think employee voice is important, the rationale for voice, and the forms of voice we deem preferable (as discussed by Heery, this volume).

For some, *employee voice* is a synonym for trade union representation linked to a very specific normative and empirical case for collective organiza-tion (Freeman 1980). However, in this book we take a much broader, looser view of voice, which recognizes that employee voice, like the closely associated idea of *worker participation*, is an 'essentially contested concept' (Lukes 1974). In short, 'voice' is not something simple and empirical, like the rate of rainfall, which social scientists can easily measure. Rather, the terms 'employee voice' and 'worker participation' define a lively intellectual and policy debate about how business organizations should be managed, and these two overarching, umbrella labels cover a much larger family of terminology. To see the wood for the trees, it is useful to distinguish three different approaches to voice or participation, each with its own supporters (loosely derived from Marchington et al. 1992).

First there is the managerial idea of *Employee Involvement* (EI). Old-fashioned 'hard' unitarists assume that employers and management share the same goals and that the best approach is for management to command and control the organization. Work rules and strong management are believed to be needed to ensure workers perform as required. However, for over a century, enlightened employers have adopted 'softer' approaches and invented new ways of involving ordinary employees in the pursuit of these putative shared goals. Many new management terms and buzzwords have emerged over the years: profit-sharing, consultation, teamwork, HRM, total quality management, empowerment, and most recently employee engagement. Sometimes different terms relate to different aspects of this approach; sometimes new terms are simply more fashionable jargon, with vague, overlapping meanings—raising what David Guest below calls the problem of 'construct validity'. The essential feature of all these concepts, however, is that they are management initiated and build a measure of voluntary employee participation around a conventional capitalist business organization, run to increase shareholder value. Indeed, the central rationale for voice here is to enhance employee—and in turn organizational—performance, however this is defined. Such EI techniques acknowledge that the employment relationship has important social and psychological dimensions and cannot be reduced to a simple economic exchange. Finally, EI techniques often focus upon the relationship between the individual employee or small groups of employees, as selected by management, rather than the overall relations between an employer and the workforce as a whole.

At the opposite end of the voice spectrum, the radical idea of *workers' control* is also in favour of voice and participation but supports something quite different. In this view, conventional capitalist business organizations are run for shareholders, against the interests of employees and thus cannot allow genuine voice; this can only develop once workers own and control the business organization. Public ownership is a necessary but not sufficient step, since ordinary employees should actively run the nationalized company, not leave this to 'expert' professional managers. Indeed, if they neglect to do so, the socialized company may soon resemble the capitalist one above. Various schemes have been tried over the years, like 'guild socialism' or 'Yugoslavian self-management', and this fundamental approach to voice and participation, which replaces the capitalist business organization, may blur into worker cooperatives such as the well-known Mondragon network. This utopian ideal has limited support in the contemporary voice debate represented in this book, which is concerned predominantly with the value and efficacy of voice in conventional capitalist businesses and public sector organizations.

The third, pluralist, approach to voice, *representative participation*, lies somewhere between unitarist EI and radical workers' control. Here the assumption is that while at times employers and employees do have different interests, there is also substantial scope for developing forms of cooperation through dialogue. Rather than simply letting employers decide how the workplace is managed or trying to replace private ownership altogether, this approach aims to balance management voice with employee voice and reach some sort of compromise between the two. Often this rebalancing was to be achieved by employees' own voluntary organizations, normally trade unions, with the support of the democratic state. Industrial democracy (Webb and Webb 1897; Clegg 1960) was supposed to expand on and broaden narrow political democracy, whether through voluntary collective bargaining with employers alone—joint regulation (Flanders 1975)—or some statutory code-termination system of employee representation on company boards and works councils (Bullock 1977). In early versions, there was little expectation that employers and unions would actively cooperate or that these democratic processes would contribute directly to business performance. However, more recent usages like workplace partnership and mutual gains stress the potential for voice to benefit both workers and organizations; the core idea is that management, unions, and workers can potentially work together to use the voice process to achieve a win–win outcome (Handel and Levine 2004; Johnstone and Wilkinson 2013). Similarly, the larger European Union (EU) conception of social partnership—which links workplace collaboration to a tripartite system of employment policy making by the state, employers, and trade unions—also claims both democratic and organizational-performance benefits from this approach. What binds together these different methods and concepts is some sense that the workforce, as a whole, should be able to express their voice to management, independently of the employer.

The key debate for employment relations is which of these three approaches 'works best'. But the quality of voice is not the only issue. In theory at least, there is no question that workers' control offers the greatest employee influence, but few academics or policy makers support this solution today because it is seen as inconsistent with an efficient business organization that delivers wealth to society. Equally, as Samuel and Bacon note below, this public concern with 'performance' also applies to public service organizations. In short, organizations are rarely run for employees alone. On the other hand, few doubt that EI in a free market economic system produces wealth, but here many questions arise over the distribution of that wealth, and what real say ordinary employees have in the running of the organization. Lastly, representative participation may promise both employee influence and organizational efficiency, but there is some doubt over whether employers or trade unions can deliver on their sides of this bargain (Thompson 2011).

The central debate is now between variants of EI and representative participation. Can EI raise its game by offering employees genuine rather than token or superficial influence; and can representative participation find some legal or voluntary methods of bringing collective representation into the heart of work organizations without damaging, or even by contributing to, their effectiveness? In real workplaces, as we shall see in this volume, there are movements between the three camps. Some commentators seek to blend EI and representative participation, while others, drawing on radical insights, wish to make closer partnership with employers conditional upon much wider changes in the regulation of shareholder capitalism. In linguistic terms at least, some employers want to give EI a utopian radical spin by calling it something much grander, like 'empowerment'.

What's changed in the voice debate? The contested role of trade unions

Voice is a long-running public policy debate. In the UK, for example, the Involvement and Participation Association (IPA) was founded in 1884 as the Labour Association for Promoting Co-operative Production based on the co-partnership of workers. The current IPA mission is to help 'managers and employees develop new ways of working, based on trust and collaboration that deliver better workplaces and better outcomes' (IPA 2014). Equally, the Chartered Institute of Personnel and Development (CIPD), which has supported the annual 'Voice and Value' conference at the LSE since 2000, has its own roots in the progressive employers of the early twentieth century. The founders of both these organizations would be familiar with many of the debates above. Trade unions have existed since the late eighteenth century and pluralist collective bargaining developed during the nineteenth. Enlightened employers, such as Robert Owen and George Cadbury, experimented with forms of consultation and profit sharing. And by the turn of the twentieth century, socialist and syndicalist ideas of workers' control were in the air. In this sense, the same conceptual cards are on the table today as there were a century ago. Yet the terms of debate have changed quite dramatically over the past three decades.

Perhaps the greatest change has been the triumph of neoliberal free market ideas in economic policy and management thinking, beginning with Thatcher and Reagan in the 1980s, but now much more widespread. Before this development, the voice debate centred on trade unions and how their role as the natural voice of workers could be extended and developed. Pluralism was taken for granted as the basis for employment relations public policy, even in the USA. For most of the twentieth century, collective bargaining was *the* method of determining pay and conditions for workers; even shaping behaviour in non-union organizations. Trade unions were assumed to be a normal and essential part of healthy workplace relations. The UK is a good example. In 1968 a Royal Commission asserted: 'collective bargaining is the most effective means of giving workers the right to representation in decisions affecting their working lives' (Donovan 1968: 27). A decade later, the 1977 Bullock Report on Industrial Democracy went further still, arguing for parity union representation with shareholders on tripartite company boards for large companies (Bullock 1977). In this era, non-union EI forms of voice were regarded as marginal to employment relations. The main question was how the representative participation strand could be further developed to give workers more say, and the main challenge to this came from radicals calling for something approaching workers' control.

In the UK, the tide turned dramatically in 1979, with the emergence of Thatcherism. Union membership and the coverage of collective bargaining peaked in that year and both have fallen ever since. Public policy stopped supporting trade unions as the central mechanism for voice, and many employers, old and new, turned to developing their own EI techniques. The academic world changed too, with the global rise of HRM and Business Schools. Often these marched hand in hand with the new unitarist EI. Trade union decline had begun decades earlier in the USA and has now spread across the world. However, unions have remained strong in certain sectors and companies, often alongside the new EI initiatives, complicating the voice picture. The industrial relations (IR) academic field was at the centre of the old pluralist, pro-union consensus, and these changes have forced both pluralists and radicals to research and assess the new, more managerial and individualistic managerial approaches to voice, which de-emphasize trade unions, democracy, and collectivism. Typically, the new EI stressed direct forms of participation such as downward communication, upward problem solving, task-based teamwork, and financial involvement through shares or bonus schemes (Marchington et al. 1992). Terms such as 'empowerment', 'high commitment management', and 'high performance work systems' became increasingly popular as firms emphasized quality and flexibility and recognized the dysfunctional nature of Taylorist approaches. Voice, in this very functional sense, was less concerned with avenues for the expression of dissatisfaction than with a desire to understand and strengthen the links between HRM practices and organizational performance. Participation techniques became increasingly task centred rather than power centred (Boxall and Purcell 2008), and more concerned with 'educating' employees and encouraging them to contribute ideas regarding business and workplace improvement, rather than as a general means to influence management policy.

However, the representative participation strand of the voice debate also revived and metamorphosed through well-publicized American experiments in mutual gains (Kochan and Osterman 1994), such as the high-profile labour management partnership at the Saturn car plant. In addition, some British trade unions entered 'single-union, no-strike deals' with Japanese inward investors, and Nissan developed a company council and voice forums that blurred bargaining and consultation (Bassett 1986). Moreover, while the neoliberal tide was flowing in one direction, European social policy prompted a counterflow from the late 1980s with statutory information and consult-ation initiatives. While many of the provisions were already a matter of routine in continental workplaces, they were quite new to lightly regulated liberal market economies like the UK and the Irish Republic. Changes in government, such as the election of Tony Blair and New Labour in 1997, also encouraged the trend towards a new version of partnership, concerned with 'modernizing' union/management relations and making enhanced business performance an explicit goal of voice (see Ackers and Payne 1998; Martínez Lucio and Stuart 2005; Johnstone et al. 2009, 2011). Some organizations also set up in-house representative structures without trade unions (Johnstone et al. 2010). As there was once a Cold War competition over democratic processes and economic outcomes, now there is a similar dual contest over EI and partnership voice regimes. Which provides the most say and which contributes most to business success? Rather than ignoring or attempting to eradicate trade unions, the new normative model of partnership promotes consultation and joint problem solving between union and employer repre-sentatives rather than arms-length adversarialism, founded on the belief that both stand to benefit from such an arrangement (Johnstone et al. 2011; see also Johnstone, this volume).

These are not 'ivory tower' academic debates. They concern politicians and map on to left and right political divisions, with many free market US Republicans and UK Conservatives supporting the exclusion of trade unions from the voice debate, while European Social and Christian Democrats and US Democrats tend to endorse their inclusion. Trade unions are still significant employment policy actors in most democratic societies, but so too are employ-ment pressure groups and professional associations such as the CIPD in Britain, which defines employee voice as: 'the two way communication between employer and employee . . . the process of the employer communicat-ing to the employee as well as receiving and listening to communication from the employee' (CIPD 2011). Mike Emmott's foreword highlights 'chan-ging the culture' of organizations. And in one sense this is crucial, since institutions alone cannot guarantee effective employee voice. However, the danger is that culture, like voice itself can become the ether of employment relations: 'a win-win solution to a central organizational problem—how to satisfy workers' needs while simultaneously achieving organisational objectives' (Strauss 2006: 778). A central role of social science research, from whichever perspective, is to subject alluring but simplistic pop management prescriptions to strenuous analysis and evidence. Voice can be many things, but it is not an easy solution to all work problems—which is why the workers' control utopia has lost credibility. Policy makers need more pragmatic, realistic answers to enduring questions: what works best in different contexts, what are the conditions of success, and what are the drawbacks?

Given different national employment relations traditions and the inherent complexity of working life, it seems unlikely that one voice blueprint will work best everywhere. Thus business and management interest groups—such as the CBI, Institute of Directors and CIPD in the UK—stress the importance of management choice and flexibility (Marchington et al. 2001). Regulation is often bemoaned by employers as 'red tape' which damages labour market competitiveness (CBI 2012). At one level this is understandable, as a 'one size fits all' approach is unlikely to be feasible. For instance, we might expect that the most appropriate forms of voice for a small or medium enterprise (SME) will differ from those of a large corporation. On the other hand, unduly loose definitions of voice as merely management 'talking to people' are soft on power and perhaps no better than 'spitting in the wind' (Strauss 2006). Modern management is particularly adept at public relations and voice can become little more than internal marketing. This is a particular danger if management alone decides whether or not workers can have a voice and which mechanisms to utilize. A management agenda concerned with increasing understanding and commitment from employees and securing an enhanced contribution to the organization may yield significant forms of real voice for certain types of employees. Yet critics question the degree of real influence that employer-sponsored voice mechanisms offer workers, because they either underemphasize or neglect completely the potential for conflicting interests to occur. As a consequence, the real potential for workplace mutual gains may not be realized. Managers who believe in the easy win–win route may only be fooling themselves.

Why does voice still matter for employment relations and society?

Just as it is important to test management voice claims against hard evidence, it is also crucial to disentangle the main rationales for giving employee voice at work. Though nowadays most cases for voice blend different arguments it is important to separate these out and decide which has priority when push comes to shove. Two competing rationales stand out.

The first makes a moral and political argument for a measure of *democracy at work* to complete political democracy. While the precise mechanisms may change, the general argument is as old and well established as Sidney and Beatrice Webb's *Industrial Democracy* (1897). It also bears a close correspondence with the modern political idea of social democracy, as a variety of capitalism regulated by voluntary trade unions and the state. Ironically, the Webbs were concerned more about the outcomes for employees, in terms of protecting them against low pay and exploitation, than with the expression of voice itself. But classic pluralists, such as Clegg (1960), felt that union voice at work was essential as a counter to management totalitarianism (see Ackers 2007). His fear was that the workplace could become like a small-scale communist or fascist state, controlled by an authoritarian business elite that imposes its interests on the employees. Hence this argument for voice is twofold, combining a case for democratic process and an argument for rebalancing the unlimited power of management, as a means to protect employee interests in good wages and working conditions. Voice must deliver real say for either of these conditions to be met.

Starting at the opposite end of the equation, the economic or *business case* argument views employee voice as an essential link in the quest for increased organizational performance, through 'high performance work systems' or 'good HRM' more generally (see Ackers 2013; Johnstone and Wilkinson 2013). For some unitarists, crudely authoritarian workplace relations, such as those in 1920s Ford factories, are counterproductive because they undermine employee motivation and commitment, and in turn the potential for cooperation. Once more, this is an old argument, promoted by Elton Mayo and the human relations movement since the 1930s (see Mayo 1933). The last two decades have seen a steady stream of articles examining the relationship between HRM practices and firm performance, which in itself has formed the new subfield of Strategic HRM (Kaufman 2010), yet our understanding of the precise links between HRM and performance remain limited (Guest 2011). Nevertheless, the current international vogue for employee engagement initiatives reflects a voracious and seemingly insatiable interest among employers in the links between employee attitudes and behaviour, and organizational performance. In the UK, the MacLeod report *Engaging for Success* (2009) was designed to open a national discussion on employee engagement, underpinned by the central notion that engaged workers are more effective and 'add value' (MacLeod and Clarke 2009; see also Guest, this volume).

Again, it is often argued that employee voice is important in raising engagement levels, though the practical recommendations tend to focus upon downwards communication and employee surveys rather than giving employees much influence or developing systems of collective employee representation. By implication, voice is only worthwhile from this perspective if it has some measurable business payoff: employees work harder, show more initiative, stay with the company longer, spend less time off work sick, or whatever. This has two logical consequences. First, voice must be effective to bring about these benefits—unless it is merely a smokescreen to evade regulation by trade unions or the state, a way of saying 'we're doing something'. Second, and more worryingly, voice is only worthwhile if and when employers stand to benefit from it, at a time when HRM research has increasingly emphasized different 'configurations' for workers contingent upon their 'strategic value' (Lepak and Snell 2002). Potentially, voice may become an optional extra for certain types of high-skilled or customer-facing workforce but not something low-skilled, low-waged workers need, when from a moral and political perspective they need it most of all.

To what extent can the 'democracy at work' and the 'business case' arguments be reconciled? In our view, the argument tends to flow one way and not the other. If you start with an argument for democracy, as a few enlightened employers such as Cadbury and John Lewis have done, and develop appropriate voice institutions, it is not hard to build a supplementary business case that becomes a virtuous circle of participation and profit. If, on the other hand, you begin with a purely instrumental business case for voice, fail to invest in long-term voice institutions and then adjust the business' commitment according to short-term market fluctuations, it seems unlikely that sustainable or strong voice will emerge (see Ackers 2013). One of the strengths of a statutory voice framework, as discussed below, is that it sends a strong signal that voice must be a priority and locks employers into serious, credible voice institutions. Budd's (2004) normative argument about the employment relationship is useful in this respect. He proposes three goals that need to be held in balance: efficiency, equity, and voice. This challenges the neoliberal view that good wages and conditions and effective employee voice should be constructed solely as a means to enhanced business performance. From this perspective, voice can be considered to be: 'an intrinsic standard of participation—participation in decision-making is *an end in itself* for rational human beings in a democratic society...intrinsic voice is important whether or not it improves economic performance and whether or not it improves the distribution of economic rewards' (Budd 2004: 13). This argument is particularly compelling in rich, advanced economies which already set minimum standards for equity, such as the UK's national minimum wage or statutory rules about unfair dismissal, race, and sex discrimination. Businesses operate within the rules laid down by democratic societies. Perhaps these should include more ambitious minimum standards of employee voice for all workers?

What are the key debates in this book?

For the past three decades the voice field has seen many employer and public policy experiments, especially within the EU. Academics have responded both by revisiting, revising, and revitalizing old arguments and by conducting major research projects. This book offers a critical assessment of the main contemporary concepts and models of voice, with each chapter written by an authority in that area. Our collection is centred on the UK and EU because that is where the main global debate about the future of voice has taken place, and in the latter case, where some of the most significant state initiatives have originated. Europe, with its great democratic traditions, has much to contribute to the world-wide development of employee voice. At the same time, the success or failure of its various voice models and initiatives are of great policy interest across the globe. The diversity of the European experience, with perhaps the most successful coordinated market economy, Germany, sitting alongside liberal market economies, like the UK, makes the comparisons and contrasts all the more compelling. An in-depth theoretical and empirical exploration of voice in the UK and Europe can take us a long way towards answering the question, why does voice matter and which versions work best? Much of this material is usually dispersed across a dozen academic journals. Here we bring it together as one cohesive collection, an accessible form that we hope will be useful to students and lecturers of employment relations, HRM, and the sociology of work, as well as to other scholars.

Clearly, employee voice has a long intellectual lineage. *Part 1, Key Concepts*, explores this along two dimensions. First, different academic fields of study have conceptualized voice differently and here we witness three in action: British IR with its strong sociological inflection; occupational psychology; and the newer field of equality and diversity studies. Second, there has been a long intellectual war over voice, which predated and has extended well beyond the community of academic specialists. Over the years, socialist intellectuals, trade union leaders, business people, and politicians have all opined about voice.

These debates have been further refined within the field of employment relations, and Edmund Heery opens with a central theoretical debate between British IR radicals, influenced by Marxism, mainstream pluralists, who have traditionally championed moderate trade unions, and unitarists, who are closer to new managerial ideas about HRM. As we have seen, this debate centres on how necessary trade unions are to effective voice, how far they should cooperate with management, and the significance of management-driven EI techniques. The debate is constantly shifting as the world of work changes. Radicals have become critical theorists as the prospect of some socialist workers' control alternative to capitalist forms of participation has waned; while, with the decline of trade unions, pluralists have become neopluralists and have had to take more seriously management and statutory forms of voice (Ackers 2002). These debates redound through the rest of the book, particularly in the next section on trade unions, and explain why the argument about voice can never be reduced to an empirical discussion about 'evidence-based policy'—important as this is.

While the academic field of IR has concentrated on workplace institutions—collective bargaining structure, committees, procedures, collective forms of representation—there have always been parallel fields of researchers exploring the microsociology or psychology of work. Notable examples include Elton Mayo on the informal work group and other 'human relations' and socio-technical scholars, such as Trist and Bamforth (1951) on coalmining teamworking. With the rise of EI since the 1980s, this type of research has gained greater prominence and is increasingly shaping management policy, leading some to question whether the traditionally multidisciplinary field of HRM is becoming increasingly 'psychologised' (Godard 2014). In this respect, the chapter by David Guest on employee engagement takes us straight into the heart of the latest policy concept heavily influenced by positive psychology. As he shows, engagement overlaps with a succession of past HRM concepts, such as EI, partnership, and voice itself, such that 'construct validity' becomes a central issue. Is this just another way of discussing voice—a new word for the same concept—or is employee voice fairly marginal to this new way of talking about involving employees? And here, once more, Guest comes face to face with a managerial and unitarist concept of employment relations and a succession of new management techniques, which may or may not benefit employees and employers.

Western societies have changed greatly since the classic voice debates about industrial democracy. Women now make up half the UK workforce and European societies are increasingly racially diverse. Other differences related to disability and sexuality have also been recognized. Of course, the old industrial society was never in any sense homogenous, especially in a country like the USA. However, real material changes have been accompanied by new social currents, such as 'multiculturalism' and 'identity politics'. This combination has begun to challenge conceptions of voice forged in a mid-twentieth-century labour movement dominated by white, male 'breadwinners'. Anne-marie Greene takes the voice debate into unchartered territories by asking precisely 'who' voice is for, and questioning whether all employees have the same voice, or even the same things to say. Whatever the true demographic realities, until recently employees were often thought of as a relatively homogenous 'standard' group, implicitly male and full time. The development of greater workforce diversity across European and North American workforces raises new questions about how they can best express their voice and how trade unions and other institutions can facilitate this. Greene's central contention is that diversity concerns should be at the heart of the employee voice debate.

As we have seen, voice is a large and complex field, but one central and fairly straightforward debate has dominated UK employment relations for the past decade: should trade unions form partnership relations with employers or should they militantly mobilize workers against them (see Kelly 1996)? This controversy over the union strategy towards voice has taken place between radicals and pluralists, across a fairly clear and defined border. *Part 2, Union Voice,* broadens the old partnership argument by exploring the wider goals of trade unions, presenting the main organizing alternative, and moving beyond black-and-white Marxist and pluralist exchanges.

Peter Ackers takes Greene's important point about the non-standard character of contemporary employees in a different direction, arguing that neither workers nor their unions have ever been 'standard'. Nor have British unions, in particular, ever been the generic workers' organizations fighting capitalism, as envisaged by many radical sociologists. Rather, they are occupational bodies whose best prospect for future advance is to transmute into professional associations that aim to raise the status of paid work. Ackers incorporates a positive attitude to partnership into his approach, pointing out that UK trade unions did not rise to power and influence in the workplace and society simply or even mainly by mobilizing workers. Instead, membership growth followed in the train of collective bargaining, as this was sponsored and spread by the state and employers. Unions need to win the support of employees, employers, the state, and, above all, public opinion if they are to recover at all their central role as voice organizations.

In the past, radicals often rejected 'class collaboration' and capitalist forms of voice *tout court* and saw trade unions mainly as a way of fighting for a different social system. As an academic perspective, this approach to researching real-life partnerships often seems a priori, as if empirical research merely confirms pre-existing theoretical assumptions. However, Melanie Simms, in making the case for union organizing and against partnership as a general strategy in the private sector, develops a more nuanced and context-sensitive (Ram and Edwards 2010) radical-pluralist argument. Hall and Soskice's (2001) *Varieties of Capitalism* thesis has been a major influence on IR theory. Simms argues that partnership may work in 'coordinated market economies', such as Germany and Sweden, but is much more problematic in 'liberal market economies' like the UK or US. Here financialization and short-term profit maximization render long-term stable, co-operative relationships between management and labour difficult to maintain. Genuine partnership is not quite impossible but extremely rare and vulnerable in this context. Trade unions cannot strike enduring deals with most private sector employers, and thus mobilizing and organizing workers is the best way forward, even if the prospects of success are not that rosy.

Stewart Johnstone challenges this argument, by noting the limited results achieved by the organizing model, and the success of partnership in some leading-edge sections of the British economy, such as financial services and high-end manufacturing. He also stresses the importance of reigniting actor interest in representative participation in the private sector, and suggests that a key strength of partnership is its potential to the win much needed support of employers, workers, and governments. While Johnstone concedes that partnership may not work everywhere, and acknowledges that it is in no way a panacea for employment relations, he concludes that its potential range in the private sector is far wider than Simms suggests, and in many contexts may be more fruitful than the organizing alternative.

Varieties of Capitalism has been one of the dominant academic frameworks of the past two decades, and, as Simms argues, it tends to circumscribe the scope for effective voice in liberal market economies. Ackers (2012, 2014) has argued that this determinist conceptual 'iron cage' is oversimplistic and misleading, and in danger of merely repackaging the 1970s 'capitalist' bête noire as 'neoliberalism' and 'liberal market'. Moreover, an abstract bipolar division between 'coordinated market' and 'liberal market' economies may not capture the rich complexity of European employment relations. And this debate leads us naturally to *Part 3, European Models and Varieties of Capitalism*, which tests these claims empirically by exploring different national employment systems and then the two main EU directives to support voice. Building upon the previous section, which addressed voluntary initiatives such as partnership and organizing in a notionally liberal market economy, the UK, these chapters look at the impact of the nation state, devolved government, and EU initiatives on the development of voice systems. Hence, the next two chapters explore different national systems within the EU.

Peter Samuel and Nick Bacon show that within the UK's liberal market model, devolution in Scotland and Wales has created new scope for partnership in the National Health Service. They argue that devolved government has allowed the construction of new small-state voice systems, approaching Scandinavian tripartite social partnership, especially in Scotland. In part, this supports the Varieties of Capitalism argument, by stressing the importance of state regulation for 'social partnership', but it also draws out the sectoral and organizational scope for different strategic choices, suggesting the need for a closer reading of institutional context. For instance, even before devolution, the liberal market in the UK included Europe's largest socialized free public medical system, with markedly different voice systems to those found in private sector organizations. Similar unionized voice subsystems exist within large manufacturing companies and financial services. In the same way, Germany's vaunted coordinated market model largely excludes the large and expanding private service sector, to the point where a statutory minimum wage is being introduced.

Michael Gold and Ingrid Artus take us to the heart of the German statutory codetermination system that has inspired other EU voice initiatives. This allows worker representatives to sit on some company boards and gives works councils in many workplaces statutory powers over certain decisions. They acknowledge the limited reach of the 'German model'—with the growing service sector looking increasingly like a liberal market model of its own—but also note the capacity of the system to rejuvenate itself. In particular, they stress the proactive role of German trade unions in shaping the level of bargaining and nature of voice, a dimension that is notably absent from US and UK discussions. Anglo-Saxon IR theory has tended to stress either the state or the employer as strategic actors in voice systems and to regard trade unions as relatively passive organizations that merely pass on collective messages from employees. This issue recurs in the two chapters on specific EU voice initiatives: European works councils and the information and consultation regulations.

Andrew Timming and Michael Whittall consider one key EU voice initiative, European Works Councils (EWCs), and suggest that these offer some scope for transnational trade union cooperation. EWCs were introduced two decades ago for large companies located in several EU countries, and represented a milestone in the fight for employment rights at a European level. Yet despite initial enthusiasm, in practice EWCs have encountered various challenges. These include the 'varieties of voice' problem, whereby difficulties arise as a consequence of the diverse composition of EWC delegates, drawing on different national union traditions, as well as the tendency for EWCs to be dominated by management. For British and Irish delegates, however, EWCs arguably provided some of the first experiences of European-style social dialogue. The authors are cautiously optimistic so long as EWCs can continue to demonstrate their relevance and potential to 'add value' to both employees and organizations. But there is a strong sense that EWCs, as statutory voice institutions, are very much what trade unions, as voluntary actors, can make of them.

Tony Dobbins and Tony Dundon note that most continental European countries already had works council systems, so that the Information and Consultation Directive (ICE) was most important for those liberal market economies, like the UK and Ireland, that have depended almost entirely on voluntary forms of voice, whether through trade unions or at management's discretion. However, in these countries, neither the state nor employers nor trade unions have pushed ICE. Weak implementation of the new voice regulations by the state, combined with unitarist management ideologies, provide an inhospitable environment for the development of pluralist mutual gains arrangements. They suggest that this leads to a 'prisoners' dilemma' of low-trust relations that does not make the most of voice. The onus is on the state to do more. However, trade unions in both countries kept the new voice initiative at arm's length for fear that it might become a Trojan horse and undermine existing collective bargaining arrangements. As Mike Emmott has argued in the Foreword, UK unions have remained ambivalent about these new forms of consultation. To us this seems short-sighted and our question here would be: had the trade unions showed greater commitment to these potential voice channels, would the outcome have been different?

Part 4, Looking Ahead, considers the future prospects for voice in Europe and the USA. Richard Hyman has charted the development of European employment relations for several decades, since the first emergence of EU social policy in the late 1980s. His contribution recalls past industrial democracy policy perspectives but is highly pessimistic about the future, positing a 'cancer stage of capitalism' brought on by financialization, neoliberalism, and globalization—arguments similar to those employed by Melanie Simms earlier. Hyman sees Europe entering a post-industrial democracy era, with strong social democratic forms of voice that are hard to maintain, and asks whether 'good capitalism' can be restored. He looks to new social movements to return some life to the voice debate.

Our closing chapter focuses on the future prospects for voice in the USA. America once had strong trade unions and a pluralist system of employment relations based on union voice. Indeed, managerial alternatives to union voice, such as company unions and consultation committees remain outlawed by US employment law. At the same time, American unions now represent a small fraction of the national workforce. So often it is the case that 'where America leads, others follow', which makes it important to grasp the predicament of and prospects for US employee voice. Bruce Kaufman picks up similar and overlapping debates to Heery's earlier chapter, but views them through the rather different lens of American academic IR influenced by institutional labour economics. The chapter builds upon earlier conceptual frameworks and models to develop a new 'employment relations model' of voice. In doing so Kaufman utilizes both frames of reference and an economics-based theory of the firm's demand for HRM practices. Without the statutory impetus of European social policy, with unions marginalized and employers increasingly disinterested in complex HRM solutions, Kaufman finds the prospects bleak for voice in the USA.

Indeed, it is hard not to be pessimistic about certain voice trends if they continue. Trade unions have always been a spur in management's side, encouraging employers to listen to employees, even in companies where unions were not themselves present. And, left to their own devices, there is little evidence that employers will initiate strong or power-centred forms of employee voice. However, in democratic societies the authoritarian work organization will always be under suspicion and there is considerable public scepticism about free market capitalism today. In our view, if politicians and trade union leaders can channel—rather than alienate—that public concern, a new chapter may open. And our hope is that this book will contribute towards putting *effective* employee voice at the centre of public policy—where it used to be.

■ REFERENCES

Ackers, P. (2002) 'Reframing Employment Relations: The Case for Neo-pluralism'. *Industrial Relations Journal*, 33(1), 2–19.

Ackers, P. (2007) 'Collective Bargaining as Industrial Democracy: Hugh Clegg and the Political Foundations of British Industrial Relations Pluralism'. *British Journal of Industrial Relations*, 45(1), 77–101.

Ackers, P. (2012) 'The Warwick School of Industrial Relations (review of Colling and Terry, *Industrial Relations*)'. *Work, Employment and Society*, 26(5), 879–82.

Ackers, P. (2013) 'Employment Ethics'. In T. Redman and A. J. Wilkinson (eds), *Contemporary Human Resource Management: Text and Cases*, 4th edn, pp. 451–65. UpperSaddle River, NJ: FT/Prentice Hall.

Ackers, P. (2014) 'Rethinking the Employment Relationship: A Neo-pluralist Critique of British Industrial Relations Orthodoxy'. *International Journal of Human Resource Management*, 25 (18), 2608–25.

Ackers, P. and Payne, J. (1998) 'British Trade Unions and Social Partnership: Rhetoric, Reality and Strategy'. *International Journal of Human Resource Management*, 9(3), 529–50.

Bassett, P. (1986) *Strike Free: New Industrial Relations in Britain*. London: MacMillan.

Boxall, P. and Purcell, J. (2008) *Strategy and Human Resource Management*, 2nd edn. New York: Palgrave MacMillan.

Budd, J. (2004) *Employment with a Human Face: Balancing Efficiency, Equity and Voice*. New York: Cornell.

Bullock, A. (1977) *Report of the Committee of Inquiry on Industrial Democracy*, CMND, 6706.

CBI (2012) *Changing the Rules: Eight Steps to a Better Regulatory Regime*. London: CBI.

CIPD (2011) *Employee Voice Factsheet*. [Online.] Available at: <http://www.cipd.co.uk/hr-resources/factsheets/employee-voice.aspx>, accessed 4 May 2014.

Clegg, H. A. (1960) *A New Approach to Industrial Democracy*. Oxford: Basil Blackwell.

Donovan, T. (1968) *Report of the Royal Commission on Trade Unions and Employers Associations*. CMND, 3623, 185.

Flanders, A. (1975) *Management and Unions: The Theory and Reform of Industrial Relations*. London: Faber.

Fox, A. (1966) *Industrial Sociology and Industrial Relations*, Royal Commission on Trade Unions and Employers' Associations, Research Papers 3. London: HMSO.

Freeman, R. B. (1980) 'The Exit-Voice Tradeoff in the Labor Market: Unionism, Job Tenure, Quits, and Separations'. *Quarterly Journal of Economics*, 94(4), 643–73.

Godard, J. (2014) 'The Psychologisation of Employment Relations?' *Human Resource Management Journal*, 24(1), 1–18.

Guest, D. (2011) 'Human Resource Management and Performance: Still Searching for Some Answers'. *Human Resource Management Journal*, 21(1), 3–13.

Hall, P. A. and Soskice, D. (eds) (2001) *Varieties of Capitalism: The Institutional Foundations of Comparative Advantage*. Oxford: Oxford University Press.

Handel, M. J. and Levine, D. I. (2004) Editors' Introduction: The Effects of New Work Practices on Workers. *Industrial Relations: A Journal of Economy and Society*, 43(1), 1–43.

IPA (2014) About Us: Who IPA Are and What IPA Do. [Online.] Available at: <http://www.ipa-involve.com/about-us/>, accessed 4 May 2014.

Johnstone, S. and Wilkinson, A. (2013) 'Employee Voice, Partnership and Performance'. In G. Saridakis and C. Cooper, *How Can HR Drive Growth*, pp. 141–69. London: Edward Elgar.

Johnstone, S., Ackers, P., and Wilkinson, A. (2009) 'The Partnership Phenomenon: A Ten Year Review'. *Human Resource Management Journal*, 19(3), 260–79.

Johnstone, S., Ackers, P., and Wilkinson, A. (2010) 'Better than Nothing? Is Non-Union Partnership a Contradiction in Terms?' *Journal of Industrial Relations*, 52(2), 151–68.

Johnstone, S., Wilkinson, A., and Ackers, P. (2011) 'Applying Budd's Model to Partnership'. *Economic and Industrial Democracy*, 32(2), 307–28.

Kaufman, B. E. (2010) 'SHRM Theory in the Post-Huselid Era: Why It Is Fundamentally Misspecified'. *Industrial Relations: A Journal of Economy and Society*, 49(2), 286–313.

Kelly, J. (1996) 'Union Militancy and Social Partnership'. In P. Ackers, C. Smith, and P. Smith (eds), *The New Workplace and Trade Unionism*. London: Routledge.

Kochan, T. and Osterman, P. (1994) *The Mutual Gains Enterprise*. Boston, MA: Harvard Business School Press.

Lepak, D. P. and Snell, S. A. (2002) 'Examining the Human Resource Architecture: The Relationships among Human Capital, Employment, and Human Resource Configurations'. *Journal of Management*, 28(4), 517–43.

Lukes, S. (1974) *Power: A Radical View*. London: Macmillan.

MacLeod, D. and Clarke, N. (2009) *Engaging for Success: A Report to Government*. London: BIS.

Marchington, M., Goodman, J., Wilkinson, A., and Ackers, P. (1992) 'New Developments in Employee Involvement', *Management Research News*, 14(1/2), 34–7.

Marchington, M., Wilkinson, A., Ackers, P., and Dundon, T. (2001) *Management Choice and Employee Voice*. London: CIPD.

Martínez Lucio, M. and Stuart, M. (2005) *Partnership and Modernization in Employment Relations*. Basingstoke: Routledge.

Mayo, E. (1933) *The Human Problems of an Industrial Civilisation*. London: Routledge.

Ram, M. and Edwards, P. (2010) 'Industrial Relations in Small Firms'. In T. Colling and M. Terry (eds), *Industrial Relations: Theory and Practice*, 3rd edn. London: Wiley.

Strauss, G. (2006) 'Worker Participation: Some Under-Considered Issues'. *Industrial Relations* 45(4), 778–803.

Thompson, P. (2011) 'The Trouble with HRM'. *Human Resource Management Journal*, 21(4), 355–67.

Trist, E. and Bamforth, K. (1951) 'Some Social and Psychological Consequences of the Longwall Method of Coal Getting'. *Human Relations*, 4, 3–38.

Webb, S. and Webb, B. (1897) *Industrial Democracy*. London: Longmans.

Part 1
Key Concepts

2 Frames of reference and worker participation

Edmund Heery

Introduction

One of the few concepts in industrial relations (IR) to attain both longevity and ubiquity is that of 'frames of reference', first popularized by Fox (1966) in the 1960s but still widely used today to identify competing interpretations of the employment relationship. In what follows, the concept of frames of reference is used to chart a route through contemporary debate over worker voice and participation. The latter is marked by sharp divisions between unitary, pluralist, and critical writers, who favour different forms of participation, interpret the functions of voice in competing ways, and have developed distinct research programmes to record, explain, and evaluate the experience of participation. The value of the concept of frames is precisely that it directs attention to these competing interpretations; it highlights the fact that the field of IR, broadly conceived, is marked by contention and perhaps nowhere is this more apparent than in work on participation.

At the core of the different frames of reference within IR are competing understandings of the relative interests of workers and their employers. Thus, for unitarists it is assumed that the interests of workers and employers are fully congruent and that this congruence can underpin ready and continuing cooperation within the employment relationship. Where conflict is encountered, for writers in this tradition, it tends to be viewed as essentially pathological: the result of management failure or of baleful external influences, such as inappropriate regulation by the state or disruptive trade unions. These unitary assumptions were once marginal to much IR scholarship but in recent years, following the emergence of human resource management as a major field of study, they have become widespread and influence a great deal of academic commentary on work and employment. They tend to be expressed in two main forms. On the one hand, there is a 'soft unitarism', typically grounded in psychology, which sees the basis for shared interests at work in management's ability to configure job roles that are intrinsically satisfying, developmental, and rewarding (Gratton 2004). On the other hand, there is a 'hard unitarism', which typically is grounded in economics and which is most fully developed in the 'the new economics of personnel' (Lazear 1995). In this formulation it is the capacity of managers to offer financial incentives on both an immediate and a deferred basis that produces the congruence of interests between workers and employers. As we will see, these two versions of unitarism tend to prescribe different forms of employee participation.

For pluralists, there is an irremovable conflict of interest at the heart of the relationship between workers and employers, which encompasses both 'market relations', issues relating to remuneration and working time, and 'managerial relations' that concern the organization of work and the deployment and control of labour (Sisson 2008). Equally, however, pluralists have identified common interests—both parties have a stake in the survival and success of the employing enterprise—and have often sought to expand the scope of these shared interests through strategies of mutual gains (Kochan and Osterman 1994). In addition, pluralists rarely regard the division of interests between workers and employers as so deep or so entrenched as to be unbridgeable. Conflict, in this tradition, is unavoidable but not chronic and can be resolved through compromise to the benefit of all. Such beneficial outcomes, however, are unlikely to be secured solely through unilateral employer action, as is assumed in the unitary tradition. On the contrary, for pluralists both maximizing the scope of shared interests in the employment relationship and the reconciliation of conflicting interests require the regulation of employer behaviour, from below through institutions of worker representation and from above through systems of employment law and wider state intervention. Differences in the pluralist camp often relate to the scale of the regulatory effort that is required to resolve conflict and promote mutual gains. In the pluralist literature of the post-war period it was assumed that beneficial outcomes could be secured through the creation of a discrete industrial relations system, founded on trade union representation and collective bargaining (Dunlop 1993). More radical versions of the pluralist argument, however, have tended to argue that mutual gains require a wholesale reconstruction of the political economy; that liberal market economies like Britain's generate a suboptimal employment relationship and will continue to do so unless subject to sweeping reform (Sisson 1993, 2008).

Adherence to the pluralist frame of reference continues to mark the mainstream of industrial relations scholarship. As the comments above suggest, however, pluralism has acquired a more radical edge in recent years and the line between this tradition and critical scholarship has blurred over time. As the kind of regulation for mutual gains promoted by pluralists has exerted less sway over state policy and business practice, so some adherents to the pluralist frame have been pushed towards a more critical position.

The hallmark of the critical frame of reference is the belief that the interests of workers and employers are starkly opposed. From this perspective the employment relationship is regarded variously as exploitative, coercive, and dehumanizing and for these reasons workers have an interest in continual resistance. Conflict, in this view, is not only the natural condition of the employment relationship, but is to be welcomed as it is only through challenging the opposed interests of employers that workers can register any improvement in their condition. This orientation can be seen both in the celebration of industrial militancy of traditional left commentators on industrial relations (Darlington and Lyddon 2001) and in the equally positive assessment of 'resistance' in the work of contemporary critical management studies (CMS) (Thomas and Davies 2005). Another defining feature of the critical frame is its very focus on critique. Unlike unitary and pluralist writers who typically are prescriptive in orientation, critical scholars have concentrated much of their activity on critiquing both the practice of actually existing employment relationships and their theoretical defence in contributions from the other traditions. On the traditional, Marxist wing of the critical frame, attack has long been targeted at reformist trade unionism, established systems of industrial relations, and their pluralist defenders (Hyman 1975; Kelly 2010). On the CMS wing, in contrast, there is primary emphasis on the critique of management and on uncovering the oppressive kernel of purportedly progressive forms of management advanced by the soft unitary exponents of HRM (Keenoy 2009). These two wings of critical scholarship are often sharply opposed in terms of their fundamental assumptions with regard to ontology and epistemology. They are united, however, in their assumption that the employment relationship in capitalist societies is a fundamentally oppressive and conflicted institution and in their appetite for scholarly critique.

Each of these three frames of reference has approached the subject of worker participation in strikingly different ways. In the remainder of the chapter there is a review of the contemporary writing of unitary, pluralist, and critical scholars on participation, which seeks to map their main lines of argument. In each case the review considers four aspects of these accounts: the prescriptions for worker participation that are offered, the standards of evaluation that are used to assess forms of participation, the research programme that has been developed to explore the empirical record of participation, and the primary explanations of why participation takes the form it does and generates a given set of outcomes. Having reviewed each frame in turn, the chapter ends by identifying their differences, what might be regarded as the chief zones of contention between the competing interpretations of worker participation that they offer.

Unitary perspectives on worker participation

The function of worker participation in the unitary tradition is to align the interests of workers and employers, though 'soft' and 'hard' variants of the unitary frame tend to prescribe different mechanisms to produce this alignment. In the softer version the typical prescription is for employee involvement, comprising information sharing, direct consultation of workers, and task-based forms of participation that grant discretionary power to individual workers or to work teams (Marchington 2007). Often measures of this kind are prescribed as part of a wider bundle of high commitment or high performance work practices that include systems of recruitment, selection, reward, development, and recognition, which reinforce the principle of direct employee involvement (Boxall and Purcell 2011). Employee involvement itself is deemed to be effective, first because it provides an opportunity for workers to contribute to business decision making by drawing upon their tacit knowledge of work processes, second because it can generate positive work attitudes such as commitment, engagement, job satisfaction, and trust in management, and third because these attitudes in turn can lead to positive work behaviours that raise business performance, such as lower absenteeism and higher productivity. While writers in the hard unitary tradition have also endorsed employee involvement, their main prescription has tended to be for systems of financial participation. They have variously prescribed profit sharing, employee share ownership, worker cooperatives, and partnerships, organizational forms that erode the distinction between workers and owners and thereby provide long-term financial incentives for cooperation (Bradley and Gelb 1983b; Bradley and Taylor 1992).

While the prescription of employee involvement has been an enduring feature of the soft unitary tradition, it has assumed different forms over time depending on the vagaries of management fashion. Thus, the quality movement of the 1980s prompted experiment with quality circles, while the later vogue for empowerment was driven by a desire to make expanding service industries responsive to their customer base (Bradley and Hill 1983; Jones et al. 1997). Today, the clearest prescription can be seen in the literature on employee engagement. According to Purcell (2010: 5), 'employee engagement can be said to exist where a sizable majority of employees are committed to their work, their colleagues, management and, overall to the organisation, and this is reflected in positive behaviour, sometimes called "organisational citizenship behavior"'. Employee involvement or 'voice' is typically identified as one of the 'key enablers' of these positive outcomes and in the prescriptive literature extensive communication, consultation, and job redesign are presented as essential supports of engagement (MacLeod and Clarke 2009; Sparrow et al. 2010). The single involvement technique which is most strongly identified with the employee engagement movement is the employee attitude survey (Guest 2014). The purpose of the latter is to measure variation and trends in the level of engagement across the workforce, allowing managers to refine their set of 'enabling' practices and so ensure that aggregate engagement remains on an upward trajectory.

The prescription of financial participation also has a long history with periodic bursts of enthusiasm for particular schemes, such as American employee stock ownership plans of the 1970s, the Mondragon cooperatives in the 1980s, and current interest in the John Lewis Partnership (Bradley and Gelb 1983a, 1986). Enthusiasm has been particularly marked in the Anglophone, liberal market economies and has translated into active state support for financial participation through tax incentives (Bradley and Gelb 1986). State-level encouragement continues to be offered in Britain. The Coalition Government has launched a number of initiatives, some of which seek to echo the experience of the John Lewis Partnership. Thus, for the private sector the government established and has largely accepted the recommendations of the Nuttall review of employee ownership, resulting in a series of measures to encourage the formation of employee-owned firms on the John Lewis model (BIS 2012). In the public sector it has espoused the creation of 'public service mutuals', endowing workers with a new 'right to provide' public services, when they are privatized, through the medium of an employee-owned social enterprise (Mutuals Taskforce 2012). Another, rather different measure has been the new entitlement for workers to exchange employment rights for ownership of shares in their employing enterprise (BIS 2013). It is widely expected that there will be limited take-up of the new 'employee shareholder' employment status but the measure demonstrates clearly the strongly unitary assumptions that often underpin proposals for financial participation.

If writers in the soft and hard unitary traditions tend to prescribe different forms of worker participation, they are more united in the criteria they apply when assessing these forms. On both wings, there tends to be a very strong assumption that the core purpose of worker participation is to improve business performance. This assumption can be seen very clearly in reports on employee engagement, employee ownership, and public service mutuals that the government has commissioned from writers with a broadly unitary perspective. These reports, by the Mutuals Taskforce (2011), Rayton et al. (2012), and Lampel et al. (2012), take as their main criterion for assessment contribution to business performance measured through a variety of indicators. The latter include efficiency, productivity, innovation, resilience in the face of shocks, profitability, customer responsiveness, and quality of service. To be sure, these reports also refer to the contribution of worker participation to employee well-being, reflecting the core unitary belief that management techniques can work to the joint benefit of workers and employers. However, the main criterion of assessment, measured through most indicators, is business performance.

The programme of research on participation developed by unitary writers has reflected these beliefs and assumptions. The focus of research has very much been on techniques of employee involvement and financial participation, with some work exploring whether these two types can mutually reinforce one another (Kessler 2010). In contrast, scant attention has been paid to other methods of participation, particularly indirect forms that rest upon systems of worker representation. The central object of study for unitary writers, therefore, has been methods of participation created by and for employers to help them run their businesses more effectively. They have mapped the incidence and trends in the use of employee involvement and financial participation and have identified the types of business and types of business context in which such techniques are used (Marchington 2007; Kaarsemaker et al. 2010; Kessler 2010). The main thrust of their research agenda, however, has been towards the outcomes of participation, with an emphasis on business performance. This interest has been pursued in two broad ways. On the one hand, researchers have sought to isolate the statistical association between the use of a particular method of participation and some measure of business performance. The succession of studies by labour economists seeking to identify the impact of employee share ownership, profit-sharing, and cooperative systems on productivity and profit provides a case in point (Oxera 2007; Pérotin 2012). Integral to much of this research have been attempts to measure the attitudinal and behavioural response of workers to these techniques, as it is through these responses that financial participation is assumed to produce its performance effect. On the other hand, researchers have focused on the 'dependent' variable, such as employee engagement, and worked backwards to identify the methods of participation, along with other management techniques, that generate this favourable complex of worker attitudes and behaviour (Crawford et al. 2014). Whether the starting point of the research is a measure of a participation input or a performance output, however, the basic purpose is the same: to identify a statistical association between these indicators when other conditions are held constant.

In developing their research agenda on participation, unitary scholars have drawn upon an array of social theory taken largely from the core disciplines of economics and psychology. Nevertheless, it is possible to identify some broad patterns which typify unitary theoretical explanation. One such pattern relates to the level of analysis at which explanation typically is developed. In much unitary work explanation is pitched at the level of the employing enterprise, with statistical regularities, such as the association between worker participation and business performance, being explained in terms of causal mechanisms that operate within the firm. For example, those seeking to account for the positive impact of employee share ownership on performance have variously attributed this to a sorting effect, in which schemes attract employees with a preference for share ownership (Lazear 2000), a retention effect in which schemes foster long-term commitment through a deferred incentive (Sengupta et al. 2007), and to schemes producing a fundamental change in employee values, characterized by 'psychological ownership' (Pierce et al. 2003). In all of these examples, psychological or economic reasoning is used to penetrate the 'black box' of the enterprise and thereby explain the link between participation and performance.

Two other features of unitary explanation relate to the context in which schemes for worker participation are developed and to agency, to the designation of the key actor initiating and shaping participation. With regard to context, it is common for unitary writers to resort to a form of benign post-industrialism, in which long-run changes in the economy and society exert a selective pressure for the introduction of more participative forms of management. The case for employee engagement rests on this type of claim, typically invoking the needs of the knowledge economy and the demands of knowledge workers for qualitatively different forms of management (MacLeod and Clarke 2009). With regard to agency, unitary writers have focused on the key role of managers in driving forward the participation agenda and have either downplayed or neglected the role of the state or of workers and their institutions. Experiments with new forms of participation, or successful 'engagement strategies', it is commonly claimed, originate with management and are dependent on senior management commitment and support if they are to be brought to fruition (Sparrow 2014). Effective leadership is one of the 'key enablers' that allow employees to 'engage with their work' (Soanes 2014).

Pluralist perspectives on worker participation

Recent years have seen a marked shift in the prescriptions for worker participation offered by pluralist writers. The classic pluralist position, exemplified in Britain by the work of Flanders and Clegg (Ackers 2010; Kelly 2010), was that the primary if not sole form of worker participation should be through collective bargaining, in which independent trade unions negotiated the terms of the employment relationship with employers. Joint regulation of this kind was considered to be the hallmark of a mature industrial relations system. As trade unionism has declined and collective bargaining shrunk to a minority of the workforce, however, pluralists have had to adjust their position. One response has been to seek to relaunch union-based participation under the rubric of labour-management partnership (Kochan et al. 2009; Samuel 2014; see also Johnstone, this volume). In Britain, attempts of this kind date back to productivity bargaining in the 1960s and the current vogue for partnership agreements is the latest in a long line of attempts to reboot the old system on a more collaborative basis. At the heart of these agreements are two kinds of impulse: one is to broaden the compass of shared interests between employers and workers by developing a new, integrative bargaining agenda around work organization, flexibility, training, and diversity; the other is to seek new ways of resolving conflict through new forms of third-party intervention or through mechanisms such as the indexation of pay, which preclude the need for bargaining at all.

While experiments with partnership have been quite widespread in the unionized segment of the British economy, they have not proved able to halt the decline of joint regulation. The second pluralist response acknowledges this fact and has embraced non-union forms of worker participation, which have become increasingly prominent through the years of union decline. Methods of worker participation that were once disregarded or treated with suspicion are now assessed in positive terms and prescribed as a means to close the 'representation gap' within UK workplaces. Statutory works councils, joint consultation, non-union forums and councils, and, indeed, employee involvement and financial participation have all been treated sympathetically by pluralist commentators in recent years (Bryson and Freeman 2007; Marchington 2007; Ackers 2010; Johnstone et al. 2010; Kaarsemaker et al. 2010; Hall and Purcell 2012). Acceptance of a plurality of institutions of worker voice, indeed, has become the hallmark of the contemporary pluralist position.

Pluralists have also shifted in terms of their understanding of the functions of participation and the standards they apply to evaluate participation in practice. Again, it is possible to identify classical and more recent positions. The classic pluralist defence of participation through collective bargaining was that it provided a means of regulating conflict and of integrating the industrial working class into stable, capitalist democracies (Kaufman 2010). Very similar views continue to be articulated by pluralist commentators today who suggest that the decline of traditional industrial relations institutions is helping to unleash new, threatening social forces on the political right, and also is contributing to levels of social exclusion and inequality that impose a severe strain on the social fabric (Standing 2011). Running alongside this preoccupation with order in the classic pluralist position, however, was adherence to two other important principles. On the one hand, there was an emphasis on the need for workers to have an independent voice through which they could articulate their legitimate, distinct, and opposed interests to those of their employers. On the other hand, there was a need for a 'power-based' system of worker participation through which employers could be compelled to address worker interests. In combination, these principles implied worker participation through trade unions equipped with the organizational and economic resources to sanction employers in pursuit of their members' interests (Ackers 2010). Adherence to these principles of independence and power-based participation has long provided the basis for a pluralist critique of the methods of participation favoured by unitarists. From Clegg's (1960) scepticism towards experiments with job enrichment in the 1950s to contemporary doubts about the sufficiency of non-union participation (Purcell and Hall 2012), pluralists have questioned the capacity of employee involvement, acting in isolation, to promote workers' interests effectively.

While classic standards for assessing participation remain in use, they have been supplemented with additional principles in recent years. Since the publication of Freeman and Medoff's *What Do Unions Do?* (1984), there has been a concerted effort to demonstrate that trade union-based systems of participation generate positive economic effects, not just for workers but for businesses as well (Metcalf 2005). On aggregate, it has been claimed unions exercise a generally benign effect within economy and society. The primary criterion by which unitary scholars evaluate methods of worker participation, therefore, has migrated to the pluralist frame and repeatedly pluralists have fashioned a 'business case' for the forms of participation that they prescribe. Running alongside and in certain respects in opposition to this essentially utilitarian standard has been an increasing tendency for pluralists to make a categorical argument in favour of worker participation. This 'social justice case' for union and associated forms of participation is most clearly apparent in the recent US literature on labour rights as human rights (Gross 2012). In this trenchant restatement of pluralism, the rights of workers to form unions, elect representatives, and participate in the running of business through works councils and collective bargaining are presented as absolute entitlements that must be respected regardless of cost. This adoption of a categorical standard for assessing participation is indicative of a more assertive pluralism coming to the fore.

The pluralist research agenda that has flowed from these prescriptions has embraced four main elements. First, there has been continuing work on trade unionism and collective bargaining, which has tracked the international decline in these institutions but also followed significant innovations, such as the growth of 'equality bargaining', the bending of this most traditional of institutions to the interests of women and minority workers (Colling and Dickens 1989). The focus on labour-management partnership identified above, however, has been the most pronounced theme. Work in this vein has mapped the incidence and content of partnership agreements but perhaps its main form has been the use of exemplary case studies of partnership to serve as models for others to follow (Rubinstein and Kochan 2001; Kochan et al. 2009). Second, there has been a broadening of the scope of pluralist research on participation to encompass non-union forms, including employee involvement and financial participation. Much of this work has been concerned with the relationship between these forms and the once dominant institution of collective bargaining (Charlwood and Terry 2007; Gumbrell-McCormick and Hyman 2010). Pluralists have tested competing replacement and reinforcement hypotheses and in the main have concluded that non-union forms of participation can coexist with a union presence and, indeed, may operate more effectively where unions are present. Many contemporary pluralists have become supporters of complex or hybrid systems of worker participation on the basis of findings of this kind (Ackers 2010; Purcell and Hall 2012; Purcell 2014). The third research theme has largely been the province of pluralist labour economists and has flowed from *What Do Unions Do?* This work has used secondary data analysis to test for statistical associations between union presence and a wide array of outcome variables, ranging from productivity, profit, investment, pay, benefits, training, accidents, dismissal, and redundancy, to flexibility and beyond (Blanchflower and Bryson 2009). In the latest iteration of this work there is an emphasis on the impact of unions on worker well-being, with researchers wrestling with the conundrum of whether or not unions enhance work quality and the experience of work (Bryson et al. 2013). The final theme is the least developed and is associated with the labour rights school. The research which has been developed in this area has typically concentrated on exposing the denial of labour rights by governments and corporations; for example, through employers hiring union busters to deny workers the right of association (Gross 2010). In its sharp emphasis on critique and revealing employer malfeasance, this wing of pluralism comes closest to the research interests of critical IR scholars.

A defining feature of pluralism has long been its predilection for institutional analysis; that is a preference for forms of explanation which emphasize the causal role of those formal institutions that comprise the national industrial relations system, trade unions, employers' organizations, state policy, the framework of employment law, and the structure of collective bargaining. Patterns of worker participation and their effects differ in countries such as France, Germany, Sweden, and the UK, it is argued, because they are embedded within the national systems of these countries, which in turn reflect enduring national industrial relations traditions (Clegg 1976). In recent years, pluralists have added a new layer of institutional explanation, identifying the causal role of supranational institutions, particularly the European Union. European legislation encouraging first the development of European works councils in cross-national enterprises and then the creation of information and consultation procedures within smaller enterprises has been a major focus of pluralist research in recent years (Waddington 2011; Hall and Purcell 2012). This European institutional impulse, however, is typically believed to be refracted powerfully through national institutions, which shape its determinate effects. Whatever the precise locus of the institutional impulse the key feature is that it originates beyond the employing enterprise and in this preference for institutional-level analysis there is a marked contrast with the predominant form of explanation of worker participation offered by unitarists.

There is also a marked contrast with unitary scholarship in the pluralist understanding of the context that shapes participation. In contemporary pluralist writing this understanding has been derived primarily from the 'varieties of capitalism' school within political economy. Forms of participation, it is often argued, reflect the wider imperatives of coordinated and liberal market economies (Turnbull et al. 2004). Indeed, the complex of institutions, which shape systems of worker participation, has been effectively extended in this work to embrace modes of corporate governance and business finance (Gospel and Pendleton 2005). The set of causal institutions, identified by pluralists, is no longer confined to a discrete system of industrial relations but includes all elements of the national business system. Another contrast between pluralist and unitary writers in this regard is the pronounced pessimism of many of the former with respect to contextual influences. The pressures within liberal market economies, in particular, especially the pressure to maximize shareholder value, are believed to generate an adversarial employment relationship and undermine attempts to build enduring cooperation, whether through employee involvement or labour-management partnership (Sisson 2008). Whereas unitarists have viewed the context for participation as essentially benign, encouraging the diffusion of techniques, those pluralists influenced by varieties of capitalism have tended to regard context as a malign influence, discouraging the adoption of desirable forms of participation.

The final aspect of pluralist theoretical explanation concerns agency, the identity of those actors with potential for significant agentic action. In contrast to unitary writing there is a marked trend in pluralist work to play down the agency of employers. The latter tend to be viewed as 'institution takers', conforming to systemic imperatives that operate above the level of the firm. There is also a marked scepticism with regard to the capacity of workers and their trade unions to engage in strategic action and exercise a determining role over the system of participation, a feature that differentiates the pluralist frame from much work on the critical wing (Gospel 2005). While unions may exert bargaining power and thus shape the operations of enterprises in which they are recognized, including shaping the process of worker participation, they are seen to exercise this influence within an institutional context of which they themselves are not the primary architect. In contemporary pluralist scholarship it is the state which is the principal actor in systems of industrial relations, fashioning the institutional context in which unions and employers operate and playing a key role in determining the rise and fall of different forms of worker participation (Howell 2005). Proposals to reform industrial relations, put forward by pluralists, even in a country like Britain with a pronounced voluntarist tradition, tend to address the state and identify public policy as the key source of innovation (Purcell and Hall 2012).

Critical perspectives on worker participation

Those writing from a critical perspective on worker participation have typically evinced a deep scepticism about the forms of participation prescribed by their unitary and pluralist rivals. While prescription is not absent from this tradition, the primary scholarly effort has been invested in critique, in identifying how and why systems that seemingly empower workers operate contrary to their interests. For critical writers, the division of interests between workers and employers is such that attempts to build cooperation through participation will either collapse through their inherent contradictions or, when successful, serve ultimately to reinforce an exploitative system of employment relations.

The main and enduring elements of this critique of participation can be seen in the response of critical writers to the spread of labour-management partnership and to the current vogue for employee engagement. The attack on partnership has come primarily from the traditional critical wing within IR, from writers who espouse an explicitly Marxist position. Through a series of case studies and reflections on partnership, critical writers have identified a variety of problems for workers and for trade unions that they believe are integral to this method (Kelly 1996a, 2004; Danford et al. 2005; McIlroy 2008; Upchurch 2009). While advancing participation may be the ostensible purpose of labour-management partnership, it is claimed that the underlying objective is to promote the restructuring of work and employment relations, essentially to raise the rate of exploitation. The primary condition that must exist for this goal to be pursued is an oligarchic and incorporated trade union organization that is able to comply with partnership initiatives because it is insulated from upward pressure from the union rank and file. The outcomes of partnership are considered to be deleterious both from the perspective of workers and their trade unions. Trade unions experience the reduction of bargaining and other rights and their replacement with weaker forms of participation, while their members are exposed to work intensification, pay restraint, and other negative changes to substantive employment conditions. The balance of outcomes from partnership agreements, it is argued, is weighted very heavily in the employers' favour. Because partnership agreements have these effects, critical writers often judge them to be unstable and liable to generate rank-and-file opposition within trade unions: a rejection both of the substantive settlement and of the leadership who negotiated it. This opposition, in turn, is welcomed because it is always believed that there is an alternative to partnership. This can take the immediate form of militant opposition to restructuring and in the longer term attempts to rebuild labour as a social movement through organizing campaigns and alliances with community organizations. Responses of this kind, which rebuild the independent power resources of the labour movement, are needed because of the division of interests that continues to exist between workers and employers, a division that is equally apparent with regard to training, flexibility, and equality, supposedly more integrative issues that lie at the heart of many partnership agreements. Labour-management partnership, according to Danford et al. (2005: 236), 'cannot mask irreconcilable conflicts that are prime characteristics of capitalist workplace dynamics'.

The response to employee engagement has come mainly from the CMS wing of critical scholarship (Jenkins and Delbridge 2013; Keenoy 2014). The provenance of this critique has led to some distinctive features. There has been a focus on deconstructing the meanings of engagement, an emphasis on its discursive function in promoting an interpretation of work that accords with the interests of politicians and employers, and in identifying the role of academic entrepreneurs and management consultants in formulating and diffusing this interpretation. There is also a lack of concern with the impact upon the labour movement, which features so prominently in traditional critical scholarship. Much of the substantive critique of engagement, however, echoes that which has been written about labour-management partnership. Thus, engagement is perceived to serve underlying goals that are at odds with its ostensible purpose, including intensifying management control and raising worker performance while controlling labour costs in the post-crisis economy. The condition of engagement, moreover, is believed to possess a 'dark side', manifest in overwork, poor work–life balance, and a diminution of well-being. Partly for this reason, critical researchers have claimed that engagement initiatives may encounter resistance and prove fragile, falling into disuse either as workers 'disengage' or as managers withdraw 'enabling' supports in the face of business pressure to reduce costs. These themes of ulterior purpose, work degradation, resistance, and fragility can be viewed as the enduring tropes of critical scholarship, rhetorical devices deployed on both wings of the critical frame in response to successive waves of worker participation.

While critique has been dominant, prescription has not been wholly absent from the writing of critical scholars on participation. The most frequent prescription has been one of resistance; a recommendation that workers should oppose methods of participation devised by employers, governments, and their own compromised trade unions. On the traditional wing of critical scholarship, such resistance is envisaged to come from the base of the trade union movement through the mobilization of the rank and file, a position that is often extended to include the broader renewal of the labour movement through organizing campaigns or the forging of union–community coalitions (Danford et al. 2005; McIlroy 2008). On the CMS wing little credence is placed in the traditional labour movement and there tends to be more emphasis on informal and individual resistance, including acts of misbehaviour at work, the preservation of autonomy from management direction and control, including cultural control, and the construction of alternative worker identities that subvert those propounded by employers (Thomas and Davies 2009). Alvesson and Willmott (1992) have interpreted resistance of this kind as a form of 'micro-emancipation'. A second response is a pragmatic acceptance of forms of participation that afford a degree of protection and influence to workers, which otherwise would be lacking. Hyman's (1996) defence of statutory works councils is a case in point, a defence which acknowledges the limitations of this form but also recognizes its potential benefits for workers in a period of union decline. This pragmatic position comes very close to pluralist reasoning and unsurprisingly has been attacked by critical writers who cleave to a more robust position (Kelly 1996b). The final prescription has been to endorse radical, worker-led experiments with alternative forms of organization and production. Examples can be seen in the enthusiasm for workers' control, exemplified by the occupation of Upper Clyde Shipbuilders in 1971, and the alternative workers' plans developed at Lucas Aerospace, Vickers, and other companies later in the 1970s (Beynon and Wainwright 1979; Ackers 2010). The attraction of these experiments for critical writers of the time lay in their strongly syndicalist character—they originated in mass worker mobilization and embodied principles of direct democracy—and in the fact that they seemed to be 'transitional', both by challenging capital in a way that mere economic militancy did not and in adumbrating forms of participation that might become dominant in some future socialist society. Of course, these experiments have long since faded from view as has the workerist prescription for participation to which they gave rise. In its wake there is mere critique.

Unlike their pluralist and unitary rivals, critical scholars generally have not employed business performance as a standard for assessing forms of worker participation. They often evince scepticism about the potential of these forms to raise performance and have been quick to identify perverse consequences of participation (Keenoy 2014), but judgements of this kind are incidental to the main thrust of critical evaluation. One yardstick that is widely used, at least on the traditional wing of the critical frame, is the impact of participation on trade unions. Critical writers have been concerned lest participation neuters trade unions, making them less effective through leadership incorporation and the reinforcement of oligarchy within union organization, and have also been alive to the possibility that many forms of participation have the potential to substitute for union voice (Kelly 1996b; Danford et al. 2005). Another standard has been the impact of participation on workers. The assessment of many critical writers is that forms of participation, such as partnership and employee involvement, have deeply negative consequences for workers, particularly with regard to 'managerial relations'. It is claimed that these forms lead to work intensification, higher levels of job strain, and increased surveillance and control (Danford et al. 2005; Jenkins and Delbridge

2013). Lurking behind judgements of this type is a belief that work can and should be a locus of emancipation (Fleming and Mandarini 2009), coupled with an insistent claim that such potential cannot be realized within capitalist enterprise. Another criterion of assessment used by critical writers concerns the extent to which forms of participation transfer real power to workers and fundamentally change the structure of governance within the economy. The typical judgement reached is that most forms fall well short on this criterion, providing mere pseudo-participation or limited influence within bounds set by the employer (Danford et al. 2005). Critical writers hold that work relations are exploitative and that workers have an interest in their transformation. The predominant forms of worker participation are regarded as at best a marginal adjustment within these relations or at worst a confirming influence that pacifies dissent and renders transformative change less likely.

An aspect of the critical research agenda on participation that sharply differentiates it from those of the unitary and pluralist frames is an absence of exemplary cases, studies of organizations or techniques which embody lessons others can learn and apply. With the exception of the now venerable studies of workers' control, critical research has eschewed the search for good practice in participation in favour of the examination of flawed systems, the main lesson from which is the need for resistance. Each new vogue in the long history of employee involvement and each new bid to relaunch pluralist industrial relations has been the subject of empirical critique. The main exception to this is financial participation, experiments with which have attracted very little attention from critical scholars, perhaps because they have very little contact with or interest in mainstream labour economics. Another distinctive feature of critical research has been its overwhelming preference for qualitative methods, such as interview-based case studies or ethnography, and a desire to examine participation from the bottom up through the voices of workers subject to these techniques (Jenkins and Delbridge 2013). On the CMS wing there has also been an emphasis on textual analysis, probing the meanings of terms like 'employee engagement' in the documents of managers, consultants, and policy makers (Keenoy 2014), together with a wider attention to discursive processes through which meanings are constructed, experienced, and challenged within the workplace (Francis et al. 2013). Whatever the precise method employed, however, the fundamental purpose of virtually all research in this tradition is critique, to expose the gap between the rhetoric and reality of worker participation.

While critical researchers have often developed complex, multi-level accounts of worker participation (Jenkins and Delbridge 2013), there is a tendency within this frame to couch explanation at a relatively high level of abstraction. Thus, the limits to worker participation are often traced ultimately to the systemic properties of the capitalist mode of production or, on the CMS side, to inescapable disciplinary processes through which worker identities are constructed and regimented (Danford et al. 2005; Fleming and Mandarini 2009). While firm-level processes and the causal impact of formal institutions are acknowledged in this tradition, explanations are typically anchored in broad social theory and interpretations of the fundamental nature of modernity. There is an ambition to reach beyond mid-range theory, dealing with how methods of participation raise worker performance or how national business systems constrain the use of these methods, which is characteristic of unitary and pluralist frames, in order to attain a deeper, more complete form of analysis.

Critical understandings of the context of participation reflect this preference for relatively abstract explanation. Thus, the form of participation, its outcomes, sustainability, and the degree to which it is contested tend to be related to the enduring and universal features of capitalism, to the latest epoch in the evolution of capitalism, such as neo-Fordism, neoliberalism or postmodernity, or to universal processes within contemporary capitalism, such as globalization or financialization. The latter process has featured prominently in recent critical scholarship on work and employment relations, including discussion of worker participation. In Thompson's (2013) 'disconnected capitalism' thesis it is suggested that the dominance of finance capital, and the imperatives for short-term profitability it imposes on business, constrains the adoption of more participative forms of management that rest on long-term commitment and mutual gains. For Jenkins and Delbridge (2013), the same pressures account for the fragility of employee engagement. These pessimistic assessments of the impact of the wider business context on worker participation echo very closely the arguments of pluralists with regard to developments within liberal market economies. There is effectively a shared critique across the two frames, which points to the constraints on management capacity to introduce effective and lasting forms of participation within contemporary capitalism.

The main difference between the pluralist and critical positions is that the latter concedes less scope for effective agency to the state. The process of financialization is viewed as systemic, not tied to a particular business system, and indeed has the capacity to unravel the national institutions of industrial relations which retain causal primacy in much pluralist thinking (Appelbaum et al. 2013). Many critical writers are also sceptical of the scope for strategic action by employers. For example, in Jenkins and Delbridge's (2013) study of a highly engaged call-centre workforce, pains are taken to demonstrate the importance of immediate contextual factors in allowing engagement to emerge. Engagement is the product of happenstance, not management purpose, and vulnerable to erosion as systemic pressures to which employers are subject act upon the enterprise. The key source of agency in much critical thought is workers and to a lesser degree their trade unions. In both traditional and CMS versions of the critical frame worker resistance is viewed as a major source of change through which malign forms of participation are broken. The clearest statement of this position can be found in Ramsay's (1977) thesis of 'cycles of control', that across UK business history experiments with worker participation have followed strike waves as employers have attempted to re-establish control over the enterprise. Very similar reasoning can be seen in the work of CMS scholars on microemancipation, with even incremental gains in worker control being dependent on resistance (Alvesson and Willmott 1992). Of course resistance may fail and employer-designed programmes prove effective but repeatedly in critical writing there is a defence of the capacity of workers to challenge and shape the form of worker participation.

Conclusion

Characterizations of the academic field of IR have often stressed its coherence. IR scholars, it is claimed, are united by shared values and perspectives (Sisson 2008) or by a common methodology (Edwards 2005). The position adopted in this chapter has been different. Using the time-honoured concept of frames of reference, it has identified three competing traditions of writing about worker participation, which, starting from fundamental assumptions about the relative interests of workers and employers, have advanced very different interpretations of this core subject matter. These unitary, pluralist, and critical traditions have formulated competing prescriptions for participation, offered different standards of evaluation, developed their own research programmes, and have favoured distinctive forms of explanation (see Table 2.1). The clash between these traditions defines contemporary debate about worker participation and reveals the field of IR to be marked as much by contention as coherence.

Although enduring, unitary, pluralist, and critical frames have been subject to change and over time there has been some realignment between the three traditions. This can be seen most clearly in the changing relationship between the central pluralist frame and its unitary and critical rivals. On the one hand, pluralists have moved closer to the unitary frame, accepting the standard of business performance as a measure of the effectiveness of participation and endorsing forms of employer and government-authored participation about which many pluralists were once deeply sceptical. For some time now, pluralist researchers have been engaged in the open-minded and generally sympathetic assessment of different forms of employee involvement and financial participation. On the other hand, there is another current within pluralist scholarship that has approached the critical frame. The social justice

Table 2.1 Unitary, Pluralist, and Critical Perspectives on Participation

	Unitary	Pluralist	Critical
Prescription	Employee involvement; financial participation	Revival of collective bargaining through partnership; hybrid systems that combine union and non-union participation	Critique of pluralist reform and progressive forms of management; union renewal; micro-emancipation through 'resistance'
Evaluation	Business performance plus employee well-being	Conflict regulation and social integration, plus business performance and social justice	Union capacity for militancy; control and discipline of workers
Research	Impact of employee involvement and financial participation on worker attitudes and behaviour and business performance	Evaluation of partnership; relationship between union and non-union forms; unions and business performance; infractions of freedom of association	Critical accounts of participation 'from below'; studies of resistance to existing forms of participation
Theory	Firm-level analysis of link between participation and performance; post-industrialism; employers as primary agent	Institutional analysis, informed by varieties of capitalism school; financialization; state as primary agent	Systemic and epochal accounts of participation; financialization; workers and their organizations as primary agent

case for labour rights, the use of research as exposé, and pessimistic assessments of business context as constraining effective participation, represent a realignment of pluralist and critical positions. The tone of writing of many pluralist commentators on industrial relations has become more critical as the practice of participation has drifted further from the principles they hold dear.

While realignment has muted some old divisions, there remain clear zones of contention between the competing frames. Between pluralists and unitary scholars there are differences over the sufficiency of employer-sponsored systems of participation and in their assessments of the need for independent worker representation through trade unions and statutory works councils. The latter are viewed as essential, as part of a complex hybrid system of participation, in the pluralist camp but are often disregarded by unitarists. Between pluralists and critical scholars another zone of contention can be seen in their competing assessments of labour-management partnership. An abiding theme of the pluralist tradition has been to reform union-based participation on a more integrative basis, a project that has met equally abiding resistance from those on the traditional wing of the critical frame. Critical writers, including but not confined to those with a CMS badge, have also maintained a relentless critique of employee involvement, attacking both the theory and practice of unitary participation. This appetite for critique shows no sign of abating as is apparent in the critical response to employee engagement. Notwithstanding realignment and dialogue between the frames, therefore, zones of contention remain clearly defined. On balance, this is to be welcomed as a means of bolstering IR scholarship. It is through advancing and defending positions against rival frames that arguments are strengthened, interpretations are clarified, and new research is born.

▓ REFERENCES

Ackers, P. (2010) 'An Industrial Relations Perspective on Employee Participation'. In A. Wilkinson, P. J. Gollan, M. Marchington, and D. Lewin (eds), *The Oxford Handbook of Participation in Organizations*, pp. 52–75. Oxford: Oxford University Press.

Alvesson, M. and Willmott, H. (1992) 'On the Idea of Emancipation in Management and Organization Studies'. *Academy of Management Review*, 17(3), 432–64.

Appelbaum, E., Batt, R., and Clark, I. (2013) 'Implications of Financial Capitalism for Employment Relations Research: Evidence from Breach of Trust and Implicit Contracts in Private Equity Buyouts'. *British Journal of Industrial Relations*, 51(3), 498–518.

Beynon, H. and Wainwright, H. (1979) *The Workers' Report on Vickers*. London: Pluto Press.

BIS (2012) *Government Response to the Nuttall Review: Next Steps for Employee Ownership*. London: Department for Business, Innovation and Skills.

BIS (2013) *Employee Shareholders*. London: Department for Business, Innovation and Skills. [Online.] Available at: <https://www.gov.uk/employee-shareholders>.

Blanchflower, D. G. and Bryson, A. (2009) 'Trade Union Decline and the Economics of the Workplace'. In W. Brown, A. Bryson, J. Forth, and K. Whitfield (eds), *The Evolution of the Modern Workplace*, pp. 48–73. Cambridge: Cambridge University Press.

Boxall, P. and Purcell, J. (2011) *Strategy and Human Resource Management*, 3rd edn. Basingstoke: Palgrave MacMillan.

Bradley, K. and Gelb, A. (1983a) *Cooperation at Work: The Mondragon Experience*. London: Heinemann Educational Books.

Bradley, K. and Gelb, A. (1983b) *Worker Capitalism: The New Industrial Relations*. London: Heinemann Educational Books.

Bradley, K. and Gelb, A. (1986) *Share Ownership for Employees*. London: Public Policy Centre.

Bradley, K. and Hill, S. (1983) 'After Japan: The Quality Circle Transplant and Productive Efficiency'. *British Journal of Industrial Relations*, 21(3), 291–311.

Bradley, K. and Taylor, S. (1992) *Business Performance in the Retail Sector: The Experience of the John Lewis Partnership*. Oxford: Oxford University Press.

Bryson, A. and Freeman, R. (2007) 'What Voice Do British Workers Want?' In R. Freeman, P. Boxall, and P. Haynes (eds), *What Workers Say: Employee Voice in the Anglo-American Workplace*, pp. 72–96. Ithaca, NY, and London: ILR Press.

Bryson, A., Barth, E., and Dale-Olsen, H. (2013) 'The Effects of Organizational Change on Worker Well-being and the Moderating Role of Trade Unions'. *Industrial and Labor Relations Review*, 66(4), 989–1011.

Charlwood, A. and Terry, M. (2007) '21st Century Models of Employee Representation: Structures, Processes and Outcomes'. *Industrial Relations Journal*, 38(4), 320–37.

Clegg, H. A. (1960) *A New Approach to Industrial Democracy.* Oxford: Basil Blackwell.

Clegg, H. A. (1976) *Trade Unionism under Collective Bargaining: A Theory Based on Comparison of Six Countries.* Oxford: Basil Blackwell.

Colling, T. and Dickens, L. (1989) *Equality Bargaining: Why Not?* Manchester: Equal Opportunities Commission.

Crawford, E. R., Rich, B. L., Buckman, B., and Bergeron, J. (2014). 'The Antecedents and Drivers of Employee Engagement'. In C. Truss, R. Delbridge, K. Alfes, A. Shantz, and E. Soane (eds), *Employee Engagement in Theory and Practice*, pp. 57–81. London: Routledge.

Danford, A., Richardson, M., Stewart, P., Tailby, S., and Upchurch, M. (2005) *Partnership and the High Performance Workplace: Work and Employment Relations in the Aerospace Industry.* Basingstoke: Palgrave MacMillan.

Darlington, R. and Lyddon, D. (2001) *Glorious Summer: Class Struggle in Britain, 1972.* London: Bookmarks.

Dunlop, J. T. (1993) *Industrial Relations Systems*, revised edn. Boston, MA: Harvard Business School Press.

Edwards, P. K. (2005) 'The Challenging but Promising Future of Industrial Relations Research'. *Industrial Relations Journal*, 36(4), 264–82.

Fleming, P. and Mandarini, M. (2009) 'Towards a Workers' Society? New Perspectives on Work and Emancipation'. In M. Alvesson, T. Bridgman, and H. Willmott (eds), *The Oxford Handbook of Critical Management Studies*, pp. 328–44. Oxford: Oxford University Press.

Fox, A. (1966) *Industrial Sociology and Industrial Relations*, Royal Commission on Trade Unions and Employers' Associations, Research Paper 3. London: HMSO.

Francis, H. M., Ramdhony, A., Reddington, M., and Staines, H. (2013) 'Opening Spaces for Conversational Practice: A Conduit for Effective Engagement Strategies and Productive Working Arrangements'. *International Journal of Human Resource Management*, 24(14), 2713–40.

Freeman, R. B. and Medoff, J. L. (1984) *What Do Unions Do?* New York: Basic Books.

Gospel, H. (2005) 'Markets, Firms and Unions: A Historical-Institutionalist Perspective on the Future of Unions in Britain'. In S. Fernie and D. Metcalf (eds), *Trade Unions: Resurgence or Demise?* London: Routledge, 19–44.

Gospel, H. and Pendleton, A. (eds) (2005) *Corporate Governance and Labour Management: An International Comparison.* Oxford: Oxford University Press.

Gratton, L. (2004) *The Democratic Enterprise: Liberating Your Business with Freedom, Flexibility and Commitment.* London: FT/Prentice Hall.

Gross, J. A. (2010) *A Shameful Business: The Case for Human Rights in the American Workplace.* Ithaca, NY, and London: ILR Press.

Gross, J. A. (2012) 'The Human Rights Movement in US Workplaces: Challenges and Changes'. *Industrial and Labor Relations Review*, 65(1), 3–16.

Guest, D. (2014) 'Employee Engagement: Fashionable Fad or Long-Term Fixture?' In C. Truss, R. Delbridge, K. Alfes, A. Shantz, and E. Soane (eds), *Employee Engagement in Theory and Practice*, pp. 221–35. London: Routledge.

Gumbrell-McCormick, R. and Hyman, R. (2010) 'Works Councils: The European Model of Industrial Democracy'. In A. Wilkinson, P. J. Gollan, M. Marchington, and D. Lewin (eds), *The Oxford Handbook of Participation in Organizations*, pp. 286–314. Oxford: Oxford University Press.

Hall, M. and Purcell, J. (2012) *Consultation at Work: Regulation and Practice*. Oxford: Oxford University Press.

Howell, C. (2005) *Trade Unions and the State: The Construction of Industrial Relations Institutions in Britain, 1890–2000*. Princeton, NJ: Princeton University Press.

Hyman, R. (1975) *Industrial Relations: A Marxist Introduction*. Basingstoke: MacMillan.

Hyman, R. (1996) 'Is There a Case for Statutory Works Councils in Britain?' In A. McColgan (ed.), *The Future of Labour Law*, pp. 64–84. London: Pinter.

Jenkins, S. and Delbridge, R. (2013) 'Context Matters: Examining "Soft" and "Hard" Approaches to Employee Engagement in Two Workplaces'. *International Journal of Human Resource Management*, 24(14), 2670–91.

Johnstone, S., Ackers, P., and Wilkinson, A. (2010) 'Better than Nothing? Is Non-Union Partnership a Contradiction in Terms?' *Journal of Industrial Relations*, 52(2), 151–68.

Jones, C., Nickson, D., and Taylor, G. (1997) 'Whatever It Takes? Managing Empowered Workers and the Service Encounter in an International Hotel Chain'. *Work, Employment and Society*, 11(3), 541–54.

Kaarsemaker, E., Pendleton, A., and Poutsma, E. (2010) 'Employee Share Ownership'. In A. Wilkinson, P. J. Gollan, M. Marchington, and D. Lewin (eds), *The Oxford Handbook of Participation in Organizations*, pp. 315–37. Oxford: Oxford University Press.

Kaufman, B. E. (2010) 'The Theoretical Foundation of Industrial Relations and Its Implications for Labor Economics and Human Resource Management'. *Industrial and Labor Relations Review*, 64(1), 817–51.

Keenoy, T. (2009) 'Human Resource Management'. In M. Alvesson, T. Bridgman, and H. Willmott (eds), *The Oxford Handbook of Critical Management Studies*, pp. 454–72. Oxford: Oxford University Press.

Keenoy, T. (2014) 'Engagement: A Murmuration of Objects?' In C. Truss, R. Delbridge, K. Alfes, A. Shantz, and E. Soane (eds), *Employee Engagement in Theory and Practice*, pp. 197–220. London: Routledge.

Kelly, J. (1996a) 'Union Militancy and Social Partnership'. In P. Ackers, C. Smith, and P. Smith (eds), *The New Workplace and Trade Unionism: Critical Perspectives on Work and Organization*, pp. 77–109. London: Routledge.

Kelly, J. (1996b) 'Works Councils: Union Avoidance or Marginalization?' In A. McColgan (ed.), *The Future of Labour Law*, pp. 46–63. London: Pinter.

Kelly, J. (2004) 'Social Partnership Agreements in Britain: Labor Cooperation and Compliance', *Industrial Relations*, 43(1), 267–92.

Kelly, J. (2010) *Ethical Socialism and the Trade Unions: Allan Flanders and British Industrial Relations Reform*. London: Routledge.

Kessler, I. (2010) 'Financial Oarticipation'. In A. Wilkinson, P. J. Gollan, M. Marchington, and D. Lewin (eds), *The Oxford Handbook of Participation in Organizations*, pp. 338–57. Oxford: Oxford University Press.

Kochan, T. A. and Osterman, P. (1994) *The Mutual Gains Enterprise: Forging a Winning Partnership among Labor, Management, and Government*. Boston, MA: Harvard Business School Press.

Kochan, T. A., Eaton, A. E., McKersie, R. B., and Adler, P. S. (2009) *Healing Together: The Labor-Management Partnership at Kaiser Permanente*. Ithaca, NY, and London: ILR Press.

Lampel, J., Bhalla, A., and Jha, P. (2012) *The Employee Ownership Advantage: Benefits and Consequences*. London: Department for Business, Innovation and Skills.

Lazear, E. (1995) *Personnel Economics*. Cambridge, MA: MIT Press.

Lazear, E. (2000) 'Performance Pay and Productivity'. *American Economic Review*, 90 (5), 1346–61.

McIlroy, J. (2008) 'Ten Years of New Labour: Workplace Learning, Social Partnership and Union Revitalization in Britain'. *British Journal of Industrial Relations*, 46(2), 283–313.

MacLeod, D. and Clarke, N. (2009) *Engaging for Success: Enhancing Performance through Employee Engagement*. London: Department for Business, Innovation and Skills.

Marchington, M. (2007) 'Employee Voice Systems'. In P. Boxall, J. Purcell, and P. Wright (eds), *The Oxford Handbook of Human Resource Management*, pp. 231–50. Oxford: Oxford University Press.

Metcalf, D. (2005) 'Trade Unions: Resurgence or Perdition? An Economic Analysis'. In S. Fernie and D. Metcalf (eds), *Trade Unions: Resurgence or Demise?*, pp. 83–117. London: Routledge.

Mutuals Taskforce (2011) *Our Mutual Friends: Making the Case for Public Service Mutuals*. London: Cabinet Office.

Mutuals Taskforce (2012). *Public Service Mutuals: Next Steps*. London: Cabinet Office.

Oxera (2007) *Tax-Advantaged Employee Share Scheme: Analysis of Productivity Effects*. London: HMRC.

Pérotin, V. (2012) 'The Performance of Workers' Cooperatives'. In P. Battilani and H. G. Schroter (eds), *The Cooperative Business Movement, 1950 to the Present*, pp. 195–221. Cambridge: Cambridge University Press.

Pierce, J., Kostova, T., and Dirks, K. (2003). 'The State of Psychological Ownership: Integrating and Extending a Century of Research'. *Review of General Psychology*, 7 (1), 84–107.

Purcell, J. (2010) *Building Employee Engagement*, ACAS Policy Discussion Papers. London: ACAS.

Purcell, J. (2014) 'Employee Voice and Engagement'. In C. Truss, R. Delbridge, K. Alfes, A. Shantz, and E. Soane (eds), *Employee Engagement in Theory and Practice*, pp. 236–49. London: Routledge.

Purcell, J. and Hall, M. (2012) *Voice and Participation in the Modern Workplace: Challenges and Prospects*, ACAS Future of Workplace Relations Discussion Paper Series. London: ACAS.

Ramsay, H. (1977) 'Cycles of Control: Worker Participation in Sociological and Historical Perspective'. *Sociology*, 11(3), 479–506.

Rayton, B., Dodge, T., and D'Analeze, G. (2012) *Engage for Success: The Evidence*. London: Department for Business, Innovation and Skills.

Rubinstein, S. A. and Kochan, T. A. (2001) *Learning from Saturn: Possibilities for Corporate Governance and Employee Relations*. Ithaca, NY, and London: ILR Press.

Samuel, P. J. (2014) *Financial Services Partnerships: Labor-Management Dynamics*. Abingdon: Routledge.

Sengupta, S., Whitfield, K., and McNabb, R. (2007) 'Employee Share Ownership and Performance: Golden Path or Golden Handcuff?' *International Journal of Human Resource Management*, 18(8), 1507–38.

Sisson, K. (1993) 'In Search of HRM'. *British Journal of Industrial Relations*, 31(2), 201–10.

Sisson, K. (2008) *Putting the Record Straight: Industrial Relations and the Employment Relationship*, Warwick Papers in Industrial Relations No. 88. Coventry: University of Warwick.

Soanes, E. (2014) 'Leadership and Employee Engagement'. In C. Truss, R. Delbridge, K. Alfes, A. Shantz, and E. Soane (eds), *Employee Engagement in Theory and Practice*, pp. 149–62. London: Routledge.

Sparrow, P. (2014) 'Strategic HRM and Employee Engagement'. In C. Truss, R. Delbridge, K. Alfes, A. Shantz, and E. Soane (eds), *Employee Engagement in Theory and Practice*, pp. 99–115. London: Routledge.

Sparrow, P., Balain, S., and Chesworth, P. (2010) 'Vodafone: Creating an HR Architecture for Sustainable Engagement'. In P. Sparrow, M. Hird, A. Hesketh, and C. Cooper (eds), *Leading HR*, pp. 231–52. Basingstoke: MacMillan.

Standing, G. (2011) *The Precariat: The New Dangerous Class*. London: Bloomsbury.

Thomas, R. and Davies, A. (2005) 'Theorising the Micro-politics of Resistance: New Public Management and Managerial Identities in the UK Public Services'. *Organization Studies*, 26(5), 683–706.

Thomas, R. and Davies, A. (2009) 'Reassessing Identity: The Relevance of Identity Research for Analysing Employment Relations'. In P. Blyton, E. Heery, and P. Turnbull (eds), *Reassessing the Employment Relationship*, p. 147–68. Basingstoke: MacMillan.

Thompson, P. (2013) 'Financialization and the Workplace: Extending and Applying the Disconnected Capitalism Thesis'. *Work, Employment and* Society, 27(3), 472–88.

Turnbull, P. J., Blyton, P., and Harvey, G. (2004) 'Cleared for Take-off? Management-Labour Partnership in the European Civil Aviation Industry'. *European Journal of Industrial Relations*, 10(3), 287–307.

Upchurch, M. (2009) 'Partnership: New Labour's Third Way'. In G. Daniels and J. McIlroy (eds), *Trade Unions in a NeoLiberal World: British Trade Unions under New Labour*, pp. 230–53. London: Routledge.

Waddington, J. (2011) *European Works Councils: A Transnational Industrial Relations Institution in the Making*. London: Routledge.

3 Voice and employee engagement

David E. Guest

Introduction

In recent years, employee engagement has attracted the interest of scholars, policy makers, consultants, and managers. For academics, it appears to offer a new concept that fits within a stream of positive psychology. For policy makers and managers it promises a way of enhancing employee motivation and commitment to the organization. And for consultants, it provides a new product to market. However, appearances can be deceptive and claims about the antecedents, the precise nature and the benefits of engagement require careful scrutiny. Furthermore, as this chapter will argue, the approaches to engagement and the meaning of engagement promoted by academics on the one hand and practitioners on the other appear to diverge quite markedly. Because of these differing perspectives, it can be difficult to offer general statements about the relationship between voice and engagement. This chapter will therefore start with an analysis and evaluation of different approaches to engagement before considering its relevance for, and relationship to, employee voice. It will then set employee engagement in the context of wider debates on human resource management, participation, and partnership. It will be argued that much of the literature on engagement is either silent or muddled about employee voice but that engagement would be strengthened as a concept and an instrument of organizational policy if it took fuller account of voice.

The concepts of engagement

Interest in the concept of engagement at work can be traced back to two rather different sources. In the USA, Kahn (1990, 1992) developed the concept of *behavioural engagement*, which he viewed as a motivational construct and suggested that 'People can use varying degrees of their selves, physically, cognitively, and emotionally, in the roles they perform ... the more people draw on their selves to perform the roles... the more stirring are their performances' (Kahn 1990: 692). He went on to suggest that engagement is 'the simultaneous employment and expression of a person's "preferred self" in task behaviors that promote connections to work and to others, personal presence (physical, cognitive, and emotional) and active, full performance' (Kahn 1990: 700). It is therefore a state in which motivated behaviour leads to high work performance. For some years there was no established measure of behavioural engagement. However, Rich et al. (2010) have developed and presented a scale which they claim provides a sound measure of behavioural engagement.

In Europe, Schaufeli et al. (2002) developed a somewhat different concept of *attitudinal engagement*. They had previously worked extensively on the concept of burnout, and the way it was reflected in, and resulted in, disengagement from work. In turning their attention to engagement, they began to focus instead on positive experiences at work. While initially considering it as the opposite of burnout, they subsequently claimed that it was a separate dimension rather than the other end of a continuum. They viewed engagement with work as an attitude or state and defined it as 'a positive, fulfilling, work-related state of mind that is characterised by vigour, dedication and absorption' (2002: 74). Vigour is defined as 'high levels of energy and mental resilience... willingness to invest effort in one's work and persistence even in the face of difficulties' (2002: 74). Dedication is defined as 'a sense of significance, enthusiasm, inspiration, pride and challenge' (2002: 74), while absorption is defined as 'being fully concentrated and deeply engrossed in one's work' (2002: 75) and draws heavily on the concept of 'flow' at work (Csikszentmihalyi 2000). Attitudinal engagement is typically measured through the widely used Utrecht Work Engagement Scale (UWES).

In addition to the two predominantly academic approaches, a third approach to engagement has been championed by consultants and embraced by commercial organizations on both sides of the Atlantic and we will term it *organizational engagement*. The reason for this is that one of its distinguishing features is its dominant focus on engagement with the organization, as opposed to the focus on an individual level of analysis in the more academic attitudinal and behavioural perspectives on engagement and their concern with engagement in work.

The Gallup organization was one of the first consultants to use the term. Drawing on statistical analysis of their extensive attitude surveys, they identified twelve key items, including a global item on job satisfaction, and badged this as a measure of employee engagement. In presenting the so-called Gallup 12, Harter et al. (2002: 269) define employee engagement as 'the individual's involvement and satisfaction with as well as enthusiasm for work'. Inspection of the items in the Gallup 12 reveals that they cover a wide range of issues, many of which are more usually viewed as antecedents of job satisfaction. It is therefore doubtful whether this provides either a conceptual or operationally useful definition of engagement.

In the UK, the government set up an enquiry in 2008 'to take an in-depth look at employee engagement and to report its potential benefits for companies, organisations and individual employees' (MacLeod and Clarke 2009: 3). There was particular encouragement 'to examine in particular whether a wider take up of engagement approaches could impact positively on UK competitiveness and performance, as part of the country's efforts to come through the current economic difficulties, take maximum advantage of the upturn when it comes, and meet the challenges of increased global competition' (MacLeod and Clarke 2009: 3).

The enquiry received more than fifty definitions of employee engagement, reflecting the diversity of views. Early on in the report, it was noted that 'you know it when you see it' or 'you can sort of smell it' (MacLeod and Clarke 2009: 7) implying that it is operationally indefinable but that certain experts can use different senses to spot it. The report acknowledged that a useful operational definition of employee engagement might be 'a workplace approach designed to ensure that employees are committed to their organisation's goals and values, motivated to contribute to organisational success, and able at the same time to enhance their own sense of well-being' (MacLeod and Clarke 2009: 9). What this definition does not do is address the determinants of engagement. This was addressed in the report which identified four antecedents or 'enablers of engagement' (MacLeod and Clarke 2009: 74), which were leadership, engaging managers, integrity, and voice. This is a first recognition that voice may have a part to play in employee engagement. The problems of definition have not stopped various consultancies offering measures of organizational employee engagement which have been widely used by organizations.

The growing international interest in the topic of employee engagement has resulted in a number of major reviews (see, for example, Macey and Schneider 2008; Peccei 2013), meta-analyses of the existing research (see, for example, Crawford et al. 2010; Halbesleben 2010; Christian et al. 2011; Cole et al. 2011), and a series of books (see, for example, Albrecht 2010; Bakker and Leiter 2010; Truss et al. 2013). As already noted, employee engagement has also provided the focus for a government-inspired review of the potential value to industry of adopting engagement in industry in the UK.

Almost all the systematic academic research has been based on the behavioural and more particularly the attitudinal approaches to engagement. This has explored the antecedents, the measurement and the consequences of employee engagement. The major concern of consultants has been with levels of organizational engagement, as identified in their surveys, often resulting in what is typically described as 'an engagement deficit', and with demonstrating an association between higher scores on engagement surveys and measures of organizational performance. Despite their much more extensive conceptual and research base, the behavioural and attitudinal approaches to employee engagement are notably silent on the topic of voice and we need to dig deeply to find inferences about voice. Therefore, in the following section, we will briefly review the evidence about their antecedents and consequences before providing an evaluation of what they have to offer, including any relevance for voice. We will treat them together since this is what has happened in most of the integrative reviews and statistical analyses. After that, we will return to a fuller exploration of organizational engagement and its relationship to voice.

Attitudinal and behavioural engagement

ANTECEDENTS OF ATTITUDINAL AND BEHAVIOURAL ENGAGEMENT

The meta-analyses have brought together the research on antecedents and consequences of engagement but in doing so they have generally not distinguished between the behavioural and attitudinal perspectives. Nevertheless, it is worth noting that the bulk of the reviewed studies use the UWES measure implying a bias towards attitudinal engagement.

The reviews generally highlight two main kinds of antecedent. The first concerns the nature of the work and is typically based on the job demands—resources model (Karasek and Theorell 1990). The meta-analysis by Halbesleben (2010) found a strong positive association between job resources and engagement and a negative, albeit weaker association between demands and engagement. Interestingly, he also included the full range of studies from both European and American research using different measures and found that the choice of measure had no impact on the outcome. The meta-analysis of Crawford et al. (2010) adopted a similar focus but reached slightly different conclusions. They again used the full range of available studies. They found a consistently positive association between resources and engagement, but a more mixed association between engagement and demands whereby demands that were perceived as hindrances had a negative association with engagement, whereas demands that were seen as challenges had a positive association. In his review of three of the main meta-analyses (Crawford et al. 2010; Halbesleben 2010; and Christian et al. 2011), Peccei (2013) identified the most important antecedents as job variety, work-role fit, task significance, and opportunities for development, all of which had a correlation with engagement of about 0.50. It is interesting to note that job control or autonomy and feedback, while both strongly associated (correlations of 0.39 and 0.35 respectively), appeared to be less important, despite their centrality to the job demands–resources model.

The second kind of antecedent concerns individual differences. Peccei (2013) again reviewed the meta-analyses and found that there was evidence of a strong association with self-efficacy, proactivity, optimism, and conscientiousness, ranging between 0.50 and 0.40. One interpretation he offers is that these can be construed as personal resources that may pre-dispose individuals to become engaged in work. A rather different perspective on individual differences concerns intra-individual differences. This is based on the argument that there may be relatively stable individual differences in the propensity to seek work engagement but each person may also vary over time in their level of engagement. This may be a function of mood, energy, or the variable nature of the work. It has been explored using diary studies in which the work of the work of Sonnentag et al. (2010) has been particularly influential. Research has generally confirmed these variations in levels of engagement over time and the role of the explanations proposed above. In addition, Sonnentag's (2003) work places some emphasis on the importance of recovery time away from work.

OUTCOMES OF ATTITUDINAL AND BEHAVIOURAL ENGAGEMENT

Much of the organizational interest in employee engagement stems from an assumption that high engagement will have positive outcomes. This has been a focus of much of the academic research and the results have been brought together in two of the meta-analyses. Research on the outcomes associated with employee engagement typically focuses on attitudes, behaviour, performance, and health.

The research exploring engagement and employee attitudes consistently reveals a strong association with job satisfaction and organizational commitment. The corrected correlations in the meta-analyses are in the region of 0.60. Since extensive separate research has shown that job satisfaction is related to performance (Judge et al. 2001) and commitment is related to lower intention to quit (Meyer et al. 2001), these are relevant findings for policy makers. However, it is unclear whether job satisfaction and organizational commitment can be clearly identified as consequences rather than operating as coexisting correlates of engagement, so we must be cautious in making any attributions of causality.

The meta-analytic reviews confirm a consistent and often quite strong association with behaviour and task performance. With respect to behaviour, employee engagement is positively associated with organizational citizenship behaviour, proactive behaviour, and job crafting with a corrected correlation in the meta-analyses of 0.34 (Christian et al. 2011). In the case of task performance, the evidence shows a positive association with engagement and the corrected positive correlation in the meta-analyses is about 0.43. Finally, a negative correlation of -0.20 is reported across the studies exploring the link between engagement and intention to quit (Halbesleben 2010).

The fourth type of outcome that has been extensively explored is employee health. This reflects the influence of burnout research which preceded and helped to stimulate the attitudinal stream of research on engagement. The meta-analyses show a corrected correlation of 0.20 between higher engagement and reported health (Halbesleben 2010). It should be noted that this is based on subjective rather than objective indicators of health and, although the association is quite small, it is nevertheless consistently in the positive direction.

As with much research, many of the reported studies are cross-sectional. However, there are a number of longitudinal studies. One of the interesting issues they raise is the possibility of a positive spiral reflecting an interaction between resources and engagement (Mauno et al. 2010; Salanova et al. 2010). There is good evidence from these studies that the availability of resources enhances engagement but it is also possible that engagement enhances resources, and notably personal resources as well as resources gained through proactive behaviour and job crafting. Taken together the various studies, both cross-sectional and longitudinal, confirm an association between engagement, often measured as attitudinal engagement and a range of positive outcomes.

BEHAVIOURAL AND ATTITUDINAL ENGAGEMENT: AN ASSESSMENT

There is no doubt that behavioural and attitudinal engagement have emerged as popular and overlapping topics of academic research. Those associated with attitudinal research and using the UWES measure have reported a systematic and evolving programme of research exploring many aspects of engagement. Nevertheless, there are many unresolved conceptual and empirical issues that offer an extensive continuing research agenda.

A first point to highlight is that despite their conceptual differences and different origins, there is considerable overlap between attitudinal and behavioural engagement. They share much the same antecedents and outcomes. The meta-analyses have tended to view them interchangeably and the meta-analysis by Halbesleben found that the choice of measure made no difference in the outcomes. This raises the question of how useful it is to maintain the distinction between the two perspectives. Acknowledging both the growing interest in the concept of engagement and the increasing confusion about how to define and operationalize it, Macey and Schneider (2008) presented an integrative review in which they identified and distinguished three broad approaches which they labelled trait, state, and behavioural engagement. In doing so, they implied that a distinction between approaches is useful. A trait approach reflects a view that engagement can best be considered as a feature of personality akin to an orientation towards positive affect and proactivity. It is, as such, a characteristic of a person and subject to persisting individual differences. For Macey and Schneider, state engagement is reflected in feelings of energy and absorption, reflecting attitudinal engagement, but it is largely viewed as 'old wine in new bottles' and explored in terms of organizational commitment, job satisfaction, and job involvement. However, they also included the approach of Kahn within this category, clouding the distinction made by most other observers. For Macey and Schneider, behavioural engagement, which they seemed to favour, was reflected in specific behaviour such as organizational citizenship behaviour and role expansion. Perhaps the most useful approach is to adopt the perspective of a number of observers by suggesting that attitudinal engagement is best viewed as an antecedent of behavioural engagement.

The charge of concept redundancy reflected in the claim that attitudinal engagement is 'old wine in new bottles' is an important one that needs to be addressed. The meta-analysis by Christian et al. (2011) reveals quite a significant overlap between engagement measures and the potentially related constructs of job involvement, job satisfaction, and organizational commitment, with correlations between 0.50 and 0.60. Nevertheless, they concluded that engagement did emerge as a distinct construct and displayed acceptable discriminant validity. In accepting this, they are challenging the assumption that attitudinal engagement is 'old wine in new bottles'.

The meta-analysis by Cole et al. (2011) focused on the relationship between engagement and burnout and raises some rather different issues. When it was originally developed, attitudinal engagement was viewed as the opposite end of the same dimension as burnout (Maslach and Leiter 1997), although more recently Schaufeli and colleagues have sought to demonstrate that they are two distinct variables. Cole et al. found a negative correlation of about -0.55 between the two variables, which suggests that they are overlapping but nevertheless distinct. However, when burnout was entered first into a regression, it was found that engagement provided only marginal additional explanatory power. This implies that in practical terms the distinction between the two constructs may not be very meaningful. A rather different point is made by Newman et al. (2010) who conducted a meta-analysis exploring the presence of what they termed an A factor. This is a higher level attitudinal construct that includes engagement as well as job involvement, job satisfaction, and organizational commitment. They argued that this A factor had much stronger explanatory power than engagement or indeed the other variables on their own. There are therefore continuing concerns about the independent status and relative significance of the construct of engagement.

A third issue that needs to be addressed concerns the measurement of engagement. The nine-item UWES, reflecting attitudinal engagement, is the most widely used measure and as a result, the associated attitudinal model has dominated research, including the meta-analyses. It is only relatively recently that Rich et al. (2010) presented their measure of behavioural commitment. However, it is not clear that it demonstrates good construct validity. In his analysis of this eighteen-item measure, Peccei (2013: 345) says 'it is not clear whether the emotional engagement items in the scale provide an appropriate behavioural operationalisation of the notion of investment of emotional energy'. He goes on to say that 'many of the items appear to be little more than a rephrasing of items designed to measure feelings of positive affect at work, thereby raising questions about their inclusion in a behavioural engagement scale'. Until we have a more extensively utilized and tested measure of behavioural engagement, it will be difficult to establish the status of the construct.

Finally, a wide range of antecedents of engagement have been identified in the research. Most of these are considered at the task or job level of analysis, based on the job demands–resources model or are concerned with individual differences in propensity to be engaged. Some studies have shown the importance of social and organizational support as well as a role for leadership, organizational climate, and rewards. However, there is no indication of a link to a wider systems perspective that might be reflected in employment relations or human resource management.

In summary, the academic research has helped to develop along two streams reflecting an emphasis on either attitudinal or behavioural engagement. However, the practical distinction between the measures for these apparently different constructs has yet to be clearly established. The more widely used measure which addresses attitudinal engagement may be subject to concept redundancy while the status of the behavioural measures has yet to be fully established. None of the studies exploring these types of employee engagement make any reference to voice. In so far as autonomy is central to these approaches to engagement, it could be argued that there is implied scope for individual-level, job-related voice. However, to explore the potential role of voice in relation to employee engagement, we need to turn to the concept of organizational engagement.

Organizational engagement

As noted previously, the growing academic interest in engagement was picked up by consultants and notably by the Gallup organization. They were soon followed by other consultancies, for example, Towers Perrin (now Towers Watson) and Aon Hewitt, that typically make extensive use of employee attitude surveys. The initial focus of these consultants is to highlight the performance benefits to organizations of having highly engaged employees while at the same time suggesting that levels of engagement are only modest. The promise is to provide a benchmark to indicate how staff engagement in your organization compares with others or how it has changed over time. While definitions of engagement were generally left vague, it was often emphasized, in line with the definition offered by Gallup, that engaged employees displayed commitment and involvement. These in turn are claimed to be associated with positive outcomes.

The concept of employee engagement has attracted the attention of academics and organizational policy makers in North America and much of Europe. The development of the Gallup measure was undertaken in the USA while the main attitudinal measure was developed in the Netherlands. However, in the UK successive governments have also endorsed engagement. The Labour Government in 1997 briefly flirted with partnership at work but showed no enthusiasm for implementing it and later only reluctantly accepted the European imposition of works councils. Instead, it adopted the increasingly meaningless rhetoric of partnership as a basis for many of its wider policy initiatives, resulting in a devaluation of the concept. By its third term, the Labour Government had endorsed an increasingly unitarist perspective and had begun to focus on the recurring concern for levels of productivity and competitiveness in the UK economy. Since employee engagement, with its claimed link to motivation at the individual level and to performance at the organizational level, appeared to be an attractive option the Secretary of State, Peter Mandelson, asked David MacLeod and Nita Clarke to assess its potential value for the UK economy.

The MacLeod/Clarke report reached the clear and unsurprising conclusion that engagement was a good thing and should be strongly encouraged. This view was accepted by the Labour Government and was subsequently endorsed by the new Coalition Government. Indeed, the Prime Minister launched the next stage of promotion of employee engagement. This has resulted in a series of activities to promote engagement, with a task force led by David Macleod and Nita Clarke, the authors of the original report; these include a web page, a blog, a number of special interest groups, and a series of road shows and conferences.

In promoting employee engagement, much use has been made of case studies from a wide range of public and private sector organizations that claim to have applied it successfully. The wide variety of reported experiences makes it difficult to draw any general lessons from these. However, in promoting engagement consistent emphasis has been placed on the four fundamental principles identified in the initial MacLeod/Clarke report that should guide effective engagement—what they termed 'enablers of engagement' (MacLeod and Clarke 2009: 74). To give a little more detail, the first is *leadership*, revealed in particular in 'a strong strategic narrative' reflected in the organization's aims, values, and culture with clear support from top management. The second is *engaging managers* who 'facilitate and empower rather than control' (MacLeod and Clarke 2009: 75) or who, in other words, provide supportive, developmental management of subordinates. The third is *integrity*, which is concerned with the consistent application of organizational values to promote trust. The final principle is *voice*. This is described as: 'an effective and empowered employee voice—employees' views are sought out; they are listened to and see that their opinions count and make a difference. They speak out and challenge when appropriate. A strong sense of listening and of responsiveness permeates the organisation, enabled by effective communication' (MacLeod and Clarke 2009: 75).

This outline of the role of voice seems highly plausible, despite the absence of any specification of channels. The report elaborates on the issue of voice by presenting a number of case studies and outlining the views of various interested parties. These include the Trades Union Congress (TUC) who emphasize the importance of developing engagement through union representatives. Evidence for the report provided by Purcell notes that there are probably as many non-union as union representatives on works councils and similar institutions. Therefore, the key is appropriate representation of workers' interests. However, the TUC emphasizes the importance of an independent voice if the process is to generate the necessary trust and commitment from employees. The section of the report on voice ends with a quote from a joint TUC/Confederation of British Industry (CBI) document from 2001 stating that 'Optimal results are achieved where there is a mix of direct employee involvement and indirect participation through a trade union or works council' (MacLeod and Clarke 2009: 103). If this is engagement, then it looks very familiar and raises the question of how, if at all, voice in this context, and indeed organizational engagement more generally, can be distinguished from established constructs such as involvement and participation.

Before turning to an analysis of the relationship between employee engagement and voice, it is important to understand why organizational engagement has become so popular in management circles.

ORGANIZATIONAL ENGAGEMENT: WHY THE INTEREST?

It is tempting to claim that employee engagement is little more than the latest management fad. This is a plausible accusation and one we return to later in this chapter but it is also one that advocates of engagement predictably deny.

One possible reason why advocates claim it is not a fad is that the problems which it is hoped engagement can address have not gone away. The government remains concerned about the stalled levels of productivity and the lack of competitiveness of much of British industry while the challenge of moving out of recession remains for most organizations, as does the need to ensure the motivation of employees over whom management has only limited control. Therefore the case for a national debate persists.

Consultants and others help to support the continuing interest in two ways. First, together with some academics, they have pointed to persistently low levels of engagement among employees or what is sometimes termed 'an engagement deficit', strongly implying that organizations should be worried. Second, they have produced evidence, some of it quoted in the MacLeod/Clarke report (see, for example, Towers Perrin-ISR 2006; Gallup 2006), showing an association across a sizeable number of organizations between higher scores on their engagement measures and higher financial performance.

There is some indication that organizations are concerned that when and if the economy returns to significant growth, a worrying number of key employees will move elsewhere and they see the promotion of engagement, with its strong implied link to organizational commitment, as a means of helping to retain them. A more troubling view, reflected in some of the comments and examples in the MacLeod/Clarke report, is that engagement can help in managing labour force reductions. There is the ironic implication that workers may wish to become engaged in making themselves redundant, although the focus appears to be at least as much on seeking to retain the engagement of those who survive the cutbacks.

Purcell (2010), writing in an ACAS discussion paper soon after the publication of the MacLeod/Clarke report, presents a helpful outline of why engagement is of interest to organizations and what its content might be. His core argument is that the nature of work has changed and that many jobs allow employees more discretion. Therefore, to increase the likelihood of high performance, employers need to find ways of encouraging 'discretionary effort' since 'command and control' is no longer effective. He notes that:

One attraction of the term 'employee engagement' is that it is simple and straightforward in a way that earlier terms like 'high performance work systems' (HPWS) or 'high commitment management' (HCM) were not. At the same time this simple term can cover a variety of meanings. It is worth remembering that engagement is a combination of an attitude and behaviour. The attitude is 'commitment' and the behaviour is action to cooperate or what is sometimes referred to as 'going the extra mile'.

(Purcell 2010: 3)

In terms of the content of engagement, Purcell suggests that:

Employee engagement is not the only term used to describe the positive attitudes and behaviour of employees at work. Other terms commonly used are 'commitment', 'organization citizenship behaviour' and 'the psychological contract'. The policy and practice implications of employee engagement are often captured in 'high involvement work practices' and 'high performance working'. This plethora of terms can sometimes confuse the debate but the fundamentals are the same.

(Purcell 2010: 2)

These comments, in the context of an ACAS discussion paper, are revealing. They appear to confirm that employee engagement is a rebadging of existing concepts but that this is justified because it has the attraction of simplicity. The potential problem is that this simplicity may be illusory since it hides the complexity of, for example, applying an effective high performance work system. At the same time, by emphasizing the combination of attitude and behaviour, it also draws us back to the earlier academic approaches.

A final factor helping to promote organizational interest in employee engagement is that the role of trade unions has declined, and in many organizations managers can develop employment relations policy and practice without having to take significant account of union concerns. This means that if they wish to promote some kind of employee voice, they can choose the form it takes. To be fair to the MacLeod/Clarke approach, the definition they endorse does acknowledge employee well-being as a key outcome of engagement and in their consideration of voice, they do emphasize the importance of listening and responding to the concerns of employees. The role of voice in employee engagement was addressed in subsequent investigations and reports presented by the Involvement and Participation Association (IPA) and the Tomorrow's Company consultancy. The IPA is supported by both employers and trade unions and has a tradition of supporting both workers' participation and, when it was in vogue, partnership at work. Both of these build on a pluralist tradition that is likely to start from an assumption that employee voice is central to any process of exchange and engagement between employers and employees. There is a separate issue of whether a pluralist perspective is reflected in action by organizations to promote engagement.

Employee engagement and role of voice

As noted earlier, the definition of voice in the context of employee engagement outlined in the MacLeod/Clarke report has some merit. It emphasizes seeking employee views, listening to employees and showing that their opinions are important and have an impact. The views of the TUC on the importance of representative channels is reported and acknowledged and a role for both direct and indirect participation appears to be endorsed based on the quote from a joint TUC/CBI policy statement.

Engaging for Success, the follow up to the report on employee engagement led by the report authors, strongly endorsed the IPA/Tomorrow's Company exploration of the role of employee voice. *Rethinking Voice* (IPA/Tomorrow's Company 2012a) reports the results of a web survey with 161 responses. The survey confirms that in the large majority of organizations the emphasis is on individual rather than collective voice. The main forms of voice used by respondents were whole team meetings (86 per cent), line manager one-to-one meetings (85 per cent), staff surveys (74 per cent), direct contact between employees and senior management (72 per cent), and, much lower down, union meetings (44 per cent). Line manager one-to-one meetings were believed to be the most important (cited by 28 per cent), followed by direct contact with senior management (21 per cent) and whole team meetings (20 per cent). Only 3 per cent rated union meetings as most important. This reinforces the perception among managers of the importance of direct voice, if indeed what they report can usefully be described as voice.

A number of barriers to voice are identified. The most frequently cited are cynicism from staff (cited by 54 per cent) and getting staff buy in (51 per cent) followed by lack of management buy in, a problem more notable in large organizations. Given the management perceptions of voice, the problem of negative staff reactions is perhaps understandable. Reflecting on perceptions of the effectiveness of voice, the authors of the report noted: 'many people referred to levels of satisfaction or employee engagement overall as indicating the strength of employee voice. This likely follows the belief that staff who are given an adequate voice are more likely to be engaged and satisfied. Engagement is therefore used as a proxy for effective voice' (IPA/Tomorrow's Company 2012a: 9).

This statement reinforces a possible link between voice and engagement. On the other hand, it also suggests that high levels of engagement indicate voice without specifying the form of voice that is present. There is therefore an implication that as long as staff display engagement, the form, content, and extent of voice may be very limited. Set against this, the report notes that many respondents thought that voice had a positive influence on organizational performance, though there was little evidence of any measures to support this claim. It is also important to bear in mind that the preferred type of voice is individual rather than collective voice. This is reinforced in the follow-up IPA/Tomorrow's Company report *Releasing Voice* (2012b), although it does acknowledge the potential benefits of using a variety of channels depending on the organizational aims in using voice and on employee preferences.

INVOLVEMENT, PARTICIPATION, AND ENGAGEMENT

The focus on direct voice draws attention to parallels with the well-established concepts of participation and involvement. Indeed, the concept of employee involvement lies at the heart of several definitions of engagement. Marchington et al. (1993) identified four main types of involvement and presented an 'escalator' of levels of involvement. The four types of involvement are downward communication, upward problem solving, task participation, and teamworking/self-management. The focus is very much on local or task-related involvement and it provides a potential agenda for organizational engagement processes. The escalator presents a hierarchy of control over decisions that might be associated with engagement ranging from communication through consultation to codetermination and control.

Marchington et al. had been sympathetic to Ramsay's (1977) argument about 'cycles of control', reflecting varying levels of power of employer and employee interests but, acknowledging the problems with the concept, prefer the metaphor of waves (Marchington et al. 1993). The underlying argument is that new initiatives typically emerge when management control is under threat. In the present context, it could be argued that the necessary passing on to workers of discretionary control amounts to one aspect of the threat that has stimulated interest in the apparently novel concept of engagement. Thus he and colleagues argue that 'newer schemes—such as partnership or engagement—may have been operating for years, although under different labels' (Wilkinson et al. 2013).

The key feature of employee involvement is its focus on direct forms of participation that typically operate under the discretion of the management of an organization. Any analysis of worker participation usually distinguishes between direct and representative participation. Strauss (2006) has argued that participation, which is often defined in terms of influence over decision making, is a stronger and preferable term to voice since the latter lacks any connotation of control. In this context, representative participation usually reflects a pluralist rather than a unitarist approach to employment relations. There seems to be little doubt that when senior managers express enthusiasm for employee engagement and when surveys, such as that of IPA/Tomorrow's Company, cited above, list and value a range of direct forms of communication as representing engagement, they view it within a unitarist framework. This helps to explain why involvement and organizational commitment often appear alongside each other in definitions of employee engagement.

Purcell and Hall (2012) in an ACAS document, outline why this view of engagement and voice is too restrictive. They cite a variety of sources to confirm that managers prefer direct communication and accept that this may be appropriate for much downward communication. But they are not convinced that it is appropriate for upward communication or voice. They assert that 'employee surveys can never be an effective means for employees to express their views and be consulted' (Purcell and Hall 2012: 6) and that at best they can be viewed as 'a weak form of voice' (2012: 5). This contrasts with the IPA/Tomorrow's Company (2012b) report which cites the growing use of attitude surveys as evidence of voice and notes that 76 per cent of the FTSE Top 100 companies used surveys in 2009.

Advocating a more pluralist view, Purcell and Hall recommend 'collective consultation' including works councils or consultative committees as well as the involvement of employee representatives in strategic issues. They suggest that 'employee engagement is not, in itself, a form of voice but a desirable outcome of good leadership and employment practices, including the extensive use of voice systems' (Purcell and Hall 2012: 5). While the case for independent voice systems as one of a number of antecedents of employee engagement is a plausible one, evidence from the 2011 Workplace Employment Relations Study (WERS 2011) (van Wanrooy et al. 2013) reveals a drop in the number of workplaces where there is any form of employee representative arrangements from 45 per cent in 2004 to 35 per cent in 2011, with only 14 per cent having a representative arrangement actually on site. At the same time there has been an increase in management controlled involvement activities such as all staff workplace meetings (up from 75 per cent in 2004 to 80 per cent of workplaces in 2011), team briefings (up from 60 per cent to 66 per cent) and provision of information on workplace finances (up from 55 per cent to 61 per cent). There has been little change in the use of attitude surveys and a decline in the use of problem-solving groups, which represent one kind of activity where employees might have an input. As a result, only 43 per cent of employees are satisfied with the overall amount of involvement in decision making while 20 per cent are dissatisfied. Despite this, the survey reveals quite marked increases in the level of organizational commitment between 2004 and 2011.

The modest level of satisfaction among employees in their involvement in decision making suggests that organizations still have a long way to go to create a sense of engagement and overcome the 'engagement deficit'. In a section on change in WERS 2011, 27 per cent of managers cited 'new employee involvement initiatives', though only 9 per cent said it was their most important initiative. Despite the focus on involvement, and perhaps because of the absence of representative voice arrangements, only 58 per cent said they were consulted about the initiative.

TRUST, EXCHANGE, AND ENGAGEMENT

In the earlier ACAS contribution in which he analyses engagement, Purcell (2010) appears to confirm the essential unitarism of the organizational perspective and notes that it has little to say about exchange or about benefits to employees. While the rationale provided by Purcell recognizes the power of workers in choosing whether or not to exercise discretionary effort, the focus is on the contribution to the organization through enhanced organizational commitment and extra role or organization citizenship behaviour. It is about the contribution of the employee to the organization without any implicit or explicit concern for how the organization can contribute to the well-being of the employee. It is assumed that employees share management interests in positive organizational outcomes even, by implication, to the denial of competing interests reflected in a traditional pluralist approach.

It is notable that much of the writing about engagement is directed to management with managers urged to do something to workers who are largely silent in the process. Thus Purcell again, in arguing that engagement is more than conducting attitude surveys, suggests that 'It is about building trust, involvement, a sense of purpose and identity where employees' contribution to business success is seen as essential' (Purcell 2010: 3). What this emphasizes is that employers need engaged employees, so engagement is a process whereby managers have to do something to employees to gain their engagement. What that might be is indicated by reference to high performance work systems and high commitment management. In other words, the emphasis is very much on the familiar ground of contemporary human resource management. This picture of employee engagement is reflected in the WERS 2011 preliminary report where it is suggested that 'engaging and involving employees with all aspects of their work is at the heart of many prominent models of human resource management including high performance work systems' (Purcell 2010: 18). A similar observation is made by Emmott (2012: 1) who argues that 'it is increasingly accepted that "organizational climate" offers the key to engagement, and it is in turn influenced by the level of trust in the senior management'.

A feature of much of the writing about, and advocacy of employee engagement is the role of trust when seeking to gain the commitment and involvement of employees. It is about the relationship between the employee and the organization to the benefit of the organization with much of the focus on individual employees. In this context, it is helpful to explore in more detail the concept of the psychological contract referred to by Purcell as something that overlaps with engagement. A common definition of the psychological contract is 'The perceptions of both parties to the employment relationship, organization and individual, of the reciprocal promises and obligations implied in the relationship' (Guest and Conway 2002: 22). This emphasizes a two-way process of exchange and it can be seen that it is deeply embedded in social exchange theory. It is reflected in Gouldner's (1960) concept of the 'norm of reciprocity' and, as developed in an employment relations context by Fox (1974), highlights the importance of trust and fairness. Guest (2004) built on this to argue that the key focus of research concerning the psychological contract should be on what is termed the state of the psychological contract, defined as 'whether the promises and obligations have been met, whether they are fair and their implications for trust' (Guest and Conway 2002: 22). This reinforces the role of an exchange relationship at the individual level of analysis at which the psychological contract operates and extends, by implication, to direct forms of participation. Parallels can be drawn at the level of representative participation where any form of negotiation implies an exchange and some level of trust.

An analysis based on social exchange theory (for a wider discussion, see Shore et al. 2012) raises again the question—why should employees wish to be engaged? Much of the analysis of engagement suggests that employees ought to be engaged, particularly if managers apply direct communication and similar systems of involvement. It is not clear what employees get in return. One answer might be autonomy and decision latitude but, as noted earlier, the nature of contemporary work makes the ceding of control to employees in many kinds of work more or less inevitable. The Macleod/Clarke report argues that engagement enhances employee well-being. Their evidence is based largely on research on autonomy and control, but the analysis of the growth of interest in engagement suggests that this may be an antecedent of management interest in the topic—management have had to cede control—rather than an outcome of moves to increase engagement where this typically takes the form of downward communication and attitude surveys.

Employees might respond positively to engagement initiatives from management if they trust management to deliver something in return—if there is a genuine exchange. This has echoes of an earlier debate on partnership at work, the difference being that partnership was typically viewed as a multi-level approach that included both direct and representative participation. In an analysis of partnership among members of the IPA, who espoused an interest in partnership, and based on responses from both management and employee representatives in forty-three organizations, Guest and Peccei (2001) found only low levels of partnership activity. In terms of outcomes such as attitudes, behaviour, and good employment relations, as judged by both parties, direct participation worked better than representative participation but a combination of both direct and representative participation worked best of all. Where there was more progress towards partnership, there was evidence of mutual gains but with the balance of advantage lying with management. This has some parallels with the study of Cox et al. (2006, 2009) on employee involvement where they found that greater breadth in forms of involvement and greater depth in their embeddedness was associated with higher satisfaction and commitment among employees.

Guest et al. (2008) had an opportunity to explore the extent of partnership activity through the 2004 Workplace Employment Relations Survey. They found that across British workplaces there was very limited development of partnership and where there was some partnership activity it was only very weakly, if at all, related to trust. In so far as there was a relationship, it was direct rather than representative forms of partnership that were positively associated with trust. On the basis of this survey, there appeared to be no strong case for partnership and no enthusiasm for it; it is not surprising that it has fallen out of favour as a concept.

One explanation for the lack of impact of partnership on trust might be found in some of the research on the psychological contract. In their study of management of the psychological contract, Guest and Conway (2002) found that managers admitted that on occasion they were quite likely to breach the terms of a psychological contract, in other words, to fail to meet their promises and obligations to employees. In a seven-country study, Guest et al. (2010), based on reports from both employer representatives and employees, found that employers were more likely than employees to breach the psychological contract. This implies that attempts to build the necessary trust to facilitate engagement may be hard to achieve in many organizations. It suggests that management behaviour rather than employee negativity may be the cause of any engagement deficit.

Conclusion: implications for engagement and voice

This analysis of employee engagement and voice has highlighted the different approaches to employee engagement, drawing a distinction between the academic perspectives that focus on attitudinal and behavioural engagement and what we have termed organizational engagement. The former has little explicitly to say about voice although it does emphasize the important role of employee autonomy which can be classified as a form of direct participation. Organizational engagement, on the other hand, does address the issue of voice and some advocates have emphasized the importance of voice. But an inspection of management-initiated engagement activities reveals that these typically take the form of downward communication and attitude surveys. This suggests little in the way of an exchange framework in which employees are encouraged to express their views or to share in decision making either directly or through representatives. Employee engagement can thus be seen as a management-controlled means of seeking to leverage the employment relationship to the benefit of the organization, with the aim of tightening the link between the individual and the organization to enhance commitment and to extract more contribution from employees by increasing their motivation. It therefore does little, if anything, to enhance employee voice; indeed, it may distract from and diminish voice and, in particular, representative voice. One manifestation of this is the emphasis on the use of engagement surveys, reflecting the consultants' attempts to capture the concept of engagement. The WERS 2011 data suggests that organizations have been successful in enhancing employee commitment since levels of commitment have been rising. However, the continuing relatively low levels of satisfaction among employees with the extent to which they can participate in decision making suggests that this may not have resulted from engagement initiatives.

Wefald and Downey (2009) reflected on whether engagement should be considered as 'fad, fashion or folderol'. They highlight the divide in the perspectives of academics and organizational managers and express scepticism about many of the measures of organizational engagement. Nevertheless, they arrive at the conclusion that it may not be a management fad. In contrast, Guest (2014) has argued that organizational engagement does have many of the characteristics of a management fad. It is a term that everyone can support; engagement is a good thing. It provides a simple catch-all term to describe some complex issues. It appeals strongly to senior management as a means of tapping in to the motivation of employees in a context where this appears to be an ever more challenging issue. At the same time, it captures an anxiety among managers, particularly in the UK, for two reasons. First, in the ongoing financial crisis, productivity has been consistently low and declining. Second, there is a concern that low wage increases and the imposition of extra demands on employees with respect to patterns of work have led to a degree of disaffection such that when and if there is an upturn, employees will be on the move and organizations will lose much of their scarce talent. At the same time, the changing nature of work places greater emphasis on the involvement, commitment, and motivation of employees and managers need to find ways of tapping in to this. In other words, organizations will need employee motivation and involvement to ensure productivity and will need commitment to increase the chances of retention.

The risk, as Purcell highlights, is that action to seek employee engagement will usually take the form of attitude surveys and benchmarking. Yet the evidence suggests that the key antecedents to higher performance are the presence of more 'high commitment' or 'high involvement' (Boxall and Macky 2009) HR practices and, in particular, greater autonomy and control for employees. Recent surveys, including the more recent WERS 2011 (van Wanrooy et al. 2013), indicate that progress in this respect is slow. Advocates of organizational engagement can probably learn from the more carefully theorized and researched attitudinal and behavioural engagement. For example, there is emerging research on engagement as implicit voice through the role of emotional contagion (Demerouti and Cropanzano 2010: 158). This suggests that positive attitudinal engagement among some employees could affect colleagues, especially in teams. This view can find support in research on mood. Recent developments include the utilization of broaden-and-build theory (Fredrickson 2001) which argues that positive affect influences behaviour in a positive way. Therefore, attitudinally engaged employees might feel more inclined to express (positive) voice. Alternatively, employees who are highly engaged in union activities or in promoting workers' interests might be more motivated to raise their voice against management. This implies a need to look at engagement in union activities or in what might be construed as counter-productive activities. It also implies that we need to be alert to what has been termed 'the dark side of engagement' (George 2010), which can include the social, family, and emotional costs of overengagement at work and the kind of proactive job crafting that can result in the 'stealing' of attractive elements of the jobs of other employees (Bakker 2010).

Organizational engagement, as Purcell and others have emphasized, can also learn from the extensive research on human resource management. Local, individual, and direct voice is an essential prerequisite for what is currently often termed engagement but what over many years has more commonly been defined in terms of motivation, involvement, and commitment. Representative voice, alongside a supportive climate and a strong HR system (Bowen and Ostroff 2004) can help to embed this and increase the chances that local line managers are monitored to minimize the gap between espoused and operational practice and to ensure appropriate implementation (Guest and Bos-Nehles 2013). The concept of organizational engagement may serve as a useful device through which to draw attention to these issues within organizations, although the evidence to date is not altogether encouraging. Once organizations tire of repeated surveys, and consultants note that this is no longer such a good generator of income, attention will turn to the next management fad. Meanwhile, the importance of good human resource management and the various forms of employee voice, perhaps best articulated in terms of workers' participation, will persist. It is to ways of promoting these that policy and research might more usefully be directed.

◼ REFERENCES

Albrecht, S. (ed.) (2010) *Handbook of Employee Engagement.* Cheltenham: Edward Elgar.

Bakker, A. (2010) 'Engagement and Job Crafting: Engaged Employees Create Their Own Great Place to Work'. In S. Albrecht (ed.), *Handbook of Employee Engagement,* pp. 229–44. Cheltenham: Edward Elgar.

Bakker, A. and Leiter, M. (eds) (2010) *Work Engagement: A Handbook of Essential Theory and Research.* Hove: Psychology Press.

Bowen, D. and Ostroff, C. (2004) 'Understanding HRM-Performance Linkages: The Role of the "Strength" of the HRM System'. *Academy of Management Review,* 29, 203–21.

Boxall, P. and Macky, K. (2009) 'Research and Theory on High-Performance Work Systems: Progressing the High-Involvement Stream'. *Human Resource Management Journal*, 19, 3–23.

Christian, M., Garza, A., and Slaughter, J. (2011) 'Work Engagement: A Quantitative Review and Test of Its Relations with Task and Contextual Performance'. *Personnel Psychology*, 64, 89–136.

Cole, M., Walter, F., Bedeian, A., and O'Boyle, E. (2011) 'Job Burnout and Employee Engagement: A Meta-Analytic Examination of Construct Proliferation'. *Journal of Management*, 37, 1–32.

Cox, A., Zagelmeyer, S., and Marchington, M. (2006) 'Embedding Employee Involvement and Participation at Work'. *Human Resource Management Journal*, 16, 250–67.

Cox, A., Marchington, M., and Suter, J. (2009) 'Employee Involvement and Participation: Developing the Concept of Institutional Embeddedness'. *International Journal of Human Resource Management*, 20, 2150–68.

Crawford, E., LePine, J., and Rich, B. (2010) 'Linking Job Demands and Resources to Employee Engagement and Burnout: A Theoretical Extension and Meta-Analytic Test'. *Journal of Applied Psychology*, 95, 834–48.

Csikszentmihalyi, M. (2000) *Flow: The Psychology of Optimal Experience*. New York: Harper and Row.

Demerouti, E. and Cropanzano, R. (2010) 'From Thought to Action: Employee Work Engagement and Job Performance'. In A. Bakker and M. Leiter (eds), *Work Engagement: A Handbook of Essential Theory and Research*, pp. 147–63. Hove: Psychology Press.

Emmott, M. (2012) *Is Collective Consultation the 'Gold Standard' for Employee Voice?* London: ACAS.

Fox, A. (1974) *Beyond Contract: Work, Power and Trust Relations*. London: Faber and Faber.

Fredrickson, B. (2001) 'The Positive Role of Emotions in Positive Psychology: The Broaden-and-Build Theory of Positive Emotions'. *American Psychologist*, 56, 218–26.

Gallup (2006) 'Engagement Predicts Earning per Share'. In D. MacLeod and N. Clarke, *Engaging for Success: Enhancing Performance through Employee Engagement*, 11. London: Department for Business, Innovation and Skills.

George, J. (2010) 'More Engagement Is Not Necessarily Better: The Benefits of Fluctuating Levels of Engagement'. In S. Albrecht (ed.), *Handbook of Employee Engagement*, pp. 253–63. Cheltenham: Edward Elgar.

Gouldner, A. (1960) 'The Norm of Reciprocity: A Preliminary Statement'. *American Sociological Review*, 25, 161–78.

Guest, D. (2004) 'The Psychology of the Employment Relationship: An Analysis Based on the Psychological Contract'. *Applied Psychology: An International Review*, 53, 541–55.

Guest, D. (2014) 'Employee Engagement: Fashionable Fad or Long-Term Fixture?' In K. Truss, K. Alfes, R. Delbridge, A. Shantz, and E. Soane (eds), *Employee Engagement in Theory and Practice*, pp. 221–35. London: Routledge.

Guest, D. and Bos-Nehles, A. (2013) 'HRM and Performance: The Role of Effective Implementation'. In J. Paauwe, D. Guest, and P. Wright (eds), *HRM and Performance: Achievements and Challenges*, pp. 79–96. Chichester: Wiley.

Guest, D. and Conway, N. (2002) 'Communicating the Psychological Contract: An Employer Perspective'. *Human Resource Management Journal*, 12, 22–38.

Guest, D. and Peccei, R. (2001) 'Partnership at Work: Mutuality and the Balance of Advantage'. *British Journal of Industrial Relations*, 39, 207–36.

Guest, D., Brown, W., Peccei, R., and Huxley, K. (2008) 'Does Partnership at Work Increase Trust? An Analysis Based on the 2004 Workplace Employment Relations Survey'. *Industrial Relations Journal*, 39, 124–52.

Guest, D., Isaksson. K., and De Witte, H. (eds) (2010) *Employment Contracts, Psychological Contracts and Employee Well-Being: An International Study*. Oxford: Oxford University Press.

Halbesleben, J. (2010) 'A Meta-Analysis of Work Engagement: Relationships with Burnout, Demands, Resources, and Consequences'. In A. Bakker and M. Leiter (eds), *Work Engagement: A Handbook of Essential Theory and Research*, pp. 102–17. Hove: Psychology Press.

Harter, J., Schmidt, F., and Hayes, T. (2002) 'Business-Unit Level Relationship between Employee Satisfaction, Employee Engagement, and Business Outcomes: A Meta-Analysis'. *Journal of Applied Psychology*, 87, 268–79.

IPA/Tomorrow's Company (2012a) *Rethinking Voice: Survey of Employers about Employee Voice*. London: Involvement and Participation Association.

IPA/Tomorrow's Company (2012b) *Releasing Voice for Sustainable Business Success*. London: Involvement and Participation Association.

Judge, T., Thoresen, C., Bono, J., and Patton, G. (2001) 'The Job Satisfaction–Job Performance Relationship: A Qualitative and Quantitative Review'. *Psychological Bulletin*, 127, 376–407.

Kahn, W. (1990) 'The Psychological Conditions of Personal Engagement and Disengagement at Work'. *Academy of Management Journal*, 33, 692–724.

Kahn, W. (1992) 'To Be Fully There: Psychological Presence at Work'. *Human Relations*, 45, 321–49.

Karasek, R. and Theorell, T. (1990) *Healthy Work: Stress, Productivity, and the Reconstruction of Working Life*. New York: Basic Books.

Macey, W. and Schneider, B. (2008) 'The Meaning of Employee Engagement'. *Industrial and Organizational Psychology: Perspectives on Science and Practice*, 1, 3–30.

MacLeod, D. and Clarke, N. (2009) *Engaging for Success: Enhancing Performance through Employee Engagement*. London: Department for Business, Innovation and Skills.

Marchington, M., Wilkinson, A., Ackers, P., and Goodman, J. (1993) 'The Influence of Managerial Relations on Waves of Employee Involvement'. *British Journal of Industrial Relations*, 31, 553–76.

Maslach, C. and Leiter, M. (1997) *The Truth about Burnout*. San Francisco, CA: Jossey-Bass.

Mauno, S., Kinnunen, U., Makikangas, A., and Feldt, T. (2010) 'Job Demands and Resources as Antecedents of Work Engagement: A Qualitative Review and Directions for Future Research'. In S. Albrecht (ed.), *Handbook of Employee Engagement*, pp. 111–28. Cheltenham: Edward Elgar.

Meyer, J., Stanley, D., Herscovitch, L., and Topolnytsky, L. (2001) 'Affective, Continuance and Normative Commitment to the Organization: A Meta-Analysis of Antecedents, Correlates and Consequences'. *Journal of Vocational Behavior*, 61, 20–52.

Newman, D., Joseph, D., and Hulin, C. (2010) 'Job Attitudes and Employee Engagement: Considering the Attitude "A-factor"'. In S. Albrecht (ed.), *Handbook of Employee Engagement*, pp. 43–61. Cheltenham: Edward Elgar.

Peccei, R. (2013) 'Employee Engagement: An Evidence-Based Review'. In S. Bach and M. Edwards (eds), *Managing Human Resources*, 5th edn, pp. 336–63. Chichester: Wiley.

Purcell, J. (2010) *Building Employee Engagement*. London: ACAS.

Purcell, J. and Hall, M. (2012) *Voice and Participation in the Modern Workplace: Challenges and Prospects*. London: ACAS.

Ramsay, H. (1977) 'Cycles of Control: Worker Participation in Sociological and Historical Perspective'. *Sociology*, 11, 481–506.

Rich, B., Lepine, J., and Crawford, W. (2010) 'Job Engagement: Antecedents and Effects on Job Performance'. *Academy of Management Journal*, 53, 617–35.

Salanova, M., Schaufeli, W., Xanthopoulou, D., and Bakker, A. (2010) 'The Gain Spiral of Resources and Work Engagement: Sustaining a Positive Worklife'. In A. Bakker and M. Leiter (eds), *Work Engagement: A Handbook of Essential Theory and Research*, pp. 118–31. Hove: Psychology Press.

Schaufeli, W., Salanova, M., Gonzalez-Roma, V., and Bakker, A. (2002) 'The Measurement of Engagement and Burnout: A Two-Sample Confirmatory Factor Analytic Approach'. *Journal of Happiness Studies*, 3, 71–92.

Shore, L., Coyle-Shapiro, J., and Tetrick, L. (eds) (2012) *The Employee-Organization Relationship*. New York: Routledge.

Sonnentag, S. (2003) 'Recovery, Work Engagement, and Proactive Behavior: A New Look at the Interface between Non-Work and Work'. *Journal of Applied Psychology*, 88, 518–28.

Sonnentag, S., Dormann, C., and Demerouti, E. (2010) 'Not All Days Are Created Equal: The Concept of State Work Engagement'. In A. Bakker and M. Leiter (eds), *Work Engagement: A Handbook of Essential Theory and Research*, pp. 25–38. New York: Psychology Press.

Strauss, G. (2006) 'Worker Participation: Some Under-Considered Issues'. *Industrial Relations*, 45, 778–803.

Towers Perrin-ISR (2006) *The ISR Employee Engagement Report*. London: Towers Perrin.

Truss, K., Alfes, K., Delbridge, R., Shantz, A., and Soane, E. (2013) *Employee Engagement in Theory and Practice*. London: Routledge.

van Wanrooy, B., Bewley, H., Bryson, A., Forth, J., Freeth, S., Stokes, L., and Wood, S. (2013) *The 2011 Workplace Employment Relations Study: First Findings*. London: Department for Business, Innovation and Skills.

Wefald, A. and Downey, R. (2009) 'Job Engagement in Organizations: Fad, Fashion, or Folderol ?' *Journal of Organizational Behavior*, 30, 141–5.

Wilkinson, A., Dundon, T., and Marchington, M. (2013) 'Employee Involvement and Voice'. In S. Bach and M. Edwards (eds), *Managing Human Resources*, 5th edn, pp. 268–88. Chichester: Wiley.

4 Voice and workforce diversity

Anne-marie Greene

Introduction

This chapter explores employee voice mechanisms from a diversity perspective.[1] Diversity here involves both demographic and/or identity strands of difference. This includes gender, race/ethnicity, sexuality, and age; but also other forms of difference that relate to contract status and hours of work. The contention within this chapter is that diversity concerns should be at the heart of the debate about employee voice. Indeed in the introduction to this volume, alongside the business case argument about how employee voice enhances organizational performance, the more fundamental social justice argument is presented, which views employee voice as a right in modern democratic society. Such language fits naturally into the field of equality and diversity, where the tension between social justice and the business case is a central dynamic (see Greene and Kirton 2009). Diversity issues should be at the heart of participatory democracy—allowing all employees to have a voice at work. Indeed for Young (1990: 92), the concept of participatory democracy *requires* that a diversity of interests has voice. Within the diversity field, employee voice therefore becomes central to concepts of inclusion (Bell et al. 2011: 136). As is discussed, however, accepting different voices, particularly within conventional voice mechanisms, is not an easy task and challenges existing power structures and hierarchies within traditional mechanisms of voice such as trade unions. Indeed, recognizing and accepting different voices might be seen to undermine some aspects of solidarity and common interest that are often at the centre of traditional trade unionism (see Ackers, this volume), which is discussed later in this chapter.

The objective is thus to place diversity concerns at the forefront of an analysis of employee voice. To this end, the chapter begins with a mapping exercise, establishing the increasing level of diversity within the workforces of most modern industrialized societies. This mapping exercise is predominantly based in the UK, Europe more widely, and the USA, where data are more readily available. However, despite increasing workforce diversity, most mainstream literature on employee voice tends to assume that employees are homogenous (Shapiro 2000; Bell et al. 2011; Syed 2014). Indeed, the chapter will discuss the ways in which conventional employee voice mechanisms and thinking about employee voice are based around an archetype of the *standard* employee. Thus a discussion of employee voice is placed within the context of the wider critique of the lack of diversity awareness within much mainstream Anglo-American industrial relations. In particular, a critique around what I have termed the *what*, the *who*, and the *how* of conventional employee voice mechanisms forms the main part of the analysis that is delivered. The chapter will end by discussing particular mechanisms that offer, or have the potential to offer, increased chances of voice to non-standard or diverse workers.

The diverse workforce in the twenty-first century

'Diversity… is now a fact of life in most UK workplaces' (Dean and Liff 2010: 422), and as they go on to argue, it has long been part of the wider critique of industrial relations that its models, typologies, and theories are based on an archetype of the male, white, full-time, permanent contract worker (one could also add heterosexual, non-disabled, and aged 25–49 years). A key question to ask therefore is to what extent this archetype of a *standard* employee is actually applicable to the twenty-first century workforce?

DIVERSITY IN CONTRACT, HOURS, OR PLACE OF WORK

Starting with the type of work or the contract situation in relation to this archetype, the nomenclature of industrial relations and wider public policy environments is in itself illuminating. The terms used still tend to be 'non-standard' or 'atypical' work to cover anything that stands outside of this standard archetype, namely part-time, fixed term, temporary, agency, self-employed workers, and so on. In support of this position, the term 'non-standard work' as the International Labour Office (ILO) define it is used to distinguish such work from the 'regular or standard model of full time, permanent and direct employment' (ILO 2012: 2). This ILO definition also includes types of work that sit outside of the standard relationship of a worker to a physical workplace, thus covering those who engage in home working or remote working, or who are freelance or self-employed. Within this chapter, the analysis is restricted to those who sit within a formal employment relationship, thus not including the self-employed.

Use of non-standard work is increasing. Data from the 2011 Workplace Employment Relations Study (WERS 2011) indicates that there has been an increase in the proportion of workplaces in the UK that use some form of what is termed 'non-standard working hours arrangement', now standing at around a quarter of all workplaces (van Wanrooy et al. 2013). Similar trends are found in the USA (BLS 2005) and across the EU (Eurostat 2012). There is of course country variation; while a quarter of those in employment in the UK work part time, the highest proportion of part-time workers is found in the Netherlands which stands at nearly 50 per cent (ONS 2013), where part-time work really has become standard rather than non-standard. There has also been a rise in the number of people who now work away from the traditional workplace. For the UK, Labour Force Survey data indicates that just over 4 million employees usually worked at home in 2012, a 12 per cent rise since 2007 (TUC 2013). In addition to those who usually work from home, many millions more work occasionally from home (see also CIPD 2012). Again, similar trends are found in the USA (BLS 2005).

DEMOGRAPHIC DIVERSITY

There is also increasing diversity on demographic characteristics, particularly around gender, ethnicity, and age. In industrialized countries, one of the most significant social and economic changes of the post-war period has been the exponential increase in women's employment participation; indeed, the female workforce is now around the 50 per cent mark in the US, UK, and most other European countries (Greene and Kirton 2009: 47). The other most significant demographic change concerns increased race and ethnic diversity, although clearly the extent of this diversity ranges highly from country to country; for example the black and minority ethnic (BME) workforce stands at 29 per cent in the USA (BLS 2011), but only 8 per cent in the UK (DWP 2010). Arguably, these different profiles render the imperative for addressing equality and diversity issues around race and ethnicity more compelling in the USA compared with the UK (Greene and Kirton 2009: 48) and concomi-tantly, the imperative to address it as an employee voice issue. The contem-porary workforce is also an ageing one. For example, the UK sees employment rates for 50–64-year-olds having increased to account for over a quarter of the total workforce, while the employment rate for people aged 65 and over has also increased significantly (DWP 2012). Such patterns are replicated in many other countries across the EU (Eurostat 2013).

HOW STANDARD IS THE STANDARD ARCHETYPE?

It is important, however, not to overplay the extent of non-standard work; indeed the majority of people are still employed in what is considered to be standard work. While there are exceptions such as the Netherlands, for some countries non-standard hours are still very much the experience of only a small minority of the workforce, for example, part-time employment is relatively uncommon in countries such as Bulgaria and Slovakia (Eurostat 2012). In addition, some countries have seen some non-standard working arrangements declining or experiencing little change over the last decade, for example the use of fixed-term and temporary contracts and the use of agency workers in the UK (van Wanrooy et al. 2013).

However, cross-referencing between the two areas of diversity, when we start to look at the demographics of non-standard work, the picture becomes more complicated. Indeed, part-time work in the UK accounts for over 40 per cent of all women workers (ONS 2013) and it is women with dependent children who are most likely to work part time, thus indicating the childcare role undertaken by women as a key determining factor (Kirton and Greene 2010). While women's employment rate after childbirth has changed enormously over time and having a family no longer restricts women's employment to quite the same extent as formerly, UK evidence indicates that 42 per cent of working women changed from full-time to part-time hours post-maternity (Aston et al. 2005). The gender effect is also obvious elsewhere, with just under a third of women employed in the EU working on a part-time basis in 2011, a much higher proportion than the corresponding share for men (9 per cent). Again there is wide country variation, with part-time work accounting for three quarters of all women employed in the Netherlands, but only 10 per cent of women in many Central and Eastern European countries (Eurostat 2012), where women tend to either work full time or not at all. With regard to homeworking, there is also gender differentiation as while nearly two thirds of people who work from home are men, the majority of home-working jobs created in the last five years have gone to women, partly due to the fact that the greater proportion of these new jobs are part time (TUC 2013). Finally, part-time working is also more common amongst older workers than those in the 25–49 age range (DWP 2012). Similarly, the non-standard archetype of work applies more to those considered 'young' in the labour market. Across the EU, young people face increasing chances of unemployment, and where they are employed young people are around four times more likely to be offered a non-standard form of contract than their counterparts aged 25–59 years (European Foundation 2011).

So what do these patterns and trends mean from a diversity perspective? Importantly, occupational segregation and patterns of discrimination (see summary in Kirton and Greene 2010: chapter 2) mean that increasing demographic diversity in the workforce does not necessarily lead to an increasing equality of opportunity for these groups of workers. Indeed, there is now a large research base demonstrating that women, BME, younger, older, disabled, and lesbian, gay, bisexual, and transgender (LGBT) workers disproportionately face systematic and persistent disadvantages, including higher unemployment, lower pay, lower promotion opportunities, and vertical and horizontal job segregation. With regard to contract and type of work diversity, while increasing use of non-standard work creates opportunities (or at least space) for previously underrepresented groups to participate in the labour market, this kind of economic change also has significant consequences for employment inequalities (Greene and Kirton 2009: 46). Whether the employment flexibility from forms of non-standard work offers a route to greater overall equality is highly debatable (Dickens 1999; Purcell 2000). Indeed, while these effects are to a great extent individually and nationally determined, non-standard workers are generally felt to experience a number of disadvantages, including lower employment security, lower quality of work, lower levels of trade union representation and collective bargaining coverage, limited social security and employment law coverage, and limited opportunities for promotion and access to training (ILO 2012). A case in point is the recent public and academic interest in the plight of younger workers, particularly in the context of recent recessionary economic conditions.

To summarize, this mapping exercise has highlighted the increasing levels of diversity in the contemporary workforce. While the term of non-standard work still seems to be applicable, the archetype of the standard worker is not necessarily applicable, particularly on a demographic basis. The chapter now moves on to explore what this means for an analysis of employee voice.

Diversity and employee voice

Discussion of the diversity perspective on employee voice has to be placed within the context of the wider critique of industrial relations research, in which employee voice provides a typical example of an industrial relations topic where most analysis is based on the standard archetype. There is now a fairly established critique of the industrial relations field that attests to its 'gender-blindness' of which Dean and Liff (2010) provide a useful summary. Here Danieli's work (2006) looking specifically at gender is instructive, although her analysis could easily be expanded to other diversity strands. She established the ways that the boundaries of the field of industrial relations have been narrowly defined, mostly without awareness of diversity issues. This analysis of the processes of 'acknowledgement and abdication' that industrial relations academics engage in is critical here. While there is acknowledgement that gender relations are important, at least in theory, they are not seen as central to industrial relations and therefore responsibility for looking at them is abdicated to other disciplines and other fields of study. With direct relevance to employee voice, therefore, it is easy to claim that the voices of those facing the most disadvantage in the labour market are often missing or ignored within 'malestream' industrial relations (Forrest 1993). In order to address this, feminist critiques call for research to be deliberately conducted outside of the standard archetype (not just focusing on traditional male-dominated industries and occupations), to look at formal and informal social processes of industrial relations (not just focusing on structures, systems, and institutions), and to use more qualitative methods that can capture the voices not usually heard (Holgate et al. 2006; Greene and Kirton 2009: 11–13; Dean and Liff 2010).

To what extent can employee voice mechanisms be seen to be representative of the diversity identified in the contemporary workforce and, perhaps more importantly, why does this representativeness matter? A key focus here is the *what*, the *who*, and the *how* of employee voice—*what* are the common forms, issues, and purposes of employee voice mechanisms, *who* are usually participants in voice mechanisms, and *how* is employee voice enacted?

THE *WHAT* OF EMPLOYEE VOICE

Conventional mechanisms of employee voice (regardless of whether they are employer- or employee-led, direct or indirect) are usually located within the formal structures of organizations, within a conventional organization or workplace, and are arguably most applicable to the standard archetype of the worker. Indeed, non-standard workers are considered to pose significant challenges to the application of regulatory regimes and the effective functioning of industrial relations systems in practice (ILO 2012: 1), of which employee voice mechanisms are one part. These challenges include characteristics which can be applied to many non-standard as compared to standard workers, such as the limited attachment to single workplaces and/or employers, exclusion from trade unions and/or bargaining units, and ambiguities about who is the employer (ILO 2012: 4).

The primary route for employee voice has been through trade unions and levels of trade union membership are therefore significant, given the overall decline in many countries which is highlighted by several authors in this volume. Taking the UK as an example, however, after two decades of substantial decline, WERS 2011 evidence indicates that trade union presence is now relatively stable in all but the smallest workplaces (van Wanrooy et al. 2013). While there has been an increase in direct forms of employee voice mechanism, the union substitution argument does not seem to apply here as there has been no significant increase in the proportion of non-union representatives. However, if the primary route for employee voice is through a trade union, there are still problems, even with a stabilization of trade union membership, because from a diversity point of view, unions can clearly be criticized for not having 'their own house in order' (Greene and Kirton 2005), as will be discussed in more detail in the next section relating to the *who* of employee voice. Suffice it to say here, looking at the representative structures of trade unions, white and male domination of union decision making is the prevalent norm. This is the case despite substantial female membership in most countries and substantial BME membership in some countries (Greene and Kirton 2005). Cockburn (1995) argued that the absence of women and other diverse groups in union decision making created a 'democracy deficit', preventing unions from fulfilling their aim of achieving social justice. In addition, the ILO (2012) and research by Heery et al. (Heery 2005; Heery et al. 2005; Heery and Conley 2007) also clearly indicate the historical and contemporary difficulties faced by trade unions in organizing and bargaining for non-standard workers. Therefore, Cockburn's argument seems as salient now as it did twenty years ago.

With regard to *what* is voiced through conventional mechanisms, WERS 2011 data indicate that the most common issues raised by union and non-union employee representatives were discipline and grievances, health and safety, and rates of pay. These are certainly what one might consider to be fairly traditional agenda items and there does not appear to be any significant increase in the incidence of diversity-related issues, despite the fact that WERS 2011 also indicates an increase in the status of formal equality/diversity policies within workplaces.

Much of the debate around employee voice within the industrial relations field concerns the level of influence over decision making that is offered by the particular voice mechanism. WERS 2011 indicates that there has been a decline in the extent to which employees in the UK feel they can have an influence (van Wanrooy et al. 2013), a fact that is also supported by the latest *CIPD Employee Outlook Report* (CIPD 2013a), which shows a serious deterioration in employee satisfaction regarding their ability to feed views upwards. Similarly, across the EU27, most of the workforce is employed in organizations that provide very limited opportunities for employees to participate in decision making (Eurofound 2013). While studies rarely include diversity characteristics within the analysis, there are some potentially interesting findings that would be worthy of further exploration from a diversity point of view. For example, survey data concerning the UK (CIPD 2013a), indicates that employee dissatisfaction with their influence is highest in the public sector where only a third of employees are satisfied, yet the public sector is one where there is a disproportionate concentration of women and BME employees. While Europe-wide analysis offers less consistent results, this demonstrates the overall poorer position of non-standard employees who are less likely to be in high involvement organizations than standard employees (Eurofound 2013: 32–3).[2] Whittle and Mueller (2009) provide a good summary of research on telephone- and home-based workers which attests to the lack of voice experienced by many.

However, concerns about the level and type of influence offered through employee voice mechanisms are extremely rarely connected to diversity issues. An exception is research conducted by Shapiro (2000) over a decade ago, but which surprisingly has not really been developed within the field since. Her qualitative case studies of total quality management (TQM) groups in organizations in eight European countries revealed an interesting relationship between the development of employee involvement, the exposure to employee diversity, and organizational capacity to positively manage diversity (Shapiro 2000: 32). The TQM initiatives in most organizations in her study were implemented with little or no cognisance of diversity concerns, for example that different groups or individuals may be motivated by different factors to become involved, or have different training or information requirements. Furthermore, problems were found to develop in most organizations around diversity issues. As organizations aimed to increase the level of involvement of employees in order to meet organizational objectives, there was often increased exposure to the different types of employees and therefore to the effects of diversity. However, these diversity concerns had not been considered, nor did the necessary managerial capabilities exist to manage diversity effectively, thus impeding the overall effectiveness of the involvement mechanism. Shapiro (2000: 315) thus identified the importance of diversity as the 'missing link' in the success of employee involvement schemes.

Furthermore, Shapiro (2000: 314) found significant negative consequences to emerge from the lack of diversity in the selection of team leaders and facilitators in her study. Similarly, the 'mixed record' (Dickens et al. 1988: 65) of trade unions on challenging discrimination and inequalities, and the fact that union bargaining agendas have not been as progressive as they might have been (Colling and Dickens 2001), is partly because the process of bargaining has been dominated by those workers who fulfil the standard archetype—the *who* of employee voice, which is discussed further in next section.

THE *WHO* OF EMPLOYEE VOICE

The characteristics of the typical trade union member have clearly changed over time. For example in the UK, when trade union membership was at its peak in the late 1970s, the typical trade union member was a male, full-time, manual worker in the production sector. Today, the typical trade union member is slightly more likely to be female than male, a non-manual than manual worker, to work in the service rather than in the production sector, and to be a highly qualified worker in the public sector (Kirton and Greene 2010). Fifty-five per cent of union members in the UK were women in 2012 and a similar profile of increasing proportions of women trade union members is found across the EU more broadly (ETUC 2012). Rates of union membership also vary according to a number of other demographic characteristics, for example ethnicity. In the UK, white workers have a higher overall membership than other ethnic groups analysed, but black women have a higher union membership rate than white women (BIS 2013). However, it is very difficult to find out levels of BME membership in many other European countries because of socio-political opposition to the collection of national data on ethnicity. Indeed, the ETUC (2009: 31) reports that less than half of the confederations in their respondent sample have any information on the number or proportion of union members by ethnicity. Trade union membership also has an older age profile. In the UK, employees aged fifty-plus are most likely to be union members, whilst among younger workers aged 25–34, only 22 per cent are members (BIS 2013). Looking at aspects of non-standard contracts, in all occupations full-time employees are more highly unionized than part-time employees (BIS 2013) and when men work part time they are far less likely than female part-time workers to be union members.

Increasing diversity in trade union membership however, as indicated earlier, is not necessarily reflected in the representative structures of trade unions, which despite decades of positive action and campaigning are still very much dominated by the standard white, male, full-time worker archetype (see comparative information in Greene and Kirton 2005; ETUC 2009; ETUC 2012). WERS 2011 indicates that a fairly high 41 per cent of senior union representatives are women (van Wanrooy et al. 2013), although still below the proportion of women members.[3] In the context of Europe more widely, there is still strong criticism of the male-dominated nature of representative structures (ETUC 2009). With regards to ethnicity of trade union representatives, as reported above, there is relatively little information available on the proportion of union members who are from BME backgrounds, so it is no surprise to find that there is virtually no information on the proportion of union activists in these categories on a European basis (ETUC 2009: 42). Looking more broadly at data for the UK, including non-trade union representatives, it appears that compared to the smaller proportion of union representatives, over 60 per cent of non-union employee representatives are women.[4] However, on the basis of other demographic characteristics, the picture is rather more negative, indeed 97 per cent are white and 85 per cent are over the age of forty years (van Wanrooy et al. 2013). With regard to non-standard working, only 13 per cent of employee representatives work part time.

Waddington's (2011) research involving European Works Council (EWC) representatives also demonstrates a lack of diversity. It is notable that 83 per cent of respondents were male in what was a statistically representative survey of the population of EWC representatives. In addition, the book has no index reference to gender or women and there are scarce references to any other diversity issue. Scouring the text finds a couple of scant mentions, the most notable being the statement that while gender balance is a formal policy objective of EWCs, 'only 3.2 per cent of current agreements make any reference to gender balance' (Waddington 2011: 69), a clear indictment on the low status of diversity concerns.

The point of the foregoing discussion is to raise the issue of the proportionately unrepresentative nature of conventional voice mechanisms in terms of *who* is participating. This is important because there is now a considerable body of research which indicates that *who* participates, affects the nature of *what* subjects are on the agenda and essentially affects the outcomes of those voice mechanisms, in other words, to paraphrase Colling and Dickens (1998), *who* is at the bargaining table affects *what* is on the bargaining table. For a variety of reasons, not least that of membership renewal in the face of decline, unions have been compelled to confront the reality of workforce diversity, what Heery et al. (2005) identify as an ideological change, raising union preparedness to represent diversity. Positive action campaigns within trade unions over the last few decades have been built on the premise that minority representation and involvement within trade unions needs to increase, in order that these groups can develop policies and agendas to address the specific concerns of their constituent identity interests and therefore to give them voice. This is arguably in direct contrast to Ackers' argument in this volume which discusses the importance of shared occupational identity to trade union renewal and points to the dangers of the 'Identity Politics Model' in highlighting internal differences. Within the equality and diversity field, the argument is nuanced differently: that it may be impossible to identify a uniform occupational identity as this will inevitably be segmented by diversity concerns. Some of the ways in which these differences emerge through separate organizing initiatives are discussed in the last section of this chapter.

THE *HOW* OF EMPLOYEE VOICE

So far, the chapter has discussed the way in which the location of conventional employee voice mechanisms within formal organizational structures and the workplace, and the unrepresentative nature of participants in them, can be criticized from a diversity point of view. In addition, *how* people participate within the voice mechanism, the processes of participation, also matter. This involves debates about the ways in which the place, time, and nature of conventional voice mechanisms favour the standard archetype of the worker.

The Conventional Requirement for Physical Participation

With regard to trade union activism, there have been arguments that the requirement for physical participation exacerbates difficulties for women

(Greene and Kirton 2003), and this could be easily expanded to other non-standard workers. While membership meetings tend to be considered as the cornerstone of union democracy (Klandermans 1992), the problem is that attendance is notoriously low, with non-attendance especially associated with women and part-time workers (Phillips 1991; Kirton 2006). In the context of the UK, Greene and Kirton (2003) discuss the barriers to participation within trade unions for those workers that fall outside of the standard archetype. At its most simplistic level this draws attention to the way that union practices having been constructed by men, and are built around men's needs and masculine ways of operating. For example, the timing and location of meetings are often inconvenient or less appealing to women, such as evening meetings in pubs. Requirements for job mobility and to be continually 'on call' are also seen as proportionately more difficult for women to meet (Bradley 1994; Kirton 1999, 2006). These structures and cultures based around the permanent workplace and the single employer also make it extremely difficult for those on non-standard contracts to participate (meetings often being held at the workplace or during core working hours, for example) (ILO 2012). This was also a finding of Shapiro (2000), where the TQM initiatives in her study included no mechanisms to support flexible working or those working non-standard hours.

Exclusive Cultures and Structures

More complex arguments revolve around the ways that conventional employee voice mechanisms are situated within exclusive cultures within organizations. Kirton and Greene (2010: chapter 4) provide a synthesis of literature 'unpacking' diversity issues within work organizations, exploring the effects of patriarchal, white-dominated, and heterosexualized cultures on employees who stand outside of the standard archetype. Looking specifically at trade union cultures, they too are infused with patriarchal ideology, which manifests itself in all kinds of subtle ways, to the extent that minority workers often describe a feeling of symbolic rather than actual exclusion from trade union domains. This clearly relates to the unrepresentative nature of *who* employee representatives are, particularly around the absence of female role models and the behaviour of some male trade unionists towards women (Cockburn 1995; Healy and Kirton 2000; Cobble and Bielski Michal 2002; Franzway 2002; Kirton 2006). There is less literature specifically about BME underrepresentation, although research on women in trade unions has now become more sensitive to crosscutting identities, including race and ethnicity (Munro 2001). There is certainly a common (historical) problem of racism inside trade unions and in the labour market (Delaney and Lundy 1996; Bradley et al. 2002; Briskin 2002; Holgate et al. 2008). However, the labour movement of each country varies in how it understands race and ethnicity and responds to racism, depending on ideological and political orientations, as well as on the ethnic structure of the labour market (Wrench 2003). Thus, the trade union movements of different countries are differentially implicated in the historical construction of racism and racial disadvantage.

Overall, certain social groups including women, BME, disabled, and LGBT workers have complained of internal exclusion within unions. For example, the processes of exclusion are often enacted by majority groups by virtue of their greater knowledge of union jargon, procedures, and rule books. Participants of meetings are often intimidated into accepting the position of the most vocal (Dorgan and Grieco 1993). In other words, participatory democracy centred on the face to face meeting generally favours those members who are most confident to articulate their views (Phillips 1991, in Greene and Kirton 2003). Those seen as or who feel like outsiders might not feel confident enough to be able to be involved or are not encouraged to be involved.

There is very limited research analysis about the workings of non-union employee voice mechanisms from the point of view of the participation of minority groups. Here, more recent analysis of the participation or non-participation of LGBT workers in employee voice mechanisms is extremely illuminating and provides theorizing around voice and silence that can be extended to a number of other diversity strands in the workplace. Historically, women and men who were either openly lesbian or gay commonly experienced overt discrimination by employers based on their sexual orientation (Snape et al. 1995). Not surprisingly then, there is evidence of widespread concealment, with Stonewall reporting that around one third of gay workers still feel unable to be open about their sexual orientation (Stonewall 2009). Bell et al. (2011: 132) point to the 'high risk of silencing at work' that is associated with concealment and feeling excluded, which can be extended beyond LGBT workers to other minority groups. This is linked to Bowen and Blackmon's (2003) work on the 'spirals of silence', the processes of which indicate how the interaction between employees' demographic and identity characteristics and the context in which the employee operates determines an individual's ability to have voice, or to make use of, or participate in, the employee voice mechanisms that may exist in any particular organization.

Towards diversity: appropriate employee voice mechanisms

Working in the equality and diversity field can often be a rather depressing experience where 'accounts can be overly negative and can often offer a disappointingly pessimistic view of the state of things' (Greene and Kirton

2009: 211). One way forward is to try and explore some alternatives to the conventional mechanisms of employee voice, to see whether there can be a more optimistic outlook.

SPECIAL ORGANIZED GROUPS

Most large unions have developed a raft of equality structures, including separate organizing, designed to include previously excluded groups (see for example, McBride 2001; Colgan and Ledwith 2002; Kirton and Greene 2002; Holgate et al. 2008; ETUC 2009). The positive effects of these campaigns on changing the *who* and the *what* of employee voice appears at least partly lived out by research studies looking at the successful campaigns and expanded bargaining agendas of unions as a result of increasing the involvement of minority participants (for example, Colgan and Ledwith 2002; ETUC 2009; Kirton 2006; ETUC 2012; ILO 2012; Kirton and Healy 2013). Heery et al.'s (2005) research concerned with non-standard workers is a good example here, where officers working in trade unions with specific and targeted arrangements for the participation of non-standard workers were more likely to report bargaining around issues specific to non-standard workers.

However overall, as previously discussed, the latest statistics and research seem to confirm the persistence of both the male-dominated nature of representative structures and the very traditional basis of bargaining agendas. Part of this may be about the level at which activity is directed. There has been a lot of rhetorical commitment to equality (primarily gender) by unions in many countries and there has been action to increase the participation of diverse groups in decision-making bodies. However, much of the effort has been directed at national level bodies, with arguably mixed and limited impact on workplace structures.

Moving to the non-union mode, take a look at any practitioner guidance on diversity management, and alongside other conventional mechanisms such as mentoring, performance management and training and the issue of diversity employee groups will feature. For example, Kumra and Manfredi (2012: 81) set out a typical formal structure supposed to enable an organization to set its strategic objectives in relation to diversity and the mechanisms through which strategic objectives will be disseminated. Part of this structure involves employee networks, which are based at organization level and, importantly, are primarily formed by employees themselves. Whilst there are examples of trade unions being specifically involved with some employee diversity networks (Greene and Kirton 2011) they are more usually non-union. Unfortunately, there is relatively little academic research exclusively on the workings of employee diversity networks (exceptions are Ibarra 1993; Friedman and Holtom 2002; Colgan and McKearney 2012) and more usually analysis of them features within broader research around equality and diversity management within organizations (for example Cunningham 2000; Creegan et al. 2003; Greene and Kirton 2009). Partly this is because they stand separately from other employee voice or involvement mechanisms, and may have quite different functions, being attached to the diversity strategy, rather than the employee involvement or employee engagement strategy. As Friedman and Holtom state, employee networks are predominantly in existence 'for community building, not advocacy' (2002: 406). Employee diversity networks are therefore not so much about employee influence or high involvement and this may be viewed negatively in terms of the impact that the network can have, and on the level of voice given to minority groups. On the other hand, the focus on career enhancement, and fostering embeddedness within the organization by offering safe spaces and conversations with people who may have similar interests, may have a role in changing organizational cultures to be more inclusive (Friedman and Holtom 2002; Colgan and McKearney 2012; Syed 2014). This, as discussed earlier would begin to address the exclusion of minority employees from voice mechanisms.

As a case example, one of the public sector case study organizations in recent research (Greene and Kirton 2009, 2011) had established four employee diversity groups on women, race equality, disability, and LGBT issues. These groups were formalized structures with reporting channels to, and representatives on, the central bodies responsible for decision making in the diversity arena. Management and non-management employees were able to participate on equal terms and the groups were resourced by the organization both in terms of budget and time off normal work duties for participants. Most importantly, the activities of these groups were seen as having some effect on policies. In terms of active voice function, group participants reported changes made to policy documents and initiatives put in place in response to feedback from the employee diversity groups. Most importantly, specific contributions from the race equality employee group led to the development of fairer criteria in a downsizing exercise requiring substantial numbers of compulsory redundancies. The interviews with other stakeholders in the organization indicated that without this input from the employee diversity group, the redundancies would have had a far greater detrimental effect on BME employees in the organization.

However, there are still a number of disadvantages or weaknesses of employee diversity groups as mechanisms of employee voice. First, that the focus and scope of issues covered by employee diversity groups are usually specifically around diversity, thus they are linked to diversity strategy rather than to broader organizational issues. In other words there is an implicit assumption that employees from diversity strands will primarily be concerned with diversity issues. Therefore, this does not deal with the representation gap in conventional voice mechanisms. Moreover, the existence of diversity groups does not necessarily lead to an improvement in the involvement of employees more broadly, indeed the numbers of employees involved in the employee diversity groups in Greene and Kirton's (2009: 217) research were very low, and most employees typically perceived there to be a representation and communication gap.

Second, employee diversity groups may not help those most in need of voice to achieve it. Friedman and Holtom (2002) also found that because of their focus on career enhancement and networking, diversity groups were less effective for employees at the highest and the lowest levels of organizations, with the most benefit being achieved for middle managers. Third, while they tend to be initiated by employees, diversity groups rely heavily on organizational support and sponsorship and Friedman and Holtom (2002) found that their success depended very much on how well they were run, and whether there was significant senior management level involvement. Indeed, the existence of separate special interest groups will not be enough to change an exclusive culture into an inclusive one if there is not the wider organizational support to sustain the mechanism. As Bowen and Blackmon (2003: 1413) state, 'it is not enough to stick diverse individuals together and hope for the best—companies must create the conditions for and actively manage group processes . . . to ensure that diversity is productive rather than destructive'. However, as is indicated by Shapiro's (2000) research on TQM groups or Hoque and Noon's (2004) finding that most organizations had little more substantial beyond the 'empty shell' of formal equality and diversity policies, this wider and very necessary support is often absent.

Finally, and perhaps most significantly given the framework of this chapter, separate organized groups still do not address the issue of the *how* of employee voice. Although trade union positive action structures and special interest groups are undoubtedly a major advance, they are often workplace-based and usually involve attendance at meetings. The same is true of employee diversity groups. This fails to recognize that the continued emphasis on physical attendance militates against the participation of those workers who stand outside of the standard archetype.

NEW SOCIAL MEDIA AS A TOOL OF EMPLOYEE VOICE

This leads to the question of whether there could be alternative ways to do employee voice and whether the use of 'social technology' (CIPD 2013b) might offer a way of addressing the problems associated with the *how* of conventional employee voice mechanisms. What is being referred to here is 'online technology for social interaction' (CIPD 2013b: 8) and includes websites, intranets, online discussion forums, blogs, and interactive surveys, amongst other things (what might often be called 'social media'). Many years ago, my colleagues and I were engaged with research around the use of social technology by trade unions and at this time there was a lot of hyperbole about the potential of social technology for the enhancement of employee voice. Almost a decade later, the enthusiasm for the idea does not seem to have waned, indeed a recent CIPD (2013b: 2–3) literature review on the subject of the use of social media and employee voice describes social media as 'a new form of collective voice that is mobile, organized and intelligent', or even as 'people-powered communication'.

From a diversity point of view, social technology might have a lot to offer. Research has directly addressed this issue with regard to women's participation in trade unions, with a view that the ability of the technology to move activism outside of the workplace into domestic space may provide solutions for the participation constraints of women (Greene and Kirton 2003). This could arguably also be extended to a number of other non-standard workers (see also Balnave et al. 2014), where social technology has the potential 'to generate shared identification and mutuality between geographically and socially separated individuals' (Saundry et al. 2007: 180). Social technology may also provide safer spaces for participation (Greene and Kirton 2003). Bell et al. (2011) provide an amended version of Dundon et al.'s (2005) typology of voice mechanisms that offers suggestions to make them more appropriate to LGBT employees. A particular point of adjustment they suggest is that forms of voice might need to be more virtual or anonymous in character to accommodate the need to conceal identity to avoid discrimination. Voice channels through social technology may offer some significant potential benefits to conventional forms including the decreased risk of speaking up where forums are anonymous (CIPD 2013b; Greene et al. 2013). Finally, it has been argued that the immediacy of communication and the archiving possibilities of social technology mechanisms have the possibility to challenge existing hierarchy and power structures. Indeed, research has investigated the ways that social technology could challenge oligarchical tendencies within trade unions (Greene et al. 2000), of which arguably the lack of participation and representation of those from minority groups is one part. Social technology channels might offer new spaces for employee voice allowing increased employee control over issues discussed (or at least less ability for managerial control) and the increased accountability of organizations to respond to or act on feedback from employees, because of the public nature of many social technology forms (CIPD 2013b).

There are many expositions of interesting examples of social technology in operation as a voice mechanism, although significantly, not many that relate to voice for minority groups and individuals. As an exception, Greene and Kirton (2003) looked at online activities of women health visitors in the UK National Health Service. Other examples that are not necessarily diversity related include dissenting factions challenging union executive discussions (Hogan and Greene 2002; Greene 2006), and the use of electronic bulletin boards in the Justice for Janitors Campaign (Newman 2005), while Saundry et al. (2007) look at electronic networks of freelance workers in the UK audio-visual industries. Overall, however, there has been relatively little academic research or debate around the use of social technology for employee voice, with Balnave et al. (2014) providing a useful recent synthesis of the literature in this area. In particular they highlight the fact that while there is a prolif-eration of writing detailing the kinds of social technology available, there is little critical analysis of its implications, leading them to state that 'the uptake of social media has outstripped analysis of its impact on employee voice'.

There has been an explosion of the use of social technology of all kinds, and a significant proportion (reportedly a fifth) of UK employees use internal social media tools in a work context at least once a week (Towers Watson 2012). It is doubtless that employees' use of social technology outside of work has increased their expectations of its use in work, and how their voice should be heard inside their organization (CIPD 2013b: 8). However, it is significant that only a minority of organizations appear to have embraced social tech-nology formally as an employee voice channel (CIPD 2013b: 3). Indeed, similar statements are made about unions being slow on the uptake of social technology today (Balnave et al. 2014), exactly as were being made in the early 2000s (Greene et al. 2000; Greene and Kirton 2003).

The lack of uptake must be partly related to the fact that social technology carries with it a number of disadvantages and weaknesses, good summaries of which are provided in the CIPD report (2013b: 14) and Balnave et al. (2014). Issues of internet access and IT competence, which were at the forefront of possible weaknesses of the use of social technology for employee voice, are clearly less salient now than they were ten years ago, although access issues may still be relevant for some segments of industrialized countries, and clearly for the developing world. Alongside access there is also the issue of employer and trade union opposition, particularly regarding the loss of control about what can be said, the increased transparency and accountability enforced, the lack of trust between managers and trade union officers/employees, and the lack of senior management/trade union officer skills in implementing social technology mechanisms.

With regard specifically to the activism of women, analysis of three case studies (Greene and Kirton 2003) indicated the way that social technology may not fulfil all the potential expectations of it in mitigating the forces that exclude minorities. One reason is that while social technology offers oppor-tunities to change the *how* of voice mechanisms, and overcome time and space constraints, cyberspace does not exist in a virtual paradise: 'Online forms encourage "time out" from everyday commitments, with the promise that you can arrange online activism in small convenient time segments, rather than the extended blocks of "time off" which are required for conventional activism. However in practice negotiating "time out" may also be problematic' (Greene and Kirton 2003: 324).

In addition, social technology forms of voice can be as dominated by the standard worker as conventional forms—the 'usurpation of cyberspace' (Greene and Kirton 2003: 325)—rather than offering space for those who are commonly marginalized. Furthermore, in the same way as separate organizing carries with it the risk that mainstream forms of employee voice mechanism are not changed, and the separate body may be marginalized, it is also important that social technology forms of employee voice do not become the home of minority groups and individuals, while the 'real' business of employee voice within an organization occurs elsewhere (Greene and Kirton 2003: 324).

In essence, while social technology can allow the enhancement of employee voice, it requires those in authority to give up some of their power (CIPD 2013b: 6). This was clearly illustrated by the case of the online network in Greene (2006), where the union officers had to accept that opening up online spaces for member comments of any kind, including the very negative, can be very uncomfortable for officials, is a direct challenge to their authority, and makes the management of union identity and member control arguably more difficult. The issue of loss of control is an interesting one, and Saundry et al. (2007: 187) report the way that the trade union within the audio-visual industry deliberately rejected the idea of a discussion forum on its website because the freedom of expression facilitated would have been difficult to allow within legal and internal policy considerations. Indeed, 'for some commentators, such virtual networks are antithetical to the notions of solidarity, cohesion and common interest that underpin trade unionism' (Saundry et al. 2007: 180).

It is a similar situation within corporate organizations, where the balance has to be struck between freedom of employee voice and possible reputational damage to the organization, which explains the rising attention of some employers around corporate gagging clauses and organizational constraints on the type and content of online comments (see CIPD 2013b and Balnave et al. 2014 for more examples).

At the present time, as Balnave et al. (2014) indicate, there is a real need for critical research that examines the operation and effects of the use of social technology for employee voice. It is interesting that Richards' (2012) article, 'What Has the Internet Ever Done for Employees? A Review, Map and Research Agenda', does not specifically discuss employee voice, even though many facets of the discussion could be connected to voice issues in one way or another. Furthermore, there is a need for diversity issues to be a specific concern of this research on voice in a way in which they are currently not. While a number of characteristics of social technology can be identified that seem to offer advantages as far as the participation of those outside of the standard archetype, there are also a number of disadvantages which are yet to be empirically analysed and properly theorized. Clearly there is a still a strong preference for face to face interaction both in trade unions and within organizations (Greene 2006; CIPD 2013b), and it is likely that the ideal situation will be a mix of conventional and social technology approaches. Social technology forms of voice should not obviate the need for more conventional forms, indeed present analysis where it exists indicates that this has been a key part of the formula for their success so far (Darlington 2003, Cockfield 2005; Greene and Kirton 2003; CIPD 2013b).

Diversity and employee voice: a summary

This chapter has presented a picture of increasing diversity in the contemporary workforce and has offered a critique of conventional study and practice of employee voice mechanisms from a diversity perspective. There have doubtlessly been improvements in the representation of those workers who fall outside of the standard archetype, and separate organizing and special employee groups have had some significant success in offering increased spaces for diverse voices to be heard. However, overall the assessment indicates that significant individuals and groups within the workforce still face a 'representation gap' and a 'democracy deficit'. It is easy to share the conclusion that 'the transformation of workforces and dominant practices render traditional mechanisms of voice ineffective in capturing the demands of workers from diverse backgrounds' (Bell et al. 2011: 139). In addition, there has been discussion of some of the difficulties that are found with the proposed solutions to this ineffective representation.

For those involved in the organization and operation of voice mechanisms, this chapter has identified key areas that should be considered if the current underrepresentation of many individuals and groups is to be encouraged. First, there should be attention to *who* stands as a representative. At the very basic equal opportunities level, is there a proportional representation of different diversity strands with regard to the bargaining unit/organizational grouping/workforce population? Second, paying consideration to the processes of participation in the voice mechanism may improve the overall diversity of representatives. Here it is important to think about the location and nature of participation. Is physical presence always a necessity, or can some virtual interactions using social technology be utilized? Has thought been given to ensuring that meetings and interactions take place at locations and times that are as inclusive as they can be with regard to diversity characteristics, including around non-standard hours of work?

In research terms, the longstanding arguments about diversity-aware industrial relations research apply (Dean and Liff 2010). There is much future work to be done in terms of highlighting the importance of research on employee voice that explicitly includes diversity concerns, allowing the necessary analysis and theorizing that may potentially lead to better policy and practice within organizations. The emerging area of the use of social technology for employee voice in particular is a potentially exciting area for future research in this regard.

▦ NOTES

1. Thank you to a number of people for comments on early drafts of this chapter, including Peter Ackers, Stewart Johnstone, and attendees at the presentation of this chapter at the BUIRA 2013 Conference in Glasgow including, in particular, Sonia McKay.
2. Although in overall terms, there is no evidence of increased polarization between regular, permanent, and full-time workers, and those employed on non-standard employment contracts. Indeed levels of task discretion improved for temporary workers 2005–10.
3. Analysis of WERS 2011 data is not sufficiently differentiated as yet to ascertain whether these women are concentrated in 'diversity'-related union roles, such as equality representative or union learning representative, which are disproportionately filled by women or other minority represented workers. WERS 2011 data analysis so far also does not differentiate between the individual unions represented, or the gender breakdown within the workplaces with female union representatives. This may be significant because BIS (2013) data indicate that women are more likely to be trade union representatives in workplaces which are predominantly female, therefore we are unable to ascertain the level of voice women have in male-dominated workplaces, where arguably their voice is more necessary to effect change.
4. It should be noted that WERS 2011 data analysis so far also makes a correlation between non-union representative roles and a much higher incidence of the representative role being on a part-time basis (all non-trade union reps fulfilling their role on this basis compared to one in six trade union reps that were full time. Moreover, union reps spent on average thirteen hours per week on their role compared to an average of three hours per week for non-union reps. This potentially indicates something about the centrality of the representative role for the individual, the time they have available to spend on their representative tasks, and their ability to have influence. Furthermore, the data analysis does not yet differentiate between male and female representatives to understand for example whether there are gender differences in the numbers who undertake their role on a full- or part-time basis.

■ REFERENCES

Aston, J., Clegg, M., Diplock, E., Ritchie, H., and Willison, R. (2005) *Interim Update of Key Indicators of Women's Position in Britain*. London: Women and Equality Unit/ Department for Trade and Industry.

Balnave, N., Barnes, A., MacMillan C., and Thornthwaite, L. (2014), 'E-voice: How Network and Media Technologies Are Shaping Employee Voice'. In A. Wilkinson, J. Donaghey, T. Dundon, and R. Freeman (eds), *The Handbook of Research on Employee Voice*. Cheltenham: Edward Elgar Publishing.

Bell, M. P., Ozbilgin, M. F., Beauregard, T. A, and Surgevil, O. (2011) 'Voice, Silence and Diversity in Twenty-First Century Organizations: Strategies for Inclusion of Gay, Lesbian, Bisexual and Transgender Employees'. *Human Resource Management*, 50(1), 131–46.

BLS (2011) *Labor Force Characteristics by Race and Ethnicity 2010*, Report 1032. Washington, DC: US Bureau for Labor Studies.

BIS (2013) *Trade Union Membership 2012: Statistical Bulletin*. London: Department for Business, Innovation and Skills.

BLS (2005) *Work at Home Summary*. Washington, DC: US Bureau of Labor Studies.

Bowen, F. and Blackmon, K. (2003) 'Spirals of Silence: The Dynamic Effects of Diversity on Organizational Voice'. *Journal of Management Studies*, 40(6), 1393–417.

Bradley, H. (1994) 'Divided We Fall: Unions and Their Members'. *Employee Relations*, 16(2), 41–52.

Bradley, H., Healy, G., and Mukerjee, N. (2002) *Inclusion, Exclusion and Separate Organization–Black Women Activists in Trade Unions*. Swindon: Economic and Social Research Council.

Briskin, L. (2002) 'The Equity Project in Canadian Unions: Confronting the Challenge of Restructuring and Globalization'. In F. Colgan and S. Ledwith (eds), *Gender, Diversity and Trade Unions: International Perspectives*, pp. 28–47. London: Routledge.

CIPD (2012) *Flexible Working Provision and Update*. London: Chartered Institute for Personnel and Development.

CIPD (2013a) *Employee Outlook Survey*. London: Chartered Institute for Personnel and Development.

CIPD (2013b) *Social Media and Employee Voice: The Current Landscape*. London: Chartered Institute for Personnel and Development.

Cobble, D. S. and Bielski Michal, M. (2002) 'Working Women and the US Labour Movement'. In F. Colgan and S. Ledwith (eds), *Gender, Diversity and Trade Unions: International Perspectives*, pp. 232–56. London: Routledge.

Cockburn, C. (1995) *Strategies for Gender Democracy*. Luxembourg: European Commission.

Cockfield, S. (2005) 'Union Renewal, Union Strategy and Technology'. *Critical Perspectives on International Business*, 1(2/3), 93–108.

Colgan, F. and Ledwith, S. (2002) *Gender, Diversity and Trade Unions: International Perspectives*. London: Routledge.

Colgan, F. and McKearney, A. (2012) 'Visibility and Voice in Organizations: Lesbian, Gay, Bisexual and Transgendered Employee Networks'. *Equality, Diversity and Inclusion*, 31(4), 359–78.

Colling, T. and Dickens, L. (1998) 'Selling the Case for Gender Equality: Deregulation and Equality Bargaining'. *British Journal of Industrial Relations*, 36(3), 389–411.

Colling, T. and Dickens, L. (2001) 'Gender Equality and Trade Unions: A New Basis for Mobilization?' In M. Noon and E. Ogbonna (eds), *Equality, Diversity and Disadvantage in Employment*. Basingstoke: Palgrave, 136–55.

Creegan, C., Colgan, F., Charlesworth, R., and Robinson, G. (2003) 'Race Equality Policies at Work: Employee Perceptions of the "Implementation Gap" in a UK Local Authority'. *Work, Employment and Society*, 17(4), 617–40.

Cunningham, R. (2000) 'From Great Expectations to Hard Times? Managing Equal Opportunities under New Public Management'. *Public Administration*, 78(3), 699–714.

Danieli, A. (2006) 'Gender, the Missing Link in Industrial Relations'. *Industrial Relations Journal*, 37(4), 329–43.

Darlington, R. (2003) 'The Creation of the E-Union: The Use of ICT by British Unions'. [Online.] Available at: <http://www.rogerdarlington.co.uk/E-union.html>.

Dean, D. and Liff, S. (2010) 'Equality and Diversity: The Ultimate Industrial Relations Concern'. In T. Colling and M. Terry (eds), *Industrial Relations Theory and Practice*, 3rd edn. Chichester: John Wiley and Sons.

Delaney, J. and Lundy, C. (1996) 'Unions, Collective Bargaining and the Diversity Paradox'. In E. Kossek and S. Lobel (eds), *Managing Diversity: Human Resource Strategies for Transforming the Workplace*, pp. 245–72. Cambridge, MA: Blackwell.

Dickens L. (1999) 'Beyond the Business Case: A Three-Pronged Approach to Equality Action'. *Human Resource Management Journal*, 9(1), 9–19.

Dickens, L., Townley, B., and Winchester, D. (1988) *Tackling Sex Discrimination through Collective Bargaining*. Manchester: Equal Opportunities Commission.

Dorgan T. and Grieco, M. (1993) 'Battling against the Odds: The Emergence of Senior Women Trade Unionists'. *Industrial Relations Journal*, 24(2), 151–64.

Dundon, T., Wilkinson, A., Marchington, M., and Ackers, P. (2005) 'The Management of Voice in Non-Union Organisations: Managers' Perspectives'. *Employee Relations*, 27(3), 307–19.

DWP (2010) *Ethnic Minorities in the Labour Market*. London: DWP. [Online.] Available at: <http://www.dwp.gov.uk/emesg/what-we-do/background/ethnic-minorities-in-the-labour/>, accessed 31 August 2013.

DWP (2012) *Older Workers Statistical Information Booklet 2012: Official Statistics*. London: DWP.

ETUC (2009) *Migrant and Ethnic Minority Workers: Challenging Trade Unions*. Geneva: ETUC.

ETUC (2012) *Report of the Fifth Annual ETUC 8 March Survey*. Geneva: ETUC.

Eurofound (2013) *Work Organization and Employee Involvement in Europe*. Luxembourg: Publications Office of the European Union.

European Foundation (2011) *Foundation Findings: Youth and Work*. Brussels: European Foundation for the Improvement of Living and Working Conditions.

Eurostat (2012) *Employment Statistics.* [Online.] Available at: <http://epp.eurostat.ec. europa.eu/statistics_explained/index.php/Employment_statistics>, accessed 31 August 2013.

Eurostat (2013) *Labour Markets at Regional Level.* [Online.] Available at: <http://epp. eurostat.ec.europa.eu/statistics_explained/index.php/Labour_markets_at_regional _level>, accessed 31 August 2013.

Forrest, A. (1993) 'A View from outside the Whale: The Treatment of Women and Unions in Industrial Relations'. In L. Briskin and P. McDermott (eds), *Women Challenging Unions: Feminism, Democracy and Militancy.* London, ON: University of Toronto Press.

Franzway, S. (2002) 'Sexual Politics in the Australian Labour Movements'. In F. Colgan and S. Ledwith (eds), *Gender, Diversity and Trade Unions: International Perspectives,* pp. 275–91. London: Routledge.

Friedman, R. A. and Holtom, B. (2002) 'The Effects of Network Groups on Minority Employee Turnover Intentions'. *Human Resource Management,* 41(4), 405–21.

Greene, A. M. (2006) 'Reflections on the Developing Activist's Network: Solidarity More Real than Imagined? Paper presented at the *Industrial Relations in Europe Conference (IREC),* workshop on 'Imagined Solidarities: Labour and the Information Age', Ljubjlana, Slovenia, 31 August–2 September.

Greene, A. M. and Kirton G. (2003) 'Possibilities for Remote Participation in Trade Unions: Mobilizing Women Activists'. *Industrial Relations Journal,* 34(4), 319–33.

Greene, A. M. and Kirton, G. (2005) 'Trade Unions and Diversity'. In A. Konrad, P. Prasad, and J. Pringle (eds), *Handbook of Workplace Diversity,* pp. 489–510. London: Sage.

Greene, A. M. and Kirton, G. (2009) *Diversity Management in the UK: Organizational and Stakeholder Perspectives.* New York: Taylor and Francis.

Greene, A. M. and Kirton, G. (2011) 'Diversity Meets Downsizing: The Case of a Government Department'. *Employee Relations Journal,* 33(1), 22–39.

Greene, A. M., Hogan, J., and Grieco, M. (2000) 'E-Collectivism: Emergent Opportunities for Renewal'. In B. Stanford-Smith and P. K. Kidd (eds), *E-Business: Key Applications, Processes and Technologies,* pp. 845–51. Amsterdam: IOS Press.

Greene, A. M., Donaghey, J., and Parker, M. (2013) 'Breaking the Silence in a UK Business School: Speaking out through the Internet'. Paper presented at the Work, Employment and Society Conference, Warwick University, 3–5 September.

Healy, G. and Kirton, G. (2000) 'Women, Power and Trade Union Government in the UK'. *British Journal of Industrial Relations,* 38(3), 343–60.

Heery, E. J. (2005) 'Sources of Change in Trade Unions'. *Work, Employment and Society,* 19(1), 91–106.

Heery, E. J. and Conley, H. (2007) 'Frame Extension in a Mature Social Movement: British Trade Unions and Part-Time Work, 1967–2002'. *Journal of Industrial Relations,* 49(February), 5–29.

Heery, E., Conley, H., Delbridge, R., Simms, M., and Stewart, P. (2005) *Trade Unions and the Representation of Non-Standard Workers.* Swindon: Economic and Social Research Council.

Hogan J. and Greene, A. M. (2002) 'E-Collectivism: On-line Action and On-line Mobilization. In L. Holmes, L. Grieco, and M. Grieco (eds), *Organizing in the*

Information Age: Distributed Technology, Distributed Action, Distributed Identity, Distributed Discourse, pp. 57–79. Farnham: Gower.

Holgate, J., Hebson, G., and McBride, A. (2006) 'Why Gender and "Difference" Matters: A Critical Appraisal of Industrial Relations Research'. *Industrial Relations Journal*, 37(4), 310–28.

Holgate, J., Pollert, A., Keles, J., and Jha, M. (2008) *Ethnic Minority Representation at Work: An Initial Review of Literature and Concepts*. London: London Metropolitan University.

Hoque, K. and Noon, M. (2004) 'Equal Opportunities Policy and Practice in Britain: Evaluating the "Empty Shell" Hypothesis'. *Work, Employment and Society*, 18(3), 481–506.

Ibarra, H. (1993) 'Personal Networks of Women and Minorities in Management: A Conceptual Framework'. *Academy of Management Review*, 18(1), 56–87.

ILO (2012) *Non-Standard Workers: Good Practices of Social Dialogue and Collective Bargaining*. Geneva: International Labour Office.

Kirton, G. (1999) 'Sustaining and Developing Women's Trade Union Activism: A Gendered Project?' *Gender, Work and Organization*, 6(4), 213–23.

Kirton, G. (2006) *The Making of Women Trade Unionists*. Aldershot: Ashgate.

Kirton G. and Greene, A. M. (2002) 'Positive Action in Trade Unions: The Case of Women and Black Members'. *Industrial Relations Journal*, 33(2), 157–72.

Kirton, G. and Greene, A. M. (2010) *The Dynamics of Managing Diversity: A Critical Approach*, 3rd edn. Oxford: Elsevier.

Kirton, G. and Healy, G. (2013) *Women and Trade Union Leadership*. London and New York: Routledge.

Klandermans, G. (1992) 'Trade Union Participation'. In J. Hartley and G. Stephenson (eds), *Employment Relations*, pp. 184–99. Oxford: Blackwell.

Kumra, S. and Manfredi, S. (2012) *Managing Equality and Diversity: Theory and Practice*. Oxford: Oxford University Press.

McBride, A. (2001) *Gender Democracy in Trade Unions*. Aldershot: Ashgate.

Munro, A. (2001) 'A Feminist Trade Union Agenda? The Continued Significance of Class, Gender and Race'. *Gender, Work and Organization*, 8(4), 454–71.

Newman, N. (2005) 'Is Labor Missing the Internet Third Wave?' *Working USA: Journal of Labor and Society*, 8(4), 383–94.

ONS (2013) *Statistical Bulletin: Labour Market Statistics*. London: Office for National Statistics.

Phillips, A. (1991) *Engendering Democracy*. Bristol: Policy Press.

Purcell, K. (2000) 'Gendered Employment Insecurity?' In E. A. S. Heery and J. London (eds), *The Insecure Workforce*. London: Routledge.

Richards, J. (2012) 'What Has the Internet Ever Done for Employees? A Review, Map and Research Agenda'. *Employee Relations*, 34(1), 22–43.

Saundry, R., Stuart, M., and Antcliff, V. (2007) 'Broadcasting-Discontent Freelancers, Trade Unions and the Internet'. *New Technology, Work and Employment*, 22(2), 178–91.

Shapiro, G. (2000) 'Employee Involvement: Opening the Diversity Pandora's Box?' *Personnel Review*, 29(3), 304–23.

Snape, D., Thomson, K., and Chetwynd, M. (1995) *Discrimination against Gay Men and Lesbians*. London: SCPR.

Stonewall (2009) *Stonewall Top 100 Employers 2009: The Workplace Equality Index.* London: Stonewall.

Syed, J. (2014) 'Diversity Management and Missing Voices'. In A. Wilkinson, J. Donaghey, T. Dundon, and R. Freeman (eds), *The Handbook of Research on Employee Voice.* Cheltenham: Edward Elgar.

Towers Watson (2012) *Global Workforce Study.* New York: Towers Watson.

TUC (2013) *Home-Working on the Increase despite the Recession.* [Online.] Available at: <http://www.tuc.org.uk/workplace/tuc-22217-f0.cfm>, accessed 31 August 2013.

van Wanrooy, B., Bewley, H., Bryson, A., Forth, J., Freeth, S., Stokes, L., and Wood, S. (2013) *The 2011 Workplace Employment Relations Study: First Findings.* London: Department for Business, Innovation and Skills.

Waddington, J. (2011) *European Works Councils: A Transitional Industrial Relations Institution in the Making.* Oxford: Routledge.

Whittle, A. and Mueller, F. (2009) '"I Could Be Dead for Two Weeks and My Boss Would Never Know": Telework and the Politics of Representation'. *New Technology, Work and Employment*, 24(2), 131–43.

Wrench, J. (2003) *Breakthroughs and Blind Spots: Trade Union Responses to Immigrants and Ethnic Minorities in Denmark and the UK.* Esbjerg: University of Southern Denmark.

Young, I. M. (1990) *Justice and the Politics of Difference.* Princeton, NJ: Princeton University Press.

Part 2

Union Voice

Competing Strategies

5 Trade unions as professional associations

Peter Ackers

The youth who has the good fortune and inclination for preparing himself as a useful member of society by the study of physic, and who studies that profession with success so as to obtain his diploma from the Surgeons' Hall or College of Surgeons, naturally expects, in some measure, that he is entitled to privileges to which the pretending quack can lay no claim; and if in the practice of that useful profession he finds himself injured by such a pretender, he has the power of instituting a course of law against him. Such are the benefits connected with the learned professions. But the mechanic, though he may expend nearly an equal fortune and sacrifice an equal proportion of his life in becoming acquainted with the different branches of useful mechanism, has no law to protect his privileges.

(Preface to the *Rules of the Journeymen Steam Engine Makers, and Millwrights' Friendly Society*, edition of 1845, quoted in Webb and Webb 1894: 218)

Introduction: trade union voice. Speaking to whom about what?

Worker voice used to mean trade unions. Academic Industrial Relations (IR) analysis, on both sides of the Atlantic, has long considered other channels, such as joint consultation or works councils, as either supplementary to or corrosive of this essential union role. Complimentary economic analysis added a generic 'voice effect' to the established 'wage effect', as an alternative to employee exit from the organization (Freeman 1980). However, as Chapter 1 made clear, the current voice debate is much more complicated, especially in Europe. Often, a substantial range of management and state-sponsored participation institutions compete for attention with trade unions, which rarely stand alone as voice institutions in the workplace and, often, do not appear there at all. Moreover, sociologists and historians have always recognized that trade unions are much more complex and varied social and political institutions than such economic discussions would allow.

In this sense, the character of trade unions is crucial to their voice role. And, for over a century, there has been a major ideological debate about the role and strategy of unions in industrial society. Outside the USA, socialists of various stripes have made the running and left an indelible imprint on contemporary IR conventional wisdom. This chapter explores and challenges these *radical* foundational assumptions and champions a *neopluralist* alternative. In my view, this would make trade unions a more credible avenue for voice in the eyes of members, employers, the state, and society in general, since how unions frame themselves is crucial to their future as voice institutions.

In the academic IR literature, particularly in Britain, trade unions are widely regarded as general 'worker' organizations, rooted in a supposedly straightforward, primary contradiction in the employment relationship between the interests of employers who hire labour and employees who work for pay. From this radical viewpoint, the basic union strategy is clear: 'unity is strength' and 'sectionalism' is a problem to be overcome. This chapter argues that this is a *sociological misconception*—a misunderstanding of what types of organizations trade unions really are and what attracts people to them—grounded partly in socialist idealism and partly in a Marxian adversarial reading of the employment relationship. In truth, trade unions formed long before the rise of Marxian socialism as a popular movement in the late nineteenth century, were influenced by it to only a limited degree—outside those movements that were actively created by socialists and communists—and have survived the demise of radical socialist politics at the end of the last century. Today, they are often middle-class professional organizations for doctors, nurses, and teachers. Yet their sociology and historiography still bears the heavy imprint of Marxian socialism, a body of ideas brought from the outside by radical intellectuals. This reading of trade unions extends from Fabian socialists, such as Sidney and Beatrice Webb (1894, 1897) to Marxist IR writers (see Hyman 1971; Kelly 1998), and a diluted version lingers on in mainstream contemporary *radical-pluralist* IR thinking.[1]

As Alan Fox (1966) once noted, an IR 'frame of reference' is not just a way of understanding reality, it also informs any approach to solving practical employment problems. Thus this sociological misconception shapes a number of putative strategies for trade union regeneration and revival, such as the merger, social movement, and organizing models, discussed below. These initiatives are predicated upon residual socialist notions that trade unions are general-purpose employee bodies, whose primary hostility is to employers and who rose to prominence by the militant efforts of an activist membership. Most of these assumptions are highly questionable and the sociological misconception about trade unions rests on *sturm und drang* mythology rather than accurate trade union history. This is especially true of Britain, where most trade unions, most of the time, have been deliberately sectional bodies who enjoyed cordial, sometimes close relations with employers, whose ordinary members were largely passive—rarely attending union meetings—and who advanced mainly with the spread of collective bargaining, encouraged by the state and employers.

Understanding this past is crucial to grasping the current decline of unions and the type of strategy that might begin to reverse this. If militancy, strikes, and independent organizing had indeed driven the original 'forward march' of labour, there would be a good case for returning to it. But, to the contrary, that twentieth century advance followed the tide of employer recognition and state sponsorship and was heavily conditioned by sympathetic public opinion. After 1979, this century-long political tide turned against British trade unions. So any realistic strategy for revival has to ask: how can trade unions regain their legitimacy, not only with employees, but also with the state, employers, and public opinion? To answer that we have to return to the 'bread-and-butter' basics of trade unionism and suggest how these might benefit society as a whole.

Below, I endeavour to construct an alternative sociological understanding of trade union identity, rooted in pluralist IR theory and the classical sociology of Weber and Durkheim. Even European trade unions are very diverse organizations (Hyman 2001), and elsewhere I've already criticised the abstract, generic idea of 'any union' (see Ackers 2014a). In the English-speaking world, trade unions developed occupational identities long before some socialists tried to reshape them in their own image. Elsewhere, in southern Europe or India, trade union movements were sometimes created by socialists and communists as transmission belts for political parties. Yet, even there, to thrive, these 'political' unions still had to follow what Gramsci called the 'contours of capital' (Hyman 1971: 12) and do a practical job for their members. Herein lies the *occupational essence of trade unions*, as organizations of employees by company, trade (craft), industry, and ultimately profession. These are inherently sectional bodies with necessary borders, and from this commonplace empirical observation it is possible to construct a professional view of trade unions that is superior to the radical model at the levels of social science, normative appeal, and public policy relevance.

The remainder of the chapter proceeds as follows. First, I discuss the various explanations of why trade unions have declined globally, as vehicles for employee voice. Next, I outline the foundational radical sociology of trade unions, before presenting a neopluralist alternative. After that I look at British trade union history, to explore which strategies really drove union advance until 1979 and how this was reversed by Thatcherism, and to consider the types of politically adept partnership policies that have been adopted by some trade unions since the 1980s to assimilate the 'lessons of defeat' and address the new realities. To illustrate the occupational and professional dynamic at the core of practical trade unionism—suggested in the opening quote—I then track several different types of British unions.

Finally, I argue that *professionalism*, in the broad sense used by Perkin (1989), is the best overarching *strategy* open to trade unions, cutting with the grain of occupational identities and the practice of partnership, while transforming the status and nature of work for manual and white-collar workers alike. Other policies may be useful and realistic for some unions at some times, but they are better understood as *tactics* whose value remains conditional on a professional vision rooted in the core occupational identity of trade unionism. Professionalism, by contrast, is a means to transform the 'corporate' occupational context into an active and persuasive normative strategy (to translate Gramsci's revolutionary concept of hegemony into the language of practical reform) that appeals not just to employees but also to employers, the state, and especially public opinion. This is no magic formula for success, but it has a proven historical track record.

The global problem of trade union decline

> Over the past thirty years, British unions have declined in power and influence on every measure.
>
> (Simms and Charlwood 2010: 126)

A generation ago, when I began my MA in Industrial Relations at Warwick University in 1980, any discussion of employee 'voice' or representation at work began and often ended with trade unions. In Britain, the 1977 Bullock Report on 'Industrial Democracy' had reaffirmed the 'single channel' view of employee voice, as collective bargaining extending right up to union representation at board level. This sustained the Anglo-American pluralist assumption that trade unions, independent of both management and the state, were the only viable mechanism for employee voice, while trying to blend this with a continental tradition of state-regulated representative structures, like German co-determination or works councils (discussed later in this volume). Some pluralists regarded Bullock as a bridge too far; one which threatened to undermine the proper independent role of trade unions. But all the participants in such British debates, before 1979, assumed that independent trade unions would remain absolutely central to employee voice.

This was equally true in northern Europe, where legal participation structures often ran in tandem with independent unions and were shaped by them. Indeed throughout the 'free world', the independent representative role of trade unions became a Cold War tenet of liberal and social democracy. Ironically, even where trade unions became an arm of the state or ruling party, most notably in socialist countries, they remained central to the idea of employee voice, however muffled the reality. In liberal democracies themselves, the hostility of communists to capitalist employers and the state ensured that they were among the strongest advocates of 'free collective bargaining' (see Seifert and Sibley 2012). Such ideas were exported round the developing world by liberal colonialists and leftist nationalists alike. Thus India inherited a version of the British pluralist model, while the rival communist parties organized their own militant trade union movements and other regional and ethnic parties followed suit, creating rival trade union centres (see Bhattacherjee and Ackers 2010). Movements like Peronism in Argentina did likewise, moulding corporatist trade union practices to their own distinctive ideology.

In short, for most of the twentieth century, trade unions and associated IR concepts, such as 'collective bargaining', became central to global society and terms like 'the labour movement' were the mental furniture of the age, used routinely by all and sundry. There were communist unions, socialist unions, catholic unions, protestant unions, nationalist unions, non-political unions, company unions, and plenty of bitter disputes between them; but few doubted the social significance of trade unions. There were huge national variations in trade union membership and in the power that unions exercised in the workplace and society, with perhaps the highest levels of union influence to be found in corporatist northern Europe. The effectiveness of trade unions as channels for employee voice was often suspect in the developing world, where official membership figures were highly misleading and these bodies became largely propaganda arms of the political national liberation movement. But this does not change the reality that, if there was a problem called 'worker voice', unions were the almost universal public policy answer. Almost everybody was for them in principle. In these terms, trade unions were part of the twentieth century 'spirit of the age' (see Kerr et al. 1973).

This is no longer true. The stark reality today is that all this has changed on a global scale, with very few national exceptions; though union retreat is uneven. This is not just a question of union membership, which was always highly variable and subject to national institutional and cultural influences. French unions developed a strong national presence and Indian unions contributed to the highest strike levels in the world, both with minority memberships. The fall in trade union membership is most telling in the USA and Britain, where membership is a more accurate measure of influence. In the former, unions are now marginal institutions with membership density of around 10 per cent, while in Britain they have fallen from 55 per cent in 1979 to around 25 per cent today. German density may be lower, but since national collective bargaining and company works council systems survive, they remain more central national institutions. In Sweden union membership has fallen from 80 per cent to about 70 per cent and collective bargaining remains almost universal, but even there a sense of uncertainty hangs over the movement.

Three related trends are taking place everywhere across the globe, albeit at greatly variable speeds. First, trade union membership and the coverage of collective bargaining are in steady decline. Second, unions are losing political influence—especially outside continental Europe—either as corporate actors or militant mobilization organizations. Third, and perhaps most important, unions are becoming marginal to the way we talk and think about work and society. They are no longer part of the 'spirit of the age'. Why? One pat radical answer is *neoliberalism*. In other words, free market political policies that have spread around the world from Thatcher and Reagan in the 1980s, inspired by the writing of Hayek and Friedman, have de-legitimized and stigmatized trade unions as enemies of freedom and prosperity. The threat is real, but begs the further question: why have these ideas been so successful that, in Marx's words, they have become a 'material force' in contemporary global society? I will consider six partial explanations for why trade unions are being marginalized. Three concern *external material changes* related to the structure of industry and the role of markets. Then two others relate to *external ideological changes* in the way people—the state, employers, employees, and the general public—think about unions and work. The sixth centres on the way unions reposition their traditional role in this new global context.

One external material change in Western societies is the development of *post-industrial society*. Modern Britain has about 10 per cent of the workforce in manufacturing and an increasingly white-collar economy. As late as the 1970s, trade unions with a manual workforce in primary and secondary industries, such as coal, steel, and engineering, were considered the *real* trade unions. Indeed, Blackburn and Prandy (1965) devised a measure of 'unionateness' against which to measure white-collar 'professional associations', which hoped to 'mature' into full-scale trade unions. Clearly the changing shape of the workforce in the West, away from the era of industrial society, has contributed to the anachronism of phrases like the 'labour movement'. Even so, it is often among middle-class, white-collar workers in the public sector that trade unions are strongest, while, in Britain, several large supermarket chains and banks are unionized. The old 'industrial' unions were largely male and the new service economy is highly feminized; but, overall, British women are now as well represented by trade unions as men. Other features of the new service economy, such as smaller workplace size and more temporary and part-time workers don't help union organization. However, small-scale employers and casualization were also characteristics of the late Victorian world from which trade unions began their great twentieth-century expansion (McKibbon 1984). And general unions of the poor have declined much more rapidly than professional or skilled organizations. Most tellingly, there has been no rapid unionization of the new industrial work-forces in the developing world. In short, there is no simple or inevitable connection between the class and gender characteristics of a given workforce and trade union membership.

A second trend, *globalization*, has grave implications for trade unions (see Brown 2010). Mobile transnational capital is much harder for nation states to regulate while international competition over labour costs undermines the effectiveness of the national unions of the low paid. In the past, unions organized local labour markets, such as the British lock, carpets, or coal industries discussed below. Working with responsible employers they established industry agreements that set minimum rates and prevented cut-price competition from those with poor labour practices. Global free trade and high levels of international migration make these local standards difficult to maintain, such that we now find even the Swedish construction industry struggling to protect national labour standards (Thornqvist and Wolfson 2012). Skilled, well-trained employees may be able to cushion themselves against low-cost competition and easy replacement, but low skilled workers cannot. Despite radical rhetoric about trade union internationalism and the existence of organizations like the European Trade Union Confederation (ETUC) and the International Labour Organization (ILO), trade unions are essentially national organizations and have few serious strategies beyond the national to deal with these problems. Organizing a mobile, unskilled, global workforce is like herding cats—and just as hopeless. So any credible union strategy must entail insulating employees from the lowest global market price by upgrading the status of jobs for a given occupation. This is the strategy of *professionalization*.

The emergence of *the flexible firm* (Atkinson 1984) is closely related to the problem of globalization. For not only do companies compete in increasingly competitive product markets and price down wages by tapping low-cost labour, but they also have developed new structures that are inimical to the old forms of trade union action, most notably strikes. The general decline in strike action has been a remarkable feature of British IR since 1979; indeed, specialist chapters on strikes have disappeared from most textbooks. Such strikes as still occur are normally found in protected sections of the public sector, whereas they have become a rarity in private manufacturing and services. One likely explanation for this is the development of complex, just-in-time supply chains and subcontracting arrangements, whereby any disruption of work would lead rapidly to workplace closure and job loss. Thus the unionized warehousing and haulage company that supplies a major supermarket chain would see its contract moved elsewhere; while the turbulent manufacturing plant, owned by a large multinational, would see production relocated; and even the small, independent firm would lose its market.

Here, old forms of collective economic power are simply too toxic to use. The effect would be instant, dramatic, and suicidal.

However, neither fragmented workplaces nor cut-throat market competition are new to trade unions. And this suggests that there are clear limits to purely material explanations for union decline. Something else is going on and two external ideological changes suggest themselves. One possibility is *post-modern affluence and consumer capitalism*, with the suggestion of different cultural identities to those found in the working-class communities of the early twentieth century. In Britain, these trends were already identified early on by the 1960s Affluent Worker studies, with the suggestion than even union members had developed an 'instrumental collectivism', geared to private leisure pursuits (Goldthorpe et al. 1968). More recently, there is the suggestion that people construct their identity around consumption rather than production. There is also evidence of a wider decline of associational forms in society, such as churches, political parties, clubs, and so on; an aspect of trade unionism stressed by Alastair Reid's (2004) recent history. Yet, people probably spend more time in paid work than ever, while some employers have turned workplaces into leisure centres and professional forms of organization remain strong. Overall then, it is oversimplistic to suggest that society is so individualized and consumer-orientated that there is no scope for trade unions. Rather this suggests that old appeals to economic interests need to be complemented by a stronger emphasis on values and identities.

Another candidate is *the end of the Cold War* and the associated decline of socialism as a major world ideology. Indeed, there is a remarkable correlation between the fall of the Berlin Wall in 1989 and the declining salience of trade unionism as a popular idea, notwithstanding the contribution made by the Polish 'Solidarity' union to the collapse of communism. In narrower terms, this may be interpreted as the death of one of the most determined sponsors of trade unionism in the capitalist world, responsible for the largest confederations in France, Italy, India, and many other countries. Without communist organization and activism one brand of trade unionism lost its vital impetus. Other socialist activists often worked with or against communists and the broader demise of any sense of an alternative socialist society, worth fighting against capitalism for, further corroded this variety of politicized union commitment. On the other side, free of the Cold War need to compete with communism, sponsors of alternative liberal and conservative models of trade unionism, such as the CIA or the Catholic Church, have tended to fade from the scene. Politics no longer needs the 'labour movement' and the impetus to plant your union brand all over the world is lost. So today the USA has many criticisms of human rights in China, but a lack of independent trade union representation rarely figures very high among them.

The employment world has changed dramatically over the past three decades. Trade union strategy cannot depend upon the return of industrial society and relatively closed national economies with large bureaucratic work organizations, or the reversal of consumer society and a socialist revival. These contextual influences are past. But that doesn't mean that trade unions are doomed to universal decline. To begin with, unions have never depended on external ideologies to find a moral purpose. As Perlman argued in 1928: 'The difficulty arises from a disposition to class as idealistic solely the profession of idealistic aims—socialism, anarchism and the like—and to overlook the un-self-conscious idealism in the daily practice of unionism' (in McCarthy 1972: 29). Any realistic contemporary sociology of trade unionism must return to these occupational basics.

Nor are trade unions without resources to influence society. Melanie Simms et al. (2013: 154) distinguish between potential *legitimacy power* and the *coercive power*.[2] Most radical commentators obsess on the latter, with discussions of group mobilization, economic bargaining power, and strike capacity (see Kelly 1998). As we have seen, the new material environment limits the scope for these crude tools. So the power to influence becomes crucial. Any trade union sits at the centre of a *diamond of stakeholders*, who together condition this power: employees, employers, the state, and public opinion. More often than not a trade union can only succeed at a national or workplace level by addressing all five stakeholders and by presenting itself as a solution to shared problems, a valuable channel of voice. Hence, whatever the external material and ideological factors constraining trade unions, they will only prosper if they define a credible, long-term social role. My argument is that one obstacle in the path of trade union revival is a radical mindset that was always misleading about the character of trade unions and is likely to lead to further errors of strategy. To return to Fox (1966), any 'frame of reference' that confuses an idealized view of organizational life with the real thing is likely to lead to bad public policy solutions. This is as true for trade union strategy as it is for the management equivalent.

The sociology of trade unions: some Marxian socialist foundations

> Wage labour rests exclusively on competition between the labourers. The advance of industry, whose involuntary promoter is the bourgeoisie, replaces the isolation of the labourers, due to competition, by their revolutionary combination, due to association.
>
> (Marx and Engels 1848/1952: 60)

To pick up from Heery's earlier chapter, Fox's (1966, 1974) three IR frames of reference succinctly link the sociology of work and organizations to the sociology of trade unions, following the headings of (1) model of the business enterprise, (2) attitudes to workplace conflict, and (3) the role of trade unions. Thus, *Unitarists* see the modern enterprise as a team, working together towards common goals (efficiency, customer service), with ordinary employees happily following management leadership. Conflict here is never more than frictional, perhaps caused by outside troublemakers or misunderstandings based on bad management communication. Policies like employee involvement can overcome these problems and restore the essentially cooperative nature of paid work. Trade unions as independent, employee organizations are viewed with great suspicion and often hostility; as outside bodies liable to introduce divisive conflict, like a virus infecting an otherwise healthy organism.

Pluralists, by contrast, see the business enterprise as a microcosm of modern society, composed of different interest groups, which are often in competition and conflict with each other. This is particularly true of large, complex organizations. These various groups share some long-term interest in the success and expansion of the organization, but there is no straightforward, natural basis for cooperation. Instead, conflict needs to be institutionalized or channelled through procedures, committees, and representative bodies. Moreover, workplace cooperation has to be negotiated and can never be total. Moderate trade unions perform this central voice role of bargaining and consulting with management on behalf of employees. As such, they represent their members, but also perform a valuable function for employees and management alike.

Radicals, and in particular Marxists, offer a third, more fundamentally conflictual view. Here the business enterprise is a system of class exploitation of labour by capital at the heart of wider capitalist society, wherein the state operates as the political arm of the capitalist ruling class. Workplace class conflict, therefore, is endemic and destructive, characterized above all by strikes. Militant trade unions 'fight' employers for better wages and conditions, but little is to be gained until the capitalist system, as a whole, is replaced by a new socialist system based on public ownership and popular control of the means of production. This bald summary conceals significant differences within the classical Marxian socialist approach, which I will now try to disentangle, beginning with the foundational Marxist sociology of trade unions. As Richard Hyman (1971) argues, these can be divided into optimists and pessimists.

Optimists see trade unions as direct agents in the destruction of capitalism and its replacement by socialism. Thus, the early Marx and Engels saw unions as 'schools of war', drawing workers into ever larger and more destructive battles with capitalists and paving the way for the final revolution. In this sense, trade unions are straightforward expressions of class conflict, ways of organizing the collective power of workers against their oppressors. They may not achieve much in the way of better wages and conditions—since capitalist economics will not allow this—but collective action and bitter struggles will raise working class consciousness and once the proletariat is fully united and aware of itself, capitalism will succumb. Early twentieth-century syndicalism translated these ideas into the strategy of 'one big union' and a general strike that would not only paralyse capitalism, but enable that union to take control of the running of industry and society.

Pessimists see another side to trade unionism, which convinces them that they can never play this socialist political role. Lenin and others wrote of the limits of 'trade union consciousness' and the extent to which unions, as sectional, practical, negotiating bodies, 'incorporated' workers into capitalism by encouraging them to believe that purely economic reforms were possible without overthrowing the entire political system. These fears grew in the twentieth century, as employers recognized trade unions for collective bargaining purposes and the two sides of industry negotiated settlements that not only improved the wages and conditions of workers but usually avoided serious outbreaks of conflict. While Marxists still valued strikes as means of raising socialist consciousness among the workers, increasingly they looked to the revolutionary party to gain state power.

Many classical Marxists foresaw a sudden, rapid revolutionary rupture with capitalism, perhaps associated with mass strikes and public disorder. Another strand of socialists, however, shared the core sociology of capitalism and socialism, but argued that a peaceful, democratic transition to socialism was possible, spread over a considerable period of time. Two of the best-known exponents of this *gradualist* viewpoint were Sidney and Beatrice Webb and their Fabian circle. The Webbs wrote the two great foundation works of trade union studies: *The History of Trade Unionism* (1894) and *Industrial Democracy* (1897), and their framework still shapes contemporary IR thinking. They differed from Marxism in some key areas.

First, they played down the conflictual aspect of the employment relationship. Yes, there was great inequality between capitalists and wage labourers, but no, the workers did not advance by heroic class struggle. Instead, given the slow 'permeation' of socialist values into capitalist society, trade unions could aid this advance, not by disrupting society through strikes, but by developing practical collective bargaining as a mechanism for 'industrial democracy', curbing the influence of the market. For the Webbs, such responsible policies raised the image of trade unions in the eyes of the public and helped to usher in the coming collective spirit. Second, capitalist society would travel towards socialist collectivism through enlightened state reform led by middle-class experts, operating through a democratic political system and a socialist political party. A final irony is that the Webbs and Lenin, for all their other political differences, shared a common suspicion about the merits of trade union activity per se and neither saw much of a role for it under full socialism.

In this way, the Webbs left a highly ambivalent legacy with regard to the sociology of trade unionism. On the one hand, they founded the social science analysis of trade unions as pragmatic, practical organizations engaged in sensible collective bargaining; an analysis that anticipated IR pluralism. On the other, they hung onto two core Marxian principles: that the capitalist employment relationship defined trade unions as general organizations of wage labourers, and that socialism would usher in another employment order under which these fundamental conflicts of interest would no longer exist. The Webbs' key works on trade unions were written before the rise of the British Labour Party or the Russian Revolution. After the First World War, this second socialist dimension of their thinking grew ever stronger.

There are grave dangers in observing trade unions through the lens of some future-orientated socialist utopia. To begin with, unions become an instrumental means to some other, higher end—socialism—rather than organizations to be understood in their own terms. New goals and methods are proposed to replace what unions already do. They are assigned new roles—to foment revolution or build a socialist society—that have little to do with their original purpose; and then judged negatively against this. Hence pessimistic Marxist theories of trade union oligarchy, integration, and incorporation represent no more than a belated, social science recognition that these were not the socialist bodies that revolutionaries had hoped for. So there is a strong case for a realist pluralist approach that begins with what trade unions actually do and then sees how this contributes to society. Utopian assumptions also make it easy to portray working life in the here and now as some sort of hell, with unions forever battling against dark employer forces. Not only does this risk negating the genuine progress that unions can make in regulating employment, but it also leads radicals to advocate highly risky forms of industrial action, like large-scale strikes, which often damage the real-life interests of ordinary employees. Once the socialist future is forfeited, these heroic suicide missions make little sense. Finally, as pluralists argue, utopian IR thinking easily becomes totalitarian practice. Under actually existing socialism, in the USSR and elsewhere, post-capitalist workplaces assumed the unitarist model with no place for independent trade unions.

Full-blown, future-oriented socialism is not the main issue in contemporary IR writing on trade unions. Most commentators concentrate on what trade unions can achieve, as pure-and-simple trade unions, by collective bargaining and industrial action in our current society. This said elements of radical thinking still float, unexamined, in the background and many of the assumptions about trade union strategy, such as the attachment to strikes as an all-purpose strategy, are saturated with old socialist myths. The central element is a Marxian reading of how trade unions arise directly from the capitalist employment relationship as organizations of wage labourers. For Marx and the Webbs, writing in the nineteenth century, wage labour was associated with the manual working classes, typically miners and factory workers, employed in private industry. However, contemporary IR writers have stretched the elastic concept of the employment relationship to include the huge contemporary white-collar and public sector workforce (see Edwards 2003). Thus everyone, from the hospital cleaner to the consultant is a wage labourer, in a position of subordination to their employer and, in some radical readings, driven by the same impetus to join a trade union. Indeed, the logic of this position is that they should all be one big union, as the syndicalists once advocated. In the same spirit, some argue that we should abandon the 'trade' prefix and speak only of 'unions'.

The sociology of trade unions: some alternative neopluralist foundations

> A trade union, as we understand the term, is a continuous association of wage-earners for the purpose of maintaining or improving the conditions of working lives.
>
> (Webb and Webb 1894: 1)

The Webbs' classic definition sounds innocuous: outlining no more than one core feature of a family of organizations that can be grouped under the heading of 'trade union'. This is how many contemporary pluralists read it. However, the Webbs were deliberately defining the general role of trade unions in capitalist society from their own socialist perspective. The definition is not wrong, but incomplete. It is a *necessary condition* for trade unionism that members are paid employees—even though there are obvious affinities with other types of associational and work interest groups, such as organizations of the self-employed or the National Farmers Union. However, in sociological terms, being in an employment relationship is not enough to foster trade unionism. It takes some sense of occupational identity to provide a *sufficient condition*. So when Fox's (1966) pluralism speaks of 'interest groups', this does not refer simply to workers versus employers, but to a variety of competing occupational groups. As Melanie Simms and Andy Charlwood (2010: 127) recognize, 'worker interests are socially constructed' by trade unions, but the material that activists build with is some shared sense of working in the same company, trade (craft), industry, or profession.

Classical British IR pluralism built on the Webbs' *Industrial Democracy*, but replaced their socialist case with a broader social democratic one (Ackers 2007, 2014c). Yes, Hugh Clegg (1951: 22) and Allan Flanders (1975) agreed, trade unions are representative bodies, not channels for mass mobilization— as Marxists had hoped. By and large, they are oligarchic, with limited membership participation, but that doesn't matter so long as they fulfil an essential pluralist role as, in Clegg's phrase, 'an opposition which can never become a government'. There are three important differences with the Webbs, however. First, unions are not on some road to state collectivism, whereby their importance would decline. Rather, they are central elements of a mature, stable, liberal democracy, as bulwarks against authoritarian state and management power. Indeed, the voluntary role of independent, if measured opposition becomes the essence of pluralist 'industrial democracy'. Second, unions are not just economic bargaining agents with beneficial effects; through collective bargaining they become rule-making bodies, creating a new political order in the workplace. Finally, unions are not converging on some general employee representation body, but remain fractured between many different employee interest groups, operating within or between official trade union organizations.

IR pluralism has rarely been developed into a full sociology of trade unionism. It is easy, however, to find some classical sociological underpinning. One is Max Weber's ideal-type model of three types of social stratification, by *market, status,* and *party* (political power). Devised in direct response to Marx's class polarization thesis, this model acknowledges that there are indeed societal divisions based on tensions in the employment relationship between employers and employees. However, this does not exhaust economic conflict, since different groups of workers and employers may be in conflict with others of their general employment kind. Moreover, divisions of status are also essential, such as differences between skilled, unskilled manual, and white-collar workers. Conflicts of interest are a feature of modern society, but in a much more complex sense than the Marxist notion of a class war between employers and employees (see Dahrendorf 1956; Parkin 2002).

At the level of trade union action, perhaps the most fertile source for developing a Weberian approach is Frank Parkin's (1974) *Strategies of Social Closure.* Once again, while this analysis runs in parallel to Turner's (1962) IR analysis of 'open' and 'closed' unions in the Victorian cotton industry, the two lines of argument are rarely connected. Parkin observes that organized employee groups have two possible strategies open to them for increasing the power of their members. One stresses building the broadest possible collective of shared interests. Yet, large general groups of workers are rarely effectively united. A more realistic strategy for many groups of employees is to define themselves in fairly exclusive terms by closing their borders against other 'unqualified' workers. This has been the dominant strategy of craft trade unions with their insistence on an apprenticeship or seniority system, as it is for professional groups like teachers who use qualifications to patrol their borders. Parkin captures the essential 'limited sympathy' of effective trade unionism: combining and excluding at the same time.

The other crucial figure for a pluralist sociology of trade unionism is Emile Durkheim (see Parkin 1992). While Fox and Flanders deployed Durkheim's concept of anomie or 'normlessness' to characterize the chaos of the 1960s British IR system (Flanders 1975: 241–76), the French sociologist's writing on professional associations is not often applied to unions. Yet Durkheim's 'profession' overlaps with the Anglo-Saxon concept of 'trade union' and becomes central to his normative theory of social integration. In brief, traditional society was bound together from above by authoritarian, *mechanical solidarity*, as under feudalism, with its rigid hierarchy and single religious focus. Modernity and the Industrial Revolution broke down these traditional structures, such that many French conservatives feared that society itself was falling apart, into a state of anomie. To the contrary, Durkheim argued, modern society develops new, more flexible forms of solidarity, including the division of labour itself, which connects many different groups of producers. The formation of professional organizations or trade unions is central to this *organic solidarity*, which prevents the emergence of an atomized society of isolated individuals.

There is still much to be learnt from classical IR pluralism, but it is no longer an adequate guide to the situation of trade unions today, for several reasons. First, interests dominate, when conflict over values can be just as important. Second, there is a narrow emphasis on conflict inside the workplace—recalling a time of full-time, male 'breadwinners' ensconced in large factories—which does little to account for the fragmented tensions between work, family life, and society today. Finally, trade unions are defined exclusively as collective bargaining agents, from an era when collective bargaining alone—as 'arms-length adversarialism'—was an adequate union strategy. *Neopluralism* (see Ackers 2002, 2014a) suggests a broader normative appeal and closer dialogue with employers, grounded in the same basic occupational identities. There are tensions in the employment relationship and sectional demands for employee voice, which may be cultivated into trade union representation. Legitimacy power is now crucial, however, not just to convert sectionalism into occupational identity, but also to convince employers, the state, and above all public opinion that union organization benefits society. This returns us to Durkheim's insight that independent forms of associational life, like trade unions, do not tear society apart—as Marxists would suggest—but bind it together through the development of responsible, professional identities. In certain circumstances, employers and the state stand to gain from this source of cohesion.

Beyond socialist trade union history: the British case

It is therefore misleading to speak of a 'labour movement' as a constant in the history of this period. The term describes an aspect revealed by the unions and their political arm from time to time... But it was often apparent only to the discerning eye, rarely visible in day-to-day union business, and only very rarely powerful enough to override the self-interest of any individual union.

(Clegg et al. 1964: 488)

Trade unions are widely misrepresented today, by both friends and foes, as militant socialist organizations, composed of poor manual workers who once built ever wider class unity and rose to power through fierce battles with employers and the state. The lesson drawn by radicals is that trade union decline is caused by just another state and employer anti-union offensive and that the only credible response is another bout of militancy. Yet, as Clegg et al. suggest for the period to 1910, this 'class' reading of the past is grossly oversimplistic. Indeed, socialist labour history has been written to justify socialist politics: whether the gradual permeation of collectivist ideas, anticipated by the Webbs, or the class struggle envisaged by Marxists. So, yes, there were some socialist militants, trade unionism did reach the poorest manual workers, and there were some big strikes; but, by and large, British trade unionism was an apolitical movement, dominated by relatively skilled and later professional workers, that expanded dramatically in the twentieth century with the support of employers, the state, and public opinion. During the 1970s British unions forfeited this support through a wave of strikes and since then the more politically perceptive sections of the movement have been trying to regain legitimacy power through a strategy of partnership.

One popular socialist caricature of British trade union history goes roughly as follows. Over the nineteenth century a 'proletariat' was forming from the disparate trades and crafts as large-scale factories deskilled those groups. This process was held back by the emergence of a 'labour aristocracy', benefiting from the golden age of Victorian industrial predominance and empire. The 1889 new unionism outbreak of strikes among unskilled dock workers and others, accompanied by the spread of socialist ideas, paved the way for the modern, united, twentieth-century labour movement, characterized by broader class forms of industrial action. A ruling class legal offensive in the early years of that century, most notably over Taff Vale in 1901, broke the old links between the trade unions and liberalism. In 1918 the Labour Party adopted a socialist constitution and from then onwards the trade unions were the industrial arm of a (highly imperfect) socialist labour movement. Overall, trade unions gained members and influence by organizing from below and forcing themselves onto hostile capitalists and the state that stood behind them.

Hugh Clegg's (1964 et al. 1985, 1994) monumental trade union history offers an entirely different picture of trade union advance. He plays down these political and ideological developments by stressing the sectional, pragmatic continuity of British trade unionism from its late eighteenth century origins. Thus, the early craft societies formed the bedrock of Victorian trade unionism, slowly expanding in their national scope. The year 1889 brought new groups of less skilled workers into the union ambit, but even here an organized skilled core formed the condensation nuclei around which the new general unions formed; and it was these skilled groups that survived the harder years ahead once the strike excitement was over. By the end of Victoria's reign, many employers had already recognized trade unions for collective bargaining purposes, encouraged by a sympathetic state and public opinion. The real turning point came after the Great War, along with universal suffrage, as the state and employers fostered both stable industry bargaining and corporatist state/employer/trade union relations. Following the next war, under a social democratic settlement, the Ministry of Labour and employers further sponsored the spread of trade unionism. On this solid institutional and sectional basis, British trade union membership followed the spread of collective bargaining, reaching peak coverage of 55 per cent and 75 per cent in 1979. By this time, collective bargaining was normative 'best practice', resisted by only a few maverick employers.

Socialism—in any Marxian sense of the word—has been a fairly superficial element in British trade unionism. Policies like big general or industrial 'fighting' unions have been achieved on paper only. As we shall see, supposedly 'general' unions, such as the General and Municipal Workers' Union (GMWU) and Transport and General Workers' Union (TGWU) in the past or Unite today, in reality are marriages of convenience, coalitions of occupational groups, each negotiating for its own patch. Big strikes against employers and the state, like the 1926 General Strike, were usually disasters for the movement, leading to a loss of union legitimacy power. Rarely did trade unions organize the unskilled from outside the company by taking on recalcitrant employers. Indeed, trade unions advanced not by becoming an active militant social movement, organizing from below, but by winning recognition from employers and the state and thus spreading the coverage of collective bargaining. Without this prior support, they would have struggled to ever reach the unskilled and low paid—as they do today. Collective bargaining fostered union membership rather than the other way round, spreading the canopy of joint regulation to these 'hard-to-organize' groups with active employer and state cooperation. With such support trade unions could widen and deepen their membership, often through a 'closed shop', which made this an involuntary condition of employment. Collective bargaining and thus union membership became a 'public good'.

This is the real story of twentieth-century trade union advance, and it also explains the dramatic decline of British trade unions after 1979 (see Howell 2005). From the 1960s onwards, British IR, especially in manufacturing, experienced unofficial strikes, restrictive practices, and chaotic inflationary wage settlements. Both major political parties—Labour and Conservative—and a growing body of public opinion saw trade union behaviour as a major cause of inflation, inefficiency, and the decline of the British economy. British pluralists sought to address this anomie by reforming bargaining structure and fostering an effective national tripartite approach to incomes policy, as found in most continental north European economies. By contrast, Marxists misread this sectional conflict as an instance of class conflict and fanned the flames, with the hope that it would break capitalism and lead to socialism. In reality, the 1978–9 'winter of discontent' merely destroyed the social democratic political settlement that had underpinned the very advance of collective bargaining and trade unions in the first place. The election of Margaret Thatcher's neoliberal Conservative Government in 1979 began the delegitimization of British trade unions. State policies and new laws turned against trade unions and further militancy merely confirmed these political prejudices.[3]

Once legitimacy power, grounded in state, employer, and public support, was lost, collective bargaining coverage and then coercive power quickly followed, leading to rapid membership loss. Old, inefficient unionized manufacturers closed or contracted and new high-tech or service organizations no longer felt any state pressure or moral obligation to recognize trade unions. All trade unions need legitimacy power to thrive. Indeed this, rather than coercive power, is their primary source of social influence. Moderate, practical trade unionists have always recognized this and, in the 1980s, the 'single-union, no-strike deal' pioneered by the electricians' union paved the way for a new partnership approach, founded upon regaining legitimacy power with all the key stakeholders (see Bassett 1986). The impetus came from increasing inward investment by Japanese companies, such as Nissan and Komatsu, opening new plants on green field sites. Unions feared these would be non-union, as foreign companies tried to avoid the conflict-ridden, multi-union IR traditions of British engineering. Japanese businesses were accustomed, by contrast, to a single company union that cooperated closely with management. The electricians' formula (shared in practice by other unions) was to represent the entire workforce as a single voice channel and operate a system of pendulum arbitration, which replaced strike action as a bargaining tool. In addition, a company council shifted from adversarial bargaining to proactive consultation. Finally, these agreements gave manual workers the same status and employment conditions as staff, while the union ran its own craft training centre, to encourage efficient multi-skilled working.

While the immediate appeal of the electricians' strategy was to employers, it also spoke to employees, the state, and public opinion by presenting trade unions as constructive organizations that could contribute to business efficiency. Partnership, as an official Trades Union Congress (TUC) strategy to woo the state, employers, and employees, emerged under the New Labour Government after 1997 (see Ackers and Payne 1998). And partnership deals, which exchanged flexibility for security and replaced adversarial, arms-length bargaining with a more proactive and consultative relationship between the employer and the trade union, spread across a substantial part of the economy. Radical critics champion a militant alternative which mobilizes workers into strike action against employers (see Kelly 1998). However, as we have seen, today neither material nor ideological conditions favour militancy—as strike statistics bear out. Even were this to prove a short-term success in certain protected sectors (courting ultimate derecognition and deunionization), its pursuit would simply deepen the legitimacy crisis for the rest of the movement. While it is easy to pick holes in partnership and measure its limitations against some heroic alternative, this remains a central element of any strategy for mobilizing legitimacy power in an era when 'mere collective bargaining' is insufficient to regain employer, state, or public support.

Constructing occupational identities: three British historical examples

> In industry professionalization has not reached down far enough to persuade the manual workers that they fully belong to the new society or to the same order of human being as the managers. The professionalization of the workers, their merger into a single status along with non-manual staff, with the same conditions of employment, paid sick leave and holidays, pension rights and the like, is far from complete.
>
> (Perkin 1989: 516)

Trade unions are not just about haggling over wages and conditions; they can change the status of labour. Harold Perkin is highly critical of British society, including its trade unions, for failing to professionalize work. However, occupational identity is the first step towards professionalization and the history of British trade unionism offers us many examples of craft or professional unionism in action. Here I have chosen four examples from my own research and experience to demonstrate how organized groups of employees have actively constructed trade union identities from the raw material of occupational commonalities and, in some cases, used these to reshape the meaning of work itself.

The National Association of Colliery Overmen, Deputies and Shotfirers (NACODS) was a coalmining trade union formed early in the twentieth century to represent underground supervisors and firemen (see Ackers 1994). The impetus for union organization came from health and safety legislation, which encouraged these men to development an identity separate from both colliery managers and ordinary colliers. Under the Mines Acts, they became legally responsible for inspecting underground conditions and deciding if it was safe to work for the all-male workforce. A central issue was the presence of gas and the danger of an explosion and both these supervisory and safety roles created the potential for trade union organization. As supervisors they were often under pressure from colliery management to drive face workers harder and work in dangerous conditions. This tension in the employment relationship with their employers was accompanied by another tension with other employees, ordinary coal miners. Since piecework was paid, either group might press to work in dangerous conditions. Occupational differences encouraged separate union organization, while the latter reshaped and consolidated the former, creating clear borders and a strong professional sense of duty. To begin with, the main industrial union, influenced by syndicalist ideas, tried to absorb these men. However, the deputies maintained a strong, separate sense of themselves as qualified men, enforcing health and safety, independent of commercial interests. Thus NACODS turned an occupational tension into a professional opportunity.

Two small manufacturing unions suggest some other dynamics (see Ackers 1988; Greene et al. 2000; Sayce et al. 2006). The British lock industry has been highly localized in the Wolverhampton area of the Midlands, with a major concentration of companies in one small industrial town, Willenhall. Good early relations with large employers, fearful of price undercutting by small firms, led to a national agreement negotiated with a single union, the National Union of Lock and Metal Workers (NULMW). This provided stable collective bargaining and very high levels of union membership throughout the twentieth century with few strikes. For many years, work was highly gender segregated, with women working on the assembly line and men working in other areas, like polishing, machine-setting, the tool room, and labouring. Over time, the union negotiated flexible team working, which began to break down gender boundaries. There were other occupational tensions, however, with skilled toolmakers wanting to join the engineering union. Even so, the strong lock maker occupational community seems to have been enough to hold this small, intimate industrial union together.

The British carpet industry had similar industrial characteristics, being largely centred in one Midlands town, Kidderminster. Again a national agreement was negotiated with an industry union, the Power Loom Carpet Weavers and Textile Workers Union (PLCWTWU). However, this was primarily a craft, weaving body, and other workers in spinning, the tool room, labouring, and other jobs joined a variety of other general and craft unions, creating a multi-union agreement. To further complicate matters, the PLCWTWU included women preparatory and finishing workers although the union was dominated by male Wilton and Axminster weavers, who had served their time in a seniority system and exercised craft controls over how many looms they would run at a time. This illustrates the pluralist theme of occupational (and gender) fragmentation and the group tensions that can arise as when, for instance, other workers refused to support a weavers' strike. By the 1990s, the craft union had neither resolved tensions with other groups nor satisfied management demands for greater flexibility, as employers began to move production to low-cost countries. So we can see the limitations of an old-fashioned, restrictive craft approach in a globalized economy. Could a more professional model, involving formal training and multi-skilling, have been more successful in securing these manufacturing jobs?

The Association of University Teachers (AUT) was an elite, professional association for academics from 'old' British research universities. Other university employees belonged to different unions, while lecturers from polytechnics (now the 'new' universities) and further education colleges were in the National Association of Teachers in Further and Higher Education (NATFHE). Unlike some professions, there was no explicit qualification, such as a Ph.D., only an academic post within the university sector. However, the narrow occupational focus of the AUT provided for a strong professional identity, distinguishing its elite academic membership from other groups working in education. Since academics moved between the 'old' and 'new' universities, there was a professional case for bringing these two groups together. The University and College Union (UCU) was formed from a merger of the two unions. From an AUT perspective, one problem was a dilution of professional identity, as traditional research academics (some from NATFHE) were combined with a larger, teaching-only group. Moreover, despite the union merger, the old and new universities and further education colleges remained in separate collective bargaining sectors, with quite different job titles and hierarchies. From a radical perspective, this might appear as an instance of growing worker unity across the larger educational sector, but that rests on the assumption that the 'old' university lecturers share an occupational identity with college lecturers, or vice versa. Was a once strong professional identity diluted in the new general 'teaching' union?

These four cases indicate how real trade unions have constructed organizations out of complex and fragmented occupational realities. They show that while, in each case, the employment relationship is a necessary condition for organization, it is very far from being a sufficient one. A common sense of 'trade' identity is crucial. In each case there were strategic choices: the deputies could have become a section within a larger miners' union; the lock union could have merged with a larger engineering union; the carpet weavers could either have become a small industrial union or restricted their membership to core weaving workers; the universities union could have remained an elite association. These choices determine the success of any trade union as it attempts to transform the base metal of occupation into the gold of an attractive professional identity that draws new members to it and attracts the respect of employers and the state.

Deconstructing general unionism

> [In the mid-nineteenth century] we have industrial society still divided vertically trade by trade, instead of horizontally between employers and wage-earners. This latter cleavage it is which has transformed the Trade Unionism of petty groups of skilled workmen into the modern Trade Union Movement.
>
> (Webb and Webb 1894: 46)

Thus the Webbs charted the forward march of the trade union movement from exclusive craft societies to ever broader forms of organizations, from sectional bodies to general employee organizations reflecting the central facture of the capitalist employment relationship. Looking at the web pages of the current British trade unions we might think that the Webbs were right after all. There are fewer and larger unions than ever before. 'Unite is Britain's biggest union with 1.5 million members in every type of workplace ... taking trade unionism out to the millions of unorganized workers'. This union is 'also active on a global scale building ever stronger links with trade unions around the world to confront the challenges of the globalised economy'. Growing size means growing power: 'The history of the union movement has been punctuated by mergers in which smaller and more specialized unions come together to combine their resources and increase their bargaining power and collective strength'. Likewise, 'UNISON is the UK's largest public service union with more than 1.3 million members', having absorbed numerous smaller organizations.

However, closer inspection tells a very different story of a patchwork of separate occupational identities beneath the 'general union' image. Thus Unite has twenty-three 'sectors', covering most of the British economy, each of which fragment into a myriad of companies and professions. Nowhere does Unite negotiate as a single union and whereas there are still some industry agreements, most are at the company level. So the 'health sector', where Unite is a secondary force working with others, breaks down into twenty 'Occupations, professions and Organising Professional Committees', including the British Veterinary Union (BVU), the Healthcare Chaplains (CHCC), the Mental Health Nurses (MHNA), the Doctors (MPU), Community Nursery Nurses (CPHVA), and so on. The 'Finance and Legal sector' is a miscellany of former staff associations, following distinctive policies as at a company level: 'Unite works with Barclays through a Partnership agreement'. A union with a strong tradition of representing the unskilled, Unite also includes the National Union of Professional Interpreters and Translators (NUPIT) and the Unite Criminal Justice Managers or Probation Officers (UCJM). UNISON's range is almost as broad, listing ten general 'occupations' but just one of these, Healthcare, includes ten 'Allied health professions', including the British Association of Occupational Therapists (BAOT). Another of the 'occupations' represented is *managers in partnership*.

We might conclude that with such occupational diversity, the employment relationship is the only basis for shared interests, as the Unite website suggests. But members join Unite not to be part of the biggest general union but to be represented in their company, industry, trade (craft), and profession. So Barclays is the focus for members there, while occupational therapists look to BAOT. Growing union size may contribute to the financial strength and professional resources of trade unions, but this adds little to the bargaining power of the constituent groups. Although Unite or UNISON project a larger organizational unity—the latter around public service—they are really 'holding groups' for a mass of separate occupational identities. A third union, Community, illustrates this by representing 'members and their families in all industries and sectors within the UK economy'. The carpet workers (discussed above) now belong to Community, as do the former National Union of Domestic Appliance and General Operatives (NUDAGO), the British Union of Social Work Employees (BUSWE), the Iron and Steel Trades Confederation (ISTC), the National Union of Knitwear, Footwear and Apparel Trades (KFAT)—the four main groups—as well as the (football) League Managers Association (LMA) and the National League of the Blind and Disabled (NLBD).[4] It is hard to imagine a more disparate group of employees.

The point of this analysis is to show that occupation is the real root of trade unionism beneath the general union rhetoric. By and large, employees combine not with other workers in general but with fellow workers who share a much more specific identity and look to see this represented through collective bargaining. In this way, trade unions need to be stripped back to their older essentials, which are much closer to Victorian craft ideals than they are to the 'workers of the world unite' radical slogan. In short, these are occupational bodies that represent the interest of employees in a particular group or trade.

Trade union regeneration: six models

So how does this revised understanding of the character of trade unionism reshape our understanding of the scope for union revitalization and revival today? Above all, it does so by jettisoning any simplistic radical assumptions about the generic employment relationship fostering general workers' organizations. This is not to glorify gratuitous sectional divisions, or to question the value of a central coordinating body like the British TUC, which addresses national employment issues. At times, British unions have been too narrowly sectional for their own good; and selfishly neglectful of broader distributional issues linked to the 'social wage' when compared to their continental counterparts (Nijhus 2011). And, while my principal focus here is on liberal market economies, such as the UK or US where the state currently offers limited support for trade unions, the professional argument also applies to coordinated market economies with national tripartite systems of 'social partnership'. Indeed, they have already travelled much further down that road. For the building blocks of occupational identity do not preclude higher levels of union cohesion at the national or industry levels, provided that we see these as political and social constructions. And occupational realities cannot be ignored even by national union movements with strong state support. The same diamond of stakeholders appears in every modern economy, conditioning the future of trade unions. Let us now compare the professional approach to several current strategies for trade union revival (see general discussions in Ackers et al. 1996; Blyton and Turnbull 2004; and Simms et al. 2013). The first three strategies make broadly radical assumptions, while four and five can be more easily integrated into a professional association model.

THE MERGER MODEL: BIG IS POWERFUL?

As we have seen, merger has been a major response to union membership decline in Britain, constantly creating new composites with evocative titles like Unite or UNISON to replace the descriptive acronyms of old. As older industries contract, such as coal, shipbuilding, steel, or lock making, there may be strong economies of scale or financial justifications for merger, though we should recall that many effective unions, like the NULMW and NACODS, have thrived on a small scale. The real problem here is when the rhetoric of merger promises some higher level of worker unity, the classic radical language of 'the workers united shall never be defeated'. In truth, trade union identity is constructed around companies, industries, trades (crafts), and professions and where merger blurs or submerges this core union identity it serves to actively weaken employee commitment to their trade union. The strongest trade unions or groups within larger trade unions—coal miners, boilermakers, teachers, or nurses—have always had a clear occupational identity.

THE ORGANIZING MODEL: BUILDING FROM BELOW?

At one level, all effective unions need to organize, since representative bodies with high membership command employer and state respect. Besides, in many cases employers will help the union to deepen its organization, as the supermarket chain, Tesco, promised as part of its partnership agreement. The problem arises when 'organizing' becomes shorthand for another radical delusion: the idea that militant conflict with the employer is the best strategy for building long-term union support, an approach that might be characterized as 'standing outside the building and throwing stones'. In the next chapter, Simms makes a robust defence of organizing, yet her own sympathetic audit of the recent British union organizing experience draws fairly bleak conclusions (Simms et al. 2013). This is hardly surprising since, as historical research shows, strong, stable trade unionism depends on employer and state support for collective bargaining, conditioned by public opinion. Any strategy that either ignores or alienates these three constituencies is doomed to heroic failure. Radical union history is full of tragic defeats, many of them self-inflicted by misunderstanding the real dynamics of union advance. Any credible organizing strategy must be a multiple dialogue with potential members, employers, the state, and the general public; what Gramsci terms 'a war of position'. Aggressive frontal assaults or 'wars of manoeuvre', had very limited success under the old twentieth-century 'socialist' dispensation and are even less likely to be successful today (see Ackers 2014b).

THE SOCIAL MOVEMENT MODEL: MOBILIZING THE PEOPLE?

This is another approach redolent with radical assumptions and close to the old 'class' mobilization modus operandi of communist-led union movements in France, Italy, Spain, Greece, or West Bengal. Here unions shift their focus beyond the workplace to develop broader community campaigns, linking together a rainbow alliance of disenfranchised groups. Ironically, the support for this strategy today, as for much of the organizing model, comes from the USA, a country with one of the most depleted and isolated union movements in the world, using examples such as 'Justice for Janitors'. As with organizing, the very American assumption is that there is little or no support to be expected from either employers or the state. This runs against the political realities elsewhere in the world—notably in Europe (including Britain) and

Latin America. This said, in certain, very specific industrial communities, such as coalmining, such an approach may have real purchase (see Ackers 2014b). Today, these settings are more likely to be in the developing world. But even in the UK, adding a community dimension to any trade union campaign is one way to win over other stakeholders and renegotiate a particular occupational interest as the general interest. In this sense, it is essential to effective professional unionism. However, to go further still and remove unions from their workplace base and transform them into general leftist campaigning organizations is another recipe for marginalization and decline. Moreover, while this strategy often focuses union energies on those who 'most need unions' in an economic sense, these people are also those least likely to form or join unions—and always have been. For contrary to radical mythology, the core of trade unionism has always been those in relatively stable, well-paid employment.

THE IDENTITY POLITICS MODEL: MANAGING DIVERSITY

Radicals have always played up the unity of worker interests and tried to transform trade unions from sectional to general worker organizations. I've argued that this is mistaken, because sectional identity of some sort—company, industry, trade (craft), profession—is the occupational magnet that draws people to trade unions in the first place. Others also point to divisions in the working population that belie simple notions of worker solidarity. However, they stress identity differences routed in gender, ethnicity, and sexuality and suggest that unions should focus on this diversity of interests and values (see Greene, this volume; Dean and Liff 2010). Since unions began as largely male, white, skilled organizations of established workers, women, and immigrants were often excluded from or marginal to them. And no one doubts the harm that racial or religious divisions can cause in trade unions, as the experience of Northern Ireland and South Africa testify. Clearly unions need to remove barriers to participation by all their members, current and potential. However, it is mistaken to suggest that a trade union can advance by highlighting internal differences. A strong sense of shared occupational identity and common purpose is their raison d'être.

THE FRIENDLY SOCIETY MODEL: INDIVIDUAL SERVICES AND CIVIL SOCIETY

There are two version of this, both deeply grounded in trade union history. The first stresses the delivery of individual services to members. The second, championed by Reid (2004), highlights the contribution of trade unions to civil society, as Britain's largest voluntary organizations. The provision of services goes back to the early craft-friendly societies, with their sickness, strike, funeral, and emigration benefits, all designed to protect fee-paying members against employment adversity and to restrict the flow of skilled labour and thus raise its price. Trade unions still offer membership benefits, credit cards, and so on, but the growth of the welfare state and a sophisticated financial services industry has reduced the distinctive attraction of these. Trade unions have also provided opportunities for participation, especially for activists. In democratic terms, this makes them a major public good, as Durkheim realized. But unions are highly distinctive voluntary associations. Their primary function is workplace voice and they attract members through effective collective bargaining and consultation. This role dwarfs individual services in importance and depends on bureaucratic competence, rather than mass participation. In short, unions need to regulate their occupations through relations with employers and the state if they are to attract and hold members.

THE PARTNERSHIP MODEL: MAKING FRIENDS AND INFLUENCING PEOPLE

As Johnstone argues in this volume, partnership is a strategy to regain support from employers, the state, and public opinion in the new employment dispensation. In Budd's (2004) language, partnership promotes voice, equity, and efficiency, forms of legitimacy rather than coercive power. Trade unions do not harness the collective economic power of workers in any simple sense. Rather the assumption is that power is relational and conditional on the response of a diamond of stakeholders: employees (including members), employers, the state, and public opinion. Trade unions reach partnership agreements with employers, but still depend for their credibility in others' eyes on strong membership support. Partnership tells us what these relationships with stakeholders should look like, but it does not, of itself, define the trade union's own identity or orientation towards work. By itself, partnership can leave a union, as a voluntary association, unduly dependent on employer recognition, without a life of its own outside of collective bargaining.

Conclusion: Professional Trade Union Voice?

Insecurity, the ever-present threat of unemployment and cessation of earnings, has been the lot of the manual worker. This accounts more profoundly than lower income or inferior working conditions for the collective psychology of the British working class, their constant fear of

> change, suspicion of management, restrictive practices, and opposition
> to any kind of labour-saving innovation.
>
> (Perkin 1989: 310)

Harold Perkin has charted *The Rise of Professional Society*. Too often we think of this purely in terms of middle-class professions—doctors, nurses, and teachers—all now citadels of professional trade unionism. 'At first sight the working class seem to have been excluded from professional society' (Perkin 1989: 463). Indeed, British 'hourly paid' manual workers have regularly been called 'hands' or 'operatives', and denied salaried job security, full sickness benefits, contributory pensions, or extended forms of skills training. By contrast, some successful economies, such as Germany and Sweden, have actively professionalized manual work as a basis for high-skill, high-productivity workplaces. In the former case, the systems of employee participation, discussed by Gold and Artus in this volume, are part and parcel of this professionalization. Under this model, professional trade unions not only bargain better wages and conditions but also seek to raise the status of labour from a cost to a resource, thereby transforming mere jobs into careers. We have caught glimpses of this already with the NACODS and electricians' 'single-union deal' examples.

As Perkin (1989: 306–16) notes, a crude radical view of labour as a class to be mobilized against capitalism is partly responsible for the failure of this professional strategy in Britain. Too often, socialist trade union rhetoric aims to turn occupational sections into a united class, whereas a professional strategy suggests recasting passive occupations as active professions, following in the footsteps of the middle classes. Partnership is a central element because professions take some responsibility not only for the quality of work but also for the success of the organization and the service it provides. Hence they need to work with the state and management, since these become sources of their wider social legitimacy. When they criticize employers it is from the moral high ground of concern for the public interest. And while mere occupations simply follow the contours of business and technology, professions are actively normative organizations, redefining the value and meaning of their members' labour. Above all, they insist, against neoclassic economics, that labour is not just a commodity to be bought and sold at the cheapest price for the shortest possible period. Instead, they endow each particular type of work or career with its own vocation, meaning, and sense of purpose.

How realistic is this as a strategy for trade union regeneration? To begin with, it is already widely in operation, as demonstrated by our brief examination of UNISON, Unite, and Community. As we saw there, the structure of many nominally general unions is chaotic, almost meaningless. However, by refocusing explicitly on the crucial subcategory of 'profession', they could more effectively mobilize around this influence. For others, like the influential

Royal College of Nursing (RCN), structure and purpose are already aligned. In addition, the professional strategy is no more than the old craft strategy writ large and super-charged by the power of education and training, as the opening quote of this chapter advocated.[5] The concept of profession can embrace many categories of employment today, building trade union strength from the strong inner core outwards. Clearly there are limits and the least skilled will struggle to professionalize their work. But trade unions, as essentially occupational organizations, cannot reach those without settled occupations or relatively secure work, except where active cooperation with the state and employers allows them to regularize that employment.

Trade unions are a declining presence in the workplace voice debate. In my view, a professional partnership strategy would make them more attractive to employees, employers, the state, and public opinion, restoring legitimacy power. However, unions should no longer be considered a one-stop panacea for employee voice at either the workplace or national levels. In the latter case, state policies such as the national minimum wage or special organizational forms, like those for domestic workers, will have to plug the gaps left by the patchwork of occupational identities. Representative bodies like the TUC and ETUC, or even conglomerates like Unite and UNISON, will need to influence public opinion and the state on broader employment issues. As in the past, a strong 'aristocracy of labour' will not stand in the way of these initiatives, as radicals have suggested, but actually make them possible.

NOTES

1. My neopluralist reading of trade unions is compatible with non-Marxian strands of Christian and ethical socialism or social democracy. Socialism is a vague and confusing term. Here 'socialist' or radical defines a broadly Marxian approach, stretching from Lenin to the Webbs, that sees 'capitalist society' in general class terms and hopes to replace it, in toto, with a new socialist economic system, however that is to be achieved. Such radical beliefs first attracted many to trade union studies, myself included. Today mainstream academic radical-pluralism in IR and the sociology of work does not embrace socialist politics in these terms, yet remains shaped by the same foundational assumptions about employment and trade unions (see Ackers 2014a and McGovern 2014). Colling and Terry 2010 and Simms et al. 2013 are representative overviews of the large British IR literature, which I've referenced sparingly. I'm generalizing mainly from British IR research about British trade unions, but the argument about the nature of trade unions has wider application, particularly in Europe, but also well beyond.

2. This distinction arises from Weber's classic sociological distinction between *power* and *authority*, the former based on coercion, the latter on legitimacy or some form of consent by the subjects of power. This relates to a similar distinction made by

Gramsci between crude domination and ideological hegemony (see Ackers and Payne 1998 and Ackers 2014b on trade union strategy).
3. Richard Whiting (2008) argues that fears about 'public order' became central to public perceptions of British unions in the 1970s. A Christian moral distaste for conflict and confrontation also lies behind some historical strands of trade union moderation (see Ackers 1994).
4. The web pages are available at: <http://www.unitetheunion.org>; <http://www.unison.org.uk>; <http://www.community-tu.org>, all accessed 13 March 2013.
5. As Alastair Reid has pointed out to me, craft unionism depended on 'non-militant coercive strategies' such as the control of training and labour supply and the withdrawal of labour from 'blacked' workplaces. Since the 1980s any such 'restrictive practices' have been de-legitimized for British manual workers, yet similar, though more subtle tactics could contribute to a professional strategy, underpinning legitimacy power by stressing training, qualifications, and the health and safety of workers, customers, and the general public. I would like to thank George Ackers, Stewart Johnstone, Bruce Kaufman, Alistair Reid, Richard Whiting, and Adrian Wilkinson for their comments on an earlier draft of this chapter.

■ REFERENCES

Ackers, P. (1988) 'Change in Workplace Industrial Relations in West Midlands Manufacturing Industry in the 1980s'. M.Phil. thesis, University of Wolverhampton.
Ackers, P. (1994) 'Colliery Deputies in the British Coal Industry before Nationalization'. *International Review of Social History*, 39, 383–414.
Ackers, P. (2002) 'Reframing Employment Relations: The Case for Neo-Pluralism'. *Industrial Relations Journal*, 31(1), 2–19.
Ackers, P. (2007) 'Collective Bargaining as Industrial Democracy: Hugh Clegg and the Political Foundations of British Industrial Relations Pluralism', *British Journal of Industrial Relations*, 45(1), 77–101.
Ackers, P. (2014a) 'Rethinking the Employment Relationship: A Neo-Pluralist Critique of British Industrial Relations Orthodoxy'. *International Journal of Human Resource Management*, 25(18), 2608–25.
Ackers, P. (2014b) 'Gramsci at the Miners' Strike: Remembering the 1984–1985 Eurocommunist Alternative Industrial Relations Strategy'. *Labor History*, 55(2, May), 151–72.
Ackers, P. (2014c) 'Game Changer: Hugh Clegg's Role in Drafting the 1968 Donovan Report and Redefining the British Industrial Relations Policy-Problem', *Historical Studies in Industrial Relations*, 25, 63–88.
Ackers, P. and Payne, J. (1998) 'British Trade Unions and Social Partnership: Rhetoric, Reality and Strategy'. *International Journal of Human Resource Management*, 9(3, June), 529–50.
Ackers, P., Smith, C., and Smith, P. (eds) (1996) *The New Workplace and Trade Unionism*. London: Routledge.
Atkinson, J. (1984) 'Manpower Strategies for Flexible Organizations'. *Personnel Management*, 16(8), 28–31.

Bassett, P. (1986) *Strike-Free: New Industrial Relations in Britain.* London: Macmillan.

Bhattacherjee, D. and Ackers, P. (2010) 'Introduction: Employment Relations in India: Old Narratives and New Perspectives'. *Employment Relations in India, Industrial Relations Journal,* 41(2), 104–21.

Blackburn and Prandy (1965) 'White-Collar Unionization: A Conceptual Framework'. *British Journal of Sociology,* 16(2, June), 111–122.

Blyton, P. and Turnbull, P. (2004) 'Unions and Their Members'. In P. Blyton and P. Turnbull, *The Dynamics of Employee Relations,* chapter 5. London: Macmillan.

Brown, W. (2010) 'Negotiation and Collective bargaining'. In T. Colling and M. Terry (eds), *Industrial Relations: Theory and Practice,* 3rd edn, pp. 125–46. Chichester: Wiley.

Budd, J. W. (2004) *Employment with a Human Face: Balancing Efficiency, Equity and Voice.* New York: ILR Press.

Clegg, H. A. (1951) *Industrial Democracy and Nationalization.* Oxford: Blackwell.

Clegg, H. A. (1985) *A History of British Trade Unions since 1989,* Volume 2: *1911–1933.* Oxford: Oxford University Press.

Clegg, H. A. (1994) *A History of British Trade Unions since 1989,* Volume 3: *1933–1951.* Oxford: Oxford University Press.

Clegg, H. A., Fox, A., and Thompson, A. F. (1964) *A History of British Trade Unions since 1989,* Volume 1: *1889–1910.* Oxford: Oxford University Press.

Colling, T. and Terry, M. (eds) (2010) *Industrial Relations: Theory and Practice,* 3rd edn. Chichester: Wiley.

Dahrendorf, R. (1956) *Class and Class Conflict in Industrial Society.* London: Basic.

Dean, D. and Liff, S. (2010) 'Equality and Diversity: The Ultimate Industrial Relations Concern'. In T. Colling and M. Terry (eds), *Industrial Relations: Theory and Practice,* 3rd edn. Chichester: Wiley.

Edwards, P. (2003) 'The Employment Relationship and the Field of Industrial Relations'. In P. Edwards (ed.), *Industrial Relations: Theory and Practice,* 2nd edn, chapter 1. Oxford: Blackwell.

Flanders, A. (1975) *Management and Unions: The Theory and Reform of Industrial Relations.* London: Faber and Faber.

Fox, A. (1966) *Industrial Sociology and Industrial Relations,* Royal Commission on Trade Unions and Employers' Associations, Research Paper 3. London: HMSO.

Fox, A. (1974) *Beyond Contract: Work, Power and Trust Relations.* London: Faber and Faber.

Freeman, R. B. (1980) 'The Exit-Voice Tradeoff in the Labor Market: Unionism, Job Tenure, Quits and Separations'. *Quarterly Journal of Economics,* 94(June), 643–73.

Goldthorpe, J. H., Lockwood, D., Bechhofer, F., and Platt, J. (1968) *The Affluent Worker: Industrial Attitudes and Behaviour.* Cambridge: Cambridge University Press.

Greene, A.-M., Black, J., and Ackers, P. (2000) 'The Union Makes Us Strong: A Study of the Dynamics of Workplace Leadership at Two Manufacturing Plants'. *British Journal of Industrial Relations,* 38(1, March), 75–94.

Howell, C. (2005) *Trade Unions and the State.* Princeton, NJ: Princeton University Press.

Hyman, R. (1971) *Marxism and the Sociology of Trade Unionism.* London: Pluto.

Hyman, R. (2001) *Understanding European Unionism: Between Market, Class and Society.* London: Sage.

Kelly, J. (1998) *Rethinking Industrial Relations: Mobilization, Collectivism and Long Waves.* London: Routledge.

Kerr, C., Dunlop, J. T., Harbison, F., and Myers, C. A. (1973, first edition 1960) *Industrialism and Industrial Man.* Harmondsworth: Penguin.

McCarthy, W. E. J. (1972) (ed.) *Trade Unions.* London: Penguin.

McGovern, P. (2013) 'Contradictions at Work: A Critical Review', *Sociology*, 48(1, February), 20–37.

McKibbon, R. (1984) 'Why Was There No Marxism in Great Britain?' *English Historical Review*, 99, 287–333.

Marx, K. and Engels, F. (1848/1952) *Manifesto of the Communist Party.* Moscow: Progress Publishers.

Nijhus, D. O. (2011) 'Explaining British Voluntarism'. *Labor History*, 52(4, November), 373–98.

Parkin, F. (1974) 'Strategies of Social Closure in Class Formation'. In F. Parkin (ed.), *The Social Analysis of the Class Stucture*, pp. 1–18. London: Tavistock.

Parkin, F. (1992) *Durkheim.* Oxford: Oxford University Press.

Parkin, F. (2002) *Max Weber.* London: Routledge.

Perkin, H. (1989) *The Rise of Professional Society.* London: Routledge.

Reid, A. (2004) *United We Stand: A History of Britain's Trade Unions.* London: Penguin.

Sayce, S., Greene, A.-M., and Ackers, P. (2006) 'Small Is Beautiful? The Development of Women's Activism in a Small Union'. *Industrial Relations Journal*, 37(4, July), 400–14.

Seifert, R. and Sibley, T. (2012) *Revolutionary Communist at Work: A Political Biography of Bert Ramelson.* London: Lawrence and Wishart.

Simms, M. and Charlwood, A. (2010) 'Trade Unions: Power and Influence in a Changed Context'. In T. Colling and M. Terry (eds), *Industrial Relations: Theory and Practice*, 3rd edn, pp. 125–46. Chichester: Wiley.

Simms, M., Holgate, J., and Heery, E. (2013) *Union Voices: Tactics and Transitions in UK Organizing.* Ithaca, NY: ILR/Cornell University Press.

Thornqvist, C. and Wolfson, C. (2012) 'When Tender Turns Tough: Posted Workers and the Tendering Regime in the Swedish Construction Industry'. *Construction Management and Economics*, 30(7), 525–33.

Turner, H. A. (1962) *Trade Union Growth Structure and Policy: A Comparative Study of the Cotton Unions.* London: Allen and Unwin.

Webb, S. and Webb, B. (1894) *The History of Trade Unionism.* London: Longmans.

Webb, S. and Webb, B. (1897) *Industrial Democracy.* London: Longmans.

Whiting, R. (2008) 'Affluence and Industrial Relations in Post-War Britain'. *Contemporary British History*, 22(4, December), 519–36.

6 Union organizing as an alternative to partnership. Or what to do when employers can't keep their side of the bargain

Melanie Simms

Introduction

The long-term decline of trade unionism in the UK is particularly evident in the private sector, where collective bargaining is now a feature of only a very small number of workplaces (van Wanrooy et al. 2012). These long-term trends have been the catalyst for a debate taking place over at least two decades about the prospects and strategies for trade union renewal. A range of alternatives has been proposed, debated, and experimented with in that time. Of particular relevance here are strategies often labelled for shorthand as 'organizing' and 'partnership' (Heery 2002) and the similarities and differences between the two approaches are discussed in more detail in later sections of this chapter. At the outset, the important thing to note is that although there is considerable debate about the precise meaning of the two terms (much of which has been captured in other chapters in this volume), in brief, 'partnership' can be understood as a renewal strategy that requires unions to build long-term, high-trust bargaining relationships with managers within organizations. This can be contrasted with 'organizing', which has as its primary focus the objective of building collectivism amongst workers to act together to identify and pursue collective interests. Action is often, although not always, directed towards challenging managerial behaviour. Where organizing campaigns seek to extend collective action beyond the workplace they can make links with wider communities to pursue objectives outside the employment relationship (Wills and Simms 2004; Martínez Lucio and Perrett 2009; McBride and Greenwood 2009). By contrast, partnership strategies tend to focus on bargaining relationships within the organization.

This chapter considers partnership to be only one of a range of activities trade unions can undertake in an effort to renew themselves, but it is one of the most debated and thus merits particular attention. The chapter argues that there are inherent challenges to establishing partnership between unions and managers in the private sector that limit the opportunities to establishing long-term, high-trust relationships. It is argued that these barriers arise from the particular form of financialized capitalism that has developed in recent years. Specifically, the analysis develops the argument of Thompson (2003, 2011) that the emergence of 'financialized' capitalism (Froud et al. 2000, 2006) has changed processes of corporate decision making and that this has had an adverse effect on the opportunities for trade unions to negotiate effectively and for managers to make long-term commitments to workers and unions. Although there is evidence that this process of financialization is spreading to public sector management (Shaoul 2008), this development is highly contested and marked by an engagement with specific institutions of public sector regulation (including, but in no way limited to the strength of collective bargaining and other forms of collective regulation of employment). Thus, our focus in this chapter is on the private sector.

This is a rather pessimistic analysis and it is important, therefore, to consider what alternatives, if any, unions can consider. It is the argument of this chapter that there are alternatives open to unions and that organizing strategies offer a way to challenge managerial decision making and to shift the locus and focus of confrontation and negotiation. That is not to say that organizing is a panacea to the challenges of union revitalization in the private sector. Strategies to challenge financialized capital are extremely difficult to develop and deliver and there is no guarantee of success. But it is the central contention of this chapter that if one's proposed 'partner' cannot commit to and deliver on a long-term, high-trust relationship, then the notion of an effective partnership is largely irrelevant. If it is essential to maintain a relationship, as it is an ongoing employment relationship, then a more assertive and confrontational approach is required for effective representation of workers' interests.

What does the evidence tell us about partnership?

Johnstone et al. (2009) undertook an important overview of at least a decade of empirical evidence regarding partnership. They differentiate between authors who are generally optimistic about the prospects for partnership and those who are more pessimistic. The optimists tend to emphasize the opportunity for union renewal through the development of long-term and high-trust relationships. These studies highlight the opportunity for unions to engage in long-term, win–win deals with managers, often securing import-ant benefits for workers such as commitment to job security and improve-ment in working conditions. By contrast, pessimists tend to emphasize the risk of union incorporation into managerial agendas and the danger that this will undermine the legitimacy of unions in the eyes of members and potential members. These authors also identify examples where partnership agreements have led to work intensification and tighter surveillance and control over workers (Johnstone et al. 2009: 264).

Importantly, there are empirical studies that illustrate both positions, leading Johnstone et al. (2009: 267) to stress several points about the existing literature in this area, two of which have particular relevance to this chapter. The first is that ideology is extremely important in understanding the inter-pretations of participants and commentators. The second is that the context within which partnership arrangements take place is a crucial factor in understanding the dynamics of particular processes and outcomes. Both of these points are important to the argument presented in this chapter because the central point is that the context within which the employment relation-ship takes place has changed (in the private sector at least). The advent of financialized capitalism means that the objectives of many companies have shifted towards privileging financial objectives and managerial decision making has therefore changed. This changed context makes it important to re-examine the prospects for partnership.

Is there common ground between organizing and partnership?

Of course there can be common ground between the two approaches, both in theory and in practice. Heery (2002) explicitly considers these two strategies as alternative futures for the trade union movement in the UK. In his conclusions, he makes a number of important points with regards to the relationship between organizing and partnership in union renewal efforts. He recognizes the inherent tensions presented by any union or union movement that seeks to pursue both strategies but he notes that, in practice, there may be ways in which the two can be combined. One way in which we can see evidence of both is that there may be a specific form of organizing that emerges in some settings (he specifically discusses 'greenfield' campaigns where unions are seeking to establish a presence for the first time) and partnership may emerge in other settings. He also notes that the two may fit together by running sequentially in a form of a representation cycle in which unions seek to build membership strength and legitimacy through organizing and subsequently establish a partnership arrangement with managers. However, he flags potential dangers and difficulties for unions in simultaneously pursuing two strategies which are in tension with each other, such as the challenge of building legitimacy simultaneously with both managers and workers.

Despite potential tensions, unions have broadly the same tasks to undertake in both organizing and partnership strategies. At a very basic level, all unions need to recruit members in order to build support to negotiate on behalf of those members. They need to establish mechanisms for ensuring members have a say in those negotiations and they need to be able to enforce any agreed outcomes of negotiation. However, amongst both academics and practitioners, there is a strong understanding of the idea that partnership and organizing take different approaches to these tasks as well as how they differ in general. As we shall see as the chapter develops, the argument here is not that partnership and organizing are inherently irreconcilable. Rather, the central point is that *all* trade union activities are difficult in the context of financialized capitalism and that this context presents *particular challenges* that make partnership arrangements especially difficult. A final strand of the argument is that in the context of financialized capitalism there are important advantages to organizing independently of managerial support and perhaps even beyond the workplace.

Why focus on the private sector?

As emphasized above, the focus of the discussion in this chapter is the private sector. This is deliberate. Evidence of the challenges facing trade unions in the private sector can be seen in the collapse of union representation and collective bargaining in the private sector. The data here are well rehearsed, but it is worth restating some of the most important developments in order to highlight how catastrophic the collapse has been and how profound are the challenges facing unions in the private sector. The most recent Workplace Employment Relations Study (WERS) establishes that in 2011 only 6 per cent of private sector workplaces bargained collectively over terms and conditions of work. Bargaining coverage in the private sector has also collapsed with only 16 per cent of private sector employees having their terms and conditions of work set by collective bargaining (van Wanrooy et al. 2012). Over time, this reflects a dramatic reduction in the influence of trade unions and collective bargaining, particularly in the private sector (see Blanchflower and Bryson

2009). And although there has been a decline in the public sector it has been nowhere near as severe as in the private sector, with many mechanisms of collective regulation of work remaining intact if somewhat weakened.

It is clear, therefore, that if trade unions are to renew themselves in any meaningful way across the UK labour market they must establish new agreements with employers in the private sector. Looking at a range of evidence, there is little evidence of any significant unmet demand by employers for trade union representation. So it seems implausible that companies themselves are actively seeking *new* partnership relationships with unions, otherwise there would be evidence of this in both the literature and data on trade unionism and human resource management. The lack of evidence, combined with the clear judgement of trade unionists expressed during interviews undertaken by the author for a longitudinal study on union revitalization in the UK (see Simms et al. 2013 for an extended discussion of the project design and methods) clearly reject this hypothesis.

It is therefore evident that if trade unions are serious about extending their influence, they must proactively establish new representation and bargaining relationships in the private sector. So any effort to (re)establish union presence in the private sector requires unions to demand recognition from managers. That necessarily, therefore, takes them on a collision course with new forms of organizational structure and corporate decision making within the context of financialized capitalism.

What's wrong with partnership?

It is important to make clear that it is not the argument of the chapter that partnership is an inherently problematic strategy for renewal. Indeed, there are notable examples of positive and effective partnership relationships (see other chapters and a later section of this chapter). But it is important to note that the most effective of these examples are in the public sector. For example, Samuel and Bacon (2010 and this volume) explore and analyse the extremely productive partnership arrangements between unions and managers in restructuring NHS Scotland. What is less evident is a widespread adoption of these ideas within the private sector.

The previous section highlighted that private sector trade unionism is a marginal activity. In some of the companies that recognize unions, it is evidently possible to establish effective and long-term relationships between managers and unions. The partnership agreement between the shopworkers' union, the Union of Shop, Distributive and Allied Workers (Usdaw) and Tesco supermarket is probably the most well known and is discussed further below. But if they are to renew themselves, UK unions must surely seek to expand their influence within the private sector. A central question therefore becomes what strategies and actions would be required to establish new bargaining and representation relationships and what opportunities and constraints act on the decisions facing unions as they seek to renew themselves in that context?

The impact of 'disconnected capitalism'

The argument of this chapter is that partnership will not and cannot become a widespread phenomenon in the private sector because of the emergence of a particular form of contemporary capitalism. To explain why I argue this, I draw on the very important work of Thompson (2003) and his identification of the phenomenon of 'disconnected capitalism'. It is a central concept for the argument presented and so is worth examining in some detail.

In two related papers, Thompson (2003, 2011) examines the ways in which contemporary capitalism presents specific challenges for the ways in which companies manage workers. He examines the ways in which corporate structures and decision making have changed in the past decade or so. He identifies important features of change as being the restructuring of corporations into semi-autonomous units with responsibility for maximizing labour productivity and which are frequently in competition with other business units for investment from the corporate centre. He also highlights how the development and spread of a particular form of financialized capitalism means that corporate decision making is frequently based primarily on the rate of return of particular investments in business units. He acknowledges that these changes are particularly evident in multinational corporations but are increasingly evident in nationally based corporations.

A particularly important contribution of Thompson's work is that he argues that these developments can be understood as the emergence of a new form of capitalism where the decisions of the corporate centre are 'disconnected' from the operationalization of decisions at the level of the business unit. Managers within business units have an understanding of and interest in securing agreements (including but not limited to union agreements) with workers that ensure the ongoing cooperation of workers. But the corporate centre has little interest in attending to these agreements either in general or in the specific details. In this context it is difficult, if not impossible, for local managers to sustain a long-term engagement with workplace bargains to secure high performance from employees.

Thompson (2011) argues that there are two dimensions of disconnection within contemporary, financialized capitalism. The first is between the sphere of work and employment. A central development here is the increased demand by employers for employees to use substantial discretionary effort while, at the same time, employers have systematically shifted risk onto employees through flexible and insecure forms of employment. Importantly, he identifies examples of employment that are insecure despite having the form of open-ended contracts. This arises as a direct consequence of the disconnection in corporation decision making between the centre and the business unit. As a result, when decisions about disinvestment are made at the corporate centre, employment contracts can be changed and terminated with minimal notice.

This takes us to the second dimension, a disconnection between managerial agents, and it is worth citing an important contribution of Thompson's 2011 paper here:

Local, unit and functional managers are tasked with responsibility for pursuing high performance from labour, but they ultimately lack the capacity to sustain the enabling conditions. Corporate agents, tied to financialised practices through measures, such as stock options, and distanced from their local consequences, control the key levers (Beynon et al. 2002).

(Thompson 2011: 362)

In other words, the ability of local managers to sustain agreements to high performance practices (including partnership agreements) risks being undermined by decisions at the corporate centre on where to invest, how to maximize value from supply chains, and how to maximize the productivity of labour. Perpetual restructuring in order to squeeze surplus value from labour (and other sources such as supply chains) has become a dominant feature of corporate life (Froud et al. 2000). For example, in a situation of union bargaining, a collective agreement to increase productivity in exchange for job security may be undermined by a decision from the centre to shift production to a new locale.

Thompson's arguments are important for a number of reasons. First, he focuses our attention on the link between HR practices and wider corporate decision making. Second, he gives a theoretical basis for understanding how different circuits of capital intersect within corporations to create competing tensions which financialize high-level decision making and create less 'patient' capital. In this respect, he is able not only to describe changes in corporate decisions that have destabilized the context for HR decisions, he also provides a theoretical basis for understanding these developments.

Financialization and the challenges for HR

In a later paper, Thompson (2011) returns to the idea of the financialization of corporate decision making and examines the ways in which these developments present problems for human resource management both in practice and in general. As with the idea of 'disconnected capitalism' it is important that we examine his argument in some detail. The title of the paper captures the line of argumentation, *The Trouble with HRM*. In it, he argues that the involvement of large firms in financialized practices mean that 'HR managers are increasingly not the main architects of key work and employment trends' (Thompson 2011: 364).

Associated with these changes in corporate structures and decision making, we have seen changes and developments in the HR profession. Increasingly, the role of HR managers is as 'business partners' (Ulrich 1997) with the objective of helping senior managers achieve their strategic objectives. These developments have a number of implications for the management of workers on a day-to-day level. There has been a shift within the corporate HR function from an ambition to provide a focus on worker well-being and to act as an intermediary or arbitrator between line managers and workers towards a focus on providing strategic support to the corporate centre, with HR advisers providing practical advice about, for example, legal issues to line managers. Kochan (2007) discusses the history and trajectory of these developments in some detail and is scathing in his evaluation of the implications for the HR function: 'As a result [of these shifts], HR professionals lost any semblance of credibility as stewards of the social contract because most HR professionals had lost their ability to seriously challenge or offer an independent perspective on the policies and practices of the firm' (Kochan 2007: 604). From a very different theoretical and political perspective, Thompson makes a similar point (2011: 39). '[I]t has become increasingly difficult to sustain optimistic HR narratives through periods of downsizing, financial re-engineering and perpetual restructuring. Organisations are increasingly dominated by the principles of "market rationalism", and normative interventions promoting commitment and focusing on cultural change are becoming less relevant or marginalised (Thompson 2003; Kunda and Ailon-Souday 2005)'.

So, if not high-trust HR management, then what? Compliance must surely be a possibility. Many of the early debates about the weaknesses of high-commitment HR policies and practices (see Legge 2005 for a compelling critique) highlighted evidence that shows how managerial innovations such as 'lean production' and 'total quality management' often rested on the compliance of workers rather than their active commitment. Many of the early case studies that helped develop a robust critique of such HR practices still have much to say in contemporary debates (see, amongst many others,

Garrahan and Stewart 1992; Delbridge 1998; Rinehart et al. 1997). They show how practices and rhetoric of high commitment can themselves be used to control workers both collectively and individually.

The argument to this point has rested on outlining and explaining shifting priorities of corporate decision making in the context of financialized capitalism. It has been argued that as we have seen the emergence of a form of 'disconnected capitalism' the role of the HR function within corporations has changed. Taken together, these changes mean that there is less opportunity to build high-trust relationships with workers and, by extension, their unions. We now turn our attention to reflecting more deeply on the implications of these developments for trade unions in the UK.

Implications for (partnership) relationships with unions

The nature of trade unionism in the UK means that dealing with the union will almost always be a line management rather than a strategic issue. UK trade unionism relies heavily on structures of workplace representation because of the emphasis on 'voluntarist' traditions to enforce collective agreements. In other words, in the absence of a legal route, for example a labour court, to enforce a collective agreement, workplace representatives take on a particular importance in systems of enforcing and extending agreements. Equally, within large corporations bargaining rights will typically be granted for a particular business unit, work group, or grade of workers and it is quite normal that a large corporation may recognize several different unions for different bargaining units. This is particularly evident in a context where outsourcing and merger and acquisition activity are increasingly routine and need to be understood as being inherently related to processes of financialization (Smith 2012).

Terms and conditions of workers who are employed in business units that are outsourced, merged, or acquired are usually protected within the transfer of undertakings (protection of employment) regulations. This means that where a union is recognized by the original employer, those arrangements usually transfer to the new employer. As a result, a large organization can 'inherit' a responsibility to recognize and negotiate with a number of different unions. Even where this kind of outsourcing arrangement is not central to the business model of a corporation, the complex demarcation arrangements of UK trade unions mean that different unions may be recognized for different groups of staff. It is therefore relatively rare that a large company would recognize only one union.

In addition, the UK largely lacks formal worker representation at the corporate or strategic levels. The information and consultation regulations might have provided such a mechanism, but a recent evaluation of the introduction and application of the regulations within large companies has revealed that many firms have not set up these bodies and, even where they have, they are often weak and ineffective (Hall and Purcell 2012). Both the chapters in this book on the information and consultation regulations (Dobbins and Dundon, this volume) and on European works councils (Timming and Whittall, this volume) show that although there are examples of unions using these new opportunities to secure a wider voice for workers in organizations, this is not widespread across the economy and, on aggregate, the impact has been less than those who advocate for worker voice might have hoped when they were introduced. In part this may well be because unions in the UK have not focused on taking advantage of these potential opportunities. But it is also clear in the work of authors such as Hall and Purcell (2012) that there is some considerable degree of managerial resistance to workers with a strong voice in this kind of managerial decision making.

Taken together, these arrangements give very few opportunities for unions (and non-union employee representatives more generally) to be involved at a strategic level in managerial decision making. As a consequence, trade union representation is, more likely than not, an issue for local managers at the level of the workplace or business unit. This sets the scene for a rather narrow bargaining agenda and, perhaps more importantly, a serious challenge in securing long-term commitment to bargaining agreements from the organization which are necessary pre-conditions for partnership arrangements. We can see the consequences of some of these developments in the kind of 'whipsawing' strategies used by managers to force competition between production sites in the international car industry, as described by Greer and Hauptmeier (2008) and Bernaciak (2010), and the challenges in generating any form of effective response between unions in different national settings.

In short, union partnership agreements rest on ensuring that both sides can deliver the commitments they make. The 'deal' from the management side is typically an ongoing commitment to principles of inclusion in decision making, job security, reasonable pay increases, and, sometimes, commitments to training and development. In the context of financialized corporate decision making and changes within the HR function it is very hard for local managers to, in the words of Thompson (2003), 'keep their side of the bargain'.

Thompson (2003) illustrates these tensions within the concept and practice of partnership citing research by Danford et al. (2002, 2004, 2005, 2008) examining restructuring in the aerospace industry. A workplace union representative captures the tensions very succinctly:

I think with partnership, you require two partners, and whereas from our point of view, and the employees' point of view, if we agree to do something then we continue to agree to do that. Now from management's point of view, they have a lot of different influences which change month by month, personnel changes, business changes etc., and basically I think it is they who have a problem with partnership because they cannot necessarily deliver on what they have promised to do.

(Danford et al. 2002: 10)

These criticisms of partnership are not new. Many previous authors have been critical both of the concept and practice of partnership from a range of perspectives (see Kelly 1996; Marks et al. 1998; Gall 2003). As Johnstone et al. (2009) summarize, more critical research on partnership typically emphasizes the danger of union incorporation into managerial objectives and the danger of work intensification, as tighter managerial control over work is exchanged for some kind of benefit, often commitment to job security. But these dangers are not inherent in partnership. As many more optimistic studies have highlighted there can be genuine benefits for workers (see Johnstone et al. 2009 for an overview of studies on both sides).

My argument takes a different starting point. I am less concerned to evaluate the short-term outcomes of partnership agreements than to consider the prospects for *sustaining* such arrangements in the longer term. Commitment to long-term agreements is at the heart of ideas about partnership but following the analysis laid out above, it is clear that capitalism—and, by extension, management—has changed in recent decades. What Thompson's work on the idea of 'disconnected capitalism' (2003) adds is an explanation of *why* partnership is so problematic in the private sector. Specifically, the financialization of decision making within corporations (Froud et al. 2006) makes it very difficult for managers to keep their side of the bargain when restructuring, outsourcing, and disinvestment might happen at any moment, leading to a series of 'disrupted and disputed bargains' (Thompson 2003: 364) in the field of human resource management and employment relations. As a consequence, even where local managers make efforts to build the kind of long-term trust-based relationships needed for partnership, they can find themselves breaking those agreements as flows of investment shift in line with corporate restructuring (Heery 2002; Ackers et al. 2005; Deakin et al. 2005; Suff and Williams 2004).

A note on why partnership sometimes works

The previous section mentioned briefly some of the evidence that partnership can sometimes produce effective bargains for both managers and unions. The partnership agreement between Tesco supermarket and Usdaw trade union is probably the most well-known and high-profile example in the private sector. So it is important to reflect on the conditions under which these more successful examples of partnership have emerged.

In previous writings, I have evaluated the strategies of Usdaw in seeking this kind of partnership arrangement (Simms et al. 2013; Simms and Holgate 2010). Drawing on that empirical research, it is clear that the most important factor explaining the persistence of the partnership arrangement in Tesco relates to the strength of the corporate centre in decision making about human resources in general and trade unionism specifically. In Tesco we see a profound commitment to the values and practice of partnership at the corporate centre that are then cascaded down to lower levels. In this regard, HR is given a high level of strategic attention and the scope to do that is largely explained by the fact that the profitability of Tesco until recent years has meant that they have not had to make decisions about disinvestment in particular locations. The business model for the UK has focused on squeezing cost out of supply chains and distribution networks, as well as managing their property portfolio, thus taking the pressure off squeezing labour costs (where hourly rates of pay are relatively low anyway) and allowing the development of effective long-term relationships with front-line staff and their union.[1]

This indicates that three factors are particularly important in explaining the ongoing partnership between Tesco and Usdaw: the commitment to partnership at corporate level; a business model that prioritizes profitability from non-staff areas of the business (here, property, supply chains, and distribution); and a labour strategy that emphasizes flexibility rather than absolute cost minimization.

So there are factors that make it more or less likely that a company might be open to a partnership agreement with unions and which do value the long-term relationship they can build with employees. Of particular importance is the extent to which the corporate centre is strategically committed to HR issues. And of course there are also organizations that have long-standing relationships with unions that have been recognized for a long time, but which are not formally branded as 'partnership' agreements. In essence, though, these agreements still require unions and managers to commit— and, importantly, to be able to deliver on—long-term agreements. These kinds of arrangements are often seen in sectors such as printing, transport, and the ex-public corporations such as BT and British Gas. I am not arguing that these kinds of arrangements do not exist. But it is important to remember the evidence presented at the start of the chapter. These arrangements are not widespread; only 16 per cent of private sector workers have their terms and conditions of work decided by collective agreements.

At the outset, I also stressed that the focus of this chapter is on partnership in the private sector. There are more examples of effective partnership arrangements between unions and organizations in the public sector, some of which are discussed in this volume. Here, of course, finance decisions are notably different from those in the private sector and these are sectors that are more sheltered from competition. These factors certainly help to create a context in which it is more feasible to create the long-term commitments needed for effective partnership.

What prospects for trade unionism in disconnected capitalism?

This broad context presents some very serious challenges to trade unions that go far beyond discussions of partnership and into the realms of much wider discussions of union renewal and questions about what unions 'do'. It is the central argument of this chapter that the pressures discussed make it nearly impossible for unions to exercise any consistent and ongoing influence over managerial decision making that would be required for an effective, long-standing partnership arrangement. In fact, it makes it very difficult for unions even where they have long-standing arrangements with managers who are already committed to taking staffing issues very seriously. It is even more difficult for unions if they want to try to speak for the 84 per cent of private sector workers who do *not* have their terms and conditions determined by collective bargaining. For those workers to have a unionized voice with their employer, unions would have to persuade managers to give the union recognition where there has not previously been a union presence.

At the heart of the 'disconnected capitalism' thesis is the argument that the interests of local and corporate managers are not always in alignment with regards to employment relations issues (in other words they are 'disconnected'). Local managers may well recognize the need to build long-term relationships with workers and, where relevant, their unions. But those relationships will be contingent on continued investment and support for the local business unit from the corporate centre. In this context, it is more rational for unions to build strategies that address the inherent conflict of interests within the employment relationship. In other words, rather than relying on a strategy such as partnership that seeks to align worker and manager interests wherever possible, unions can start to focus on the logic of pluralism and radicalism (see Heery, this volume) and accept that there are conflicts of interest that are inherent within the employment relationship. In doing so, rather than building legitimacy with managers, I argue that there is a growing rationale for unions to focus on building legitimacy with workers and potential members. In this regard, the argument is an extension of the view that union incorporation in managerial objectives potentially weakens union effectiveness. The contribution of this chapter has been to explain *why* and what alternatives unions therefore have.

Organizing as an alternative

The ideas underpinning union organizing rest on building collective interests between workers with the intention that those interests can be transformed into collective action (Simms et al. 2013). This section will look at what organizing means in practice and how some of the underpinning assumptions are different from the ideas within partnership. In doing so, I will argue that these ideas and assumptions form the basis of a more effective long-term renewal strategy for trade unions in the UK. Before moving on to explain why organizing presents a more effective focus for renewal activities, it is important to outline the main differences between the two approaches. Three main points of difference emerge from both practitioner and academic discussions: legitimacy, interests, and collective action.

First, ideas about how unions should build *legitimacy* are directly contrasting (Simms and Charlwood 2010). Embedded in ideas about partnership is the notion that unions should seek to prioritize establishing their legitimacy with managers. That legitimacy comes from a number of sources, not all of which are exclusive to partnership arrangements. So, for example, having a significant number of members might help build the legitimacy of a union in the eyes of both managers and workers so this is not exclusively a concern for partnership arrangements. But in order to secure a partnership agreement, the union has to agree to give priority to dialogue with management within a context where the union focuses on understanding the business context within which managers are making decisions. This does not necessarily undermine the idea that this might be followed by negotiations around issues of relevance to members, and sometimes workers more widely, but it does make it essential for unions to secure an effective high-trust dialogue with managers.

Organizing, by contrast, starts with the idea that there are inherently differences of interest between workers and managers (pluralism or radicalism, as discussed by Heery, this volume). The focus is therefore on unions building legitimacy with workers and potential members. And this is even more of a priority when unions focus their attention beyond the workplace in what has come to be known as 'community unionism' (Wills and Simms 2004; McBride and Greenwood 2009). This is an important difference of focus as it emphasizes the work unions can do to identify issues of relevance to members and potential members and how they can work to influence whoever can make changes in those areas. Often that will be managers, but it might also include local councils, businesses, and other groups. An example of organizing beyond the workplace might be a concern about public transport routes to work that might be more effectively addressed by a local council than managers within the workplace.

The second dimension on which partnership and organizing can be contrasted relates to ideas about whose and which *interests* unions should seek to represent. Because of the focus on building legitimacy with managers, unions engaged in partnership agreements explicitly agree to incorporate the interests of the company or organization into their bargaining and representation. That is not to say that workers' interests are secondary. Rather, that the focus is on finding the common ground of interests that are shared between employers and employees. By contrast, the principles underpinning ideas about organizing assume the conflict of interest within the employment relationship (see Heery, this volume). The objective of unions taking this approach is to build collective interest around whatever issues are relevant to members and potential members. There is no assumption that managers and workers necessarily share interests although, of course, any successful bargaining process requires some agreement on common ground.

The third important area of difference is the importance (or not) of *collective action* in unions' activities. A partnership approach requires a high trust from both parties that is difficult to sustain if collective action is regularly targeted at managers. By collective action, I do not necessarily mean strike action or other forms of industrial action, although those can sometimes be included. More relevantly, I am referring to activities such as demonstrations, petitions, and low level acts of disobedience described in studies of organizing campaigns (Simms et al. 2013). The purpose of these actions is to help build collectivism between workers and to demonstrate that collective action can sometimes be effective in changing (managerial) behaviour. It would be difficult to imagine how a joint commitment to partnership might be sustained in the face of such activities. Indeed, the purpose of these actions is often to highlight inconsistencies or perceived unfairness in managers' actions.

Debates about partnership do not typically rule out collective action (although some early partnership agreements did rule out collective industrial action such as strikes; see Kelly 2004 for further discussion). But there is a notable absence in debates about partnership as they often do not say very much at all about the role of collective action in trade union renewal. This is a strange omission given that collectivism is inherent within ideas about the purpose of trade unionism. This focus on collective action and collective interests is considered further in the final sections of this chapter.

What is organizing in practice?

As we can see, the principles of organizing are different from those of partnership. But what does organizing look like when unions try to implement those ideas? This is a surprisingly difficult question because lots of different unions have developed lots of different approaches to organizing in the UK (see Simms et al. 2013 for further discussion and detailed examples). Briefly, we can identify two main different forms of organizing: organizing where the union already has a relationship with managers, and organizing where they are trying to establish a relationship for the first time.

A good example of the kind of organizing that can be done when a union already has a long-standing relationship with managers can be seen in the TSSA union which represents workers in the transport and travel sector. They have long-standing relationships with a wide range of companies and their strategy has focused on building and strengthening representation within those companies. To do this, they have shifted the focus of the union towards the membership and activists. They hold regular sessions and discussion forums where members can express their views and highlight issues that are important to them. Getting members enthused so that they can recruit and involve their friends and colleagues is central. In building the membership and making sure that the issues that the union decides are its priorities, the intention is to bring more influence to collective negotiations with managers.

A good example of the second kind of organizing can be seen with the RMT union that also represents workers in the travel and transport sector. The objectives of the union's very clear strategy has been to build up membership, to make members more active within the union, and to try to shift the union from simply reacting to whatever managers do towards trying to set the agenda themselves. It has been a long process to move the union towards this set of objectives but there is some evidence that they have been successful.

The union has expanded the focus of its membership to include a range of workers who work on the railways but who were not previously represented, including contract cleaners. Contract cleaners are subcontracted so do not work directly for the train operator; they work for a specialist cleaning company that has a contract to clean trains and stations. Cleaners have much worse terms and conditions of work than, say, drivers and other crew who work on the trains, in part because the contracts between the cleaning company and the train operating company are regularly renegotiated putting downward pressure on wages and other terms and conditions. The union has made good efforts at organizing these staff by recruiting them and by launching protests and actions. The RMT recognized that it could not only pressure the contract cleaning company, but that it could also use its pre-existing relationship with the rail company to try to ensure that the contracts were not always decided based on the cheapest wages. There have even been a series of strikes of cleaners on London Underground towards these objectives and they have had some success.

Importantly, and reinforcing a point made in a previous section of this chapter, the rail transport sector where both of these unions have their core membership base is a sector that is relatively protected from fierce competition, so the pressures towards financialization of managerial decision making are, in some respects, less intense than in other sectors. An example of organizing in a cut-throat competitive sector can be seen in the low-cost airlines. There, Unite (a large, general union) has been successful at securing recognition agreements with some of the leading employers to ensure that employment standards (including safety standards) are maintained. This has been a long campaign lasting many years and is still ongoing. And the intention is that with a few key employers having been persuaded to bargain with the union, others will follow suit. But it is a risky strategy and could still be very difficult for the union to enforce.

The point here is that there are examples of where unions have been able to focus on workers and build collective interests. Not all organizing campaigns are successful and employers can counter-mobilize to try to persuade workers that they should not join the union. And, clearly, there are risks for unions. These campaigns are risky and they take a lot of resources: both money and time.

Organizing to negotiate

The differences between partnership and organizing mean that the approach to bargaining and negotiation between unions and managers is different in a partnership context as compared to an organizing context. Organizing takes for granted that the differences of interest between workers and managers are inherent within the employment relationship. Not only that, but any effective bargaining and compromise around those conflicting interests requires both parties to be strong and organized. Importantly, extensive fieldwork and interviews with organizers (see Simms et al. 2013 for a brief description) suggest that they usually accept that it may be an entirely legitimate outcome of bargaining to fail to agree. Organizing does not assume that bargaining will necessarily be 'win–win', or that a compromise mid-point can be reached.

By contrast, negotiations in a partnership context typically prioritize areas where managers and unions can share some basic understanding and objectives. And here it is important to return to the point about the challenges presented by 'disconnected capitalism'. It is not the argument of this chapter that these points of agreement can never be identified. Nor is it my intention to argue that taking such an approach inherently undermines and weakens the union. Rather, the point is to say that even where such deals can be done, there is a very real risk that they will be undermined in a process of business restructuring or reorganization.

Of course, the same is true of organizing. It is quite possible that a union may invest significant time, energy, money, and effort in organizing a bargaining unit only for that unit to be closed or restructured some time after. But the advantage of organizing is that, where it is done effectively, it can act to build future capacity for trade unionism. In short, it does not rest on managers choosing to work with unions. It requires workers to organize collectively and to identify what levers can most usefully be used to achieve bargaining and negotiating objectives. They may well require the support, resources, and specialist skills of professional union organizers and negotiators to identify and to achieve these objectives, but ultimately organizing rests on identifying issues of concern and acting collectively to address them.

Examples given by interviewees in some recent research I have undertaken as part of a wider longitudinal project on organizing in the UK (see Simms et al. 2013 for details) relate to organizing and negotiating in the care home and catering sectors. Both sectors are dominated by a small number of large multinational providers and a very large number of very small providers. Unions, and in particular the GMB as a large UK general union organizing in the private sector, have focused their organizing activity on the large corporates and the national organizer of that union reported that they frequently come across situations where managers of smaller bargaining units are subject to being undermined by decisions taken at much higher levels. Specific examples given were where a catering service contract was rapidly re-outsourced when the union became involved at the workplace. Similarly, a care home was subject to significant pressure from the UK corporate centre to resist unionization on the basis of the need to provide a high rate of return to the financiers investing in the purchase of that business unit because of the fear that union involvement would push up staff costs.

The response of the union has been multifaceted. One response has been to understand and map the financial strategies of target employers in detail. One organizer commented 'I never thought I'd have to gen up on corporate finance in this job... But it explains a lot [of employer behaviour towards unions] and helps us plan [campaigns] better'. Simultaneously, the union has had to build strategies that are increasingly known as 'corporate campaigns' (Clawson and Clawson 1999), for instance campaigns that evaluate strategic levers within workplaces, wider communities, and the larger corporate context, that can help secure the objectives of the organizing campaigns. Furthermore, the union has increasingly turned its attention to attempting to negotiate at the level of managerial decision making, even where that is outside the UK. Although examples of this kind of 'corporate campaign' are relatively rare—not least because of the resource intensive nature of this kind of activity—it illustrates how some unions at least have begun to understand and strategically address the challenges presented by disconnected capitalism.

Importantly, the examples above highlight that negotiation and bargaining are still central objectives within union organizing and these relationships undoubtedly require ongoing relationships with managers. However, the starting point is different to that within partnership deals. The main objective for organizers in these campaigns is to work out how to pull any necessary lever to achieve the objectives for workers. Negotiation with managers at various levels of the corporation may well be an important lever but it is unlikely to be the only one. Worker and/or member activism is also important, as are links with local communities and user groups. Some of these tactics undoubtedly take the union on a collision course with managerial objectives. The national organizer is clear that this is not problematic, although these kinds of campaigns are highly risky and can generate profound tensions within the union.

Although there are some examples of unions thinking much more broadly than just workplace level, there is relatively little evidence that UK unions have widely adopted the idea that they should become 'social movements' (Turner and Hurd 2001) that extend beyond the workplace into issues of community and social justice. This is largely because in the UK trade unions have focused so much on the centrality of collective bargaining and enforcing collective agreements. Which is not to say that unions are uninterested in wider issues. They have long campaigned for equal rights for black and minority ethnic workers, women workers, workers with disabilities, and a whole range of workers with other forms of potential disadvantage. But the institutional structures of UK employment relations mean that these will always be secondary to the main objectives of regulating terms and conditions of employment.

The limitations of organizing

It is not the intention of this chapter to argue that organizing is a panacea for trade union renewal. There are many challenges to organizing strategies both within the union and within the wider context of financialized capitalism. Elsewhere (Simms et al. 2013) I have highlighted extensive research findings illustrating some of the tensions that organizing strategies create within unions. In brief, these are that these campaigns are extremely expensive and time consuming with no guarantee of success even where the union already has an established presence. Further, there can be an important tension with respect to where unions can and should draw an appropriate balance between actions intended to build collectivism between workers and the need to negotiate and agree improvements in terms and conditions of employment, especially where those negotiations are through formal collective bargaining mechanisms.

By definition, institutionalized collective bargaining requires unions and managers to build ongoing and open-ended relationships. This can be difficult to do if workplace unions are engaged in ongoing actions to challenge workplace managers. But these tensions are not new; they were written about extensively by the Webbs (Webb and Webb 1897) in the early development of industrial relations theory. In many respects, decisions about how to balance these competing objectives are integral to the work of trade unions. The central point here is that organizing continually focuses the attention of unions and their officers on building—and answering to—collectivism amongst members.

As I highlighted in the opening sections of this chapter, some unions try to pursue different strategies at the same time; organizing in some sectors while building partnership with other employers. This is perfectly possible, and in some regards it is sensible. Why would a union turn down an opportunity to establish a partnership arrangement if it were offered? My point is that although it is possible to adopt different strategies in different sectors of the workforce, there is a risk that the tensions that it brings makes it a very difficult approach to take. Multiple strategies within any organization can bring the risk that the people who speak for the organization (in the case of unions both the activists and the officers who work for the union) can become confused by the multiple messages and approaches. It is also possible that other stakeholders (employers, government, for example) may be confused about what the union 'stands for'. Obviously, in practice, many organizations do pursue multiple strategies simultaneously. And I am certainly against the fad of management consultants who sometimes impose strategic 'solutions' on organizational problems that either do not exist or which are made worse by the proposed strategy. But planning a future for a declining organization such as a trade union does require some 'vision' about what that organization's values and objectives are and that requires some kind of strategic planning. So although there are potential barriers to the success of organizing, I argue that it is a strategy that makes much more sense than partnership within the context of 'disconnected capitalism'.

Prospects for organizing: or why organizing makes sense when managers can't uphold their side of the bargain

Despite the limitations and tensions inherent within any union renewal strategy, it is the contention of this chapter that organizing offers a more sustainable and pragmatic response to the challenges of (re)establishing trade union strength in the extremely difficult external context presented by financialized capitalism. In previous sections of this chapter, Thompson's concept of disconnected capitalism has been used to highlight and to explain the particular problems presented to unions seeking to build long-term and high-trust relationships with managers within large corporations.

In that context, it is rational for unions to seek to build organizational capacity amongst members and workers more widely that take as the starting point the inherent conflict of interest in the employment relationship. Those organizing efforts can be within the workplace and increasingly there is evidence that unions are thinking more strategically about developing their presence and relevance in the wider community. This makes sense in a context where workplace deals can be undermined through the financialized rationales of corporate decision making. If the deals done in workplaces and other bargaining units are always contingent then it makes sense to have strength beyond the employer.

Is this only a UK phenomenon?

The focus of this chapter has been on the UK specifically, although the implications of the debates are relevant for unions in other countries. Ideas about 'organizing' originated in the USA (see Simms et al. 2013 for a more detailed explanation of the transfer of organizing ideas and practices), where relationships between managers and unions are often extremely hostile. There, unions have had to develop innovative tactics to counter managerial strategies to avoid having to deal with unions. Because of the hostility, those tactics are often quite secretive until the union and the activists are confident they have enough support to challenge managers. They are also typically focused on building strong relationships between workers so that there is some chance to counter the anti-union tactics and rhetoric of managers and so-called 'union-busters'. In the UK, there is a less confrontational managerial culture and as the ideas about organizing have transferred to the UK, they have often not had to be so secretive and assertive.

However, both the UK and the USA can be contrasted with some other European Union countries, such as Germany, which have a much more deeply embedded culture of partnership in employment relations. Importantly, in Germany there are strong structures at the workplace, company, and sectoral levels that support unions and managers in partnership. These include legal separation between unions and works councils which represent workers at different levels and on different issues. Works councils have a legal responsibility to consider the future of the company when they discuss workers' concerns with managers. And there has been a stronger emphasis on ensuring that companies are managed for long-term success. Added to this, there have been systems of financing companies that focus much more on long-term investment and success rather than short-term shareholder return (see Keller and Kirsch 2011 for a more detailed explanation of the German employment relations system; see also Gold and Artus, this volume). Despite this, these systems are under pressure from the culture of global finance and it is not clear what future there may be for institutions of 'social partnership' in these countries. Even some of the most high-profile writers seem to swing between optimism and pessimism (Streeck 2009).

In countries such as Germany, Denmark, and Sweden we have seen trade unions become very interested in organizing practices for a number of reasons. Partly because some of the systems and institutions that support a 'partnership' approach at company, sectoral, and national levels are under a lot of pressure from global finance. But also, in these countries there has been a danger that unions focus more on negotiating within the system than focusing on what their members want. As social attitudes towards unions have changed, membership has declined even in these countries and some union leaders have developed strategies that focus on building up relationships with members and potential members. Although the end result is often strategies that look very different from organizing in the UK or the USA, they have explicitly been inspired by those ideas. And sometimes, the campaigns look remarkably similar to those run overseas. In the Netherlands, for example, there has been a big campaign to organize part-time, mainly immigrant cleaners which directly echoes similar campaigns in the UK (Justice for Cleaners) and the USA (Justice for Janitors).

What we have tended to see is that as pressures of global finance have put similar pressures on employers around the world to squeeze labour costs and terms and conditions, unions have tried to use a range of ways to challenge those trends. In some cases that is to use the existing institutions and infrastructure of employment relations and in other cases unions have looked for new and innovative ideas on how to challenge those developments. As ideas move between countries and unions, it is not surprising that they end up as very different practices. But the appeal of organizing strategies across national boundaries is remarkable and has provoked intense debate even in countries where partnership is deeply embedded in the practices of employment relations.

Conclusions

This chapter has made an argument that is importantly different from previous critiques of partnership. It is not only a critique of the potential for union incorporation into managerial objectives, nor does it focus on the danger of work intensification or increased control, although it is evident that all of these can be dangers of partnership arrangements agreed in conditions of union weakness. Equally, this chapter does not deny the evidence from more optimistic analyses that, in some circumstances, partnership can deliver genuine improvements for workers including, importantly, the possibility of greater job security.

Instead, this chapter presents a more strategic analysis of the serious weaknesses of partnership which focuses our attention on the reasons *why* it is difficult to create sustainable, long-term, high-trust relationships with managers in contemporary capitalism. In doing so, the chapter draws heavily on Thompson's notion of 'disconnected capitalism' (2003, 2011), which helps to explain how the financialization of corporate decision making makes it difficult for managers to keep their 'bargains' with workers because of the constant risk and threat of restructuring and disinvestment.

Since the financial crisis in 2008 and the election of the Conservative–Liberal Democrat Coalition Government in 2010, the context within which unions are operating in the UK has become notably more challenging. Despite early predictions, there has been little effective and organized pressure on 'capitalism' to change, despite the best efforts of social movements such as Occupy. Although the current government has made clear that it is not a priority to further limit the influence of trade unions, there are pressures within the Conservative party to do so. Since 2008, companies have faced growing pressures to become and remain competitive, which are likely to intensify the move towards financialized decision making. And downward pressure on wages has intensified since 2008 such that most UK workers have experienced a backwards step in their standard of living.

One potential criticism of the argument made here is that it could be read as being rather deterministic. Not all companies are equally driven to financialize managerial decision making in the same way. There are some large UK companies that are still privately owned which means that their decision making is less exposed to the tyrannies of short-term stock market pressures. Similarly, there are companies such as Tesco which have developed a distinctive approach to HR management and competition within sectors and labour markets vary. These contexts put different pressures on managers in different settings. But it is undoubtedly true that the general trend in corporate decision making in the recent past has been towards prioritizing financial imperatives over other interests and this has had—and continues to have—profound implications for the management of people within those organizations.

Taken together, these developments have made it even more challenging for unions to seek to extend their influence. In this difficult environment of a particularly financialized form of neoliberal capitalism, it is the central contention of this chapter that trade unions cannot and should not rely on the deals they can do with managers. Indeed, Thompson (2011) argues that *employees* more widely cannot and should not rely on the deals they do with their employers. At the very least, this means that unions in partnership arrangements with large corporations should regard deals as contingent and likely to be subject to disruption. Particularly problematic disruptions for unions and employees might involve requiring additional productivity, tightening performance regimes, or removing investment from a business unit. Unions will inevitably find it difficult to make headway negotiating in these circumstances. Organizing at least offers a strategically viable option for how to build strength both within the workplace and beyond by focusing on building collectivism and the capacity for collective action amongst workers.

■ NOTE

1. Tesco have not pursued the same business model in their international expansion.

■ REFERENCES

Ackers, P., Marchington, M., Wilkinson, A., and Dundon, T. (2005) 'Partnership and Voice, with or without Trade Unions: Changing UK Management Approaches to Organisational Participation'. In M. Stuart and M. Martínez Lucio (eds), *Partnership and Modernisation in Employment Relations*, pp. 23–45. London: Routledge.

Bernaciak, M. (2010) Cross-Border Competition and Trade Union Responses in the Enlarged EU: Evidence from the Automotive Industry in Germany and Poland. *European Journal of Industrial Relations*, 16(2), 119–35.

Beynon, H., Grimshaw, D., Rubery, J., and Ward, K. (2002) *Managing Employment Change*. Oxford: Oxford University Press.

Blanchflower, D. and Bryson, A. (2009) 'Trade Union Decline and the Economics of the Workplace'. In W. Brown, A. Bryson, J. Forth, and K. Whitfield (eds) *The Evolution of the Modern Workplace*, pp. 48–73. Cambridge: Cambridge University Press.

Clawson, D. and Clawson, M. (1999) 'What Has Happened to the U.S. Labor Movement? Union Decline and Renewal'. *Annual Review of Sociology*, 25, 95–119.

Danford, A., Richardson, M., Stewart, P., Tailby, S., and Upchurch, M. (2002) 'High Performance Work Systems and Workplace Partnership: An Aerospace Case Study'. Paper prepared for the 20th Annual Labour Process Conference, University of Strathclyde, 2–4 April.

Danford, A., Richardson, M., Stewart, P., Tailby, S., and Upchurch, M. (2004). 'High Performance Work Systems and Workplace Partnership: A Case Study of Aerospace Workers'. *New Technology, Work and Employment*, 19(1), 14–29.

Danford, A., Richardson, M., Stewart, P., Tailby, S., and Upchurch, M. (2005) 'Workplace Partnership and Employee Voice in the UK: Comparative Case Studies of Union Strategy and Worker Experience'. *Economic and Industrial Democracy*, 26(4), 593–620.

Danford, A., Richardson, M., Stewart, P., Tailby, S., and Upchurch, M. (2008) 'Partnership, High Performance Work Systems and Quality of Working Life'. *New Technology, Work and Employment*, 23(3), 151–66.

Deakin, S., Hobbs, R., Konzelmann, S., and Wilkinson, F. (2005) 'Working Corporations: Corporate Governance and Innovation in Labour-Management Partnerships in Britain'. In M. Stuart and M. Martínez Lucio (eds), *Partnership and Modernisation in Employment Relations*, pp. 63–82. London: Routledge.

Delbridge, R. (1998). *Life on the Line in Contemporary Manufacturing*. Oxford: Oxford University Press.

Froud, J., Haslam, C., Johal, S., and Williams, K. (2000) 'Restructuring for Shareholder Value and Its Implications for Labour'. *Cambridge Journal of Economics*, 24(6), 771–97.

Froud, J., Leaver, A., Johal, S., and Williams, K. (2006) *Financialization and Strategy: Narrative and Numbers*. London: Routledge.

Gall, G. (2003) *The Meaning of Militancy*. London: Ashgate.

Garrahan, P. and Stewart, P. (1992) *The Nissan Enigma: Flexibility at Work in a Local Economy*. London: Mansell.

Greer I. and Hauptmeier M. (2008) Political Entrepreneurs and Co-Managers: Labour Transnationalism at Four Multinational Auto Companies. *British Journal of Industrial Relations*, 46(1), 76–97.

Hall, M. and Purcell, J. (2012) *Consultation at Work: Regulation and Practice*. Oxford: Oxford University Press.

Heery, E. (2002) 'Partnership versus Organising: Alternative Futures for British Trade Unionism'. *Industrial Relations Journal*, 33(1), 20–35.

Johnstone, S., Ackers, P., and Wilkinson, A. (2009) 'The British Partnership Phenomenon: A Ten Year Review'. *Human Resource Management Journal*, 19(3), 260–79.

Keller, B. and Kirsch, A. (2011) 'Employment Relations in Germany'. In G. Bamber, R. Lansbury, and N. Wailes (eds) *International and Comparative Employment Relations*, pp. 196–223. London: Sage.

Kelly, J. (1996). 'Union Militancy and Social Partnership'. In P. Ackers, C. Smith, and P. Smith (eds), *The New Workplace and Trade Unionism*. London: Routledge.

Kelly, J. (2004) 'Social Partnership Arrangements in Britain'. *Industrial Relations*, 43(1), 267–92.

Kochan, T. (2007) 'Social Legitimacy of the Human Resource Management Profession: A U.S. Perspective'. In P. Boxall, J. Purcell, and P. Wright (eds), *The Oxford Handbook of Human Resource Management*. Oxford: Oxford University Press.

Kunda, G. and Ailon-Souday, G. (2005) 'Managers, Markets and Ideologies: Design and Devotion Revisited'. In S. Ackroyd, R. Batt, P. Thompson, and P. Tolbert (eds), *The Oxford Handbook of Work and Organization*. Oxford: Oxford University Press.

Legge, K. (2005). *Human Resource Management: Rhetorics and Realities*. Basingstoke: Palgrave Macmillan.

McBride, J. and Greenwood, I. (eds) (2009) *Community Unionism: A Comparative Analysis of Concepts and Contexts*. Basingstoke: Palgrave Macmillan.

Marks, A., Findlay, P., Hine, J., McKinlay, A., and Thompson, P. (1998) 'The Politics of Partnership? Innovative Employee Relations in the Scottish Spirits Industry'. *British Journal of Industrial Relations*, 36(2), 209–26.

Martínez Lucio, M. and Perrett, R. (2009) 'Meanings and Dilemmas in Community Unionism: Trade Union Community Initiatives and Black and Minority Ethnic Groups in the UK'. *Work, Employment and Society*, 23, 693–710.

Rinehart, J., Huxley, C., and Robertson, D. (1997) *Just Another Car Factory? Lean Production and Its Discontents*. Ithaca, NY: ILR/Cornell University Press.

Samuel, P. and Bacon, N. (2010) 'The Contents of Partnership Agreements in Britain, 1990–2007: Modest Aims of Limited Ambition?' *Work, Employment and Society*, 24 (3), 430–48.

Shaoul, J. (2008) 'The Political Economy of the Private Finance Initiative'. In P. Arestis and M. Sawyer (eds), *Critical Essays on the Privatisation Experience*. Basingstoke: Palgrave Macmillan.

Simms, M. and Charlwood, A. (2010) 'Trade Unions: Power and Influence in a Changed Context'. In T. Colling and M. Terry (eds), *Industrial Relations: Theory and Practice*. London: Wiley.

Simms, M. and Holgate, J. (2010) 'Organising for What? Where Is the Debate on the Politics of Organising?' *Work, Employment and Society*, 24(1).

Simms, M., Holgate, J., and Heery, E. (2013) *Union Voices: Tactics and Tensions in UK Organizing*. Ithaca, NY: Cornell University Press.

Smith, J. (2012) Outsourcing, Financialisation and the Crisis. *International Journal of Management Concepts and Philosophy*, 6(1–2), 19–44.

Streeck, W. (2009) *Re-Forming Capitalism: Institutional Change in the German Political Economy*. Oxford: Oxford University Press.

Suff, R. and Williams, S. (2004) 'The Myth of Mutuality? Employee Perceptions of Partnership at Borg Warner'. *Employee Relations*, 26(1), 30–43.

Thompson, P. (2003) 'Disconnected Capitalism: Or Why Employers Can't Keep Their Side of the Bargain'. *Work, Employment and Society*, 17, 359–78.

Thompson, P. (2011) 'The Trouble with HRM'. *Human Resource Management Journal*, 21(4), 355–67.

Turner, L. and Hurd, R. (2001) 'Building Social Movement Unionism: The Transformation of the American Labor Movement'. In L. Turner, H. Katz, and R. Hurd (eds), *Rekindling the Movement: Labor's Quest for Relevance in the 21st Century*. Ithaca, NY: Cornell University Press.

Ulrich, D. (1997) *Human Resource Champions: The Next Agenda for Adding Value and Delivering Results*. Boston, MA: Harvard Business Review Press.

van Wanrooy, B., Bewley, H., Bryson, A., Forth, J., Freeth, S., Stokes, L., and Wood, S. (2012) *The 2011 Workplace Employment Relations Study: First Findings*. London: Department for Business, Innovation and Skills.

Webb, S. and Webb, B. (1897) *Industrial Democracy*. London: Longmans.

Wills, J. and Simms, M. (2004) 'Building Reciprocal Community Unionism in the UK'. *Capital and Class*, 82.

7 The case for workplace partnership

Stewart Johnstone

Introduction

For many years industrial relations scholars have normally associated employee voice with employee representation, and especially representation through formal industrial relations institutions such as trade unions, joint consultation, and collective bargaining. For much of the twentieth century, voice in Britain was synonymous with trade unions. The central idea is that the inherent imbalance of power between most individual employees and their employer means that independent collective representation is likely to be more effective and safer than speaking up individually. However, the decline of trade unions over the last thirty years in Britain has raised important questions about the future of employee voice. Union membership has fallen from a peak of 13 million in 1979 to around 6.5 million today, or around 26 per cent of all employees (BIS 2012). Union decline has been particularly severe in the private sector where trade union representation is now very much the exception to the rule; only 14 per cent of employees are union members compared to 57 per cent of their public sector counterparts. In 2011, 6 per cent of private sector workplaces bargained over pay for some of their employees and one sixth of private sector employees have their pay set by collective bargaining (van Wanrooy et al. 2013). This is compounded by the evidence which suggests that even where unions continue to be recognized they are increasingly 'hollowed out' (Millward et al. 2000). This has led to vigorous debates in both policy and academic circles regarding the future of trade unions. Many commentaries are pessimistic regarding the prospects for a revival of trade unions, especially in the private sector. Howell (1999: 26), for example, declared that 'British trade unions are in crisis' and a report by Metcalf (2005: 28) concluded that 'the future for private sector unionisation is bleak indeed...perdition is more likely than resurgence'.

The most recent Workplace Employment Relations Study (WERS) confirms divergence between employment relations in the public and private sectors in several areas, including patterns of employee voice (van Wanrooy et al. 2013). But is the decline of unions a problem for employment relations and worker voice in the private sector? It could be argued that most modern employers now recognize the value of 'good' people management, employees enjoy a range of individual employment rights, and might also have access to an array of alternative employee voice mechanisms. Trade unions are thus superfluous: either relics of a bygone era when workers were at real risk of exploitation from unscrupulous employers but which no longer applies in advanced economies, or more critically as destructive forces. Of course most employment relations specialists would reject such unitarist arguments as ill-conceived, oversimplistic and naïve at best, or as a ruse to further bolster managerial prerogative at worst. An employment relations perspective generally rejects viewing the employment relationship as a straightforward economic exchange. The employment relationship is believed to be multifaceted, with various social, psychological, legal, and political dimensions (Colling and Terry 2010). Labour is not simply a commodity which can be traded on the free market like any other resource, and maximizing 'economic efficiency' is not the only goal. A pluralist approach recognizes the potential for both overlapping and divergent interests in the employment relationship, as well as a power relationship which is normally tipped in favour of employers. Representative participation is considered to be important in order to redress this imbalance. Constructive and cooperative employment relations are believed to be possible but by no means automatic, and again representative participation can help lubricate workplace relations. From this perspective, union decline is a worrying trend for both workers as well as the overall shape of the societies in which we live.

The prospects for union voice in the private sector are likely to depend upon a combination of external factors, such as state policy, as well as internal factors such as union strategies, policies, and actions. However, the most appropriate strategies for union revitalization have divided opinion in recent years, and this divide has often been presented as a choice between a 'partnership' approach on the one hand, and an 'organizing' approach on the other (Heery 2002; see also Simms, this volume). The aim of this chapter is to evaluate the notion of workplace partnership. The central argument is that partnership is a strategy that merits serious consideration and has a much wider potential reach as a model of employee representation in the private sector than many critical commentators suggest.

The chapter is structured as follows. I begin by exploring the meaning of workplace partnership given the ambiguous and contested nature of the term. The second section then evaluates polarized conceptual debates regarding partnership, and in particular the contrasting views of industrial relations radicals and pluralists regarding the viability and desirability of partnership approaches to employment relations. The third section then assesses the prospects for partnership, and the extent to which partnership may represent an opportunity to revitalize and reconstruct collective employment relations by regaining employer and employee support. The chapter ends by briefly considering the merits of alternative approaches to workplace partnership, such as union organizing. The focus of the chapter is primarily upon the prospects for workplace partnership in the context of the British private sector, where the development of partnership has normally been argued to be the most challenging, and where union decline has been most acute.

What is workplace partnership?

Partnership was once described as 'an idea with which almost anyone can agree without having a clear idea what they are agreeing about' (Guest and Peccei 2001: 207). It has also been described as terms which have become 'too diffuse to carry much meaning' (Oxenbridge and Brown 2004: 389). It is therefore important to attempt to clarify at the outset exactly how workplace partnership is interpreted, especially as the term is often used in an ambiguous way with the precise meaning dependent upon the user (Bacon and Storey 2000). Despite this fluidity, several common themes can normally be discerned. In its most general sense, workplace partnership can be used to refer to a *particular style of collective employment relations*: a style associated with an explicit emphasis upon fostering cooperative workplace relations and an attempt to avoid or at least minimize adversarial and conflictual relations, especially in unionized settings. Huzzard et al. (2004) describe this as the difference between 'boxing' and 'dancing', while Harrison et al. (2011: 412) define partnership as 'agreements between competing actors who deliberately choose to co-operate instead of maintaining adversarial relations'.

Though perhaps capturing the spirit or guiding philosophy of a partnership approach, this interpretation is problematic for several reasons. First, it could be argued that it views partnership as an employment relations outcome (for example, cooperation) but reveals little about the policies, practices, or processes associated with the approach. An emphasis upon shifting from conflict to cooperation means partnership can be interpreted as a unitarist philosophy which downplays the potential for conflict and seeks to galvanize unions, employers, and workers around a vision of collaborative and harmonious employment relations and mutual gains. The philosophy of partnership may have little appeal to unitarists who assume cooperation to be the natural state of organizational life, requiring strong leadership and communication rather than developing relationships with trade unions.

However, from a pluralist perspective, disagreements and conflicts of interest are a normal and inevitable part of organizational life. Differences of interests are believed to be both inevitable and legitimate, and the aim is to promote constructive dialogue which provides the opportunity to pre-empt and resolve differences of interest when they do arise and before they spill over into outright conflict. The partnership model of unionism is concerned with an attempt to reconcile inherent social and economic tensions (Martínez Lucio and Stuart 2002). The key proposition is that it can be both economically effective and socially responsible for unions and employers to work together on important issues such as organizational change, and that the two are not necessarily mutually exclusive. For pluralists, partnership recognizes potential differences of interest; however, all parties are believed to have some common interests including the sustainability of the organization, and that in part hinges upon fostering positive employment relations. So partnership may represent an aspiration to construct high-trust and cooperative employment relations even if it is not fully realized. It also raises several other questions. If the employment relationship is characterized by ongoing and dynamic tensions between conflict and cooperation (Edwards 2003), what do 'cooperative employment relations' look like? Does partnership require a wholesale shift from adversarial and arms-length relations to cooperative relations? Would periods of conflict mean the failure or end of partnership? Such questions highlight the weaknesses of simply viewing partnership as a management style or a cultural characteristic.

Partnership is more than an employment relations style or philosophy with aspirations of cooperation. In more tangible and practical terms, partnership is normally associated with a particular set of *HR policies, practices, and commitments*, and these policies are helpful in understanding how a partnership might translate into particular HR systems 'on the ground'. Typical HR practices include commitments to some degree of job security, workforce flexibility, and employee voice. In some respects these may be viewed simply as a repackaging of the various HR policies and practices typically associated with 'best practice', 'high performance work system', and 'high commitment management', or more prosaically as 'good personnel management'. However, from a pluralist perspective, workplace partnership differs, in part because it is underpinned by the philosophy of reciprocity and mutuality. As a result, proponents of workplace partnership usually stress the importance of representative participation as an essential part of employee voice. Some US commentators prefer the term 'mutual gains' (for example, Kochan et al. 1986; Kochan and Osterman 1994) because it:

Conveys a key message: achieving and sustaining competitive advantage from human resources requires the strong support of multiple stakeholders ... employees must commit their energies to meeting the economic objectives of the enterprise. In return, owners must share the economic returns with employees and invest in those returns in such a way as promotes the long-term economic security of the workforce.

(Kochan and Osterman 1994: 46)

Despite this broad agreement concerning management style and HR practices, there is still some debate regarding the prerequisites required to qualify as a prima facie case of workplace partnership. One matter of contention is whether partnership requires a *formal* 'partnership agreement' or whether an informal identification with the approach is sufficient. For example, Bacon and Samuel define partnership as 'formal collective agreements to enhance cooperation between employers and independent trade unions and staff associations' (Bacon and Samuel 2009: 232), thus excluding the possibility of more informal workplace partnerships. It is estimated that 248 formal union/management partnership agreements were signed between 1990 and 2007, covering 10 per cent of all British workers (Samuel and Bacon 2010). Clearly there are merits to establishing some boundaries and a formal agreement between unions/staff associations and management seems sensible, otherwise any organization could claim to be 'working in partnership'. Again, this reinforces the challenges of viewing partnership in more nebulous terms as a 'cooperative culture'. On the other hand, it does seem feasible that some organizations may exhibit many of the day-to-day characteristics of working in partnership, but without a formal agreement. Similarly, is workplace partnership only possible in unionized organizations? To be sure, much of the research evidence and almost all of the high profile cases of partnership focus upon arrangements in unionized environments, yet as Ackers et al. (2004: 16) state in relation to participation more generally, 'it seems unreasonable and sociologically unproductive to rule out non-union forms before examining the evidence'. *Workplace partnership* can also be contrasted with other uses of the term 'partnership', such as the John Lewis partnership in the UK, which is more concerned with a particular system of financial ownership as opposed to a model of employment relations. Finally, workplace partnership can be contrasted with the *social partnership* associated with several continental European nations, and which represent a distinctive tripartite and institutionalized approach to national policy issues such as skill, training, and employment strategy. Workplace partnership focuses more upon the nature of the relationships and interactions between individual employers and trade unions operating within a voluntarist framework.

For the purposes of this chapter, it is proposed that a more useful conceptualization of workplace partnership is as both an overarching employment relations style and philosophy, as well as a particular (and more tangible) bundle of HR policies, processes, and outcomes. In terms of practices, employee voice is central to all definitions of partnership, but especially representative participation, normally involving trade unions. In terms of processes, partnership is usually associated with a highly consultative style of decision making, requiring early consultation and an opportunity for employee representatives to genuinely influence decisions. This style is related to a particular form of actor relationships requiring high levels of trust and openness. Employment relations outcomes, such as cooperation and high levels of trust, might be key aspirations of partnership which need to be explored empirically, but are not an integral component of partnership per se. Partnership may concern an attempt to achieve these outcomes irrespective of whether or not they are achieved. It is proposed that it is this particular framework of mutually reinforcing philosophies, practice, and process which underpin a prima facie case of workplace partnership (see Johnstone et al. 2009).

Conceptual debates

Workplace partnership has divided opinion and generated contentious conceptual debates. The most vocal critique of partnership has come from those writing from radical industrial relations and labour process traditions. From these perspectives, the idea of labour management partnership is simply fraught with inherent contradictions and paradoxes, as the interests of employers and unions are so sharply opposed. Radicals note how workers are simultaneously a cost to be controlled as well as a resource requiring investment, and how the balance of power in most capitalist workplaces is typically heavily skewed in favour of the employer. This renders attempts at 'partnership'-style relations deeply contradictory and naïve. As Danford et al. (2005) state, 'partnership cannot mask irreconcilable conflicts of interest that are prime characteristics of capitalist workplace dynamics'. The fundamental dynamics of capitalist societies simply undermine any meaningful notion of workplace 'partnership' between workplace actors. As Kelly (1996: 88) argues 'it is difficult, if not impossible to have a partnership with a party who would prefer you didn't exist'. This perspective assumes employer hostility to trade unions and a desire to protect and preserve managerial prerogative. By implication, developing partnerships with unions is likely to be a low priority for employers unless it offers some other attraction, such as an opportunity for employers to contain unions within tightly defined parameters.

Moreover, the nature of contemporary political economy and capitalist relations is likely to hinder attempts at fostering long-term collaborative relations, characterized by mutual trust and employment security, envisaged by partnership advocates. Even where employers are not actively hostile or seeking to exploit workers, the dynamics of modern capitalism mean even good-willed and well-intentioned employers 'cannot keep their promises' because of the preponderance of short-term financial concerns at the expense of long-term societal concerns (Thompson 2003, 2011; see also Simms, this volume). By implication, the notion of mutual gains is little more than an illusion, and even where some gains are seemingly achieved, they are likely to benefit employers more. As a consequence, it is argued that the reality of partnership is likely to be a compliant model of unionism, which makes it more difficult for unions to demonstrate credibility or effectiveness to members and potential members. For IR radicals, the 'counter-mobilisation thesis' stresses an irreconcilable and fundamental antagonism of interests between workers and employers, meaning militant forms of unionism are more appropriate than the 'moderation' strategies supported by partnership enthusiasts (Kelly 1996, 1998).

Assessments of partnership by IR pluralists have tended to be more equivocal. The political nature of the employment relationship means pluralists are sceptical about the likelihood or capacity of employers to balance countervailing tensions without regulatory mechanisms and institutional support setting out some basic 'rules of the game' (see Heery, this volume). Pluralists also believe organizations are characterized by complex tensions which need to be managed in order to reconcile different opinions and keep conflict within accepted bounds, though they differ from radicals in their perceptions of the nature and extent of class conflict and power imbalance in society and work (Ackers 2014). The key challenge is the effective regulation of employment and the representation and moderation of these different interests (Johnstone and Ackers 2014). Some regulation of behaviour is believed to be necessary in setting out fundamental rules employers are required to follow and clarifying expectations they must meet. For many years, classic IR pluralists assumed institutions such as trade unions and collective bargaining were the most appropriate process of employment regulation, combined with state policies and employment law where necessary. However, the decline of unions in recent decades means unions are no longer a taken-for-granted part of the employment relations scene in many private sector workplaces (van Wanrooy et al. 2013), leading to important concerns regarding the appropriate means of regulating the contemporary employment relationship.

One option is a relegitimization of trade unions based upon proactive partnership relations (Ackers and Payne 1998), but industrial relations pluralists are divided regarding the potential reach, feasibility, and sustainability of the partnership model. On the one hand, radical-pluralist commentators, which Ackers (2014) describes as the mainstream perspective for British and European industrial relations scholarship, tend to be pessimistic regarding the potential development of enduring partnership relations in Britain, especially in the private sector. This is not necessarily because they are ideologically opposed to partnership per se, or because they think partnership is inherently and inevitably flawed, but perhaps because radical pluralism has a default bias towards conflictual rather than cooperative dimensions of the employment relationship, rather than the other way round (Ackers 2014).

For example, Heery (2002) suggests that the British business environment provides a lack of incentive for employers to pursue partnership, due to corporate governance systems which prioritize short-term performance and shareholder value, rather than developing long-term cooperative relationships with the workforce. In addition, a focus on cost reduction, a desire to preserve managerial prerogative, as well as a weak HR function and default bias in favour of individualistic human resource management (HRM) are all barriers to the spread of partnership. Where unions are recognized, the priority may be keeping traditional but narrow relations. As Heery concludes, 'The dominant characteristics of British business, therefore, seemingly do not furnish an environment in which a union strategy of partnership can flourish' (Heery 2002: 26). Similarly, Simms (this volume), suggests that meaningful and sustainable partnerships require specific conditions to be successful. Key ingredients are likely to include a strong commitment from the corporate centre to partnership working, as well as a business model and labour management strategy which is not predicated upon cost minimization. Such environments might offer a favourable context for the development of a high-trust partnership relationship. However, Simms is concerned that the dominant contemporary financialized capitalism means that such favourable contexts are likely to be very rare in the private sector. Again, building on Thompson's (2003) notion of 'disconnected capitalism', the argument is that even where managers *are* able to build good local relations, these are always at risk of disruption and derailment by decisions made by the corporate sector rendering any partnership relations precarious and fragile. In short, the antagonistic nature of the employment relationship, combined with short-term systems of corporate governance, are not believed to offer the conditions required for partnership to flourish or become widespread (see also Heery 2002). As a result, alternative approaches to union renewal such as union organizing are generally recommended (Heery and Simms, this volume).

In contrast, a *neopluralist* perspective suggests greater grounds for optimism regarding the prospects of workplace partnership. This perspective acknowledges the potential for conflict over both the processes of employment regulation and the distribution of employment outcomes, but is more sanguine about the potential to reconcile these tensions through proactive partnership relations characterized by commitments to joint working with the aim of achieving mutual gains (Johnstone and Ackers 2014). Budd (2004) notes how the aim of 'striking a balance' between competing interests is central to the pluralist frame of reference, and that the normative agenda of IR pluralists and their preferred public policy responses can be described as those which facilitate an attempt to balance the interests of individuals, stakeholders, and institutions. This is compatible with the 'mutual gains thesis' which rejects the view that collective employee representation must be an adversarial zero-sum game, and stresses the prospects for mutually beneficial collaboration and problem solving, as well as expanding the agenda to include issues such job quality, work–life balance, and employee well-being. It also rejects the view that representative participation and trade union representation inevitably damage productivity or contribute to high levels of conflict. The core argument is that it is better to encourage stakeholders to work together to 'increase the size of the pie' and to resolve tensions before they spill over into conflict, rather than focusing on the distribution of gains and conflict resolution which tends to dominate in a more adversarial pluralist model (Cooke 1990; Kochan and Osterman 1994). In short, neopluralism is much more positive about the potential scope for the development of cooperation at work (Ackers 2014).

Prospects for partnership

Given the contested conceptual debates outlined above, which lead to us very different conclusions regarding the prospects for partnership, it is useful to now consider some of the research evidence in order to shed some empirical light on the processes and outcomes of partnership in practice. The most fundamental criticism of partnership is that it is highly unlikely to achieve the putative mutual gains suggested by more optimistic analyses. However, a review of the extensive research evidence suggests that in certain circumstances partnership can deliver gains to stakeholders (see Johnstone et al. 2009 for a detailed review). Though the specific benefits identified vary between studies, several benefits can be discerned for different stakeholders. For trade unions, the potential gains of a partnership approach have included greater facility time, access to a wider range of information, access to senior decision makers, improved consultation, stronger relationships, enhanced legitimacy and negotiating position with employers, an increase in perceived union effectiveness, employee support, and in turn higher membership and greater worker commitment to the union. Studies also report how partnership has allowed trade unions to extend their sphere of influence beyond a traditional but narrow focus upon issues such as pay and conditions and discipline and grievance, into broader issues of HRM such as work organization and organizational change. Reported benefits for employees have included enhanced work–life balance, reduced stress, increased job satisfaction, opportunities for employee voice, job security, higher wages, increased opportunities for participation in decision making, work autonomy, job security, and flexible job design. Finally, the more positive studies of partnership also identify various gains from the employer perspective including greater employee commitment and productivity, enhanced product/service quality and innovation, lower industrial relations conflict, lower absenteeism and labour turnover, support for change, flexibility, and higher levels of trust (see Johnstone et al. 2010b; Oxenbridge and Brown 2004; Whyman and Petrescu 2013). In many ways, these have the potential to be mutually reinforcing as the mutual gains thesis suggests. For example, partnership can help improve the general industrial relations climate, in turn improving firm competitiveness and financial performance, leading to greater job security for employees and an increased membership base for trade unions.

However, not all analyses of partnership identify such positive results. For example, Kelly (2004) found that while employers appeared to benefit in some ways from partnership, there were negligible gains for workers or trade unions when evaluated against criteria such as wages, hours worked, holidays, or job losses. Employee gains were only found to be achieved where unions were strong, and where the firm was performing well. His findings in relation to wage levels, influence in the company, and employment security were negative. Various other studies also find very little support for the mutual gains thesis, and suggest a range of negative outcomes that are actually more likely including difficulties demonstrating union effectiveness, greater distance between unions and their members, work intensification, job insecurity, and labour outcomes no better than non-partnership firms (see for example Danford et al. 2005; Kelly 2004; Upchurch et al. 2008). Much of the interest in mutual gains appears to relate to the balance of advantage, or the issue of who gains most. From this perspective, even broadly positive studies of partnership report evidence of 'constrained mutuality', suggesting that while employees may well stand to benefit from partnership, typically the 'balance of advantage' will be tipped in favour of the employer (Guest and Peccei 2001). Whether or not this represents a problem is where ideological differences emerge, with radicals generally seeking gains which flow equally to employers, employees, and unions, while pluralists take the view that the aim is one of levelling the playing field and having sufficient influence to make a difference. Much depends upon the criteria we employ to judge the 'success' or 'failure' of partnership, and what we believe the process is supposed to achieve (Johnstone et al. 2009).

Nevertheless, the mixed nature of findings suggests that some of the arguments of the most ardent partnership critics may be overly deterministic. Instead, they lend support to the view that partnership outcomes are contingent upon a range of conditions which determine the favourability of the context to partnership working and moderate the outcomes. Much will depend upon the precise configuration of strategic, structural, and institutional factors (Butler et al. 2011). In other words, it is too simple to dismiss partnership as a strategy which cannot deliver mutual gains in a liberal market economy, because in some cases partnership does seem capable of generating mutual gains. However, the partnership research also suggests that there is no straightforward or automatic cause and effect relationship. In practice, it seems partnership is neither intrinsically 'good' nor 'bad' as the divided conceptual debates imply, and suggests that in supportive contexts partnership can deliver positive outcomes to a range of stakeholders (see for example Johnstone et al. 2010a, 2010b, 2011). The key issue, then, becomes one of developing our understanding of the factors associated with the success and failure of partnership, in order to consider how and whether these seemingly exotic 'islands' of partnership and cooperation can be transfused across the private sector economy.

Of course, this assumes that private sector employers would be receptive to notions of partnership, or amenable to the idea of working with unions, yet a key criticism is that employers generally do not want to work with trade unions, in part because there are very few incentives for them to do so. This would suggest that there are limited opportunities to develop partnership across the British economy, and attempts by unions to promulgate the partnership model are likely to encounter employer resistance. Undoubtedly, from an employer perspective, debates concerning employee voice have evolved in recent years, and for the majority of private sector employers voice no longer necessarily means working with trade unions or indeed engaging with any form of collective employee representation. Post-war terms such as joint consultation, industrial democracy, and collective bargaining have been superseded by a new managerial language of employee involvement, empowerment, and employee engagement. Even where unions are present 'local union representatives—shop stewards—are not the negotiators or co-authors of "joint rules" that we have typically taken them for since the late 1960s' (Terry 2003: 488). Employers now also have a myriad of fashionable HR techniques from which they can choose as part of their approach to managing work and employment. Simply put, the reality is that unions are no longer the default option for worker voice outside the public sector in any Anglophone country (Boxall et al. 2007). Few British employers with established union relationships have derecognized unions, but for many non-union employers, HRM and employee voice have moved beyond traditional industrial relations institutions. Employers may not have completely lost their appetite for employee voice, but their tastes do seem to have changed in favour of more 'modern' approaches to voice which are often direct and individualistic (Willman et al. 2007). Even where employers do sense a need for collective voice infrastructure, there may be a preference for the development of in-house representative structures such as employee forums and committees rather than union voice (Johnstone et al. 2010a). This could be interpreted as providing support for the view that the UK offers an unfavourable environment for the widespread development of partnership relations with unions.

However, as Willman et al. (2010) argue, unions can be thought of as an 'experience good'. It is perhaps unsurprising that non-union employers might be concerned about the potential costs and risks of entering into new relations with unions. Experience of employment relations in unionized contexts may be limited, and perceptions may be influenced by negative media coverage which is more likely to report episodes of conflict and militancy rather than evidence of workplace cooperation. Yet, as Freeman and Medoff (1984: 179) stated over thirty years ago that 'unionism per se is neither a plus nor a minus to productivity. What matters is how unions and management interact at the workplace.' Given the plethora of voice options available to employers, this is perhaps where a partnership approach offers potential benefits as a way of gradually influencing the attitudes of employers. This might involve, for example, ways of demonstrating to employers the positive benefits of working in partnership with trade unions, as well as how partnership relationships can actually complement other HR and direct voice techniques. In the 1960s, the Donovan Commission suggested that trade unions can act as a 'lubricant not an irritant' in the management of workplace relations (McCarthy 1967), but such a view may no longer be shared by employers and managers who hold negative attitudes towards unions influenced by the industrial relations strife of the 1970s and 1980s, or have no strong feelings either way. As Metcalf (2005: 26) states: 'The challenge for the union movement is to demonstrate that they can come through for workers without putting employers at a disadvantage and/or deliver for employers while simultaneously looking after worker interests'.

Partnership approaches present such an opportunity for unions to reposition themselves as organizations that can add value rather than as destructive forces, and there are several research studies which confirm that this can indeed be the case. Charlwood and Terry (2007), for example, found that productivity outcomes are better in dual voice systems which combine direct and indirect mechanisms, while other studies have also suggested that unions can enhance productivity where management are supportive of the union (Freeman and Medoff 1984; Bryson et al. 2006). Voice systems which combine 'embedded' direct forms of involvement with indirect voice through representative bodies are also associated with higher levels of organizational commitment (Purcell and Georgiadis 2007). Further studies have revealed the benefits of combining high-performance work practices with trade union representation (Bryson et al. 2006), and the most recent WERS evidence reveals that around a quarter of British managers agreed that unions helped them to find ways to improve workplace performance (van Wanrooy et al. 2013), a figure which showed no significant change from the last WERS conducted before the global financial crisis hit (Kersley et al. 2006). Studies also reveal that the number of workplace problems falls when management and union work cooperatively, while more adversarial relations are not only stressful but can also hinder the ability of unions to deliver for members (Bryson and Freeman 2006; Freeman and Medoff 1984). The above evidence can be used by unions to demonstrate the value they can add.

Besides the findings of various quantitative research studies, further benefits of working cooperatively with trade unions are sometimes more qualitative and difficult to measure through raw economic analysis (Purcell and Georgiadis 2007). Nevertheless, a review of the recent policy literature alludes to some of the more difficult-to-measure benefits of employers working cooperatively with unions to address the challenges of the recession, and to boost employee engagement. For example, the EEF, the manufacturers' organization, note how there has been evidence among their member organizations of employers and unions working together to take a long-term view to identify imaginative and innovative ways of working and to avoid job cuts (Podro 2010). The Advisory, Conciliation and Arbitration Service (ACAS) and the Involvement and Participation Association (IPA) also report a desire on the part of many unions to avoid rushing into confrontation, and to work with employers as 'partners in change' to seek mutually acceptable solutions to the challenges of recession. Finally, the Chartered Institute of Personnel and Development (CIPD) acknowledge that it can be the collective dimension which stands to 'undermine or support engagement strategies'. A similar—but often overlooked—point is made in the 2009 *MacLeod Review* on employee engagement, which specifically suggests 'synergies between engagement approaches and partnership working between unions and employers where trust, co-operation, and information are key... many organisations with partnership agreements emphasised to us that it complemented and enhanced their engagement strategies' (MacLeod and Clarke 2009). In other words, while critics often highlight the lack of a latent employer demand for developing partnership relations with unions, it could be argued that it is the partnership model of unionism which is likely to be most appealing to employers, because this also suggests the potential to add value to the business, as well promoting the interests of workers.

Of course, any consideration of the potential reach and merits of partnership as a model of employee voice must also consider the extent to which it is compatible with what modern workers want from voice. Comparative research by Boxall et al. (2007) found that, while employees want some form of voice which will help them deal with problems at work, workers across Anglophone countries are now increasingly indifferent to what unions offer and often express a preference for direct over indirect forms of voice. Other studies reveal that many workers doubt the effectiveness of union voice, and also suggest worker satisfaction with direct non-union forms of representative voice (Bryson 2004; Bryson et al. 2006). Again, if unions are an 'experience good' this can make it difficult to attract new members who typically give reasons such as perceived union ineffectiveness and social norms to explain not joining unions, as well as the potential to 'free ride' and enjoy many of the benefits in unionized workplaces without incurring the financial cost of membership. Either way, these findings suggest that as well as considering how they can demonstrate legitimacy in the eyes of employers by adding value to the business, unions also need to consider how they can increase their appeal to modern workers, many of whom are apathetic or indifferent regarding the value of trade union membership.

One potential solution to the challenge of falling membership and worker apathy is the organizing approach, which is often presented as an alternative to partnership. As with partnership, organizing can refer to a wide range of different approaches and techniques and can be difficult to define with much precision. However, most definitions of organizing normally refer to an approach which prioritizes extensive recruitment efforts by unions, as well as 'empowering' workers so they can resolve workplace issues without external representation (Heery 2002). Organizing has been defined as 'an attempt to rediscover the social movement origins of labour, essentially by redefining the union as a mobilising structure which seeks to stimulate activism among its members, and generate campaigns for workplace and wider social justice' (Heery et al. 2000: 996). In contrast to partnership strategies, the focus of organizing is normally upon trade unions building networks and strengthening relationships with their members (and potential members) rather than attempting to develop partnership relations with managers and employers. While partnership is largely predicated upon aspirations of greater levels of cooperation and the achievement of mutual gains, organizing returns the focus to the potential conflicts of interest between employers and employees. With organizing, the interests of workers on issues such as pay and conditions or employment security are centre stage, rather than attempting to find ways of aligning or balancing these with employer priorities. Particular aims include defending and promoting the interests of workers, building collectivism among workers to work together and pursue their interests, as well as tackling broader societal issues of injustice and inequality (Simms, this volume). Organizing is also associated with a desire to embed a broader cultural change within the union movement towards one which is significantly more participative and also representative of its members. This is said to require attracting new people to work in the union movement as specialist professional organizers, as well as a culture of workplace activism rather than passivity among union members (Simms et al. 2013). More practical concerns of organizing campaigns typically include winning new recognition deals and increasing membership and participation where unions are already recognized (in-fill recruitment). A range of techniques might be used including person-to-person recruitment, raising the union profile at the workplace, establishing organizing committees, using employee grievances as a basis for recruitment, as well as high-profile public campaigns against anti-union employers (Simms et al. 2013).

There are at least two important limitations of organizing. First, the evidence suggests that despite significant union investment in organizing activity in recent years, the evidence of a recovery in union membership is limited. Research has identified various internal and external constraints which are encountered and act as barriers to successful organizing. On the one hand, organizers have encountered employer opposition to trade unions, especially where recognition was being sought or where the union only had a weak presence (Heery and Simms 2008). This often resulted in a 'spiral of mutually hostile activity' and blocked organizing efforts (Heery and Simms 2010: 10). Gall (2005) has also identified employer resistance as a major factor hampering union attempts to winning recognition rights in various 'new economy' firms, including Orange, Egg, and Amazon. Interestingly, organizing efforts have tended to enjoy greater support where unions already have established relationships with employers (Heery and Simms 2010). This leads to a paradox of organizing, in that one of the main aims is to get a foothold in new workplaces, yet the approach often does not succeed unless the door is already open or at least ajar. Yet because organizing typically favours an overtly worker-focused and adversarial approach over building positive relationships with employers, it is unsurprising that many employers prefer to keep the door latched firmly shut.

Finally, it is not only employers who may be wary of organizing attempts. Targeted workers may be resistant to the encouragement to join a union. Such resistance has been attributed to the individualistic values of non-members, the poor reputation and image of unions, and a perception that unions do not reflect the interests and diversity of modern workers, or adopt counterproductive and damaging militant strategies. In addition, while much union organizing activity is conflictual in character (Heery and Simms 2008), evidence has suggested that many workers no longer support adversarial union strategies. Rather, the majority of UK workers now express a preference for cooperation, where unions 'work with management to improve the workplace and working conditions', rather than unions which focus more narrowly upon 'defending workers against unfair treatment by management' (Bryson et al. 2006). Indeed, employee preferences for 'more cooperative styles of engagement with management which help improve their firm performance and their working lives' have been found in comparative research across the Anglophone countries (Bryson and Freeman 2007). In summary, many organizing campaigns are blocked by resistant employers or fail to ignite the interest of the very workers they are seeking to target. In such cases, a partnership model which offers value to employers and also chimes with worker preferences for cooperative rather than conflictual workplace relations may be more fruitful.

Conclusion

The purpose of this chapter was to assess the prospects for the development of workplace partnership in the British private sector, where union representation is now very much the exception to the rule, as well as where the challenges to partnership relations are argued to be most acute. At a national level, partnership enjoyed a brief spell in the limelight towards the end of the 1990s but the interest of senior politicians and union leaders quickly evaporated in the first few years of the new millennium. Partnership has continued to divide the opinions of both academics and public policy makers, with views ranging from those suggesting partnership remains an important opportunity to revitalize collective employee representation and trade unions (Johnstone et al. 2010a, 2010b), while others have highlighted perceived inadequacies and contradictions (Upchurch et al. 2008).

The central argument of my analysis is that, despite polarized conceptual debates, in practice partnership does appear to provide a valuable model of employment relations which can work in certain contexts. Deciding what constitutes success, however, is complex and depends on our expectations of what partnership is meant to achieve. Partnership is also a very loose term used to refer to many different types of arrangement, so there is always the risk we cannot easily compare like with like. However, it appears that a range of positive outcomes *are* achievable for employers, unions, and employees, thus calling into question pessimistic accounts which suggest that partnership simply cannot work. Partnership may have fallen out of fashion in national political debates, but at a workplace level many flagship partnership agreements appear to be robust (Bacon and Samuel 2009). A review of key quantitative indicators such as collective bargaining coverage, union membership, union density, or number of partnership agreements signed means it is easy to be pessimistic about both the achievements and potential of partnership unionism in the UK private sector. However, aggregate statistics ignore the fact many of these have been signed in high-profile private sector firms including Barclays, Jaguar Land Rover, Rolls-Royce, and Tesco. These are exactly the type of organizations we often find in mainstream HR textbooks as exemplars of 'strategic' and 'best practice' HRM, and which proclaim that 'people are our greatest asset' on glossy corporate websites. A more optimistic interpretation would suggest that the development of partnership in such organizations confirms first that partnership is compatible with other HRM concepts and techniques and not at the expense of organizational performance, and second that there is scope to encourage the diffusion of partnership across the different sectors in which 'flagship' agreements are located.

Partnership is also valuable because it focuses attention on the nature and value of collective employee representation, which is increasingly absent from contemporary HR debates and textbooks. The WERS series has documented the decline of employee representation and trade union membership over several decades (van Wanrooy et al. 2013), and the partnership debate is important because it rejects the unitarist assumptions of many HRM techniques, and emphasizes the value of pluralist conceptualizations of the employment relationship. This is especially important at a time when employment relations as both a field of study and area of management practice is under threat from the increasing 'psychologization' of HR (Godard 2014). This is epitomized by the current vogue for employee engagement, which as Guest (this volume) notes, underemphasizes notions of reciprocity which are at the heart of partnership and mutual gains. Interestingly, some HR commentators have also acknowledged the need for a more balanced agenda in HR, especially as HR professionals no longer see themselves as 'employee champions' but strategic 'business partners' (Francis and Keegan 2006). A particular strength of partnership is that it sets out a normative, pluralist vision of the employment relationship, and views strong employee voice as a means of moderating the tensions between business efficiency on the one hand and equity and fair treatment of workers on the other (Budd 2004; Johnstone et al. 2011).

This is not to suggest that partnership is a solution for all the ills of employment relations. Certain conditions appear to be associated with more robust instances of partnership, and arrangements which fail to deliver regular gains to the various stakeholders are unlikely to be sustainable. The factors typically associated with more robust partnerships include strong trade unions and HR departments, the commitment and competence of all actors, and integration within a wider suite of supportive HR practices. Others include the need for a high-quality workforce, a high involvement culture, and the ability to take a longer-term perspective. Of course there are contexts where few of these features are likely to be present. Some employers express overtly anti-union sentiments, and others appear to operate on the basis of tight control and cost-minimization rather than high commitment. In such contexts the notion of developing partnership may seem inappropriate or unrealistic, at least in the short term, and organizing may be viewed as a more viable strategy. Different contexts might require different strategies, or as John Monks (1997) put it, 'partnership with good employers and organise the bad employers'. With anti-union employers there might be few short-term alternatives to organizing strategies, but as noted above such approaches have had limited success when faced with the employer hostility they are likely to encounter.

The relationship between partnership and organizing is therefore complex. Partnership with existing employers might lead to organizing, and organizing new workplaces might lead to opportunities to develop partnership in the long term (see Heery 2002). However, for many other employers who have established union management relations, partnership might be something to which they can aspire. In the long term, partnership could also be a model of unionism which is more attractive—or at least less worrying—to organizations which do not currently recognize trade unions. Successful high-profile case studies of union–management partnership can be used by unions to reassure employers that positive relations with unions can actually add value and lubricate employment relations. In such circumstances, partnership could be used as a strategy to neutralize employers' concerns, to win support and recognition in new workplaces, and in turn help organizing efforts. A form of unionism which recognizes the need to balance economic competitiveness and performance, on the one hand, with employee well-being and broader societal priorities on the other may also help in winning the support of public policy makers. Howell (2005) notes the importance of government policy in influencing employer behaviour, and it is the promise of the mutual gains associated with partnership which is more likely to attract state support. It is perhaps no coincidence that both advocates of partnership and organizing approaches often highlight the impressive success of the approach adopted by Tesco and Usdaw. In the Tesco/Usdaw case, partnership and organizing have operated in parallel, and membership reportedly increased by 17 per cent between 1999 and 2009, in a sector where staff churn means unions must recruit vigorously to stand still.

The central argument of the chapter is that it would be short-sighted to dismiss partnership in the British private sector as something which cannot work within the context of a liberal market economy. Inevitably, workplace partnership is challenging. However, with the appropriate support, partnership can deliver mutual gains and also offer unions the opportunity to reinvent themselves in the eyes of employers, workers, and the general public as constructive organizations that lubricate workplace relations and make a positive contribution to society. Partnership might not work everywhere, at least in the short term, but its long-term reach is likely to be far wider than the critics admit. Finally, partnership demonstrates the advantages of a shift towards a more pluralist reading of HRM, and the potential value of an employment relations model which aspires to mutual gains for employers, workers, and society as a whole.

■ REFERENCES

Ackers, P. (2014) 'Rethinking the Employment Relationship: A Neo-Pluralist Critique of British Industrial Relations Orthodoxy'. *International Journal of Human Resource Management*, 25(18), 2608–25.

Ackers, P. and Payne, J. (1998) 'British Trade Unions and Social Partnership: Rhetoric, Reality and Strategy'. *International Journal of Human Resource Management*, 9(3, June), 529–50.

Ackers, P., Marchington, M., Wilkinson, A., and Dundon. T. (2004) 'Partnership and Voice, with or without Trade Unions'. In Stuart, M. and Martínez-Lucio, M. (eds), *Partnership and Modernisation in Employment Relations*, pp. 20–39. London: Routledge.

Bacon, N. and Samuel, P. (2009) 'Partnership Agreement Adoption and Survival in the British Private and Public Sectors'. *Work, Employment and Society*, 23(2), 231–48.

Bacon, N. and Storey, J. (2000) 'New Employee Relations Strategies in Britain: Towards Individualism or Partnership?' *British Journal of Industrial Relations*, 38 (3), 407–27.

BIS (2012) *Union Membership 2012*. [Online.] Available at: <https://www.gov.uk/government/publications/trade-union-statistics-2012>.

Boxall, P., Haynes, P., and Freeman, R. (2007) 'What Workers Say in the Anglo-American World'. In R. B. Freeman, P. F. Boxall, and P. Haynes (eds) (2007), *What Workers Say: Employee Voice in the Anglo-American Workplace*. Ithaca, NY: Cornell University Press, 206–20.

Bryson, A. (2004) 'Managerial Responsiveness to Union and Nonunion Worker Voice in Britain'. *Industrial Relations: A Journal of Economy and Society*, 43(1), 213–41.

Bryson, A. and Freeman, R. (2007) 'What Voice Do British Workers Want?' In R. Freeman, P. Boxall, and P. Haynes (eds), *What Workers Say: Employee Voice in the Anglo-American Workplace*, pp. 72–96. Ithaca, NY: Cornell University Press.

Bryson, A., Charlwood, A., and Forth, J. (2006) 'Worker Voice, Managerial Response and Labour Productivity: An Empirical Investigation'. *Industrial Relations Journal*, 37(5), 438–55.

Budd, J. W. (2004) *Employment with a Human Face: Balancing Efficiency, Equity, and Voice*. Ithaca, NY: Cornell University Press.

Butler, P., Glover, L., and Tregaskis, O. (2011) '"When the Going Gets Tough"...: Recession and the Resilience of Workplace Partnership'. *British Journal of Industrial Relations*, 49(4), 666–87.

Charlwood, A. and Terry, M. (2007) '21st-Century Models of Employee Representation: Structures, Processes and Outcomes'. *Industrial Relations Journal*, 38(4), 320–37.

Colling, T. and Terry, M. (2010) *Work, the Employment Relationship and the Field of Industrial Relations*. Chichester: Wiley.

Cooke, W. N. (1990) *Labor-Management Cooperation: New Partnerships or Going in Circles?* Kalamazoo, MI: Upjohn Press.

Danford, A., Richardson, M., Stewart, P., Tailby, S., and Upchurch, M. (2005) 'Workplace Partnership and Employee Voice in the UK: Comparative Case Studies of Union Strategy and Worker Experience'. *Economic and Industrial Democracy*, 26(4), 593–620.

Edwards, P. (2003) 'The Employment Relationship and the Field of Industrial Relations'. *Industrial Relations: Theory and Practice*, 2, 1–36. Oxford: Blackwell.

Francis, H. and Keegan, A. (2006) 'The Changing Face of HRM: In Search of Balance'. *Human Resource Management Journal,* 16(3), 231–49.

Freeman, R. and Medoff, J. (1984) *What Do Unions Do?* New York: Basic Books.

Gall, G. (2005) 'Union Organising in the New Economy in Britain'. *Employee Relations,* 27(2), 208–25.

Godard, J. (2014) 'The Psychologisation of Employment Relations?' *Human Resource Management Journal,* 24(1), 1–18.

Guest, D. E. and Peccei, R. (2001) 'Partnership at Work: Mutuality and the Balance of Advantage'. *British Journal of Industrial Relations,* 39(2), 207–36.

Harrison, D., Roy, M., and Haines III, V. (2011) 'Union Representatives in Labour–Management Partnerships: Roles and Identities in Flux'. *British Journal of Industrial Relations,* 49(3), 411–35.

Heery, E. (2002) 'Partnership versus Organising: Alternative Futures for British Trade Unionism'. *Industrial Relations Journal,* 33(1), 20–35.

Heery, E. and Simms, M. (2008) 'Constrains on Union Organising in the United Kingdom'. *Industrial Relations Journal,* 39(10), 24–42.

Heery, E. and Simms, M. (2010) 'Employer Responses to Union Organising: Patterns and Effects'. *Human Resource Management Journal,* 20(1), 3–22.

Heery, E., Simms, R., Delbridge, R., Salmon, J., and Simpson, D. (2000) 'Union Organising in Britain: A Survey of Policy and Practice'. *International Journal of Human Resource Management,* 11(5), 986–1007.

Howell, C. (1999) 'Unforgiven: British Trade Unionism in Crisis'. In G. Ross and A. Martin (eds), *The Brave New World of Labor: European Trade Unions at the Millennium,* pp. 26–74. New York: Berghahn.

Howell, C. (2005) *Trade Unions and the State.* Princeton, NJ: Princeton University Press.

Huzzard, T., Gregory, D., and Scott, R. (eds) (2004) *Strategic Unionism and Partnership: Boxing or Dancing?* Basingstoke: Palgrave Macmillan.

Johnstone, S. and Ackers, P. (2014) 'Partnership at Work and Mutual Gains'. In D. Guest and D. Needle (eds), *Wiley Encyclopedia of Management.* Chichester: Wiley.

Johnstone, S., Ackers, P., and Wilkinson, A. (2009) 'The British Partnership Phenomenon: A Ten Year Review'. *Human Resource Management Journal,* 19(3), 260–79.

Johnstone, S., Ackers, P., and Wilkinson, A. (2010a). 'Better than Nothing? Is Non-Union Partnership a Contradiction in Terms?' *Journal of Industrial Relations,* 52(2), 151–68.

Johnstone, S., Wilkinson, A., and Ackers, P. (2010b) 'Critical Incidents of Partnership: Five Years' Experience at NatBank'. *Industrial Relations Journal,* 41(4), 382–98.

Johnstone, S., Wilkinson, A., and Ackers, P. (2011) 'Applying Budd's Model to Partnership'. *Economic and Industrial Democracy,* 32(2), 307–28.

Kelly, J. (1996) 'Union Militancy and Social Partnership'. In P. Ackers, C. Smith, and P. Smith (eds), *The New Workplace and Trade Unionism,* pp. 77–109. London: Routledge.

Kelly, J. (1998) *Rethinking Industrial Relations: Mobilisation, Collectivism and Long Waves.* London: Routledge.

Kelly, J. (2004) 'Social Partnership Agreements in Britain: Labor Cooperation and Compliance'. *Industrial Relations: A Journal of Economy and Society*, 43(1), 267–92.

Kersley, B., Alpin, C., Forth, J., Bryson, A., Bewley, H., Dix, G., and Oxenbridge, S. (2006) *Inside the Workplace: Findings from the 2004 Workplace Employment Relations Survey*. London: Routledge.

Kochan, T. A. and Osterman, P. (1994) *The Mutual Gains Enterprise: Forging a Winning Partnership among Labor, Management, and Government*. Boston, MA: Harvard Business Press.

Kochan, T. A., Katz, H., and McKersie, R. (1986) *The Transformation of American Industrial Relations*. Ithaca, NY: Cornell University Press.

McCarthy, W. E. J. (1967) *The Role of Shop Stewards in British Industrial Relations*, Royal Commission on Trade Unions and Employers' Associations Research Paper No. 1. London: HMSO.

MacLeod, D. and Clarke, N. (2009) *Engaging for Success*. London: Department for Business, Innovation and Skills.

Martínez Lucio, M. and Stuart, M. (2002) 'Assessing Partnership: The Prospects for, and Challenges of, Modernisation'. *Employee Relations*, 24(3), 252–61.

Metcalf, D. (2005) *British Unions: Resurgence or Perdition?* London: Centre for Economic Performance.

Millward N., Bryson A., and Forth, J. (2000) *All Change at Work: British Employment Relations 1980–1998 as Portrayed by the Workplace Industrial Relations Survey Series*. London: Routledge.

Monks, J. (1997) 'Press Conference'. In *Monks Looks Forward to Constructive Congress*, Local Government Chronicle. [Online.] Available at: <http://www.lgcplus.com/monks-looks-forward-to-constructive-congress/1491168.article>, accessed 20 August 2014.

Oxenbridge, S. and Brown, W. (2004) Achieving a New Equilibrium? The Stability of Cooperative Employer–Union Relationships. *Industrial Relations Journal*, 35(5), 388–402.

Podro, S. (2010) *Riding out the Storm: Managing Conflict in a Recession and Beyond*. ACAS Policy Discussion Papers. London: ACAS. [Online.] Available at: <http://www.acas.org.uk/media/pdf/9/6/pdp-riding-out-the-storm-accessible-version-July-2011.pdf>, accessed 20 August 2014.

Purcell, J. and Georgiadis, G. (2007) 'Why Should Employment Bother with Employee Voice?' In R. Freeman, P. Boxall, and P. Haynes (eds), *What Workers Say: Employee Voice in the Anglo-American Workplace*, pp. 181–97. Ithaca, NY: Cornell University Press.

Samuel, P. and Bacon, N. (2010) 'The Contents of British Partnership Agreements in Britain 1990–2007', *Work, Employment and Society*, 24(30), 430–48.

Simms, M., Holgate, J., and Heery, M. (2013) Union Voices: Tensions in UK Organising. Ithaca, NY: ILR/Cornell Paperbacks.

Terry, M. (2003) 'Can "Partnership" Reverse the Decline of British Trade Unions?' *Work, Employment and Society*, 17(3), 459–472.

Thompson, P. (2003) 'Disconnected Capitalism: Or Why Employers Can't Keep Their Side of the Bargain'. *Work, Employment and Society*, 17(2), 359–78.

Thompson, P. (2011) 'The Trouble with HRM'. *Human Resource Management Journal*, 21(4), 355–67.

Upchurch, M., Danford, A., Tailby, S., and Richardson, M. (2008) *The Realities of Partnership at Work*. Basingstoke: Palgrave Macmillan.

van Wanrooy, B. Bewley, H., Bryson, A., and Forth, J. (2013) *Employment Relations in the Shadow of Recession*. Basingstoke: Palgrave Macmillan.

Whyman, P. B. and Petrescu, A. I. (2013) 'Partnership, Flexible Workplace Practices and the Realisation of Mutual Gains: Evidence from the British WERS 2004 Dataset'. *International Journal of Human Resource Management*, 1–23.

Willman, P., Bryson, A., and Gomez, R. (2007) 'The Long Goodbye: New Establishments and the Fall of Union Voice in Britain'. *International Journal of Human Resource Management*, 18(7), 1318–34.

Part 3

European Models and Varieties of Capitalism

Social partnership in devolved nations

Scotland and Wales

Peter Samuel[†] and Nick Bacon

Introduction

A growing body of literature on the 'varieties of capitalism' has developed over the last twenty years or so (see, for example, Dore 1987; Hall and Soskice 2001). This literature has drawn attention to important and persistent differences in the industrial relations and voice systems of advanced industrial economies. Perhaps the best known distinction is between 'coordinated market economies' (Germany or the Scandinavian countries, for example) and 'liberal market economies' (mostly the Anglo-Saxon systems) (Soskice 1989, 1998). The industrial relations systems of coordinated market economies are characterized by long-standing national-level institutions which bring together the social partners (the state, employers, and unions) to discuss economic and social affairs, arrangements that are often labelled as neocorporatist approaches. In addition, national legislation in such countries may also provide opportunities for trade unions to have a say in organizational decision making through representation in works councils at the establishment level and in some countries through employee directors at the corporate level. The result is usually greater cooperation and less conflict in the industrial relations system. In contrast, the industrial relations and voice systems of liberal market economies lack long-standing national-level institutions for social partners to discuss economic and social issues. Legislation in these countries does not provide equivalent levels of support for trade unions to play a role in organizational decision making at the establishment or corporate levels. The result is unilateral employer decision making in most organizations and usually greater adversarialism and conflict in the industrial relations system where unions are able to gain a foothold.

The advantage of regarding industrial relations systems as embedded in different varieties of capitalism is that it helps to explain the continuity and persistence of key industrial relations institutions and outcomes over time. Differences between liberal market economies and coordinated market economies persist in a number of respects, including the range of establishments and the type of issues covered by collective bargaining, the legislation that regulates industrial relations activity, and the degree of industrial relations conflict (such as the incidence of strikes). National industrial relations systems from this perspective therefore appear relatively fixed and unchanging, suggesting they are appropriately described as path dependent, reflecting the historical and political circumstances of nations, and to a degree also reflecting the strategic choices made by key actors in response to important historic events. The disadvantage of the varieties of capitalism approach is that industrial relations systems can be viewed as 'static so that it is difficult to grasp changes taking place internally to each model, the tensions within them and the mechanisms that may upset their equilibrium and give rise to institutional change' (Regini 2003: 253). Although it is helpful to explain continuity by reference to the institutional constraints which minimize changes from developing in industrial relations systems, innovation may be required to improve national economic performance and it may therefore also be helpful to understand the mechanisms that may encourage and support change (Gospel and Pendleton 2003: 571–5). As we shall explain in this chapter, important historic and political events provide opportunities for innovations intended to improve industrial relations systems.

This limitation in the varieties of capitalism approach—the emphasis on continuity rather than change—has appeared particularly problematic in the recent past because an important feature of the 1990s was the emergence of important innovations and experiments in industrial relations and voice systems in liberal market economies. Many countries without a tradition of long-standing national-level institutions for bringing together the social partners to discuss economic and social affairs (a process termed social dialogue), perhaps surprisingly, found it necessary to develop new institutions to encourage social dialogue in order to improve economic performance. In many EU countries this involved developing social pacts—national-level agreements between the state, employers, and unions to adjust wage setting, the labour market, and welfare policies (Avdagic et al. 2011: 3). These arrangements emerged during the 1990s in countries such as Ireland, Italy, Portugal, and Spain which lacked traditional neocorporatist institutions to negotiate reforms necessary for economic adjustment to meet the required fiscal convergence for EU monetary union.

In other countries less emphasis was placed on a national-level approach although changes to industrial relations also appeared necessary to improve economic performance. In order to improve industrial relations, governments in several countries encouraged employers and unions at the enterprise or establishment level to work together to introduce the changes required to improve organizational performance. This often led to voluntary labour–management partnership/mutual gains arrangements—collective agreements which are developed at enterprise or establishment level—to encourage union cooperation with initiatives to improve organizational performance, in return for which managers offer unions an enhanced role in organizational decision making (Kochan and Osterman 1994; Kelly 2004). Labour–management partnership arrangements emerged in many liberal market economies, such as the USA, UK, Ireland, Canada, Australia, New Zealand, and even South Korea, despite their seemingly inhospitable institutional contexts for union involvement in organizational decision making. Several countries developed unique combinations of approaches, for example, Ireland developed social pacts at national level and later encouraged labour–management partnership at enterprise level, and the Netherlands developed social pacts overlaying a more developed system of works councils at the enterprise level.

A further important development in some liberal market countries has been the emergence of higher-level social partnership in specific parts of the public sector at the sector, regional, or national levels. Social partnership is closer to social pacts, as described above, in the respect that it involves tripartite meetings between the state, employers, and unions, in contrast to the bipartite meetings involved in labour–management partnership. It differs, however, in that social pacts involve representatives of all employers and trade unions reaching a potentially one-off agreement covering a broad range of labour market and social policies. Social partnership in contrast is a continuous process of consultation of narrower scope which is focused on the important issues affecting a particular part of the public sector such as health, education, or the civil service, for example. With this sharper focus it involves only the relevant government department, employers, and unions representing the specific employees affected. Such focus may offer unions increased access to the relevant government decision makers and arguably an appropriate role in government policy making to represent their members. This contrasts with the broader issues discussed in social pacts or the lack of access to government involved in labour–management partnership at enterprise level. Governments and employers may also benefit from social partnership where it involves specific commitments by unions to cooperate with sharply defined initiatives to improve a public service (Work Foundation 2004; Cabinet Office 2009). Partnership arrangements of different types in the public sector emerged from the 1990s onwards as governments in several countries sought to increase union cooperation with plans to reform public services, perhaps most notably in Britain, Ireland, the USA, and New Zealand (Bach 2002; Masters et al. 2006; Doherty and Erne 2010; O'Donnell et al. 2011). In Britain, for example, social partnership became an important feature of public sector industrial relations covering approximately one third of public sector employees by 2007 (Bacon and Samuel 2009), with social partnership in the National Health Service (NHS) alone bringing together government, NHS employers and trade unions representing approximately 1.5 million employees. Both social pacts and labour–management partnership have been extensively studied, and the proportion of the labour force covered by social partnership and their intrinsic potential suggests it is important in the years ahead to understand these distinct arrangements.

An important feature of the emergence of social partnership in the public sector recently has been an apparent connection to changes in national sovereignty and the desire for increased political independence. One way to understand why such different approaches (social pacts, labour management partnership, and social partnership) have emerged is to regard social pacts as national responses to EU political and economic integration. This was required in countries seeking to meet the exacting requirements for fiscal convergence for economic and monetary union. Meeting these challenges appeared to require national coordinated action involving representatives from across the economy, usually because governments did not appear sufficiently strong themselves to force through the changes required unilaterally. However, an important counter-trend to the requirements for European convergence in the last twenty-five years are the shifts in several nation states towards the devolution of political power and responsibilities to subnational, regional, and area levels (Andrews and Martin 2010). This trend appears in several debates within the EU, not least the concept of subsidiarity enshrined in Article 5 of the Treaty on European Union whereby decisions should be made as close as possible to the national, regional, or local levels. It also reflects the rise of nationalist and regionalist movements seeking greater autonomy or self-determination at the regional level, examples including Flanders and Wallonia in Belgium, Catalonia and Basque nationalism in Spain, and the Northern League in Italy. Such changes may constitute important sources of innovation in industrial relations systems and may encourage social partnership within the regions of existing nation states, not least because regional governments, employers, and unions may perceive they share common interests.

The questions of national sovereignty and political independence raised by subsidiarity and nationalist/regionalist movements are interesting from an industrial relations perspective because, if successful, such demands may lead to unique historical opportunities to re-evaluate and modify the industrial relations institutions inherited from the national industrial relations system, or to construct new institutions. In particular, the creation of smaller states or autonomous regions may bring together locally based political parties, employers, and trade unions into more frequent interaction and provide the potential for social partnership to emerge if shared interests and a common cause are perceived to have developed. Arguably, a national/regional focus and the creation of small nation states are conducive for developing social partnership along the lines of the small nation Scandinavian models. This links to a wider argument that partnership works better in small cohesive countries as part of a broader social democratic approach (Judt 2010). To the extent that the politics of European integration-subsidiarity shifts towards national sovereignty and political independence, such changes may have important implications for industrial relations across Europe.

This chapter provides an initial exploration of some of these themes, focusing on the potential for social partnership to develop in countries reconsidering questions of national sovereignty and political independence. In particular, we illustrate these issues by drawing on an analysis of social partnership arrangements in the public sector which emerged in Scotland and Wales following political devolution in Britain. We focus on social partnership in the NHS—one of the largest employers in the world. The chapter provides details on the nature and scope of employee voice and participation in decision making in over fifty national-level social partnership meetings which we observed over a decade. The next section describes how social partnership operated in each of these countries following devolution, before considering the potential and future of innovative social partnership arrangements.

Political devolution and social partnership

Issues of national sovereignty and political independence have continued to occupy political parties and the electorate in Britain for the past forty years, as they have in many other European countries. Although it is readily observed that Britain at times appears to be a reluctant member of the EU, perhaps more unnoticed across Europe (until recent debates on the implications of Scottish independence) have been the internal challenges to British sovereignty and reactions against the perceived dominance of England and the government from Westminster. Britain's historic devolution settlement in 1998 represented the recent high point of these challenges to date, with Westminster acceding to pressure from nationalist and secessionist movements for greater autonomy and local accountability by establishing new governments for Scotland, Wales, and Northern Ireland. Such radical constitutional change may be expected, over time, to have significant consequences for the institutional structure, actors, and processes of industrial relations. The most immediate changes have emerged in the public sector over which devolved governments have direct impact as employers, and specifically the nationalized health service (the NHS), where devolved governments in Scotland and Wales gained significant legislative powers and embarked on a social partnership approach to improve industrial relations and health service performance.

The social partnership arrangements that emerged in the NHS are important because it is difficult to overestimate the political significance of health services for the devolved Scottish and Welsh Assembly Governments, not least in Wales because a prominent Welsh Labour politician (Nye Bevan) was pivotal in creating the NHS post-Second World War, and in Scotland because some of its regions are among those with the lowest life expectancy in Britain. NHS performance and hospital waiting lists are constantly scrutinized, with keen attention paid to the impact of government decisions on the health of more than 5 million people in Scotland and 3 million people in Wales. The economic and fiscal importance of the NHS for the devolved governments is also significant with health expenditure constituting the largest component of devolved government budgets (over 40 per cent of their total budgets). The NHS is also the largest employer in both countries, with NHS Scotland employing around 132,000 staff and NHS Wales employing 71,817 staff. The respective health ministers in the Scottish and Welsh Assembly Governments are high-profile politicians and their decisions have significant electoral consequences.

The NHS inherited by the devolved governments was organized along similar quasi-market lines across Britain prior to devolution in 1998. This involved an internal market with district health authorities purchasing services from competing NHS Trusts (the main employers) who provided health care. Devolution, however, launched NHS Scotland and NHS Wales on divergent trajectories from the quasi-market system inherited to create distinct NHS systems within the UK tailored to meet the needs of their populations (Keating 2005: 460; Greer 2008, 2009). Most authors describe NHS Scotland's approach as reintegrating coordinated services and working in partnership with medical professionals (Blackman et al. 2009: 762–3), and NHS Wales as focusing on public health, localism, and reducing health inequalities (Greer 2008: 125), in contrast to the continued focus on quasi-markets and 'managerialism' in the NHS in England (Greer 2009: 78–9; see also Donnelly 2010: 164).

Prior to devolution, industrial relations in the NHS had come to reflect features of the internal market with NHS Trusts continuing to experiment with local bargaining over some aspects of terms and conditions, and outsourcing the activities and staff which employers regarded as non-essential such as catering, cleaning, and security. Successive Westminster governments had provided the private sector with a greater role in providing and financing health services. Trade unions in the NHS had opposed all of these developments as undermining their members' terms and conditions, potentially harmful to the quality of patient care and part of a process of gradual privatization. NHS unions in both Scotland and Wales felt largely excluded from policy discussions during eighteen years of Conservative Government in Westminster (1979–97) given such disagreements, with such feelings exacerbated by their geographical distance from Westminster. Unions could not penetrate policy-making circles, industrial relations had become 'strained' in each country, and structures for consultation and negotiation appeared 'moribund and outdated'. Unions in

NHS Wales, for example, reported the All Wales Joint Consultative Committee had 'just ceased to function' because NHS Trusts preferred to negotiate local terms and conditions where possible. The industrial relations climate in NHS Scotland was described as 'one of conflict and confrontation', with a lack of regular consultation on key decisions leading to a high level of grievances and disputes (Scottish Executive 2005; UNISON 2010).

Against this background, NHS Scotland and NHS Wales, following devolution in 1998, developed social partnership arrangements to support their aspirations to improve industrial relations (Bacon and Samuel 2009). These arrangements emerged from discussions in preparation for devolution. Social partnership appeared attractive to the new governments because it provided an opportunity to engage in an inclusive manner with local policy communities and helped to satisfy local electorate demands for greater accountability, including demands from local union representatives for increased policy influence. Demonstrating accountability to local stakeholders also helped to build the democratic legitimacy of devolved institutions. However, as the next section reports, the nature and scope of employee voice and participation differed between the social partnership meetings we observed in Scotland and Wales.

Comparing social partnership structures and operation

Over the following decade we observed the extent to which social partnership in NHS Scotland and NHS Wales provided for employee voice and participation, examined the scope of issues covered, and explored whether partnership encouraged joint problem solving and helped to overcome adversarialism. Throughout this process we identified the main factors that explained similarities and differences in the social partnership process and will share these lessons after first describing how social partnership operated.

SOCIAL PARTNERSHIP STRUCTURES

NHS Scotland and NHS Wales both initially decided to implement partnership top-down, establishing social partnership structures initially at national level, providing for tripartite consultation between the devolved government, NHS employers, and trade unions. The Scottish Partnership Forum (SPF) met for the first time in October 1998 and the Welsh Partnership Forum (WPF) met for the first time in 2001. Reflecting the procedural emphasis in British partnership agreements of different types (Samuel and Bacon 2010), the agreements established forums for debate and potentially for increased union participation in decision making, but employers did not at the outset offer substantive commitments on employment security or assurances about terms and conditions in return for trade union cooperation.

The initial aims and membership of the SPF and the WPF were broadly comparable on paper. The SPF involved the parties 'sitting around a table rather than across the table' for the first time in thirteen years, with a remit to 'work together to improve health services for the people of Scotland'. It had broad aims to 'inform thinking around national priorities on health issues; inform and test delivery and implementation plans in relation to national strategies; advise on workforce planning and development' (Scottish Executive 2005). The WPF constitution describes itself as 'the forum where the Welsh Assembly Government, NHS Wales employers and trade unions and professional organisations work together to improve health services for the people of Wales . . . key stakeholders can engage with key policy leads from across the Welsh Assembly Government to inform thinking around national priorities on health issues' (Welsh Partnership Forum 2008).

Both forums involve large meetings—the SPF provides forty-two seats for fourteen representatives from government, employers, and unions, and the WPF provides forty-eight seats for sixteen representatives from government, employers, and unions. Holding approximately four full meetings each year, the SPF met forty-seven times between 1999 and 2011, and the WPF met thirty-three times between September 2004 and 2011. Although both sets of meetings were jointly chaired by the lead union representative, an important difference was the degree to which the devolved governments were directly involved and appeared to rely on seeking cooperation with unions to achieve policy objectives. The Scottish Government was more directly involved in the SPF, indicated by the joint-chair role of NHS Scotland's Chief Executive (or a nominee if unavailable). In contrast, the Welsh Assembly Government was less directly involved in the WPF, which was chaired by the lead NHS employers' representative. This difference suggests the SPF provided a venue for dialogue between the Scottish Government and trade unions, whereas the WPF provided a venue for dialogue between NHS employers in Wales and trade unions in the presence of Welsh Assembly Government representatives. The NHS Wales Chief Executive and the Chief Medical Officer did not attend the WPF, and the British Medical Association (BMA, the powerful professional association representing doctors) in Wales stopped attending after the first few meetings. This contrasts with attendance at the SPF by the Chief Executive and the Chief Medical Officer of NHS Scotland, and the BMA in Scotland, indicating the importance of social partnership for delivering improvements to the service.

SOCIAL PARTNERSHIP IN OPERATION: VOICE, SCOPE, AND PROCESS

Reflecting the arrangements for chairing meetings described above, in SPF meetings (1999–2011) speakers from the Scottish Government Health Department (SGHD) accounted for almost 60 per cent of the debate, staff-side representatives for almost 30 per cent, and employers the remaining 10 per cent. In WPF meetings (2004–11), government representatives accounted for 42 per cent of debates, staff-side representatives for 42 per cent, and employers the remaining 16 per cent. The Scottish Government was therefore noticeably more involved in social partnership debates.

Considering the opportunities for voice provided also raises the question as to which issues are actually discussed that unions may influence—the scope of social partnership. The scope of social partnership is assessed by the attention paid to each of a range of issues calculated as the proportion of the overall meeting. The scope of issues discussed differed noticeably between the SPF and the WPF. The SPF concentrated on strategic issues and provided opportunities for union input into these issues. Three quarters of all SPF debates covered 'big ticket' issues—health policy (21 per cent), health service governance (20 per cent), modernization (21 per cent), and finance (13 per cent). In contrast, the WPF concentrated on workforce issues. Only one third of WPF debates addressed health policy (3 per cent), modernization (21 per cent), and finance (9 per cent). Health service governance was not discussed in the WPF.

The WPF's focus on workforce issues included ongoing and contentious debates on workforce planning, accounting for more than one fifth (22 per cent) of debate in the WPF compared to only 7 per cent of SPF debates. This involved unions in NHS Wales continually challenging workforce plans in the WPF and seeking to defend their members from proposed organizational restructuring. This reflected concerns about employment security, a key aspiration for most unions when seeking partnership arrangements which they are rarely able to realize. This issue was largely resolved in the SPF's first substantive discussions which produced an organizational change policy in 1999 applying across the service in advance of reconfiguring NHS Trusts. This policy required all NHS Scotland employers to 'seek to avoid compulsory redundancy' with a 'no detriment' clause protecting the terms and conditions of staff redeployed into new roles (including senior managers who also benefited from this protection). As a result, workforce numbers and organizational change were much less contentious issues in NHS Scotland.

Thus far we have considered the scope of social partnership in national-level meetings. Both meetings had a keen interest in developing partnership at lower organizational levels, although the depth of social partnership differed between the cases. Debates on health service governance in the SPF encompassed the broader role of unions and professional associations in the governance of NHS boards in Scotland (the local employers in NHS Scotland that replaced NHS Trusts). The Scottish Government passed legislation requiring each NHS board to develop Area Partnership Forums (APFs) to provide for local union input into enterprise-level decisions. According to the Scottish Government, APFs 'must be fully involved in the development of Local Health Plans' and in implementing the national policies developed in the SPF. In order to facilitate these aims, a union representative from the SPF and from the local APF were directly involved in assessing the performance of NHS boards during the Cabinet Secretary for Health's annual review of each NHS board. The Cabinet Secretary also appoints the chair of each NHS board's own multi-union committee to serve as an employee director (a non-executive director) on each NHS board (Scottish Executive 2001: 22). As these details suggest, social partnership in NHS Scotland has created the types of institutionalized roles for union voice (codetermination at national and establishment levels supported by employee directors) that are more commonly associated with coordinated market economies. In contrast, social partnership did not run as deep in NHS Wales. Local partnership forums in Welsh NHS Trusts had limited roles in policy making, differing little from the consultative committees before devolution. Unions rejected the initial suggestion to develop employee directors, although some trade union representatives attended NHS board meetings in Wales. As a result of these factors, health unions in Wales are not institutionally embedded at enterprise level to the same degree as in Scotland.

All of these differences contributed towards marked variation in the amount of joint problem solving and cooperation at national level. Although debates in both the SPF and the WPF generally started in a similar manner with government policy leads introducing an agenda item for debate, the response to the presentation was markedly different in each forum. The Scottish Government generally anticipated a warm reception and presented background thinking around early-stage policy development in order to seek partnership input. Unions and employer representatives generally responded positively, expressing support for the overall direction and nominating representatives to join working groups taking the policies forward. Policies in development returned several times for further comment and to build commitment to the key decisions taken. Almost seven in ten union contributions to SPF meetings involved a positive contribution towards joint problem solving.

In contrast, in WPF debates the Welsh Assembly Government representatives anticipated a critical union response when they presented policies at late stages of development. Almost six in ten union contributions to WPF meetings involved criticism of the Welsh Assembly Government or NHS employers. Trade union representatives criticized the lack of partnership involvement in developing policy and the assumptions underlying many proposals. When union representatives in the WPF sought to debate 'big ticket' issues the Welsh Assembly Government and employers' representatives blocked debate, arguing such matters were ministerial preserves and outside the purpose of the forum, which they regarded as to concentrate on workforce issues. Cooperation was greater in the SPF than the WPF on both 'big ticket' issues and workforce policies, highlighting the wide-ranging consensus that developed in NHS Scotland after devolution.

Discussion: explaining the types of social partnership

The findings highlight a distinction between two types of social partnership with differences in the extent to which the state relies on joint working with trade unions to develop and deliver key policies. These differences are best explained by the political factors that shaped national sovereignty and political independence, with the politics of Scottish and Welsh devolution differing in important respects. Differences in the democratic mandates for these new devolved governments affected the trajectories of social partnership. The Scottish electorate had expressed a stronger desire for devolution than the Welsh electorate—74.3 per cent of Scottish voters supported devolution in a referendum, compared to 50.3 per cent in Wales. Such considerations resulted in the Scottish Government being acceded greater legislative powers than the Welsh Assembly Government. The Scotland Act 1998 invested powers to the Scottish parliament to pass primary and secondary legislation on health matters. In contrast, the Government of Wales Act 1998 invested powers to the National Assembly for Wales to pass only secondary health legislation. The Scottish Government intended to use these primary health legislation powers and the SPF provided a venue and focus for the social partners to work together in developing the National Health Service Reform (Scotland) Act 2004, which discarded the purchaser/provider split, dismantled the internal NHS market, and abolished NHS Trusts in Scotland. Subsequent Scottish Governments continued to exclude the private sector from the NHS. Dismantling the internal market established a consensus to encourage the social partners to work together and introduce standard terms and conditions of employment across NHS Scotland, and to bring back in-house outsourced activities and staff in areas such as catering, security, and cleaning.

In contrast, the Welsh Assembly Government's limited devolved powers required the retention of the internal NHS market. This restricted the scope of the WPF and protected the decision-making autonomy of NHS Trusts in Wales, including developing some local terms and conditions. Limited national sovereignty and political independence in Wales restricted the scope for social partnership to debates on the employer's terms, which unions criticized in WPF meetings. Cooperation remained limited until the Welsh Assembly Government gained enhanced legislative powers in the National Health Service (Wales) Act 2006 and the Labour–Plaid Cymru Coalition Government developed plans to dismantle the internal health market. Cooperation in the WPF subsequently increased to develop all-Wales workforce policies. The WPF produced an organizational change policy for NHS Wales in 2009 as plans accelerated to end the internal market and dissolve NHS Trusts. Formal appointments of trade union representatives as independent board members to local health boards in Wales also followed the 2009 reforms to increase stakeholder engagement. As a result of these changes, cooperation gradually increased in the WPF, although as we finished our observations it had not yet reached the levels of cooperation achieved by the SPF.

Conclusions: social partnership, national sovereignty, and political independence

This chapter has provided an initial exploration of the potential for social partnership as it has developed in two countries, reconsidering questions of national sovereignty and political independence. Social partnership arrangements represent notable attempts to develop innovative industrial relations and voice systems within liberal market economies to be considered alongside studies of social pacts and labour–management partnership. In particular, the chapter analysed the most notable social partnership arrangements which emerged in Scotland and Wales following political devolution in Britain. The findings highlighted differences in the types of arrangements that developed in terms of the scope and depth of union voice. These differences reflected variation in the extent to which the devolved governments relied on joint working and cooperation with trade unions to develop and deliver key policies. Such variation was explained by the political factors that shaped the journey to national sovereignty and political independence which had resulted in different legislative powers. The politics of Scottish and Welsh devolution differed in important respects with issues of national sovereignty and political independence producing different pathways for social partnership, with distinct industrial relations and voice implications.

The social partnership arrangements described here which developed in Britain emerged following political devolution and reflected the impact of the desire for national sovereignty and political independence. These dynamics contrast with the social pacts developed in response to increased economic and monetary union in the EU. Both types of historic and political events—increased independence and interdependence—provided new opportunities for change in industrial relations systems. Debates surrounding national sovereignty and political independence versus economic and political integration thus appear to provide unique historical opportunities to re-evaluate and change industrial relations institutions. In particular, the creation of smaller states or autonomous regions may bring together locally based political parties, employers, and trade unions into more frequent interaction and provide the potential for social partnership to emerge if shared interests and a common cause are perceived to have developed. As the cases of social partnership in Scotland and Wales suggest, a national/regional focus and the creation of small states are conducive for developing social partnership along the lines of the small-nation Scandinavian models. In the cases presented, social partnership also formed part of a social democratic approach in regions without established institutions for tripartite dialogue between the social partners.

These observations invite further reflection on the politics of EU integration-subsidiarity and the implications for industrial relations in Europe. In response to the financial crisis, EU political leaders have developed plans for closer fiscal integration. However, electorates in several countries have responded by questioning the desirability of closer political and economic integration in favour of greater subsidiarity and the devolution of political power and responsibilities to subnational, regional, and area levels. The rise of nationalist and regionalist movements seeking greater autonomy and local decision making may constitute important sources of innovation in industrial relations and voice systems, as suggested by the emergence of social partnership.

The industrial relations impact of the desire for national sovereignty and political independence on voice and participation, however, appears contingent upon two further political factors—devolved powers and partisan politics/electorate preferences—both of which may also limit the prospects for social partnership. On the first issue, the scope of national sovereignty matters with political independence and extensive legislative powers for new governments appearing more permissive of strategic choice to engage in radical industrial relations experimentation and potential transformation. In contrast, restricted sovereignty appears to limit the scope for encouraging greater representative voice and participation in policy development. Developments in Wales following political devolution, however, suggest that restricted sovereignty is a temporary solution to increased demands for political independence and voice. Further demands for enhanced voice in the policy-making process and changes to the industrial relations system are likely to follow.

The feasibility of devolved power and the scope for working with social partners is closely intertwined with broader economic considerations. Unless the broader economic context makes social partnership affordable even governments gaining greater political independence may find they cannot deliver the improvements required by social partners. The social partnership arrangements described in this chapter developed in the NHS during a period of economic growth and significantly increased public sector spending on health. Even during this period, social partnership did not develop in many other parts of the public sector following devolution that did not receive such generous public funding. Downward pressure on costs continued to generate adversarial and decentralized industrial relations in areas such as local government, for example, where any forms of partnership appear unlikely to develop. Public sector expenditure restrictions since 2008 appear to further limit the prospects for social partnership and social democratic levels of state expenditure, with all forms of cooperative industrial relations tested in more demanding circumstances. Such calculations concerning the affordability of a social democratic approach and high levels of public sector expenditure featured prominently in the vote against Scottish independence in September 2014. Although social partnership in Britain's devolved health systems has survived the long-term future of this approach is also likely to depend on delivering continued improvements in health service performance within a context of declining real-terms expenditure.

Second, party politics and electorate preferences matter for the nature of reforms to industrial relations systems during periods of increasing national sovereignty and political independence. Social partnership requires a social democratic political agenda which is shared by devolved governments, public sector trade unions and the electorate. Both Scottish and Welsh electorates share a natural affinity with the welfare state and produce governments to the left supportive of developing social partnership with unions. In the cases described, this resulted in enhanced employee voice in the industrial relations system and an imaginative and constructive role for unions in the post-independence state. Unions may rationally seek to align themselves with sovereign governments to pursue a progressive political agenda in such circumstances.

The importance of party politics and electorate preferences for reforms to industrial relations systems involves some dangers for trade unions and labour interests during periods of increasing national sovereignty and political independence. There is nothing inherently left wing about national sovereignty and political independence per se. Right-wing political parties also seek greater subsidiarity or withdrawal from the EU in order to reverse key features of the European Social Charter such as labour rights, full employment, social protection, and anti-discrimination measures. Other secessionist movements seek to restrict immigration or wealth redistribution to less economically developed areas. It also should not be assumed that trade unions are always on the progressive side of these debates. Electorates that pull governments to the right as further national sovereignty and political independence develop may encourage reforms against trade unions and labour interests, with such considerations pertinent to Britain given much recent progressive labour legislation in Britain originating from EU integration. An important unintended consequence of Scottish and Welsh devolution is that Westminster governments are increasingly accountable to the English electorate which is to the right, favours greater subsidiarity from the EU, and may lead to the roll-back of key features of the European Social Charter implemented into British law. Political devolution for Scotland and Wales may ultimately restrict the prospects for electing Social Democratic Governments in Westminster, with negative implications for social partnership in England.

More broadly, the impact of national sovereignty continues to develop in debates over EU integration-subsidiarity for several nation states. Inevitably, such debates include consideration of the feasibility and limits of sovereignty in an interconnected global economic and political system. The ongoing economic and financial crisis in Europe continues to raise questions concerning the devolution or integration of economic and political power in the years ahead with unknown consequences for industrial relations systems. Successful or partial resolution of these matters appears likely to affect the European project and industrial relations across the continent, we encourage industrial relations scholars to join this debate.

▓ REFERENCES

Andrews, R. and Martin, S. (2010) 'Regional Variations in Public Service Outcomes: The Impact of Policy Divergence in England, Scotland and Wales'. *Regional Studies*, 44(8), 919–34.

Avdagic, S., Rhodes, M., and Visser, J. (2011) *Social Pacts in Europe*. Oxford: Oxford University Press.

Bach, S. (2002) 'Annual Review Paper 2001: Public-Sector Employment Relations Reform under Labour: Muddling through on Modernization?' *British Journal of Industrial Relations*, 40(2), 319–39.

Bacon, N. and Samuel, P. (2009) 'Partnership Agreement, Adoption and Survival in the British Private and Public Sectors'. *Work, Employment and Society*, 23(2), 231–48.

Blackman, T., Elliott, E., Greene, A., Harrington, B., Hunter, D., Marks, L., McKee, L., Smith, K., and Williams, G. (2009) 'Tackling Health Inequalities in Post-Devolution Britain: Do Targets Matter?' *Public Administration*, 87(4), 762–78.

Cabinet Office (2009) *Public Services Forum: The First Five Years*. London: Cabinet Office.

Doherty, M. and Erne, R. (2010) 'Mind the Gap—National and Local Partnership in the Irish Public Sector'. *Industrial Relations Journal*, 41(5), 461–78.

Donnelly, P. (2010) 'Differences in UK Healthcare after Devolution'. *British Medical Journal*, 340, 164–5.

Dore, R. (1987) *Taking Japan Seriously: A Confucian Perspective on Leading Economic Issues*. Stanford, CA: Stanford University Press.

Gospel, H. and Pendleton, A. (2003) 'Finance, Corporate Governance and the Management of Labour: A Conceptual and Comparative Analysis'. *British Journal of Industrial Relations*, 41(3), 557–82.

Greer, S. (2008) 'Options and the Lack of Options: Healthcare Politics and Policy'. *Political Quarterly*, 117–32.

Greer, S. (2009) 'Devolution and Divergence in UK Health Policies'. *British Medical Journal*, 338, 78–80.

Hall, P. and Soskice, D. (eds) (2001) *Varieties of Capitalism*. Oxford: Oxford University Press.

Judt, T. (2010) *Ill Fares the Land*. London: Allen Lane.

Keating, M. (2005) 'Policy Convergence and Divergence in Scotland under Devolution'. *Regional Studies*, 39(4), 453–63.

Kelly, J. (2004) 'Social Partnership Agreements in Britain: Labor Cooperation and Compliance'. *Industrial Relations*, 43(1), 267–92.

Kochan, T. A. and Osterman, P. (1994) *The Mutual Gains Enterprise*. Boston, MA: Harvard Business School Press.

Masters, M. F., Albright, R. R., and Eplion, D. (2006) 'What Did Partnerships Do? Evidence from the Federal Sector'. *Industrial and Labor Relations Review*, 59(3), 367–85.

O'Donnell, M., O'Brien, J., and Junor, A. (2011) 'New Public Management and Employment Relations in the Public Services of Australia and New Zealand'. *International Journal of Human Resource Management*, 22(11), 2367–83.

Regini, M. (2003) 'Tripartite Concertation and Varieties of Capitalism'. *European Journal of Industrial Relations*, 9(3), 251–63.

Samuel, P. and Bacon, N. (2010) 'The Contents of Partnership Agreements in Britain, 1990–2007: Modest Aims of Limited Ambition?' *Work, Employment and Society*, 24(3), 430–48.

Scottish Executive (2001) *Rebuilding Our National Health Service: Guidance to NHS Chairs and Chief Executives for Implementing Our National Health*. Edinburgh: Scottish Executive Health Department.

Scottish Executive (2005) *Partnership: Delivering the Future: Taking Stock of Partnership Working*. Edinburgh: Scottish Executive.

Soskice, D. (1989) 'Reinterpreting Corporatism and Explaining Unemployment: Coordinated and Non-Coordinated Market Economies'. In R. Brunetta and C. Dell'Aringa (eds), *Markets, Institutions and Corporations: Labour Relations and Economic Performance*, pp. 170–211. London: Macmillan.

Soskice, D. (1998) 'Divergent Production Regimes: Coordinated and Uncoordinated Market Economies in the 1980s and 1990s'. In H. Kitschelt, P. Lange, G. Marks, and J. Stephens (eds), *Continuity and Change in Contemporary Capitalism*, pp. 101–34. Cambridge: Cambridge University Press.

UNISON (2010) *UNISON Health Service Group Executive Report on Devolution in Health*. London: UNISON.

Welsh Partnership Forum (2008) *NHS Wales Working in Partnership: Constitution*. Cardiff: WPF, 2 April.

Work Foundation (2004) *Trade Union and Employee Involvement in Public Service Reform*. London: Office of Public Services Reform.

9 Employee participation in Germany

Tensions and challenges

Michael Gold and Ingrid Artus

> Article 14 of the German Constitution (Property, Right of Inheritance, Expropriation): 14(2) Property imposes duties. Its use should also service the public good.
>
> (Conradt 2009: 302)

Up until the early 1990s, the German model of industrial relations was widely regarded as a great success. It had contributed to the reconstruction of the German economy since the Second World War by establishing a structured framework for collective bargaining and employee participation, which gave unions and employees alike a critical stake in running industry and services. The framework consisted principally of a 'dual system' that channelled the integrative aspects of industrial relations through employee-based works councils and the redistributive aspects through collective bargaining between employers and unions at sector level. Collective bargaining was relatively centralized, and the system led to a close partnership between the two sides of industry. Indeed, as the extract from the German constitution above demonstrates, embedded in the German model is the idea that property implies duties as well as rights. In practical terms, this means that the interests of a wide range of stakeholders—particularly those of workers—are taken into account when running a company, rather than those primarily of shareholders. Historically, the system has been derived from ideas of 'economic democracy' (*Wirtschaftsdemokratie*), which aims at equal participation of capital as well as labour in industrial management. Hence, widely admired for the social consensus that it generated, the model has been regarded as a paradigm of the coordinated market economy in the 'varieties of capitalism' literature, and has been imitated on occasion both by national governments and by the European Union (EU).

However, in recent years the system has come under pressure from a variety of sources, including reunification in 1991, privatization, foreign direct investment, labour market liberalization, changes in employment structures, and the growth of new economic sectors, not to mention recession and rising unemployment. This chapter, which is aimed at the non-specialist reader, examines the effects of these pressures on the development of employee participation and collective bargaining in the German private sector (it excludes the public sector). It does not seek to evaluate either the contribution of employee participation to the German economy (for which see, for example, Addison 2009) or the changing dynamics of the German business system itself (for which, see Streeck 2010). Following an outline of the traditional industrial relations framework, the chapter examines the pressures for change and union responses, particularly in relation to the decentralization of collective bargaining and its impact on works councils. It concludes that the erosion of collectivism in certain sectors of German employment relations undermines to some extent its paradigm status as a coordinated market economy. Since it is unlikely that such erosion will prove to be reversible, much depends in the future on the interpenetration of the layers of institutional development and on the success of union responses in adapting the changes to their own interests.

Background to the German economy

The German economy is the fourth largest in the world in terms of Gross Domestic Product, and the largest in the EU. Exports comprise over one third of the country's national output, with those of high value-added products underpinning its growth for many years (Trading Economics 2013). Even so, hit by the costs of reunification in the 1990s as well as by the legacy of earlier, structural deficiencies and recession, Germany was for a while regarded as the 'sick man of the Euro' (*Economist* 1999). Its lack of global competitiveness seemed to be symbolized by the hostile takeover of Mannesmann by Vodafone in 1999/2000 (EIRO 1999). Rising unemployment—which reached 10 per cent by the end of the 1990s, a post-war record—stoked the pressure to reform the traditional German model by adapting neoliberal policies. In 2003, the Social Democrat Government of Gerhard Schröder, with the backing of the Christian Democrats, enacted Agenda 2010, a legislative package designed to cut taxes, decrease expenditure on social welfare, and reduce regulations on businesses. Subsequently, the so-called 'Hartz' laws, named after Peter Hartz, former personnel director of the VW automobile company and chairman of a commission on reforming the labour market, substantially reduced unemployment benefit and created enhanced opportunities for temporary employment and part-time work on very reduced hours.

Wages have generally continued to grow consistently since 2003, at a year-on-year rate higher in 2012 than the Eurozone average—2.5 per cent against 1.7 per cent (Lichtenberg 2013). However, the percentage of low wage earners has grown as well at a pace above the Eurozone average (Bosch and Weinkopf 2008). Real wages have also declined nearly every year since 2000 (WSI–Tarifarchiv 2013), a tendency which, as a long-term-development, is unique in German history after the Second World War. Nevertheless, the successful crisis management of 2008–9 reinstated the reputation of the German model as a well-functioning coordinated market economy. Works councils and unions have collaborated closely with many company managements to find ways—including working-time flexibility, short-time compensation, and the lay-off of temporary workers—to bridge the months of acute crisis without substantial redundancies of the core workforce. By May 2013, Austria and Germany recorded the lowest rates of unemployment amongst EU member states (4.7 per cent and 5.3 per cent respectively), against a rate of 11.0 per cent across the EU-27, and 7.6 per cent in the USA (Eurostat 2013). Volkswagen emerged as the most profitable car manufacturer in the world in 2012, and in a recent analysis of the German economy, one American commentator concluded overall: 'Demonstrating impressive resilience, the German economy has withstood the global economic uncertainty and the European sovereign debt crisis' (Heritage Foundation 2013).

The traditional model

The characteristics of national business systems vary greatly according to the nature of the firm, market organization, and regulatory systems (Whitley 1992). The German national business system has drawn much attention in the literature as the paradigm of a 'co-ordinated market economy' (Hall and Soskice 2001). Also referred to as the 'Rhine model' (Albert 1993), or as an example of the 'continental European model' (Amable 2003), there is general agreement in the 'varieties of capitalism' literature that the German business system combines long-term orientation with the representation of broad stakeholder interests, including banks, employees, and even competitors. The role of the stock market is comparatively limited, with low levels of trading in stocks and shares in contrast to the UK and the USA (Walter 2000). Stocks and shares have been generally retained by the company or a limited range of stakeholders, notably banks, which are a key source for finance and growth. The system therefore encourages long-termism—the development of 'patient capital'—which has led to high levels of innovation in traditional sectors of the economy like manufacturing, as well as high levels of productivity and wages (Allen and Gale 2000).

The German industrial relations system, as an integral element of the country's business system, has been based on various mutually reinforcing pillars (Jacobi et al. 1992). Perhaps the most important is the 'dual' nature of the system, comprising the system of collective bargaining between unions and employers' associations at sector level (*Tarifautonomie*) on the one hand, and interaction between company management and works councils representing all employees, irrespective of union membership (*Betriebsverfassung*), on the other. Conflictual areas, which are generally zero sum, such as pay, hours of work, holidays, and pensions, are dealt with principally by trade unions through collective bargaining. Meanwhile, legislation guarantees the rights of works councils to information, consultation, and co-determination over significant areas of employee relations. Although works councils do deal with conflictual issues, such as flexibility, redundancies, and working time, they are more concerned with consensual areas. For example, codetermination—the right of the works council veto—covers areas like social matters, personnel issues, pay systems, work schedules, holiday arrangements, and monitoring workers' performance. At the same time, works councils are legally obliged to cooperate in 'good faith' (*vertrauensvolle Zusammenarbeit*) with company management, and they have no right to strike. Furthermore, in companies above certain size thresholds, employees also have the right to elect a proportion of their own representatives on to the supervisory board that oversees the strategic direction of the company's management board.

Collective bargaining remains relatively centralized by European standards, though there is no tradition of intersectoral-level bargaining. Since the end of the Second World War, bargaining in the Federal Republic of Germany—which since reunification has also covered the territory of East Germany, the former German Democratic Republic (GDR)—has taken place generally at the sectoral level. Unions, too, are organized by sector. Following a wave of mergers, there are now only eight affiliated to the Confederation of German Trade Unions (DGB)—down from eighteen in the immediate post-war period—each with its responsibility to negotiate terms and conditions for its members with the appropriate employers' association (for example, IG Metall negotiates with GesamtMetall in engineering). As Germany is a federal republic divided into sixteen 'states' (*Länder*), sectoral bargaining takes place at state level, with key states setting the standard for those following in the sector. Unions are not allowed to strike while an agreement remains in force. Sector-level agreements have historically bound all parties, whatever their size and level of profitability. Large German companies supplement these agreements with their own company-level accords, and a growing percentage of companies use 'opening clauses' in collective agreements to adapt collective norms to company conditions, an issue to which we return below.

Subject to various conditions, the terms of sectoral collective agreements may be extended across the appropriate sector by ministerial order to cover workers who are not union members and employers who are not affiliated to the signatory association, whereupon they become legally binding on the parties. Historically, the importance of extension procedures has remained quite limited, focusing on specific sectors (such as construction, hotels, and restaurants), but during the 2000s it has increasingly been used as a means to create minimum wage levels within certain sectors. However, this will no longer be required in the future as, from 2015, a statutory national minimum wage will be introduced.

Overall, then, the system attempts to restrict the 'contested terrain' within the company and to engender a sense of industrial citizenship, in which employees elect works councils with rights to information, consultation, and codetermination, much as all citizens have the right to vote in political elections at varying levels. A significant consequence of the 'dual' system is that it has engendered a close partnership between employers and works councils as well as unions. In contrast to the adversarial, low-trust environment that has historically characterized industrial relations in the UK (Fox 1974), the German system encourages cooperation on a long-term basis. Employees in German companies enjoy a stake in their success through their works councils and employee board-level representation. Potentially disruptive activity, like collective bargaining, has been kept well apart from the day-to-day operation of the works council, and the personnel involved in each is also separate. Although works councillors may well be also members of a union, the law guarantees the separation of their interests as works councillors on the one hand and trade unionists on the other.

Significance and changing perceptions of the traditional model

The historic success of the German system of employee participation has led to its serving as a model for emulation on numerous occasions by both the EU and by individual countries. Its system of employee board-level representation was imitated both in the European Company Statute (eventually adopted in 2001) and in the early drafts of the Fifth Directive (that was eventually withdrawn in 2004), while its works councils system served partly as the basis of the European works councils directive (1994), along with the development of similar voluntary arrangements in a number of French and German multinational companies by the early 1990s (Sorge 2008). German works councils were also the inspiration for the Information and Consultation of Employees Directive (2002).

From the perspective of individual countries, the German dual model played a prominent role during reform discussions in Eastern Europe after 1990 and was extended without discussion to the four new German *Länder* of the former GDR. In most of the other East European countries, the unions opposed the establishment of union-independent works councils and promoted unitary 'union representation structures'. Nevertheless, the German works council model inspired, at least partly, the new institutional regulatory regimes in countries like the Czech Republic, Hungary, Latvia, Lithuania, Slovakia, and Slovenia (Kohl and Platzer 2004). More recently, Germany served as a model for Croatia prior to its accession into the EU in July 2013. The German dual system was incorporated into the Croatian labour code in 1996 as a means to give the country credibility during accession negotiations, though it was later amended in favour of the unions (Eurofound 2012).

The UK and France are further prominent examples. In the UK, the Bullock Report proposed the introduction of an adapted form of German employee board-level representation into British corporate governance in the late 1970s, a proposal that was quashed by the Conservative Government elected in 1979 (Gold 2005). Within a similar time frame, the Sudreau Report in France also advocated employee board-level representation on supervisory boards. However, given the resistance of most unions and employers, its proposals were never realized (Sauviat 2006), though an amended system has since been adopted (Auberger and Conchon 2009).

The dominance of the German system is based largely on the longevity and stability of its legal framework (Dukes 2005). Indeed, following the defeat of the Nazi regime in 1945, the Allies successfully adapted the pre-war framework as the foundation for the new, post-war settlement between employers and unions (Dartmann 1996). Unsurprisingly, the system has been subject to changing interpretations over its history, with Jackson (2005) identifying four principal stages, to which Haipeter (2011) has subsequently added an emergent stage, 'conflictive partnership':

- coercive paternalism (Imperial Germany);
- contested authority (Weimar);
- social partnership (Post-war);
- co-management (of restructuring, since reunification);
- conflictive partnership.

Jackson (2005: 236) points out that, despite the 'remarkable continuities' in German codetermination since the nineteenth century, 'the stability of legal rules contrasts with its diversity as a social institution that has coevolved with shifts in ideas, power relationships, and coalition building among company stakeholders'. The contrasts centre on the developing role of the state, management, unions, and employees. For example, the role of the state has developed from 'further democratisation' in the post-war period to 'regime competition' in the 1990s, while management perspectives over the same period have shifted from 'increasing recognition of labour' to 'challenging the shareholder value paradigm'. The attention of unions similarly refocused from 'political demands enabling codetermination as a long arm of the unions' to 'framework agreements, decentralisation', and employees from 'experience of reconstruction, quality of life issues' to a stark 'individualisation'. The extension of the former West German legal regulation to East Germany is a further striking example of the way in which the same institutional rules may be variously interpreted and have very different effects according to the circumstances (Artus 1999). In the most recent phase, Haipeter (2011) argues that codetermination is now embracing forms of workplace concession bargaining.

This typology is a reminder that there are both continuities and contrasts historically observable in the German system, with the continuities based principally on legally based institutions and the contrasts reflecting changes in their internal dynamics and perceptions. Even then, as we shall see, generalizations are made difficult by the contrasts between sectors and industries.

Current state of employee participation

Union membership in Germany stands at around 7.4 million, an estimated 19 per cent of the working population, a decline of five percentage points over ten years (Dribbusch and Birke 2012). Eight unions covering 6.15 million workers are affiliated to the DGB, the largest three being IG Metall (with members principally in metalworking), ver.di (service workers), and IG BCE (chemical and energy workers). Together, these three unions cover 81 per cent of workers in DGB-affiliated unions. Remaining union members belong either to unions affiliated to DBB (civil servants) or to the CDU (Christian Democratic Union Confederation). Though the density of DGB-affiliated unions has fallen markedly since 1991—the peak year of membership immediately following reunification—membership has broadly stabilized, with four of the eight affiliates, including IG Metall, recording increases in 2012 (EIRO 2013).

Under the 1952 Works Constitution Act, *works councils* may be established on request in all private sector workplaces with at least five workers (for the development of this legal framework, see Box 9.1). The 2010 works council elections revealed a turnout of 80.3 per cent amongst workers entitled to vote. Thirty-two per cent of works councillors elected were women, and 66 per cent

---

BOX 9.1 SUMMARY OF LEGAL FRAMEWORK FOR EMPLOYEE PARTICIPATION

- *1951 Codetermination Act*
  - Parity representation of capital and labour on supervisory boards in coal and steel industries
- *1952 Works Constitution Act*
  - Works councils rights to information, consultation, and codetermination
  - Employee board-level representatives granted one third of seats on supervisory boards of companies with over 500 employees replaced in 2004 by the One Third Participation Act
- *1972 Works Constitution Act*
  - Broadened the scope of works council codetermination rights and recodified the works constitution
- *1976 Codetermination Act*
  - Employee board-level representatives granted half the seats on supervisory boards of companies with over 2,000 employees
- *1989 Works Constitution Act*
  - Improved rights of minorities to be represented on works councils
  - Improved information and consultation over introduction of new technology
- *2001 Works Constitution Act*
  - Simplified voting procedure for works councillors in small and medium-sized enterprises
  - Elections for blue- and white-collar candidates merged
  - Composition of works councils enlarged
- *2004 One Third Participation Act*
  - Supersedes 1952 Works Constitution Act in its application to employee board-level representation

Source: Adapted from EIRR 1989; Weiss 1992; EIRR 2001; Keller and Kirsch 2011.

---

were members of DGB-affiliated unions (Greifenstein et al. 2011). Though this latter figure is down from 73 per cent in the 2006 elections, it reveals that works councils continue to provide a significant platform for union voice at workplace and company level. In particular, it should be noted that part-time workers and workers on fixed-term contracts enjoy the same rights as full-time workers with respect to works council representation, with no minimum length of service. Part timers may vote in works council elections and stand as candidates, while those on fixed-term contracts must simply be employed on the day of the election. The position of workers employed through temporary agencies is a little more complex and is dealt with separately below.

Overall, 43 per cent of employees in the West German private sector are represented by a works council, with 36 per cent in East Germany (Ellguth and Kohaut 2013). However, these figures obscure wide divergence in coverage by sector, company size, and region. In 2012, for example, 78 per cent of workers in refuse, water, energy, and mining and 66 per cent of workers in the finance and insurance services were covered by a works council, but only 15 per cent in construction and 13 per cent in hotels and other services (Hans-Böckler-Stiftung 2013). Size of company too remains significant in

Table 9.1 Works Councils and Other Forms of Worker Representation by Company Size, 2012 (Percentages)

Size of company (number of employees)	5–50	51–100	101–99	200–500	501+	Total
West Germany (percentages)						
Companies with w/c	6	38	62	77	86	9
Companies with other forms of w/rep	12	16	16	15	17	13
Workers covered by w/cs	10	39	63	79	88	43
Workers covered by other forms of w/rep	15	17	15	14	20	16
East Germany (percentages)						
Companies with w/c	6	39	54	68	85	9
Companies with other forms of w/rep	7	8	10	14	16	7
Workers covered by w/cs	11	43	55	69	88	36
Workers covered by other forms of w/rep	8	8	11	15	17	10

Source: Ellguth and Kohaut (2013: 285).

determining the presence of a works council; indeed, as it determines joint consultation committees in the UK (van Wanrooy et al. 2013).

Table 9.1 summarizes the position with respect to both West and East Germany. It also gives an overview of the quantitative relevance of 'other forms of worker representation', which include quality circles, group leader assemblies, round tables, and other forms of direct involvement, all sharing the characteristic that they cannot exercise legal rights of codetermination (Hertwig 2011). Table 9.1 reveals that these direct forms have little influence in East Germany, while their significance in West Germany is restricted to smaller companies.

A third element of employee participation in Germany—along with trade union membership and coverage of works councils—involves *employee board-level representation*. Since 1951, legislation has provided for parity representation of employee and shareholder representatives on the supervisory boards of companies in the coal, iron, and steel industries (the *Montan* industries), with a neutral member—the labour director (*Arbeitsdirektor*)—appointed by the employee representatives to hold the balance between them. However, the number of *Montan* companies has fallen from 105 in 1951 to thirty-one in 2011 (Hans-Böckler-Stiftung 2011).

Similarly, since 1976, companies with over 2,000 employees have been required to implement parity representation of employees and shareholders on their supervisory boards. By the end of 2011 (excluding European companies or SEs), there were 648 companies in this category in Germany, a number in continuous decline since 2002 (Fulton 2013). In these companies, the chair of the supervisory board represents the shareholders and has a casting vote in case of a tie. Finally, there are 1,477 companies with between 500 and 2,000 employees, which are required to have a third of employee representation on their supervisory boards (Bayer 2009). The relevant legislation, which dates from 1952, was superseded in 2004 by the One Third Participation Act, which introduced minor changes, such as expanding the rights of the supervisory board to information and clarifying procedures for the election of its members.

In the early 2000s, the system of employee board-level representation came under attack. Employer associations argued that they acted as a competitive disadvantage for German enterprises and the Schröder government initiated a reform commission in 2005. But the commission—in dissent from the employer representatives—proposed only marginal reforms. Debate ended when the Christian Democrat Chancellor, Angela Merkel, declared publicly in 2006 that the German system of codetermination was an integral part of the German social market economy and would remain so (Biedenkopf et al. 2007: 22).

Last but not least, the national system of employee representation in larger companies has been completed by the creation of European works councils (EWCs), which create a multinational industrial relations system. Recent research reveals that there are basically two types of EWC structure: the first, found mostly in enterprises rooted in French bargaining culture, is dominated by union representatives, while the second is dominated by the German works councils culture (Rüb et al. 2013). As a result of the flexible rules enshrined in the EWC directive and a strong country-of-origin effect on EWCs in practice, the strength of the German economy has 'exported' the model of German codetermination to the European level, at least to some degree.

Current state of collective bargaining

Between 1996 and 2012, the coverage of sector-level collective bargaining fell from 70 per cent to 53 per cent in West Germany and from 56 per cent to 36 per cent in East Germany, though coverage varied greatly by sector. In the private sector, this ranged in West and East Germany respectively from 79 per cent and 64 per cent in financial and insurance services, and 75 per cent and 30 per cent in energy, water, refuse, and mining, down to 20 per cent and 10 per cent in information and communications. Meanwhile, 7 per cent of West German and 12 per cent of East German workers were covered by company-level agreements (Ellguth and Kohaut 2013: 282).

A 'strong' indicator of collective representation combines coverage of workers by both collective bargaining and by works council. Table 9.2 reveals overall a marked decline since 1998. This decline reflects mainly a significant drop in membership of employers' associations. Many associations have

Table 9.2 Percentage of Workers in Private Companies Who are Covered by Both Collective Bargaining and by Works Councils

	1998	2002	2006	2010	2012
West Germany	39	37	32	31	29
East Germany	25	23	19	18	15

Source: Hans-Böckler-Stiftung 2013.

reacted to this drop by creating new forms of 'unbound' employers' associations, which offer the normal range of services but without taking part in collective bargaining. One result is that large companies, in which unions remain significant, have maintained their affiliation to the 'bound' associations, whilst small and medium-sized enterprises (SMEs) have migrated to the 'unbound' associations: 'the heterogeneous interests of large and small firms, having long been brought together by the employers' associations, are now being represented by different organisations' (Haipeter 2011: 182).

The position becomes still more dramatic when it is realized that companies that do continue to comply with collectively agreed standards nevertheless increasingly use 'opening clauses' (*Öffnungsklauseln*), which provide the opportunity to bargain at a decentralized company level. The tendency to transfer certain bargaining competences from the unions to the works councils began when the metalworking agreement in 1984 gave works councils the competence to adapt shorter working hours to company requirements. Since then, starting with the East German metalworking agreement in 1994 and under pressure from reunification and economic recession, 'opening clauses' have become increasingly widespread, now targeting wages as well. Opening clauses, inserted into a general agreement (*Flächentarifvertrag*), normally define a certain 'space' within which company agreements may be amended, usually in reference to economic circumstances. The Pforzheim Agreement of IG Metall (2004) specified that exemptions from sector-level agreements would be permitted only if they promoted the company's competitiveness, protected or created jobs, and had *the consent of the union*. It was intended to end a fragmented and partly illegal practice of company-based deals, that is, works councils frequently conniving with employers when hit by crisis to save jobs and even the company itself by agreeing to pay cuts and longer hours, a phenomenon sometimes known as 'wildcat cooperation' (Keller and Kirsch 2011: 212). Indeed, such complementary bargaining processes at company level had become quite common, doubtlessly undermining the strength of sectoral collective bargaining.

The legal basis of opening clauses varies by sector and has also evolved since their introduction. In construction, the union and employers often identify pay-related items, such as bonuses, for potential reduction in opening clauses included in the collective agreement. Management and works councils may then invoke these opening clauses autonomously by concluding their own agreement at company level without further involvement of the union or employer associations. Opening clauses in the chemical industry—that restrict the potential items for renegotiation to wages and working time— are defined in a similar way. Management and works councils are the main bargaining partners, but they have to submit their agreement to the union for ratification and signature. In metalworking, however, IG Metall plays a much more active and strategic role in the process of decentralized collective bargaining. Following some 'bad experiences' when works councils came under massive pressure from management to agree to wage reductions and the union arrived too late on the scene to intervene in a meaningful way, IG Metall drew up a set of coordinating guidelines in 2005 to strengthen procedural control: the works council generally has to inform the union *before* opening negotiations with management. The local union must then notify the regional level, which in turn notifies IG Metall at national level. The economic background of the company is checked and it is decided whether or not to begin negotiations for a 'supplementary company agreement'. Negotiations take place in the presence of the works council *and* a union representative. Union members within the company should also be informed and involved. IG Metall takes the final decision as to whether or not to accept the agreement (Haipeter 2010: 49).

It should be noted that no legal changes have been necessary to secure the application of 'opening clauses' or special company agreements. As agreements (*Tarifverträge*) have 'legal character' in Germany, the unions can use their right to 'create' law through collective bargaining, transferring 'their' right to conclude agreements on certain issues to the works council. Employers in metalworking would have preferred the same legal procedure that applies in construction, transferring the responsibility for company-level agreements directly to the works councils, but IG Metall was resistant. It should also be noted that the legal opportunity to use 'opening clauses' exists only in companies that are affiliated to their employers' association and therefore recognize the general agreement. Any other kind of contract between management and works councils concerning collective bargaining issues remains illegal, as they always have been.

Union involvement in opening clauses may not take place along these lines in every case, but it is generally agreed that the capacity of IG Metall and IG BCE, the chemicals union, to coordinate decentralized bargaining effectively has been significantly enhanced. Faced by these developments, the attitudes of works councillors have remained cooperative (Frege 2003), though they may not always feel prepared, not least because they lack the bargaining power of unions in not being legally entitled to call a strike. On the other hand, as we see below, the unions may discover new opportunities for organization and mobilization. Overall, then, collective bargaining has—in common with many other industrialized countries (Visser 2005)—become increasingly decentralized. In contrast with the UK, where decentralization has been termed 'disorganized', Germany has experienced at least partly 'organized decentralization' (Traxler 1995).

The qualification—'at least partly'—is required because decentralization has engendered a certain rise of conflict within the German system. The former clear division of responsibilities between unions and works councils has been disturbed, thereby threatening its consensus-building consequences at shop-floor level. The rise in conflict has also been intensified by union efforts to organize the expanding 'peripheral' service sectors, as well as by new patterns of competition between DGB-affiliated unions and small 'occupational' unions (such as train drivers, pilots, and doctors). Although the frequency and extent of strike activities in Germany remain low by international standards, industrial action escalated during the 2000s, until the economic crisis (2008–09) put an end to this development. Nevertheless, short-term token strikes have increased and spread into the service sectors (Dribbusch 2013: 222).

These trends have provoked lively debate amongst commentators, with some arguing that the German system remains stable and others arguing that trends demonstrate its erosion. Hassel, for example, has argued that the German system is eroding (1999, 2002), while Klikauer has robustly questioned this view (2002), arguing that major changes reflect, rather, the pressures of reunification and developments in the public sector. Commentators more recently have generally concurred that codetermination by works councils remains relatively stable, whereas collective bargaining has undergone major changes. The result is a new 'dualism' (Palier and Thelen 2010) or 'segmentation' (Artus 2010) of industrial relations: certain 'core segments' of the economy—namely larger, export-oriented manufacturing companies, where the traditional German dual system of industrial relations still broadly predominates—coexist alongside a growing segment of mainly atypical service work and SMEs characterized by very different, strongly decentralized, and often deficient forms of employee participation.

Pressures for change

German reunification might seem to be an appropriate starting point for an analysis of these emerging pressures within the German model: 'There is no denying that reunification—its costs and difficulties, the unemployment it has engendered in the East and the tax increases it has necessitated in the West—has placed an unprecedented strain on German resources' (Watson

1992: xiii). However, a longer-term perspective argues that reunification merely consolidated or reinforced the economic, political, and social pressures that had already been gathering pace in the 1970s and 1980s, such as declining union membership, the withdrawal of SMEs from employers' associations, privatization and the crumbling of the German company network. As Streeck (2010: 209) argues: 'the institutional crisis that became manifest following unification in the 1990s cannot really be considered exogenous, as its substance and extent were importantly affected by the endogenously formed and historically conditioned behaviour of actors beholden to the political and institutional traditions of the West German system.'

This section examines some of the factors that have affected current trends in employee participation against the macro-economic backdrop of high interest rates induced by reunification, the introduction of the Eurozone, liberalization of financial markets, and (then) rising unemployment. The factors we examine include labour market liberalization and changes in the structure of employment, the emergence of new economic sectors outside traditional manufacturing, the transfer of Anglo-American industrial relations practices into Germany, and the steps taken by certain companies to reduce the influence of works councils and trade unions.

Government measures to liberalize labour markets, for example through the abolition of workers' protection rights and the reduction of unemployment benefits, have underpinned significant increases in 'non-standard' forms of employment. Part-time work, for example, rose from 14 per cent of overall employment in 1991 to 26 per cent in 2008, while temporary agency work rose from 0.4 per cent to 2.3 per cent of employment over the same period, and fixed-term contracts from 7.5 per cent to 9.6 per cent (Keller and Kirsch 2011: 219). The low-wage sector has expanded to 22 per cent of all employees (in comparison with 17 per cent in Europe): in 2010, about 8 million German workers earned less than €9.15 per hour (Schulten 2013: 131). Although 'actors in the "core" economy have been relatively well positioned to defend traditional institutions and practices for themselves..., they are no longer able to serve the leadership functions they once did of providing crucial collective goods for all' (Palier and Thelen 2010: 120).

This fragmentation of the employment structure has been exacerbated by the growth of new sectors in the German economy, which have nurtured these forms of working and pose serious challenges to union organization and the formation of works councils. In fast food, for example, Burger King (Rosenberger 2013) strenuously resisted the collective regulation of any of their work practices, while McDonalds set up its own employers' association of fast food providers and allied itself with Ganymed, a 'yellow' union, in an attempt to circumvent the legislation (Royle 2000: chapters 4–5). Walmart, too, another American multinational known for its anti-union labour practices, resisted the introduction of works councils and trade unions, and eventually pulled out of the German market having misread a number of its dimensions, including customer preferences and supply chain organization as well as employment relations (Christopherson 2007). In service industries, such as parcel delivery or retail sale, companies have introduced a variety of irregular forms of worker representation in place of works councils or by perverting its practice (Artus 2010, 2013).

Other new sectors that are difficult to organize include call centres, cleaning services, ICT, security services, and mail order, with research revealing—as noted in Table 9.1—the presence of non-statutory forms of employee representation across a variety of sectors (Hertwig 2011). A potent criticism of the 'varieties of capitalism' literature is that it focuses on manufacturing rather than on the service sectors (Blyth 2003). By 2012, only 25 per cent of the German working population still worked in manufacturing, while 74 per cent worked in 'other sectors, services' and the miniscule remainder in agriculture (Destatis/WZB 2013). The challenges facing unions organizing in services, where individualized management techniques are prevalent, are illustrated in recent cases reported by ver.di, the services union. Ver.di was able to negotiate an agreement covering Libri, a book wholesaler, but failed with GLS, a parcel carrier business. Since then it has been focusing on Amazon, the online retailer, which uses fixed-term contracts, particularly foreign agency workers in the run up to Christmas, who are insecure and hard to organize because of high levels of turnover (Reimann 2013).

Evidence for transfer of 'Anglo-Saxon' industrial relations practices into German companies is otherwise generally mixed. On the one hand, there is evidence that 'reverse diffusion' may sometimes take place, that is, 'vanguard' subsidiaries of German companies located in the UK engage in transferring 'Anglo-Saxon' practices, in areas such as performance management and training and development, back to Germany (Ferner and Varul 2000). On the other hand, there appears to be little evidence that subsidiaries of American or British multinationals import their practices on to their sites in Germany, which implies that the high-profile cases of anti-union employers tend to be untypical of the 1,800 US subsidiaries operating in the country (Schmitt 2003).

There are broader issues involved too when other countries are involved in foreign direct investment. There is evidence that businesses from Brazil, Russia, India, and China (the BRIC countries) may also experience difficulties with the German industrial relations system. This may reflect hierarchical management styles or lack of preparation as the bosses of 'asset-heavy BRIC corporations... often have no understanding of Germany's culture of co-determination' (Molitor 2012). Though there are positive cases of success, there are also many failures. When Hindalco, an Indian aluminium producer, took over Novalis Deutschland GmbH, the company began to be run increasingly from the centre, and the works council has found that 'enforcing their statutory rights to co-determination has become a miserable, time- and energy-consuming process that frequently produces disputes and not infrequently ends up in court' (Molitor 2012).

Amongst the traditional German manufacturing sector, meanwhile, recent commentators have observed that the 'vertical disintegration' of companies has become a serious challenge for the unions. The observation is based on the premise that: 'The German corporation is said to have a significantly higher degree of vertical integration than its British counterpart' (Lane 1992: 82). The process of vertical disintegration involves '[t]he creation of new intermediate markets in a previously integrated production process' (Doellgast and Greer 2007: 56) and may challenge the role of collective bargaining in German companies in a variety of ways, including subcontracting to other firms, the creation of independent subsidiaries, and the use of temporary work agencies for staffing. All these processes involve market-based relations dominated by a single influential customer, which weakens union activity. Employers move jobs from a well-organized core to poorly organized peripheries, such as SMEs without trade unions or coverage by collective agreements. Work might be shifted to new sectoral agreements, typically negotiated by different trade unions (hence fragmentation of bargaining structures). In these ways, vertical disintegration erodes the sectoral and company-level bargaining institutions traditionally central to German industrial relations, as unions find it hard to maintain pressure on employers outside core areas.

The fragmentation of core and peripheral workforces has led to the increasing significance of non-union 'exclusion zones' and the use by employers of the threat of outsourcing—both domestically and abroad—to bring the unions into line. As noted above, one conclusion that may be drawn from these developments is that the German system is 'layering' (Streeck and Thelen 2005). That is, there is a process of bifurcation underway which has led to a new employment relations regime emerging alongside or within the traditional, dominant regime (Deeg 2005). The new regime, which is evident particularly in emerging sectors of the economy, reflects the more unregulated characteristics of the neoliberal, Anglo-American model, which discourages trade unionism and collective employee representation.

Nevertheless, the German 'model' has always harboured 'exclusion zones'. Indeed, we have already noted above variations in work council density by company size. Research reveals four ideal-type patterns of works council absence (Artus 2013): first, in knowledge-based enterprises in the 'new economy' where both employers and employees believe that works councils are 'relics of an industrial past which "strong" and highly qualified employees do not need'; second, in middle-sized industrial firms in rural areas, 'where labour relations are characterized by mutual recognition (but with the clear dominance of management)'; third, in former family businesses that have grown or been acquired, where the absence of a works council is a 'relic of

"older times"'; and fourth, in areas of precarious service work where employers are hostile to the creation of works councils.

Indeed, the idea of liberalization as 'letting things happen that are happen-
ing anyway' (Streeck and Thelen 2005: 33) may require a corporate shove or
two. The processes of vertical disintegration outlined above require strategic
decisions by companies (for example, to outsource or create independent
subsidiaries). And what is of great concern to unions is the development of
avoidance strategies amongst larger companies. A project into the scale of
anti-works council activities amongst employers reveals that: 'efforts to avoid
and hamper union representation are much more prevalent in companies that
do not (yet) have organised employee representation—and that's 90 per cent
of employers—than in companies that already have a works council (Behrens
and Dribbusch 2012).

Findings show that candidates for election may be intimidated or 'bought
off' with benefits if they withdraw. Though hostility of this kind is most
common in companies with 'considerably fewer than 200 employees', which
are in many cases owner managed, half of all trade union branches in
manufacturing had also experienced efforts to prevent elections. There is
clearly a split between the generally positive attitudes expressed by those
companies with experience of works councils and by those without, which
fear their allegedly damaging consequences: they are too costly, ideologically
motivated, and undermine industrial relations. As the authors point out:
'these reasons for rejecting a works council are based not on actual experience
of working with one but purely on the respondent companies' expectations of
working with one' (Behrens and Dribbusch 2012). In other cases, works
councillors have reported dismissal, allegations of drug taking, and harass-
ment by private detectives as means of wearing them down (Kraft 2012).

Union responses

This analysis allows us to identify four trends within the system of German
employee participation. The first is the gradual decline in the density overall
of industrial relations institutions; the density of works councils is declining
only very slightly, but union membership and coverage of collective agreements have decreased markedly, a trend that Germany shares with most other
industrialized countries. The statutory basis of all these institutions remains
intact, but there is a decline in participation in them and/or new ways of
interpreting their means of operation. Second, within the traditional manufacturing sectors of German industry, some companies are restructuring in order
to hinder the operation of works councils and trade unions. Furthermore, the

increasing use of temporary work and service contracts reduces the influence of works councils even within the 'core segments' and creates new tensions between 'core' and 'peripheral' workers. Third, there is an emergence of new sectors of the economy remaining outside the scope of collective influences, such as unions, works councils, and collective bargaining. Fourth, SMEs remain 'exclusion zones' as far as collective representation at work is involved—but it is likely that they always have done. The costs of reunification, economic recession, market liberalizing policies, and the role of foreign direct investment—particularly from the USA but also from the BRIC countries, amongst others—underpin these individualizing tendencies.

However, union responses to these macro-institutional developments must also be considered. Union agency remains a critical element in any discussion about the nature of change in industrial relations (Gumbrell-McCormick and Hyman 2013), and it is clear that German unions are still influencing outcomes in company-level industrial relations in a way that their UK counterparts are not (see also Simms, this volume). Union densities in Germany remain moderate by EU standards (19 per cent), but the key question is their ability to defend their members' interests or otherwise, in such rapidly changing circumstances. Haipeter, in a significant argument, refers to the possible 'simultaneity of erosion and renewal' (2011: 176). Restricting his analysis to developments in German metalworking, he draws attention to the Pforzheim Agreement (2004) and the drafting of its accompanying coordinating guidelines (2005), as outlined above, which he interprets as signs of union renewal.

Research reveals that in exchange for concessions *to* employers—notably extensions of working time (almost 60 per cent of cases)—there have also been important counter-concessions offered *by* employers, including job security, investment, location, improvements in information disclosure, and training (Haipeter 2011). Haipeter interprets these trends as moves towards a stage of 'conflictive' partnership between unions and employers. The conflict emerges from employers' attempts to undercut collective agreements or withdraw from them completely, and then compel concessions from the union at company level, while the union in turn seeks counter-concessions. Yet exemptions from sector-level agreements have also been used as a launch pad for recruitment at local level, as they involve members in negotiations and allow the union to reconnect with members. Indeed, other commentators too have noted that declining membership has encouraged the unions to engage in membership campaigns (Turner 2009). For example, ver.di, the main German service sector union, has launched organizing campaigns in the retail sector, in hospitals, and in the security sector. Although its results in terms of mobilizing and recruiting new members have been mixed (Birke 2010), ver.di at least partly continues to adopt strategies of 'organizing by conflict' (Kocsis et al. 2013).

IG Metall has also reacted to the new problem of 'core' and 'peripheral' workers by initiating a campaign on temporary work in the car and automotive supply industries (compare the situation in the UK analysed in Greene, this volume). It included a publicity offensive, distinguishing 'good' from 'bad' temporary work, with the slogan 'equal pay for equal work'. Works councillors have been trained to address the interests of temporary workers to a greater extent and to include them in their representation policies, despite restricted legal rights to do so. By law, agency workers may request a works council at their agency company, though in practice this occurs only in the largest agencies with most having none at all. Temporary workers may also vote in elections for works councils in their host companies, provided that they have at least three months' service in the host, but they may not themselves stand for election. Overall, the campaign has had a significant impact on the re-regulation of temporary work in Germany. The union, along with others, has concluded sectoral agreements that define maximum periods of host-company service, gradually align pay between temporary and 'standard' workers in cases of long-term assignments, and even give works councils in host companies certain limited rights to represent temporary workers. The campaign also raised the (nevertheless still low) density of their union membership. In consequence there has recently been a certain shift in management strategies in favour of service contracts over temporary work, which IG Metall now has to address as well.

A further significant response by German unions to the fragmentation of labour markets has been the powerful political campaign for a statutory national minimum wage. This initiative originally stemmed from the service sector unions, ver.di and NGG, but IG Metall was also later persuaded to join. Following the elections in 2013 to the lower house of the German parliament (*Bundestag*), the Social Democrats—now in coalition with the Christian Democrats—successfully pushed through the introduction from 2015 of a statutory national minimum wage, set at €8.50 an hour (a rate well below negotiated pay rates). An element of state intervention has therefore been let back into collective bargaining, though employers and unions retain a central role in implementing and enforcing the minimum wage itself.

Conclusions

The German system of employee participation has been subject to considerable change since the early 1990s. New sectors have emerged characterized by low-pay, non-unionization, and precarious forms of work. The traditional 'dual' system, itself in a process of change, exists alongside a newer, unorganized system, based on emerging sectors and new forms of working. There are clear signs of erosion of collectivism in traditional sectors of German employment relations. There will clearly be no return to the traditional model as such, but much depends on the interpenetration of the 'layers' of institutional development, that is, whether the traditional layers of employment will tend towards the emerging layers based on individualized forms of working. To some degree this depends on the success of union responses, and their ability to instil countervailing understandings of the long-term 'sustainable company'. If they do succeed, then 'erosion' may well have proved a helpful catalyst for 'renewal'. The process of sector-level bargaining is generally remote from the lives of most workers, and evidence suggests that decentralization may well help to re-engage them in negotiations at local level over basic issues like pay and working time. Unions have already begun to organize and mobilize more effectively as a result, and recent figures indicating rises in union membership—though small—are encouraging.

Unlike the case of the UK, where long-term trends towards declining union densities were exacerbated by the overtly anti-union policies of the Thatcher governments in the 1980s, employers in Germany have not fiercely sought to undermine the existing industrial relations legal framework (though they certainly opposed its strengthening, for example in 1976 and in 2001, and they attacked the system of employee board-level representation for a while in the early 2000s). However, German employers have both retained a commitment to 'core' workers and attempted to weaken them at same time by moving work to the periphery through outsourcing and vertical disintegration. Unfortunately for the unions, German employers are not required to consult over outsourcing or spinning activities off to new companies. Overall, harsh trade union busting tactics are not very widespread and are restricted mainly to the US multinationals and the precarious service sector. But there is an expanding segment of the economy without union organization and collective bargaining or with bargaining practices deviating from collective standards. Even works councils, normally more easily accepted by employers as bargaining counterparts than union representatives, exist only for the minority of workers.

Concerns continue to focus on levels of participation within the institutions (such as the density of works councils within eligible companies and the coverage of collective agreements). Furthermore, while the legal basis for institutions may not change, their internal functions may change considerably. For example, works councils have been drawn into negotiating works agreements through the expansion of opening clauses. On the one hand, there is evidence that recruitment may follow from such decentralization and lead to greater member involvement in collective bargaining. On the other hand, many works councils are not very happy with their new tasks, not least because they lack the same bargaining power as the unions and the right to call strikes.

The role of actors is critical: trade unions are not passive, and they themselves react as they always have. The questions—whether they will be able to adapt the model to their advantage through concession bargaining and the extent to which they will manage to organize currently non-organized sectors—remain open. However, the attitudes of works councillors remain cooperative and the increasing flexibility within the German system has been negotiated within the existing legal and institutional frameworks. Opening clauses are defined at sector level—the traditional bargaining level—but then implemented at local level. This implies that works councils and unions remain significant actors, at least in those sectors and companies where works councils exist and unions have members.

▓ REFERENCES

Addison, J. T. (2009) *The Economics of Codetermination: Lessons from the German Experience*. Basingstoke: Palgrave Macmillan.

Albert, M. (1993) *Capitalism against Capitalism*. London: Whurr Publishers.

Allen, F. and Gale, D. (2000) 'Corporate Governance and Competition'. In X. Vives (ed.), *Corporate Governance: Theoretical and Empirical Perspectives*, pp. 23–94. Cambridge: Cambridge University Press.

Amable, B. (2003) *The Diversity of Modern Capitalism*. Oxford: Oxford University Press.

Artus, I. (1999) 'The Unification of Bargaining Systems in East and West Germany'. In P. Pochet (ed.), *Monetary Union and Collective Bargaining in Europe*, pp. 245–59. Oxford: Peter Lang.

Artus, I. (2010) 'Interessenhandeln jenseits der Norm: Ein deutsch-französischer Vergleich betrieblicher Interessenvertretung in peripheren und prekären Wirtschaftssegmenten'. *Industrielle Beziehungen*, 17(4), 317–44. [Online.] Available at: <http://www.hampp-ejournals.de/hampp-verlag-services/get?file=/frei/IndB_4_2010_317>, accessed 19 December 2013.

Artus, I. (2013) 'Precarious Delegates: Irregular Forms of Employee Interest Representation in Germany'. *Industrial Relations Journal*, 44(4), 409–24.

Auberger, M.-N. and Conchon, A. (eds) (2009) *Les administrateurs salariés et la gouvernance d'entreprise*. Collection les etudes, Paris: La documentation française.

Bayer, W. (2009) *Drittelbeteiligung in Deutschland: Ermittlung von Gesellschaften, die dem Drittelbeteiligung unterliegen*. Jena: Friedrich-Schiller-Universität.

Behrens, M. and Dribbusch, H. (2012) 'How Companies Keep Works Councils out'. *Mitbestimmung*, June. [Online.] Available at: <http://www.boeckler.de/36196_42116.htm>, accessed 24 July 2013.

Biedenkopf, K., Streeck, W., and Wissman, H. (2007) 'A Core Element of Europe'. *Mitbestimmung*, 8(August), 20–5.

Birke, P. (2010) *Die Grosse Wut und die kleinen Schritte. Gewerkschaftliches Organising zwischen Protest und Projekt.* Berlin: Assoziation A.

Blyth, M. (2003) 'Same as It Never Was: Temporality and Typology in the Varieties of Capitalism'. *Comparative European Politics*, 1(2), 215–25.

Bosch, G. and Weinkopf, C. (eds) (2008) *Low-Wage Work in Germany.* New York: Russell Sage Foundation.

Christopherson, S. (2007) 'Barriers to "US Style" Lean Retailing: The Case of Wal-Mart's Failure in Germany'. *Journal of Economic Geography*, 7, 451–69.

Conradt, D. P. (2009) *The German Polity.* Boston, MA: Houghton Mifflin Harcourt Publishing Company.

Dartmann, C. (1996) *Redistribution of Power, Joint Consultation or Productivity Coalitions? Labour and Postwar Reconstruction in Germany and Britain 1945–53.* Bochum: Universitätsverlag Dr N. Brockmeyer.

Deeg, R. (2005) 'Change from Within: German and Italian Finance in the 1990s'. In W. Streeck and K. Thelen (eds), *Beyond Continuity: Institutional Change in Advanced Political Economies.* Oxford: Oxford University Press.

Destatis/WZB (2013) *Datenreport 2013. Ein Sozialbericht für die Bundesrepublik Deutschland.* Berlin: Destatis [Federal Statistical Office], p. 122. [Online.] Available at: <https://www.destatis.de/DE/Publikationen/Datenreport/Datenreport.html>, accessed 19 August 2014.

Doellgast, V. and Greer, I. (2007) 'Vertical Disintegration and the Disorganisation of German Industrial Relations'. *British Journal of Industrial Relations*, 45(1), 55–76.

Dribbusch, H. (2013) 'Organisieren am Konflikt. Zum Verhältnis von Streik und Mitgliederentwicklung'. In A. Kocsis, G. Sterkel, and J. Wiedemuth (eds), *Organisieren am Konflikt. Tarifauseinandersetzungen und Mitgliederentwicklung im Dienstleistungssektor*, pp. 202–34. Hamburg: VSA.

Dribbusch, H. and Birke, P. (2012) *Trade Unions in Germany: Organisation, Environment, Challenges.* [Online.] Available at: <http://library.fes.de/pdf-files/id-moe/09113-20120828.pdf>, accessed 19 June 2013.

Dukes, R. (2005) 'The Origins of the German System of Worker Representation'. *Historical Studies in Industrial Relations*, 19, 31–62.

Economist (1999) 'The Sick Man of the Euro'. 3 June.

EIRR (1989) 'West Germany: Round-up of Important Law Changes'. *European Industrial Relations Review*, 182(March), 19–20.

EIRO (1999) 'Vodaphone's Hostile Takeover Bid for Mannesmann Highlights Debzte on the German Capitalist Model'. November. [Online.] Available at: <http://www.eurofound.europa.eu/eiro/1999/11/feature/de9911220f.htm>, accessed 19 June 2013.

EIRR (2001) 'New Works Constitution Act Enters into Force'. *European Industrial Relations Review*, 333(October), 27–8.

EIRO (2013) *Union Membership Holds up Well.* [Online.] Available at: <http://www.eurofound.europa.eu/eiro/2013/04/articles/de1304019i.htm>, accessed 24 July 2013.

Ellguth, P. and Kohaut, S. (2013) 'Tarifbindung und betriebliche Interessenvertretung: Ergebnisse aus dem IAB-Betriebspanel 2012', *WSI Mitteilungen* 4, 281–8.

Eurofound (2012) *Croatia: Industrial Relations Profile*. European Foundation for the Improvement of Living and Working Conditions. [Online.] Available at: <http://www.eurofound.europa.eu/eiro/country/croatia.pdf>, accessed 19 June 2013.

Eurostat (2013) *Unemployment Statistics*. May. [Online.] Available at: <http://epp.eurostat.ec.europa.eu/statistics_explained/index.php/Unemployment_statistics>, accessed 16 July 2013.

Ferner, A. and Varul, M. (2000) '"Vanguard" Subsidiaries and the Diffusion of New Practices: A Case Study of German Multinationals'. *British Journal of Industrial Relations*, 38(1), 115–40.

Fox, A. (1974) *Beyond Contract. Work, Power and Trust Relations*. London: Faber and Faber.

Frege, C. (2003) 'Transforming German Workplace Relations: Quo Vadis Co-operation?' *Economic and Industrial Democracy*, 24(3), 317–47.

Fulton, L. (2013) 'Worker Representation in Europe: Board-Level Representation'. *Labour Research Department and ETUI, with the assistance of the SEEurope Network.* [Online.] Available at: <http://www.worker-participation.eu/National-Industrial-Relations/Countries/Germany/Board-level-Representation>, accessed 24 July 2013.

Gold, M. (2005) 'Worker Directors in the UK and the Limits of Policy Transfer from Europe since the 1970s'. *Historical Studies in Industrial Relations*, 20, 29–65.

Greifenstein, R., Kißler, L., and Lange, H. (2011) *Trendreport Betriebsratswahlen 2010*, Arbeitspapier 231, August. Duesseldorf: Hans Böckler Stiftung.

Gumbrell-McCormick, R. and Hyman, R. (2013) *Trade Unions in Western Europe: Hard Times, Hard Choices*. Oxford: Oxford University Press.

Haipeter, T. (2011) '"Unbound" Employers' Associations and Derogations: Erosion and Renewal of Collective Bargaining in the German Metalworking Industry'. *Industrial Relations Journal*, 42(2), 174–94.

Hall, P. A. and Soskice, D. (2001) 'An Introduction to Varieties of Capitalism'. In P. A. Hall and D. Soskice (eds), *Varieties of Capitalism: The Institutional Foundations of Comparative Advantage*, pp. 1–68. Oxford: Oxford University Press.

Hans-Böckler-Stiftung (2011) *Montanmitbestimmung damals und heute*. [Online.] Available at: <http://www.boeckler.de/pdf/magmb_2011_05_molitor1.pdf>, accessed 16 July 2013.

Hans-Böckler-Stiftung (2013) 'Böcklerimpuls, Ausgabe 10/13'. *Vertretung auf Branchen- und Betriebsebene—der aktuelle Stand*. [Online.] Available at: <http://www.boeckler.de/impuls_2013_10_6.pdf>, accessed 16 July 2013.

Hassel, A. (1999) 'The Erosion of Industrial Relations in Germany'. *British Journal of Industrial Relations*, 37(3), 483–505.

Hassel, A. (2002) 'The Erosion Continues: Reply'. *British Journal of Industrial Relations*, 40(2), 309–17.

Heritage Foundation (2013) *2013 Index of Economic Freedom: Germany*. [Online.] Available at: <http://www.heritage.org/index/country/germany>, accessed 16 July 2013.

Hertwig, M. (2011) 'Patterns, Ideologies and Strategies of Non-Statutory Employee Representation in German Private Sector Companies'. *Industrial Relations Journal*, 42(6), 530–46.

Jackson, G. (2005) 'Contested Boundaries: Ambiguity and Creativity in the Evolution of German Codetermination'. In W. Streeck and K. Thelen (eds), *Beyond Continuity:*

Institutional Change in Advanced Political Economies, pp. 229–54. Oxford: Oxford University Press.

Jacobi, O., Keller, B., and Müller-Jentsch, W. (1992) 'Germany: Codetermining the Future?' In A. Ferner and R. Hyman (eds), *Industrial Relations in the New Europe*, pp. 218–69. Oxford: Blackwell.

Keller, B. and Kirsch, A. (2011) 'Employment Relations in Germany'. In G. J. Bamber, R. D. Lansbury, and N. Wailes (eds), *International and Comparative Employment Relations*, pp. 196–223. London: Sage.

Klikauer, T. (2002) 'Stability in Germany's Industrial Relations: A Critique on Hassel's Erosion Thesis', *British Journal of Industrial Relations* 40(2), 295–308.

Kocsis, A., Sterkel, G., and Wiedemuth, J. (2013) (eds) *Organisieren am Konflikt. Tarifauseinandersetzung und Mitgliederentwicklung im Dienstleistungssektor.* Hamburg: VSA.

Kohl, H. and Platzer, H.-W. (2004) *Arbeitsbeziehungen in Mittelosteuropa. Transformation und Integration. Die acht neuen EU-Mitgliedsländer im Vergleich'*, 2nd edn. Baden-Baden: Nomos.

Kraft, A. (2012) 'Spying on the Works Council'. *Mitbestimmung*, June. [Online.] Available at: <http://www.boeckler.de/36196_42117.htm>, accessed 24 July 2013.

Lane, C. (1992) 'European Business Systems: Britain and Germany Compared'. In R. Whitley (ed.), *European Business Systems: Firms and Markets in their National Contexts*, pp. 64–97. London: Sage.

Lichtenberg, H. (2013) *German Wages Grow Faster than Euro Area Average: Spring 2013 Review.* [Online.] Available at: <http://www.bruegel.org/nc/blog/detail/article/1084-german-wages-grow-faster-than-euro-area-average-spring-2013-review/>, accessed 16 July 2013.

Molitor, C. (2012) 'Alternative Proposals? No Thanks!' *Mitbestimmung*, March. [Online.] Available at: <http://www.boeckler.de/181.htm>, accessed 24 July 2013.

Palier, B. and Thelen, K. (2010) 'Institutionalizing Dualism: Complementarities and Change in France and Germany'. *Politics and Society*, 38(1), 119–48.

Reimann, H. (2013) 'Shining a Spotlight on Dreadful Conditions'. *Mitbestimmung*, March. [Online.] Available at: <http://www.boeckler.de/32214_42683.htm>, accessed 24 July 2013.

Rosenberger, M. (2013) 'Die Kunden sollen wissen, bei wem sie essen'. *Mitbestimmung*, June. [Online.] Available at: <http://www.boeckler.de/43284_43302.htm>, accessed 24 July 2013.

Royle, T. (2000) *Working for McDonald's in Europe: The Unequal Struggle?* London: Routledge.

Rüb, S., Platzer, H.-W., and Müller, T. (2013) 'Europäische Vereinbarungspolitik auf Unternehmensebene. Entwicklungsdynamiken und Prozessmuster im Metallsektor'. *Industrielle Beziehungen*, 20(3), 221–44.

Sauviat, C. (2006) *Le rôle des salariés dans la gouvernance des entreprises en France: Un débat ancien, une légitimité en devenir.* IRES Document de travail Nr. 06.02, April, Noisy-le-Grand.

Schmitt, M. (2003) 'Deregulation of the German Industrial Relations System via Foreign Direct Investment: Are the Subsidiaries of Anglo-Saxon MNCs a Threat for the Institutions of Industrial Democracy in Germany?' *Economic and Industrial Democracy*, 24(3), 349–77.

Schulten, T. (2013) 'WSI-Mindestlohnbericht 2013—Anhaltend schwache Mindes-tlohnentwicklung in Europa'. *WSI-Mitteilungen*, 66(2), 126–32.

Sorge, A. (2008) 'Industrial Democracy: The Post-War European Career of a Concept'. Paper presented at LSE workshop, *Economic Democracy: Historical and Contemporary Issues in a European Perspective*, 22–23 May, London.

Streeck, W. (2010) *Re-Forming Capitalism: Institutional Change in the German Political Economy*. Oxford: Oxford University Press.

Streeck, W. and Thelen, K. (eds) (2005) 'Introduction: Institutional Change in Advanced Political Economies'. In W. Streeck and K. Thelen (eds) , *Beyond Continuity: Institutional Change in Advanced Political Economies*, pp. 1–39. Oxford: Oxford University Press.

Trading Economics (2013) *Germany GDP Growth Rate*. [Online.] Available at: <http://www.tradingeconomics/germany/gdp-growth>, accessed 16 July 2013.

Traxler, F. (1995) 'Farewell to Labour Market Institutions? Organised versus Disorganised Decentralisation as a Map for Industrial Relations'. In C. Crouch and F. Traxler (eds), *Organised Industrial Relations in Europe: What Future?* Aldershot: Avebury.

Turner, L. (2009) 'Institutions and Activism: Crisis and Opportunity for a German Labor Movement in Decline'. *Industrial and Labor Relations Review*, 62(3), 294–312.

van Wanrooy, B., Bewley, H., Bryson, A., Forth, J., Freeth, S., Stokes, L., and Wood, S. (2013) *The 2011 Workplace Employment Relations Study: First Findings*. London: Department of Business, Innovation and Skills. [Online.] Available at: <https://www.gov.uk/government/uploads/system/uploads/attachment_data/file/175479/13-535-the-2011-workplace-employment-relations-study-first-findings1.pdf>, accessed 23 April 2013.

Visser, J. (2005) 'Beneath the Surface of Stability: New and Old Modes of Governance in European Industrial Relations'. *European Journal of Industrial Relations*, 11(3), 287–306.

Walter, I. (2000) 'Capital Markets and Control of Enterprises in the Global Economy'. In S. Cohen and G. Boyd (eds), *Corporate Governance and Globalization: Long Range Planning Issues*, pp. 95–128. Cheltenham: Edward Elgar.

Watson, A. (1992) *The Germans: Who Are They Now?* London: Thames Methuen.

Weiss, M. (1992) *European Employment and Industrial Relations Glossary: Germany*. London: Sweet and Maxwell/Luxembourg: Office for Official Publications of the European Communities.

Whitley, R. (1992) 'Societies, Firms and Markets: The Social Structuring of Business Systems'. In R. Whitley (ed.), *European Business Systems: Firms and Markets in Their National Contexts*, pp. 5–45. London: Sage.

WSI–Tarifarchiv (2013) (ed.) *Statistisches Taschenbuch Tarifpolitik*. Frankfurt am Main: Hans-Böckler-Stiftung.

10 The promise of European works councils

Twenty years of statutory employee voice

Andrew R. Timming and Michael Whittall

Introduction

Twenty years ago, the Council of the European Union (EU) passed Directive 94/45/EC on the establishment of European works councils (EWCs) 'for the purposes of informing and consulting employees' (Official Journal of the European Communities 1994). Over the last two decades, several books (Lecher et al. 2001a, 2001b, 2002; Fitzgerald and Stirling 2004; Whittall et al. 2007; Waddington 2011) and hundreds of articles and chapters have digested, debated, and deconstructed the significance of the directive and its transposition into national labour legislations (Blanks 1999; Carley and Hall 2000). With the directive now firmly in the rear-view mirror, now is as good a time as any to take stock of its influence on both firms and employees and to assess 'the current state of play' (Waddington and Kerckhofs 2003) of EWCs.

To start with, the most obvious question to ask is: has the EWC directive been helpful, and if so for whom, in what way, and to what extent? The evidence in view of this question is really a mixed bag. Unfortunately, there are no easy answers even twenty years on from the implementation of the directive. Because Europe's employees were meant to be the main beneficiaries of the legislation, this chapter focuses on the impact of EWCs on labour and its representatives. It seeks to evaluate the extent to which EWCs can really be said to 'add value' to employees and their representatives and assess the degree to which EWCs have enabled workers to have a 'voice' in multinational corporations operating across Europe.

Some writers have argued, quite persuasively, that EWCs are stepping stones towards the Europeanization of industrial relations (Marginson and Sisson 2006), and that, as a corollary, EWCs have forged some positive headway on the promises of labour internationalism (Lecher et al. 2001a; Whittall 2000; Kotthoff 2006) in spite of the many obstacles (Timming 2010). But it is also true that EWCs have failed to deliver for labour on many levels. Accordingly, Streeck (1997) has famously called EWCs 'neither

European, nor works councils'. In a similar vein, Ramsay (1997) has branded them mere 'fool's gold'. Waddington's (2003) empirical research reports widespread dissatisfaction amongst workers' representatives in respect to EWC practices. Timming (2007) provides case study evidence that managers use the EWC as a tool by which to proactively fragment nationally diverse groups of workers' representatives. In short, the evidence on the impact of EWCs on workers is still not entirely clear.

The purpose of this chapter is to take stock of twenty years of research on EWCs, offering an overview of the current state of EWCs as potential vehicles of statutory employee voice. It will synthesize what the literature suggests are the effects of EWCs on both workers and organizations, as well as draw on the authors' research in this area spanning many years. It will also take up some problematic issues that, to date, remain generally unanswered, among them: can EWCs facilitate the development of transnational labour solidarity, or are they irrelevant? To what extent do EWCs really add value to the experiences of employees and their representatives? And based on the last twenty years, what can we expect of EWCs in the coming twenty years?

We begin by providing a brief review of the function and purpose of EWCs. This section is particularly important for those readers who are not familiar with the European tradition of works councils. It will sketch out some important background details, including a brief history of statutory information and consultation in the EU and a summary of EWC prevalence. We then turn to the ever important question of the impact of EWCs on labour. EWCs are, by definition, transnational institutions that bring together, into one forum, workers' representatives from various European countries. In order to grasp the obstacles to labour internationalism, we must first understand what it is that divides workers. To this end, we present an analysis of the varieties of capitalism framework (Hall and Soskice 2001; Hancké 2009) in the context of the EWC. It will be argued that, because of the diversity of industrial relations practices and corporate governance systems, workers' representatives are still quite often failing to find each other on the same level (Timming 2009) as far as the interaction of industrial relations practices are concerned. The chapter then goes on to take a stab at the important question of whether or not EWCs can be said to add value for employee representatives. We not only focus on the directive, a piece of legislation designed to provide employees with information and consultation rights at the European level, but we also go beyond the directive. Here, we are concerned with the question of whether the EWC represents a platform for developing cross-border solidarity in the context of the Euro-company. Finally, we conclude the chapter by teasing out some of the more important lessons learned through this research and making some very tentative predictions about what the future holds for statutory information and consultation in the EU and perhaps beyond.

The arrival of the European works council

Twenty years since the EWC directive was passed, a total of 1,254 EWCs have been created, of which 1,026 are still active according to the European Trade Union Institute's EWC database. The top three countries with EWCs are Germany, France, and the UK with, respectively, 341, 256, and 185 bodies each. The figures also suggest that most EWC agreements specify a maximum number of employees' representatives at thirty. Management-chaired EWCs outnumber employee-chaired EWCs by a ratio of three to one, suggesting that employers tend to use the EWC as a tool of human resource management (Timming 2006, 2007).

EWCs are company-level statutory information and consultation forums. All multinational corporations with at least 1,000 employees in EU member states (and at least 150 employees in two or more member states) are required by law to set up and fund the operations of an EWC whose purpose is to inform and consult employees' representatives on issues of 'transnational' importance. Although these forums are mandated by law (by virtue of the transposition of the EWC directive into national labour and employment law), the vast majority of EWCs were voluntary Article 13 agreements (Rivest 1996), meaning that the contents of the EWC agreements were reached voluntarily between workers' and employers' representatives, instead of being imposed by virtue of the legal force of the directive. In this light, EWCs resemble what are referred to in the United States as 'labor management committees' (Champagne 1982), in which workers' and employers' representatives 'meet and confer', so to speak.

It is worth noting that neither the EWC nor the US equivalent of the labour management committee is meant to be an adversarial forum, but rather a vehicle for positive sum relations between the representatives of capital and labour. They are very much aligned with the ideas of social partnership and cooperative employment relations (Johnstone et al. 2009 and Johnstone, this volume), as well as the concept of unitarism (as articulated by Heery, this volume). In other words, the logic of the EWC is to promote mutuality in the employment relationship, but they are not always successful in this respect (Timming and Veersma 2007).

What does an EWC look like? There is no standardized composition because every company has a unique distribution of employees across the EU. But there are some commonalities in terms of process. For any given company, the EWC convenes typically once or twice per year. For each meeting, the company flies in employees' representatives from the different European operations. The EWC meeting typically lasts up to three days. There is often an employee-only meeting in which the labour side can discuss and exchange views. The EWC usually culminates on the final day where the employees' representatives meet face to face with employers' representatives in order to be informed and consulted. It is not uncommon for the CEO and/ or Chairman of the multinational firm to be in attendance. EWCs often follow either the French or German model, where the former is chaired by management and the latter by a workers' representative, respectively.

The remit of the EWC is to compel employers' representatives to inform and consult employees' representatives on matters of 'transnational' importance. According to the guidelines of the directive, employees' representatives are entitled to knowledge about: 'the structure, economic and financial situation, the probable development of the business, and of production and sales, the situation and probable trend of employment, and substantial changes concerning organization, introduction of new working methods or production processes, transfers of production, mergers, cut-backs or closures of undertakings, establishments or important parts thereof, and collective redundancies' (Official Journal of the European Communities 1994). As we shall see later on in the chapter, there are huge variations on the extent to which employees' representatives are informed and consulted on these matters. Some companies choose to share some information, but not consult before key decisions are taken. Others offer genuine information and consultation concomitantly. The 'degree' (Marchington 2005) of employee voice offered is largely at the discretion of the employer, as long as the company conforms to the minimum statutory requirements as spelt out in the EWC directive (Platzer et al. 2001). Dobbins and Dundon provide more details about information and consultation in this volume.

In large part because of the ambiguities surrounding the wording of the 1994 directive, it underwent a revision, or 'recasting' (Jagodzinski 2009; Schomann 2011) in 2009. This was a multiyear process, during which time the European social partners (BusinessEurope representing employers' interests and the European Trade Union Confederation (ETUC) representing the interests of labour) vacillated back and forth until they finally agreed to begin the revision in 2008. According to Lücking (2009), the recast EWC directive (2009/38/EC): (i) provided clearer definitions of information and consultation; (ii) more clearly differentiated EWCs from national works councils; (iii) provided a greater role for unions in the forums; (iv) gave EWC delegates the right to paid training; and (v) imposed rules on how EWCs handle structural change. For all practical purposes, it is still too early to assess the impact of these changes, but we will return to this issue in the final section of this chapter.

In sum, EWCs are a uniquely European animal. Nowhere else in the world are statutory, legally required information and consultation forums to be found. All large, multinational corporations operating within the EU are obligated to operate and to fund a company-level EWC in order to inform and consult workers' representatives employed by the firm. This chapter differs from others in the book in as much as it presents a discussion of a politically, that is to say, a legally mandated form of transnational employee voice.

Varieties of capitalism in one geographical space

Interesting things happen when different varieties of capitalism (Hall and Soskice 2001; Hancké 2009) are brought together into one geographical space. Among the many critiques made of the varieties of capitalism framework (Schmidt 2003; Allen 2004; Deeg and Jackson 2007; Kang 2010), not enough fuss has been made of the fact that it is, ultimately, just a dry, comparative model. So what if firms operating in liberal market economies pursue a set of corporate strategies that are qualitatively different from firms operating in coordinated market economies? Who cares if corporate governance unfolds one way in the UK and another in Germany? This may be analytically interesting in the abstract, but there is not much 'action' in asking these questions. However, when varieties of capitalism meet, converge, and overlap in an EWC, sparks fly. There are, accordingly, huge implications for cross-national labour relations.

IDENTITY AND EMPLOYMENT SYSTEMS

It should not be surprising to learn that employees' representatives in EWCs identify closely with their own national employment system. For this reason, identity has become an important topic in the EWC literature (Timming 2006; Whittall 2010; Whittall et al. 2007, 2009b). Employees' representatives inevitably identify with their respective (home country) variety of capitalism (Hall and Soskice 2001), national business system (Whitley 1999), industrial order (Lane 1995), employment relations system (Bamber et al. 2010), or whatever else scholars have chosen to call these nationally defined and delineated models over the years. The home country employment system serves as a point of reference for EWC delegates in respect to how industrial relations are 'supposed' to unfold (Timming 2010). Needless to say, there is a strong normative element to this frame of thinking. Furthermore, different countries have provisions for different levels of employee voice (Frege and Godard 2010).

The salience of identity in EWCs is best illustrated with a practical example. Timming and Veersma (2007) provide an interesting case study of the effects of the merging of different varieties of capitalism into a single geographical space: the EWC at Corus, an Anglo-Dutch steel firm. This is a fitting example because it involves the two main varieties of capitalism: the liberal market economy (UK) and coordinated market economy (the Netherlands). In the early 2000s, Corus was in severe financial turmoil and needed to raise cash quickly to stay afloat. The British-based management team decided (unilaterally and without any consultation in the EWC) to sell the Dutch aluminium operations in a deal reportedly worth over 700 million Euros. The British side of the EWC viewed this move as a viable alternative to savage cuts in the UK steel operations, so were supportive. But the Dutch employees were not happy at the lack of consultation and voice in the decision-making process. The Dutch leveraged their power in the Corus Netherlands Supervisory Board effectively to block the sale of the aluminium operations. The deal, of course, then went down in flames, inevitably resulting in further layoffs in the UK operations.

This example goes some distance in illustrating what we mean by varieties of capitalism in 'action'. It does not make a dry comparison between the systems of industrial relations and corporate governance in the UK (Edwards 2003; Marchington et al. 2010) and the Netherlands (Visser 1995). Rather, it shows what happens when the two systems meet each other face to face. These kinds of confrontation are commonplace in EWCs precisely because varieties of capitalism enable what might be called 'varieties of voice'. In this case, the Dutch employees' representatives enjoyed far greater nationally regulated employee voice than the British employees' representatives, effectively enabling the former to leverage their power to block the sale of the aluminium assets via the supervisory board. Moreover, the Dutch employees' representatives were much better able to resist any layoffs in the Netherlands, again because of nationally regulated employment protection. By the same token, as a result of the comparatively greater labour market flexibility in a liberal market economy, the British workers were destined at the time to be on the receiving end of the savage, cost-saving layoffs. They had insufficient voice to resist the cuts, unlike their Dutch counterparts.

In sum, employees' representatives in EWCs do not often find each other on a level playing field, owing in large part to nationally regulated relations of power between workers' and employers' representatives. Employees' representatives inevitably and understandably identify with their home country variety of capitalism. In the hypothetical case of, for example, a predominantly German–Dutch EWC, the level of dissonant cognitions is low as a result of the similarities between the two national systems of employment, corporate governance, and labour law. But where there are two (or more) varieties of capitalism in an EWC, as was the case at Corus, the employees' representatives fall back on what we have called different 'varieties of voice' that enable some actors to leverage more power in the employment relationship than others.

TRUST, SOLIDARITY, AND LABOUR INTERNATIONALISM

So what? Why would it even matter that some employees' representatives command a stronger 'voice' in the employment relationship than others? It matters because such voice disparities within the EWC, twenty years on, can obstruct the development of inter-personal trust, solidarity, and labour internationalism between national delegations of workers' representatives (Kotthoff and Whittall 2012).

Although it has been argued previously that employee involvement and participation in organizational decision making improves employees' trust in management (Timming 2012), it is equally important to understand the development (or indeed the erosion) of trust between workers' representatives in the context of statutory employee voice mechanisms like EWCs. Timming (2009) specifically examines the relations of trust between employees' representatives in the context of the EWC. He concludes that the presence of varieties of capitalism in an EWC generally erodes cross-national trust where it exists. He argues that trust and solidarity are not simply a question of divergent or contradictory material interests, but also of divergent 'cognitions', or ways of thinking about the employment relationship. Because employees' representatives will inevitably hold different tacit, taken-for-granted 'background assumptions' (Garfinkel 1963) about how industrial relations are 'supposed' to unfold in their respective home country, they generally speaking lack 'common cognitions', which are said to be foundational to the development of trust within and between organizations (Lane 2002).

All of this discussion has led some writers to believe that EWCs are not only failing to deliver on the promise of labour internationalism (see also Ackers' scepticism about internationalism in this volume), but in some cases may even be exacerbating divisions between national delegations of employees (Wills 2001; Streeck 1997; Timming 2007). Marginson and Sisson (2006) have referred to this phenomenon as re-nationalization, whereby attempts to promote Europeanization end up sending workers further back into the trenches. This is, of course, not to suggest in any way that EWCs only impact labour internationalism negatively. Instead, what we are arguing here is that, to the extent that the effect of EWCs on workers is positive, it has not been particularly notable as yet. In short, EWCs may have tempered workers' thirst for labour internationalism, but they certainly have not quenched it.

Do European works councils add value to employees?

The question of 'added value' has dominated EWC research ever since the passing of the directive in 1994. As most writers in this area note, the EWC research community is quite divided over this contentious issue. Not wishing to go over old trodden ground (see Whittall (2000) and Waddington (2011) for an in-depth review of these positions), the optimists and pessimists ultimately differ in their assessment of how EWC delegates can influence managerial decisions at a multinational level. It is in this area that the value-added question should be situated.

With European member states moving towards economic integration with the signing of the Maastricht Treaty in 1991, the European Commission was alert to the fact that such a political and economic change had the potential to undermine national industrial relations institutions and practices. Marginson (2000) takes up this very issue in his work dealing with the notion of a Euro-company. Here, economic integration results in the increased development of international business structures as a consequence of greater market penetration and corporate expansion through a mergers and acquisitions strategy. Moreover, the arrival of the Euro-company also signals the beginning of a greater centralization of corporate decision making and the potential disenfranchising of employee representatives reliant on nationally constituted institutions.

Encouraged by the European Trade Union Confederation (ETUC), the commission saw the need to counter this potential asymmetrical development by offering employees a voice at European level. The EWC directive put into place a structure designed to complement existing national representative practices by offering employees within European undertakings access to top management. The directive not only requires management to inform workers about European-wide developments, but equally to listen to their views as part of the right to consultation.

As Waddington (2006a) and Whittall (2010) suggest, the question of the EWCs' added value is to be found in the directive itself, namely the question of whether or to what extent EWC delegates are informed and consulted over Europe-wide management decisions. However, as the following pages will demonstrate, this represents only one side of the EWC added-value coin. An extra facet, one which is implicit rather than explicit in the EWC directive, involves cross-border solidarity and the ability of EWC delegates to coordinate their actions as a means of bringing pressure to bear on management and managerial decision making. Some writers have even gone as far as suggesting that the emergence of the EWC represents the foundations for a European system of industrial relations (Lecher et al. 2001a; Marginson and Sisson 2006; Whittall 2010). Certainly, the recent explosion of international framework agreements signed by EWCs (Telljohann et al. 2009) would suggest that there is some limited credence to this train of thought.

INFORMATION AND CONSULTATION

A number of data sets exist which have addressed the issue of the added value of employee representatives receiving information and being consulted via EWCs. In the first data set, Waddington (2006a: 561) was able to draw data from 473 questionnaires completed by EWC delegates, representing a return rate of 19.8 per cent. In the second, he conducted a questionnaire of EWC delegates solely in the chemical sector. Altogether 250 questionnaires were completed, and this represents a considerably higher return rate of 31.7 per cent (Waddington 2006b: 333) A similar research project was conducted by Whittall et al. (2009b), with the one key exception: they focused only on German companies covered by the EWC directive. Emphasizing particularly what factors lead or do not lead employee representatives to set up an EWC, the researchers hypothesized that the perceived lack of an added value might represent a factor which explains the low EWC density rate in Germany. Although in total Germany has the most EWCs, when considered in terms of implementation rate this stands at 27 per cent, representing one of the lowest levels in the whole of Europe.

Waddington's (2006a, 2006b) data present a diffuse picture about the benefits to be associated with EWCs. He notes in his study of chemical EWC delegates, for example, that the data 'shows that neither the expectations of critics [pessimists] of the Directive nor of those who emphasised its potential [optimists] have been realized' (Waddington 2006b: 329). In terms of being a source of information, the EWC does appear to have its benefits, although, as will be demonstrated below, there is a strong correlation between added value and country of origin. Utilizing a five-point scale system to test how delegates valued the EWC (5 representing high and 1 low appreciation), Waddington's (2006a: 563) general survey of EWCs uncovered an average of 3.85 in terms of the EWC as a source of information, but a mere 2.64 average when it came to delegates' ability to influence managerial decisions. This leads him to note, 'that the information flow works. But this does not, however, mean that the EWC can be used as a recognised consultation body' (563).

The question of EWC involvement in managerial decision-making processes was considered in greater detail when addressing the experience of restructuring within Euro-companies. According to Waddington (2006a), the results were quite alarming. Although 81.4 per cent of respondents reported restructuring measures had occurred within their company in the last three years, a mere 20 per cent stated that they had been consulted. Furthermore, in cases where delegates were either informed or consulted, this usually occurred 'late in the day', 'usually after a final decision had already been taken, just before management went public' (Waddington 2006a: 564). In his study of EWCs in the chemicals sector, Waddington (2006b: 335) uncovered virtually identical results: 'It is apparent that managements do not meet their obligations arising from the Directive. For example, more than 30 percent of EWC representatives report that changes to working methods, new technology policy, reorganisation of production lines, employment forecasts and research and development policy had not been raised at the EWC.' In their research into the non-implementation of the EWC directive by German multinationals, Whittall et al. (2008, 2009b) discerned that one issue which could explain the relatively low EWC density rate concerned the added-value issue; others involved resource and knowledge deficits, a lack of time required to set up an EWC, as well as an unawareness of the EWC's existence.

In a two-year study of six companies without an EWC, as well as a survey of all German firms covered by the directive, a high percentage of interview and survey respondents pinpointed the added-value factor. Interview respondents, for example, indicated that both the knowledge and resource deficit were not insurmountable problems. The question remained, though, whether they could gain any real value by clarifying if they were covered by the directive. With one exception, all case study respondents were unequivocal in their belief that their interests were best served by existing national arrangements. When questioned about the perceived benefit of a possible EWC, a mere 19 per cent of survey respondents without such a structure answered positively (Lücking and Whittall 2013), 23 per cent saw no value in an EWC, 2 per cent felt it would worsen their situation, and 56 per cent were so taken with what could be achieved through an EWC that they refused to answer the question. One can only assume that the EWC is not viewed as an instrument that complements the national industrial relations setting. Interestingly, only 21 per cent of survey respondents with an EWC felt that the forum had a positive impact on their work, whilst 36 per cent failed to answer the question and 44 per cent felt it had no impact on their work (Lücking and Whittall 2013).

The study by Whittall et al. (2009b) has to be treated with a certain amount of caution, however. Due to the codetermination rights that German employees' representatives have at their disposal (see also Gold and Artus' explanation of German codetermination, this volume), referred to above as the added-value and country-of-origin correlation, the tendency to undervalue the EWC, an institution endowed with mere information and consultation, should not come as a surprise. Even Waddington (2006b) observed the existence of quite interesting differences concerning how EWC delegates valued the information flowing down from management. Discussing the situation in the chemical sector, he noted: 'There is an inverse relationship between the range and force of national information and consultation provisions and the perception of EWC effectiveness. Anglo-Irish representatives tend to rate the EWC as most effective, whereas German-Dutch and, in particular, Nordic representatives rate it the least effective' (339). A similar principle would also seem to apply to the relationship between delegates from the home country and those from foreign subsidiaries. This concerns less the industrial relations practices in southern and northern Europe, but more the question of access to top management on the part of EWC delegates based in the country in which the headquarters are based. According to Waddington (2006a), delegates from foreign subsidiaries view the EWC as an important source of information. Various EWC case studies have reached similar conclusions (Whittall 2000; Kotthoff 2006).

In brief, with the exception of EWC delegates from Ireland, the UK, and the accession countries, all of which are countries where information and consultation rights are a relatively new phenomenon, the EWC appears to serve very little purpose. Even in those cases where the EWC complements national institutions, there still pertains huge question marks about the quality and timing of the information that delegates receive. However, case study research in recent years indicates a silver lining is associated with EWCs, one that is more implicit rather than explicit in the directive, and one which even German–Dutch and Scandinavian delegates might benefit from: international solidarity.

INTERNATIONAL SOLIDARITY AS VALUE ADDED

Although the term 'council' implies the EWC is a structure for representing the collective interests of all employees within European-wide holdings, Streeck (1997) offers a word of caution here. According to him, the EWC has been constituted in such a way that national interests are likely to prevail, and this institution is nothing more than an extension of national practices rather than a fully-fledged European-level structure. Certainly, the legal framework set down by the directive pushes the EWC in this direction, favouring national employee representative procedures as opposed to developing a comparable set of European practices. Hence, from the outset the EWC is nothing more than an amalgamation of competing industrial relations practices. In addition, the situation is complicated by the fact that employee representation by its very nature tends towards parochialism (Hyman 2004), especially when forced to leave the confines of its *heimat.* In fact, the last twenty years of EWC research has been committed to disproving, proving, or at least making recommendations on how employees can speak with a common European voice.

A couple of important studies in the last two decades have been successful in attempting to classify EWCs according to their ability to collectively represent employees at a European level (Kotthoff 2006; Whittall 2003; Lecher et al. 1998; Deppe et al. 1997). Although slight differences between the authors can be observed, generally the studies depict EWCs as complying with one of the typologies in Table 10.1.

In the main, a general consensus exists that very few EWCs have become collective bodies, what Kotthoff (2006) terms a *mitgestaltendes arbeitsgremium* (a body actively involved in managerial decision-making processes). The majority of EWCs appear to be marooned at levels 1 and 2, national and host structures. As we note above, there are certain benefits associated with

Table 10.1 European Works Council Typology

Typology	Trust level	Characteristics
National body	Low	Predominance of national interests/setting up of EWC
Host body	Intermediate	Improving EWC delegate relations, tendency of host country to dominate the EWC
Collective body	High trust	Development of a collective identity, joint consultation and negotiation

these two EWC forms. The EWC is a useful source of access to top management as well as influence for delegates from countries not possessing legally enforceable information and consultation procedures. However, for EWC representatives equipped with wide-ranging codetermination rights and adequate resources, this European body has to develop beyond being a mere structure for informing and consulting employees. The benefit for such delegates involves the EWC developing into a body which can coordinate employee interests in an attempt to neutralize managerial investment and production strategies designed to promote concession bargaining. Discussing this very problem in the case of German EWC delegates from German firms, Kotthoff (2006: 133–4) noted that although most were sceptical about the value of the EWC, quite a few believed, 'the only value to be gained was in the fact that employee representatives could get to know each other'.

Kotthoff (2006) convincingly demonstrates that a sea change can be observed amongst some German EWC delegates, a realization that the internationalization of their company, and the emergence of a Euro-company, demonstrates how bilateral approaches favoured in the past no longer appear to be contemporary. For this very reason, the priority turns to surpassing the legal parameters set by the EWC directive, transforming the EWC from a mere information and consultation body to one that can take on negotiation responsibilities. This transformation process, though, depends on developing common positions, which, as the literature on EWCs demonstrates, is a giant and often impossible task. It involves delegates who are initially strangers, jointly constructing a new representative space (Kotthoff and Whittall 2012), what Knudsen et al. (2007) refer to as the development of a European mindset, and what psychologists call groupthink.

Recent work undertaken by Kotthoff and Whittall (2012, 2013) has gone some way to considering factors that underpin the development of international solidarity. In a study of five EWCs, Kotthoff and Whittall (2012) discerned that a mere two of the five EWCs they examined, Unilever and Kraft Foods, demonstrated characteristics deemed to comply with the characteristics associated with a *mitgestaltendes* EWC. Although the other three EWCs (Ford, Sanofi, and Burger and Miller (whose name has been changed)) occasionally demonstrated facets of a *mitgestaltendes* EWC, the Unilever and Kraft Food EWCs on the other hand 'demonstrated a willingness and ability to live and breathe solidarity, the means to co-operate and mutually support each other with the aim of achieving an effective representation policy' (Kotthoff and Whittall 2012). It is important to note, however, in the case of Unilever and Kraft Foods, the authors stipulate that their findings apply mainly to members of the EWC steering committee, individuals they refer to as the 'European cadre'. The emergence of a European identity is shown to be very much a top-down process, with executive members of the EWC responsible for mobilizing the workforce at plant level. Although the European cadre is committed to the European cause, European identity amongst employees and their representatives at the local level remains fragile. This should not be seen as besmirching the value of the EWC. The fact that we can now talk of a European cadre is, in itself, evidence that the EWC has made huge progress in the last twenty years.

In discussing what contributes to the success of both EWCs, the authors refer to the importance of the interrelated factors of frequency and trust. In both cases, this inner circle of EWC representatives, the steering committee, meets once a month, usually at the company's headquarters. At these meetings, they coordinate the teams' ongoing activities as well as meet management to discuss any issues they are jointly working on, for example, the production of a code of conduct to be applied when transferring production between sites. Such regular contact, even more intensive than many German joint-works councils (these meet four times a year on average), is complemented by intensive communication between the steering committee meetings. Such a context has helped to cultivate strong personal friendships between steering committee members, and a strong feeling of mutual trust (Timming 2009).

Members of the Unilever and Kraft Food steering committees are no longer marooned within national industrial settings; they now have additional means of representation at their disposal. Of course, their ability to influence management decisions depends on mobilizing, or at least the threat of mobilizing, their local constituencies. Although this might not always be feasible, the Unilever and Kraft Food EWCs indicate it should not be excluded. Certainly, the centralization of managerial decision-making processes and the emergence of a Euro-company in the case of Unilever and Kraft Foods resulted in a disenfranchising of local management and employee representatives, as predicted by Marginson (2000). According to Kotthoff and Whittall (2012), such a situation initially led to the development of utilitarian forms of solidarity, an acknowledgement that one's own interests can be best served through a centralization of representation practices.

Although pragmatism underlies the initial interest in the EWC, the catalyst so to say, the Unilever and Kraft Food case studies also demonstrate that another form of solidarity can emerge over time, what Kotthoff and Whittall (2012) have called *Verbundheitssolidarität* (strong bonding). This form of solidarity describes the existence of a community characterized by a strong sense of trust, cohesion, and identity. Prevalent amongst members of the Unilever and Kraft Foods steering committees, *Verbundheitssolidarität* sees friendships develop and a strong sense of responsibility for each other's plight:

Our research established that the eight members of the Unilever EWC steering committee are looking through 'Europe-tinted glasses' and share a sense of responsibility for solving social problems in other countries. In short, they have a European consciousness. Intensive and principled engagement with problems at plants in other countries is now a key element in their day-to-day conduct as employees, indeed became a reality for these individuals.

(Kotthoff and Whittall 2012: 56)

As Kotthoff and Whittall (2012) note, though, there exists the need to consider factors which support the potential (eventual) development of such strong friendships. According to the authors, a key factor concerns the question of intensity. Intensity is analysed at two key levels, face to face and virtual. In terms of face to face contact, both the Unilever and Kraft Food EWC steering committees meet on a regular basis, on average once a month for two to three days. If we add to this the arrival and departure days, members of the steering committees allocate around a week's working time to EWC business. Discussing the situation at Unilever, the authors noted:

The group has a high degree of individual continuity. It meets every month for one or two days of joint work. Although there are no truly close friendships within the group, there is a high degree of familiarity between members on which trust has been built. In particular, the numerous contacts that take place alongside the official agenda, such as during coffee breaks and after the meeting has finished, and during the shared dinner and drinks at the bar, where meetings involve an overnight stay, all offer scope for members to become better acquainted. The fact that the EWC secretary, who speaks English, French and Spanish [and German], and that there is no inhibition about speaking very directly, all contribute to creating the preconditions for a free exchange of views.

(Kotthoff and Whittall 2012: 58)

At the virtual level, steering committee members make wide use of the information communication technology (ICT) at their disposal: internet, email, mobile phones, and Skype. As Whittall et al. (2009a) exemplify, ICT has the advantage of not only making distance obsolete, but also of helping to incorporate developments within the group into delegates' daily and weekly routines. Hence, information networks are no longer limited to the national setting. Furthermore, by exchanging information, ideas not only remain up to date, but they are equally strengthen the bonds between countries and notions of mutual responsibility. Discussing the situation at Kraft Foods, Kotthoff and Whittall (2012: 66) note the following:

This high level of individual continuity led to a correspondingly high degree of mutual social commitment and cohesion. Five of the eight members spoke English. For the others, a 'personal' interpreter was available during meetings. Between meetings, the members maintained a lively interchange via e-mail and (for the English speakers) by phone. We [Whittall and Kotthoff] took part in two meetings and noted that the committee was very cohesive. The EWC chair said: 'We now have good contact between the countries. At the start, it was difficult to work together, we didn't really know what to do and how to do it...We got to know and trust each other. The most important thing was that we drew closer together. We held discussions on how we could work together using examples—for example, how we would deal with the case of production being moved from one country to another.

Of course, a pre-requisite of such a functioning system is the existence of a common language, often English, as well as a high degree of continuity. In addition, Kotthoff and Whittall (2012) discerned the necessity to mutually respect each other's industrial relations practices and traditions. Although neither the Unilever nor the Kraft Food EWCs are shown to have completely mastered this problem, they have made huge strides in attempting to partly neutralize the 'national representation' factor. On the one hand, this involves comprehending the national traditions that lead individuals to act or think in such a way. On the other hand, this concerns delegating responsibility to individuals so as to ensure that the varying ideological tendencies are incorporated within the EWC. Added to this, individuals are forced to take responsibility for all employees within the holding and not merely members within their home country. This involves the development of familiarity between delegates and a common sense of mutual trust and responsibility for each other; here the notions of brotherhood and sisterhood come to mind.

SOLIDARITY MATTERS

In summary, the added value of an EWC, beyond merely receiving information and being consulted, is closely linked to the emergence of a structure able to promote a common front: a body management is forced to acknowledge and that represents the interests of the European 'workforce'. Seen from this perspective, such a European institution can even serve the interests of delegates endowed with strong information and codetermination rights in their home country.

A number of factors have to be raised here, though. The first concerns the nature of solidarity. Solidarity involves certain limitations. In both the Unilever and Kraft Food cases, employees were ready to protest in favour of plants threatened by closure, but such support rarely extended to industrial action.

Where redundancies occurred, the EWC would attempt to use its access to top management to ensure affected employees received good redundancy packages. The second factor concerns the fact that the EWC is a living system which requires delegates to constantly readjust its agenda if it is to persist as an effective vehicle of employee voice. A multifaceted body made up of potentially divergent interests (competition over investment and product) and normative contexts (competing industrial relations practices), this type of EWC is faced with numerous challenges. Delegates not only have to discern areas of common interest, but equally what strategic paths exist which can lead to a joint stance and thereby have influence over managerial decision making.

Conclusions

Twenty years ago, the passing of the EWC directive was received with much fanfare, a milestone in the fight for employee rights at the European level. This European institution potentially laid the foundation from where a European system of industrial relations (Marginson and Sisson 2006) could flourish; a European industrial relations system that could hopefully complement its national counterpart, struggling to fend off employers' neoliberal deregulation agenda. The option of a transnational approach to employee representation in the form of an EWC structure suggested labour could match capital's main source of power in a global world economy: mobility.

The optimism associated with the passing of the EWC directive, however, quickly encountered an array of obstacles which suggested a more pessimistic interpretation was far more fitting. Questions arose about the conceptual validity of talking about the 'labour movement', or the notion of international solidarity. No sooner had employee representatives jointly moved to convene a special negotiating body than arguments over seat allocation, chairing of EWC meetings, and the role of unions within such bodies broke out between delegates. The employee faction often appeared riven. As indicated earlier in the chapter, this concerns the 'varieties of voice' problem, an acknowledgement that EWC members are the product of various forms of capitalist employee and employer relations. As a consequence, EWC delegates arrive on the EWC scene in possession of a whole set of normative tools specific to their own industrial relations heritage. Whilst some delegates might be perceived as management lackeys because they favour social dialogue, their counterparts appear too adversarial and so unaware of the benefits of a constructive relationship with management.

A further hurdle involves the issue of independence, the fact that many EWCs are chaired and, by default, controlled by management. In contrast to legislators' original aim, the EWC is considered in some quarters to be a body that promotes a human resource management agenda (Timming 2006), rather than offers employees a collective European platform to meet management on something like equal terms. Where such a scenario prevails, there is a tendency that the EWC develops into what some writers have ironically termed 'international nationalism', where delegates are encouraged to use the EWC to promote their own national interests rather than build European-wide bridges. Consequently, the EWC promotes, rather than debilitates, parochialism.

As Hyman (2000) noted in a special edition of the *European Journal of Industrial Relations* on EWCs, though, there is a silver lining which might give some credence to the optimists' position. Although its lack of codetermination rights makes the EWC potentially a less appealing institution for employee representatives from member states in which the principle of co-manager has a long history and is underpinned by legislation, for the UK and Ireland, two countries with a tradition of voluntarism, the EWC directive represented a welcome change in industrial relations. Prior to the passing of the 2002 Information and Consultation Directive, the EWC directive offered employees within a voluntarist industrial relations environment their first taste of continental social dialogue. Certainly, the last twenty years has involved an interesting and at times difficult learning curve for these EWC delegates. Although it would be an exaggeration to claim that by moving within EWC circles this has led in some quarters to a sea change in British and Irish industrial relations, it cannot be denied that access through the EWC to other ways of doing business has left its mark, at least more so than in countries with an already strong tradition of social dialogue.

Then there is the question of EWCs that have reportedly surpassed the so-called 'meet and confer' stage. There are now a number of established EWCs that have begun to collectively contest the employment relationship with management, to have an influence over investment decisions and the allocation of product. In some cases, this has even resulted in European-wide industrial action. Undoubtedly, reaching this stage in their development has not been without its difficulties. Many EWC delegates are quite surprised at how far they have progressed, both personally by improving their foreign language skills (usually English) and structurally in developing transparent communication avenues that help to coordinate joint action as well as develop a sense of European identity amongst EWC delegates. For these advanced EWCs, the next major challenge concerns sustainment, especially if one considers that the closure of workplaces and the exporting of jobs only serve to remind EWC members of the delicate nature of international solidarity.

What does the future hold for EWCs? We are under no illusions and realize that information and consultation will never displace bargaining over wages and terms and conditions of employment in importance to workers. A fatter pay cheque will always trump any abstract access to company information or consultation over strategic decision making. But the fact of the matter is that unions are declining institutions (see Ackers' analysis in this volume) and the employment relationship is becoming increasingly individualized, even within the EU. It is possible that EWCs and national works councils may someday be the predominant form of collective employee voice. This is even more likely given the fact that employers have not been as resistant to information and consultation as they have been to unions. But in order to preserve their relevance well into the future, they must continue to 'add value' to both employees and organizations.

▓ REFERENCES

Allen, M. (2004) 'The Varieties of Capitalism Paradigm: Not Enough Variety?' *Socio-Economic Review*, 2(1), 87–108.
Bamber, G. J., Lansbury, R., and Wailes, N. (eds) (2010) *International and Comparative Employment Relations*, 5th edn. London: Sage.
Blanks, T. (1999) 'European Works Councils as an Institution of European Employee Information and Consultation: Overview of Typical Features of National Transposition Provisions, Outstanding Legal Questions and Demands for Amendments to EWC Directive 94/45/EC'. *TRANSFER*, 5(3), 366–83.
Carley, M. and Hall, M. (2000) 'The Implementation of the European Works Councils Directive'. *Industrial Law Journal*, 29(2), 103–24.
Champagne, P. J. (1982) 'Using Labor/Management Committees to Improve Productivity'. *Human Resource Management*, 21(2/3), 67–73.
Deeg, R. and Jackson. G. (2007) 'Towards a More Dynamic Theory of Capitalist Variety'. *Socio-Economic Review*, 5(1), 149–79.
Deppe, J., Hoffmann R., and Stützel, W. (1997) *Europäische Betriebsräte-Wege in ein soziales Europa*. Frankfurt: Campus, pp. 216–32.
Edwards, P. (ed.) (2003) *Industrial Relations: Theory and Practice in Britain*. Malden: Blackwell.
Fitzgerald, I. and Stirling, J. (eds) (2004) *European Works Councils: Pessimism of the Intellect, Optimism of the Will?* London: Routledge.
Frege, C. and Godard, J. (2010) 'Cross-National Variation in Representation Rights and Governance at Work'. In A. Wilkinson, P. J. Gollan, M. Marchington, and D. Lewin (eds) *The Oxford Handbook of Participation in Organizations*. Oxford: Oxford University Press.
Garfinkel, H. (1963) 'A Conception of, and Experiments with, "Trust" as a Condition of Stable Concerted Actions'. In O. J. Harvey, *Motivation and Social Interaction: Cognitive Determinants*. New York: Roland Press.

Hall, P. A. and Soskice, D. (2001) 'An Introduction to Varieties of Capitalism'. In P. A. Hall and D. Soskice (eds), *Varieties of Capitalism: The Institutional Foundations of Comparative Advantage*. Oxford: Oxford University Press.

Hancké, B. (ed.) (2009) *Debating Varieties of Capitalism: A Reader*. Oxford: Oxford University Press.

Hyman, R. (2000) 'Editorial'. *European Journal of Industrial Relations*, 6(1), 5–7.

Hyman, R. (2004) 'Solidarity Forever?' In J. Lind, H. Knudsen, and H. Jørgensen (eds), *Labour and Employment Regulation in Europe*, pp. 35–45. Brussels: College of Europe.

Jagodzinski, R. (2009) 'Recast Directive on European Works Councils: Cosmetic Surgery or Substantial Progress?' *Industrial Relations Journal*, 40(6), 534–45.

Johnstone, S., Ackers, P., and Wilkinson, A. (2009) 'The British Partnership Phenomenon: A Ten Year Review'. *Human Resource Management Journal*, 19(3), 260–79.

Kang, N. (2010) 'Globalisation and Institutional Change in the State-Led Model: The Case of Corporate Governance in South Korea'. *New Political Economy*, 4(15), 519–42.

Knudsen, H., Whittall, M., and Huijgen, F. (2007) *Tillidsrepræsentanter i multinationale selskaber—betydningen af IKT i europæiske samarbejdsudvalg*. Odense: Kritisk Debat. [Online.] Available at: <http://www.kritiskdebat.dk/articles.php?article_id=77>.

Kotthoff, H. (2006) *Lehrjahre des Europäischen Betriebsrats: Zehn Jahre transnationale Arbeitnehmervertretung*. Berlin: Edition Sigma.

Kotthoff, H. and Whittall, M. (2012) *Wege zur transnationalen Solidarität*. Report for Hans-Boeckler Stiftung. April. Dusseldorf.

Kotthoff, H. and Whittall, M. (2014) *Paths to Transnational Solidarity*. Oxford: Peter Lang.

Lane, C. (1995) *Industry and Society in Europe: Stability and Change in Britain, Germany and France*. Aldershot: Edward Elgar.

Lane, C. (2002) 'Introduction'. In C. Lane and R. Bachmann (eds), *Trust within and between Organizations: Conceptual Issues and Empirical Applications*. Oxford: Oxford University Press.

Lecher, W., Nagel, B., and Platzer, H. W. (1998) *Die Konstituierung Europäische Betriebsräte- Vom Informationsforum zum Akteur?* Baden-Baden: Nomos Verlagsgesellschaft.

Lecher, W., Nagel, B., Platzer, H. W., Jaich, R., Rub, S., Weiner, K. P., Fulton, L., Rehfeldt, U., and Telljohann, V. (2001a) *The Establishment of European Works Councils: From Information Committee to Social Actor*. Aldershot: Ashgate.

Lecher, W., Platzer, H. W., Rub, S., and Weiner, K. P. (2001b) *European Works Councils: Developments, Types and Networking*. Aldershot: Gower.

Lecher, W., Platzer, H. W., Rub, S., and Weiner, K. P. (2002) *European Works Councils: Negotiated Europeanisation, between Statutory Framework and Social Dynamics*. Aldershot: Ashgate.

Lücking, S. (2009) *European Parliament and Council Adopt Recast Works Council Directive*. [Online.] Available at: <http://www.eurofound.europa.eu/eiro/2009/01/articles/eu0901029i.htm>.

Lücking, S. and Whittall, M. (2013) 'Ansatzpunkte und Hindernisse für die Gründung eines Europäischen Betriebsrats: Das Beispiel deutscher multinationaler

Unternehmen'. In T. Mueller and S. Rüb (eds), *Arbeitsbeziehungen, Wirtschafts-und Sozialpolitik unter den Bedingungen der Globalisierung und Europäischen Integration*. Baden-Baden. Nomos Verlag.

Marchington, M. (2005) 'Employee Involvement: Patterns and Explanations'. In B. Harley, J. Hyman, and P. Thompson (eds), *Participation and Democracy at Work* Basingstoke: Palgrave Macmillan.

Marchington, M., Waddington, J., and Timming, A. R. (2010) 'Employment Relations in Britain'. In G. J. Bamber, R. Lansbury, and N. Wailes (eds), *International and Comparative Employment Relations*, 5th edn. London: Sage.

Marginson, P. (2000) 'The Eurocompany and Euro Industrial Relations'. *European Journal of Industrial Relations*, 6(1), 9–34.

Marginson, P. and Sisson, K. (2006) *European Integration and Industrial Relations: Multi-Level Governance in the Making* (with forword by H. C. Katz). Houndmills: Palgrave Macmillan.

Official Journal of the European Communities (1994) *Council Directive 94/45/EC of 22 September 1994 on the establishment of a European Works Council or a Procedure in Community-Scale Undertakings and Community-Scale Groups of Undertakings for the Purposes of Informing and Consulting Employees*. OJ L 254 of 30.9.94, 243–51.

Platzer, H. W., Rub, S., and Weiner, K. P. (2001) 'European Works Councils, Article 6 Agreements: Quantitative and Qualitative Developments'. *TRANSFER*, 7(1), 90–113.

Ramsay, H. (1997) 'Fool's Gold? European Works Councils and Workplace Democracy'. *Industrial Relations Journal*, 28(4), 314–22.

Rivest, C. (1996) 'Voluntary European Works Councils'. *European Journal of Industrial Relations*, 2(2), 235–53.

Schmidt, V. (2003) 'French Capitalism Transformed, yet Still a Third Variety of Capitalism'. *Economy and Society*, 32(4), 526–54.

Schomann, I. (2011) 'EU Integration and EU Initiatives on Employee Participation and Social Dialogue'. *TRANSFER*, 17(2), 239–49.

Streeck. W. (1997) 'Neither European Nor Works Councils: A Reply to Paul Knutsen'. *Economic and Industrial Democracy*, 18(2), 325–37.

Telljohann, V., da Costa, I., Müller, T., Rehfeldt, U., and Zimmer, R. (2009) 'European and International Framework Agreements: Practical Experiences and Strategic Approaches'. Luxembourg: Office for Official Publications of the European Communities.

Timming, A. R. (2006) 'Identity and Trust in European Works Councils'. *Employee Relations: The International Journal*, 28(1), 9–25.

Timming, A. R. (2007) 'European Works Councils and the Dark Side of Managing Worker Voice'. *Human Resource Management Journal*, 17(3), 248–64.

Timming, A. R. (2009) 'Trust in Cross-National Labour Relations: A Case Study of an Anglo-Dutch European Works Council'. *European Sociological Review*, 25(4), 505–16.

Timming, A. R. (2010) 'Dissonant Cognitions in European Works Councils: A "Comparative Ethnomethodological Approach"'. *Economic and Industrial Democracy*, 31(4), 521–35.

Timming, A. R. (2012) 'Tracing the Effects of Employee Involvement and Participation on Trust in Managers: An Analysis of Covariance Structures'. *International Journal of Human Resource Management*, 23(15), 3243–57.

Timming, A. R. and Veersma, U. (2007) 'Living Apart Together? A Chorus of Multiple Identities'. In M. Whittall, H. Knudsen, and F. Huijgen (eds), *Towards a European Labour Identity: The Case of the European Works Council*. London: Routledge.

Visser, J. (1995) 'The Netherlands: From Paternalism to Representation'. In J. Rogers and W. Streeck (eds), *Works Councils: Consultation, Representation and Cooperation in Industrial Relations*. Chicago: University of Chicago Press.

Waddington, J. (2003) 'What Do Representatives Think of the Practices of European Works Councils? Views from Six Countries'. *European Journal of Industrial Relations*, 9(3), 303–25.

Waddington, J. (2006a) 'Was Leisten Europäische Betriebsräte? Die Perspektive der Arbeitnehmervertreter'. *WSI Mitteilungen*. 10, 560–7.

Waddington, J. (2006b) 'Contesting the Development of European Works Councils in the Chemical Sector'. *European Journal of Industrial Relations*. 12(3), 329–52.

Waddington, J. (2011) *European Works Councils: A Transnational Industrial Relations Institution in the Making*. New York: Routledge.

Waddington, J. and Kerckhofs, P. (2003) 'European Works Councils: What Is the Current State of Play?' *TRANSFER*, 9(2), 322–39.

Whitley, R. (1999) *Divergent Capitalisms: The Social Structuring and Change of Business Systems*. Oxford: Oxford University Press.

Whittall, M. (2000) 'The BMW European Works Council: A Cause for European Industrial Relations Optimism?' *European Journal of Industrial Relations*, 6(1), 61–84.

Whittall, M. (2003) 'European Works Councils: A Path to European Industrial Relations? The Case of BMW and Rover'. Unpublished Ph.D. thesis, Nottingham Trent University.

Whittall, M. (2010) 'The Problem of National Industrial Relations Traditions in European Works Councils: The Example of BMW'. *Economic and Industrial Democracy*, 3(4), 70–85.

Whittall, M., Knudsen, H., and Huijgen, F. (eds) (2007) *Towards a European Labour Identity: The Case of the European Works Council*. London: Routledge.

Whittall, M., Lücking, S., and Trinczek, R. (2008) 'Understanding the European Works Council Deficit in German Multinationals'. *TRANSFER*, 14(3), 453–68.

Whittall, M., Knudsen, H., and Huijgen, F. (2009a) 'European Works Councils: Identity and the Role of Information and Communication Technology'. *European Journal of Industrial Relations*, 15(2), 167–85.

Whittall, M., Lücking, S., and Trinczek, R. (2009b) 'The Frontiers within: Why Employee Representatives Fail to Set up European Works Councils'. *Industrial Relations Journal*, 40(6), 546–62.

Wills, J. (2001) 'Uneven Geographies of Capital and Labour: The Lessons of European Works Councils'. *Antipode*, 33(3), 484–509.

11 The EU information and consultation directive in liberal market economies

Tony Dobbins and Tony Dundon

Introduction

This chapter considers the implementation of the European Union (EU) Information and Consultation Directive (ICD) in liberal market economies (LMEs); in particular, the impact of transposing the directive into domestic information and consultation of employees (ICE) regulations in the UK in 2004 and the implications for employee voice in workplaces. The chapter is structured in five parts. The next section briefly sets the scene by context-ualizing the ICD within the different historical 'varieties of capitalism' pathways of LMEs and coordinated market economies (CMEs). It also discusses the changing dynamics of *voluntarism*,[1] and the fact that employee voice here and in one other EU member state (Ireland) was expected to be impacted most by transposition of the directive at nation state level (Dundon et al. 2006; Dundon and Collings 2011; Hall et al. 2013). The third section considers the main elements of the directive and the transposed UK national ICE regulations (2004). Section four reviews some recent empirical studies examining the impact of the directive and UK ICE regu-lations since their inception, suggesting that reliance on voluntarism and freedom of employer choice has meant that legal measures have had little impact at workplace level in terms of encouraging employers to share decision-making power or engage in meaningful consultation with employ-ees or their representatives, as the original directive intended (Hall et al. 2010, 2013). Some real-life organizational case study examples of informa-tion and consultation are provided to give readers a sense of what consult-ation looks like in practice.

Section five advances the conceptual idea of the prisoner's dilemma to help explain the picture presented by the preceding sections, drawing on labour economics perspectives relating to employee voice and cooperation (notably Leibenstein 1982). These perspectives suggest that many organizations in liberal-based economic regimes operate below their peak level of productive efficiency with regard to consultation and voice power sharing, thereby reducing the 'potential' for mutual gains to both employer and employee.

The chapter concludes that, when viewed through the analytical lens of the prisoner's dilemma, transposition of the directive within distinctly voluntarist liberal market regimes like the UK has meant that the state and employers have redistributed insufficient voice power to employees and/or their workplace representatives. Some implications are raised concerning (re-)regulation of employee information and consultation rights.

Historical pathways of capitalist institutional voice variety

LIBERAL VERSUS COORDINATED ECONOMIES

It is useful to contextualize ICE regulations within the historical pathways of institutional voice variety in liberal capitalist employment relations systems such as the UK, but also other LMEs such as the US, Australia, or Ireland (among others). While accepting insights from radical frames of reference that employee participation under capitalism as an economic system of profit accumulation is part of a structural dialectic of managing conflict and consent within a hierarchical authority relationship (Edwards 1990; Martínez Lucio 2010; Spencer 2012), it is important to acknowledge that individual capitalist economies have different institutional starting points and pathways for employee participation. Hall and Soskice's (2001) well-known typology distinguishes between institutional contexts in LMEs and CMEs. LMEs refer to comparatively uncoordinated economies, including the UK, US, Canada, and Australia, in which (1) the economy primarily operates according to free market principles and short-term shareholder value; (2) there is little engagement of employers or worker representative organizations in national social pacts governing macro-economic issues; and (3) regulatory institutions promoting workplace cooperation and employee voice are weak. Provision of employee voice has historically been voluntarist in LMEs and employers possess the primary authority to initiate it. In contrast, CMEs (including Austria, Belgium, Denmark, Finland, Germany, Netherlands, and Sweden) have encompassing and coordinated linkages between institutions promoting employee voice across various levels, and patient longer-term collaborative relations occur between employers, workers, their representatives, and other institutions. In particular, many CMEs have mandatory independent work council representative systems embedded by protective laws, and/or very high-trade union/collective bargaining coverage, ensuring that there is some equalization of power balance in workplaces.

However, despite the usefulness of LME versus CME typologies, economies broadly characterized as LMEs and CMEs can vary considerably and are subject to ongoing change (Goergen et al. 2012; Hancké et al. 2007). Within CMEs, for instance, not all countries are characterized by heavy statutory voice regulation, with Swedish and Danish employment relations character-ized by high levels of voluntarism, but with high trade union and collective bargaining coverage encouraging high levels of bargained cooperation between trade unions and employer associations (Gallie 2009). With regard to LMEs also, there are differences, for example, between Ireland and the UK: Ireland had centralized social pacts between 1987 and 2009, whereas the UK has had no history of such pacts since the failed 'social contract' in the 1970s (McDonough and Dundon 2010). Further, even light-touch, legally backed consultative employee voice structures remain unpalatable to many in other LME contexts like the USA, where there is vehement opposition to collectiv-ism (Patmore 2010).

CHANGING HISTORICAL PATTERNS OF EMPLOYEE VOICE IN LIBERAL MARKET ECONOMIES

As noted above, an important shared characteristic of LMEs (and some CMEs) is the historical pre-eminence of liberal voluntarism in the employment relationship. Historically, governments regulated aspects of employment rela-tions to import a semblance of counterveiling power by making various legal interventions to support voluntarism. For many years, voluntarist employment relations in the UK were based on pluralist collective bargaining negotiations between employers and trade unions, which was the main form of employee participation.

In recent decades, however, decline and erosion of the once dominant model of voluntary collective bargaining in many LMEs has given way to a highly fragmented employment relations system characterized by increased diversity and experimentation (Freeman et al. 2007). Driven by new political circumstances and intensifying market pressures, the 1980s onwards saw a very different agenda for workplace participation, one focused on reducing union power and promoting more individualistic, anti-collectivist philoso-phies. This agenda was particularly pronounced and indeed highly politicized in the UK (under Thatcher), in Australia (with the Howard government's work choices reforms), and in the US (under Reagan's free market econom-ics). The UK context was also influenced by the import of so-called new management practices from overseas—notably from countries like Japan and the USA—terms like 'empowerment', 'involvement', and 'human resource management' (HRM) became more fashionable. The employment relations philosophy became much more overtly managerialist and unitarist, thereby increasingly superseding traditional pluralism. The managerialist rationale for employee participation stressed direct communication with individual employees which, in turn, often bypassed or marginalized trade unions. Unlike notions of industrial democracy in the 1970s, employee involvement from the 1980s stemmed from a drive for enhanced efficiency and flexibility from labour supply, rather than worker rights per se (Streeck 1987). This new wave of involvement was neither focused on, nor indeed accommodated, robust employee participation in areas of managerial decision-making prerogative (Wilkinson et al. 2013). In effect this was, and remains, a period of employee participation on management's terms, and objectives were predicated on assumptions that what is good for business must be good for employees. Many specific mechanisms to tap into labour as an organizational performance resource became enshrined in models of best-practice HRM and high-commitment management largely originating in the USA (Wright et al. 2001). Individual employer experimentation with a myriad of so-called high-involvement work practices reflected the need to exploit employee discretionary effort to facilitate profit accumulation, by creating cooperative alternatives to simply controlling the wage-effort bargain.[2] This was particularly necessary in product market contexts focused on quality competition and input of skilled knowledge workers, as competitive pressures from places like East Asia intensified. But employee creative input was less required in product market contexts where competition on cost reduction was dominant; here 'bleak house' or 'low road' scenarios of negligible participation were more evident (Godard 2004; Sisson 1993).

Finally, and also originating in the USA, from the 1990s onwards there was increased interest in what Kochan and Osterman (1994) termed mutual gains bargaining between employers and unions/employees, in an era when union power was on the wane in LMEs. Although no agreed definition of mutual gains exists, it can be interpreted as follows (Kochan and Osterman 1994; McKersie et al. 2008; Cullinane et al. 2013):

(1) management and workers are conscious of the shared consequences of their actions and therefore openly exchange information in a cooperative fashion to highlight areas of joint interest;
(2) they then generate decision-making options, through problem-solving structures; and
(3) choose those options that offer the highest joint returns.

In the UK context, interest in the mutual gains concept found favour among advocates of social partnership (Guest and Peccei 2001). The literature is not entirely definitive on what aspects of employment relationships are assigned to mutual gains or partnership territory, though it is generally perceived to encompass issues like pay, employment security, training, job redesign, and participative or involvement structures. Management and workers are still held to maintain their own distinct interests but seek accommodations through cooperative trade-offs, which can be either robust or weak in terms of power sharing, often encompassing newer individualized HRM-type practices alongside cooperative collective information and consultation arrangements (Cullinane et al. 2013; Dobbins and Gunnigle 2009; Johnstone et al. 2010; Oxenbridge and Brown 2004). Further interest in cooperative mutual gains partnership has been legitimized as a more permanent and embedded feature of employment regimes with the advent of European-level regulations for employee voice, notably the *European Directive on Employee Information and Consultation 2002*, the subject of this chapter.

THE RISE OF NEOVOLUNTARISM IN LIBERAL MARKET ECONOMIES

At the same time as traditional patterns of employee voice were changing in LMEs like the UK, growing ideological emphasis on economic competitiveness, market liberalization, and HRM coincided with reassessment by the state (at EU and national level) of the purpose of legal regulation of the employment relationship (Barry 2009; Martínez Lucio and MacKenzie 2004). This reassessment of regulatory purpose can now be partly interpreted as a means of protecting managerial prerogative to make decisions about governing their own workplaces. In particular, EU regulations have gravitated in recent times from 'harder' laws (such as those promoting equal pay or health and safety) towards 'softer', lighter-touch measures allowing EU member states greater latitude to transpose arrangements fitting different national cultures (Gold 2009). What distinguishes emerging EU social policy is its 'low capacity to impose binding obligations on market participants, and the high degree to which it depends on various kinds of voluntarism . . . in the name of self-regulation' (Streeck 1995: 45–9). This neovoluntarism in a contemporary context has provided employers with greater choice in shaping their 'preferred mode of intervention' (Barnard and Deakin 2000: 341). Indeed, light-touch legal regulation, combined with the unitarist advance of HRM, makes it easier for employers in LMEs to shape practice and determine policy options regarding workplace participation for and on behalf of workers than in CMEs (Thompson 2011, 2013). This neovoluntarism has constituted what can be termed a permissive system in LMEs because it places fewer constraints, aside from a tendency towards minimalist regulations, on employer actions (Dobbins 2010).

The European information and consultation directive and the UK ICE regulations

THE EU INFORMATION AND CONSULTATION DIRECTIVE

The European ICD (2002/14/EC) *establishing a general framework for inform-ing and consulting employees in the European Community* can be viewed against this contemporary backdrop of varieties of capitalism, neovoluntar-ism, and light-touch labour law. The directive has its origins in the European Community Charter of Fundamental Social Rights for Workers, adopted in 1989, which establishes the major principles on which the present European labour law model is based. The charter explicitly promotes workers' rights to information and consultation at the workplace. Directive 2002/14/EC was subsequently adopted in March 2002 and was intended to enhance employee rights to information and consultation on a range of business, employment, and restructuring issues. But it is highly significant that, in Article 1 of the directive, EU members are permitted under this general framework to cus-tomize national laws in the transposition process to suit local arrangements, which is better known as the 'subsidiarity principle' and mechanism of 'open coordination'.[3] The scope of the directive applies to undertakings with at least fifty employees or establishments employing at least twenty employees. The directive was designed to promote social dialogue, mutual trust, and elements of shared decision making across workplaces in EU member states, but requirements are stipulated in quite generalist terms.[4] It requires member states to introduce permanent arrangements so managers would support dialogue at workplace level in three broad areas: (1) provide *information* pertaining to the economic situation of the company; (2) enable *information and consultation* concerning developments or threats to employment; and (3) *inform and consult employees, with a view to reaching agreement*, on decisions likely to lead to changes in work organization or contractual arrangements. It is notable that the directive is 'without prejudice to those systems which provide for the direct involvement of employees as long as they are always free to exercise the right to be informed and consulted through their representatives' (paragraph 16). This reference to direct involvement notwithstanding, there is endorsement for information and consultation to occur through the conduit of elected employee representatives on informa-tion and consultation forums. In some countries, particularly in those CMEs like Germany and the Netherlands with (compared to the UK) long-established mandatory regulations for workforce representation, the directive did not require major regulatory or institutional reform. However, in LMEs like the UK and Republic of Ireland, (RoI) without a historical pathway of institution-alized employee information and consultation rights, major legislative reform was envisaged.

Indeed, there was a perception that the directive was introduced with specifically the UK and RoI in mind, given that they were the only two EU member states at the time lacking legislation for generalized employee information and consultation voice (Dundon and Collings 2011; Hall and Purcell 2012). However, despite having a centralized social pact at the time, the Irish did not reach agreement on the directive through social partnership. Rather, events were more controversial, due to the overriding concern of employers and government to prevent legislation advancing mandatory collective voice systems perceived to jeopardize inward investment by (non-union) US multinationals (Lavelle et al. 2010; McDonough and Dundon 2010). Such was the growing powerful influence of US multinationals over the Irish political economy, the government were very receptive to employer lobbying aimed at restricting the content of the directive and national ICE regulations. Numerous meetings occurred between Irish government officials and employers to discuss the ICE regulations, with trade unions excluded despite this being an era of tripartite social partnership. In part, unions opted out of seeking to actively influence the regulatory space for ICE because they were concerned such regulation might be used by employers to undermine traditional collective bargaining. In comparison, in the UK, which has no recent history of centralized social partnership pacts, for the first time in three decades, the Confederation of British Industry (CBI), government, and Trades Union Congress (TUC) negotiated a tripartite agreement on the ICE regulations. Yet, like their Irish counterparts, fear among British unions of being marginalized by ICE arrangements outweighed any drive to deepen engagement with the ICE regulations. Such is the complexity of political economy that static typologies such as LMEs or CMEs can ignore other nuances and realities.

THE UK ICE REGULATIONS

Facilitated by the previously mentioned subsidiarity principle of open coordination and the permissive general framework of the directive endorsed at EU level, both the UK and the Irish Governments transposed their provisions in a way (while preserving voluntarism) that reflected variation in their national customs relative to many continental European nations (Dundon and Collings 2011; Hall et al. 2013). The next part will now consider the design of the UK regulations specifically. The *Information and Consultation of Employees Regulations 2004* (SI 2004/3426) presents the legislation in the UK, which constitutes a light-touch mandate. The main provisions are outlined in Box 11.1.

The transposed regulations in the UK remain contentious in at least two principle areas: the elective nature of legislation and its scope for promoting

---

BOX 11.1 PROVISIONS OF UK INFORMATION AND CONSULTATION OF EMPLOYEES (ICE) REGULATIONS 2004

➤ *Coverage*: The legislation applies to 'undertakings' in Great Britain with fifty or more employees. There is equivalent legislation for undertakings situated in Northern Ireland.

➤ *Trigger*: The legal requirement to inform and consult employees is not automatic. It is triggered by a formal request from employees for an information and consultation agreement, or by employers choosing to start the process themselves (employer notification).

➤ An employer must establish information and consultation procedures where a valid request has been made by employees.

➤ Such a request must be made in writing by 10 per cent of employees in an undertaking (subject to a minimum of fifteen and a maximum of 2,500 employees).

➤ Where the employees making the request wish to remain anonymous, they can submit the request to an independent body (usually the Central Arbitration Committee (CAC)).

➤ The employer would have the opportunity to organize a secret ballot of employees to endorse or reject the initial request.

➤ *Pre-existing arrangements*: An employer can continue with pre-existing information and consultation arrangements, provided that such arrangements have been agreed prior to an employee's written request and:
  i. the agreement is in writing, including any collective agreements with trade unions;
  ii. the agreement covers all employees in the undertaking;
  iii. the agreement sets out how the employer is to provide the information and seek employee views for consultation; and
  iv. the arrangements have been agreed by the employees.

➤ *Standard provisions*: Where a valid request (or employer notification) has been made, but no agreement reached, standard information and consultation provisions based on ICE Regulation 18 would apply.

➤ Where the standard information and consultation provisions apply, the employer shall arrange for a ballot to elect the employee representatives. Regulation 19 states that there shall be one representative per fifty employees, or part thereof, with a minimum of two and a maximum of twenty-five representatives.

➤ Consultation should take place with a view to reaching agreement on decisions.

➤ Information must be given in such time, and in such fashion and with such content as are appropriate to enable the information and consultation representatives to conduct an adequate study and, where necessary, prepare for consultation.

➤ The maximum penalty for failing to comply with a declaration made by the CAC is £75,000.

➤ ICE Regulations 25 and 26 provide for the confidentiality of sensitive information given to ICE representatives.

➤ ICE representatives, and employees making a request, are protected against discrimination/unfair dismissal for exercising their rights under the ICE regulations.

➤ ICE representatives are to be afforded paid time off to carry out their duties.

Source: Department for Business, Innovation and Skills [Online.] Available at: <http://www.bis.gov.uk/files/file25934.pdf>.

(favouring) direct involvement rather than indirect (collective) representation, as specified in the original directive. The UK legislation effectively defines the right of employees to company information and managerial consultation as an elective and not fundamental automatic right. As specified in the UK ICE regulations, employees must obtain sufficient support (at least 10 per cent of the workforce, capped at 2,500 employees) to formally 'trigger' their mandatory rights by making a written request to an employer, or to the state Central Arbitration Committee (CAC). The elective process is in practice a hurdle that many employees will find difficult, especially for those already denied access to union protection and representation. Even when triggered, voluntary 'pre-existing' arrangements can continue if the employer can show that employees (or unions) are agreeable to pre-existing arrangements. There is considerable scope for employers to establish organization-specific ICE arrangements, including direct involvement and non-union employee representative systems.

In addition to the minimalist voluntarist traditions embellished in the transposed ICE regulations, it is equally important to note what is not covered. First, in summary form, it can be said the ICE regulations in the UK (and RoI) are not aimed at creating co-decision-making or works-based committee structures for industrial democracy, as might be found with German codetermination or representative systems in Nordic countries. Second, while the directive endorses employee representation as the preferred form of employee engagement, it does not make any particular type of representation compulsory. It is therefore possible that the UK and RoI have created their own institutional pathways that may be characterized as 'dualistic channels': recognizing unions where they already exist, while simultaneously legitimizing direct and more individualized involvement processes. Third, unlike schemes in Belgium and the Netherlands, there is no provision for injunctive relief to revert to standardized informational and consultation models if regulations are not followed.

Empirical research on information and consultation practices and outcomes

National-level statistical data charting the impact of the directive or the UK ICE regulations are not widespread. Apart from the UK Workplace Employment Relations Study (WERS) 2011 (van Wanrooy et al. 2013), statistics reporting the incidence of ICE practices are rare. First findings from WERS 2011 (van Wanrooy et al. 2013: 14–15) track incidence of employee representation between 2004 and 2011. The prevalence of joint consultative committees (JCC) remained the same, with 7 per cent of all workplaces having a JCC for

Table 11.1 Changing Patterns of Employee Representation in UK Workplaces (2004–11)

Percentage of workplaces with the following employment relations provisions	2004	2011
Union recognition	24	21
Workplace JCCs	7	7
Higher-level JCCs	29	18
European works councils (multinational firms)	21	18
Non-union	7	7
Any employment relations structure	45	35

Note: Weighted based: workplaces with five or more employees.
Source: van Wanrooy et al. (2013: 14–15).

consultative purposes. However, there was a decline in higher-level JCCs in multi-site organizations from 29 per cent in 2004 to 18 per cent in 2011. Meanwhile, there was no change in stand-alone non-union employee representation (not connected to a union or JCC), which occurred in 7 per cent of all workplaces in 2004 and 2011. The proportion of workplaces with any form of employee representation fell from 45 per cent to 35 per cent between 2004 and 2011, meaning that 65 per cent of all workplaces did not have *any* collective employee representation structure in 2011. The data are summarized in Table 11.1.

The WERS 2011 findings (van Wanrooy et al. 2013: 18–19) also indicate that methods for sharing information increased between 2004 and 2011, but more robust consultative measures have decreased or stayed the same. The most widely used direct communications were workplace meetings involving all staff, used in 80 per cent of workplaces in 2011, up from 75 per cent in 2004, and team briefings, which rose from 60 per cent to 66 per cent. In relation to consultation over workplace change, van Wanrooy et al. (2013: 20–1) suggest it appears that discussions in consultative committees like JCCs may be 'more circumscribed by managers' than in 2004, with management narrowing options over which employees are consulted. Among employee representatives on JCCs, the percentage who perceived that managers typically focused consultation around their own preferred option rose from 8 per cent in 2004 to 30 per cent in 2011. Outcomes of redundancy consultation were mixed. The consultation process created alternatives to redundancy or reduced the number of redundancies in 22 per cent of workplaces where consultation occurred. Changes were made to the employer's means of preparing employees for redundancy in 19 per cent of cases. Other changes were less common: strategies for redeployment were identified or changed in 14 per cent; redundancy payments were increased in 10 per cent; and criteria for selection were changed in 5 per cent. In terms of other areas of consultative workplace change, changes in work techniques and introducing new technology were—along with new products or services—items on which managers were least likely to consult with employees or their representatives. Consultation was more frequent over changes affecting terms and conditions of employment and organization of work than over higher-order strategic business decisions like product innovation. In relation to stages of decision making, half (52 per cent) of employees considered that management were 'very good' or 'good' at seeking their views. However, this is the lowest level step in the consultative decision-making process. Employees were less likely to rate managers as 'very good' or 'good' at responding to suggestions (46 per cent) and, in particular, allowing employees influence over final decisions at a higher consultative level (34 per cent).

Other important research on information and consultation practice several years post the EU directive points to variable and uneven impacts (see Koukiadaki 2010; Hall and Purcell 2011, 2012; Hall et al. 2013). Drawing on an EU network of national experts and the 2009 European Company Survey, Hall and Purcell (2011) conclude that, overall, evidence on the extent, oper-ation, and impact of ICE arrangements across Europe is mixed and it is difficult to provide measured assessment of the overall impact of the directive. It is apparent, they argue, that flexibilities built into the directive are widely reflected in variability in national legislation giving effect to its provisions. This is most acute outside the group of countries with mature systems of ICE, reflected in national provisions in countries like the UK and Ireland that make ICE rights dependent on employee application and provide great scope for local decentralized variation. This flexible regulatory approach, coupled with the relative absence of active promotion of ICE by governments, appears to have blunted the impact of the directive in spurring diffusion of ICE arrange-ments and setting clear standards for ICE practice. Although data on inci-dence of ICE bodies are not comprehensive, it is apparent, Hall and Purcell (2011) observe, that countries with higher coverage of ICE bodies, including Austria, Belgium, Denmark, France, Germany, and the Netherlands, tend to be those with mature and embedded ICE systems, where in most cases establish-ment of ICE bodies is technically mandatory and/or backed by strong unions. In contrast, in countries like the UK and Ireland, there is little indication of widespread uptake of ICE arrangements. Their report also identifies practices deemed important in underpinning effective consultation, including scope for calling special meetings of ICE bodies, protection and facilities for employee representatives, and access to external advice. It is notable that provisions on such matters in the ICD are limited compared with those contained in the recently 'recast' European Works Council directive.

There are also a small number of qualitative studies examining the impact of ICE regulations and practices, mainly in the UK (Hall and Purcell 2012; Hall et al. 2013; Koukiadaki 2010; Taylor et al. 2009). These studies add to the statistical picture of minimal and variable impact patterns. These deeper micro-level case studies show how employers respond to, or capture, regulation by engendering a minimalist approach which favours managerial authority at the expense of diffusing power-sharing voice arrangements. The extent to which ICE regulations can be a spur for mutual trust social dialogue, as envisaged in the directive itself, remains an important empirical issue. In this regard, the overall evidence would suggest that while there may be elements of mutuality and cooperation, it is generally not robust or enduring (Cullinane et al. 2013). Generally speaking, management continues to dominate ICE arrangements and control the agenda (Hall et al. 2013). Drawing on evidence from longitudinal case studies in twenty-five organizations, Hall et al. (2010, 2013) assess if ICE bodies established in the shadow of the UK ICE regulations have been a vehicle for robust effective consultation via what they term the 'legislatively prompted voluntarist procedure'. Assessed against the regulations' default provisions that mention ICE concerning strategic business issues and major organizational change, a minority of participating organizations were categorized as 'active consulters', but a majority were only 'communicators'. ICE primarily occurs on management's terms and is mostly direct communication rather than active consultation, which is not sufficiently robust to embed lasting cooperative mutuality. Beyond providing the catalyst for managerial moves to introduce ICE, the influence of the UK ICE regulations were deemed largely peripheral. While the legal framework remains at the periphery, differing patterns of ICE evident in the twenty-five case organizations primarily reflected internal organizational dynamics, especially management style, and company histories. Drawing on research by Hall et al. (2010), Box 11.2 provides a selection of real-life organizational case examples of information and consultation in practice.

Other research confirms the limited impact of the UK ICE regulations. As Wilkinson and Gollan (2007: 1138) argue, 'the I&C regulations could easily result in 'weak' employer-dominated partnerships and non-union firms using direct communications and information while marginalizing collective consultation'. Taylor et al. (2009) question the capacity of the ICE regulations to influence redundancy outcomes in the context of six unionized case studies. Koukiadaki (2010) identifies mixed outcomes with some mutual gains that are reflective of a specific business and management consultancy context. Yet, she argues that 'much work remains to be done on the ways in which such information and consultation arrangements can evolve as effective mechanisms for the exercise of the "voice" rights that the Directive confers' (Koukiadaki 2010: 366).

However, despite their valuable insights, existing studies do not offer comprehensive or explicit theoretical explanations of *why* information and consultation legislation largely fails to generate cooperative mutuality in the employment relationship. In the next section, we suggest that the concept of the prisoner's dilemma in game theory offers a useful tool to help explain why there will be tendencies towards non-cooperation more than cooperation in LME institutional contexts like the UK.

BOX 11.2 REAL-LIFE CASE EXAMPLES OF INFORMATION AND CONSULTATION IN PRACTICE

Engineering company

A major US-based engineering multinational employing around 5,000 employees in several UK plants, the organization is highly unionized with a strong tradition of workplace collective bargaining and an effective European works council. Management commitment to extend consultation led to union agreement on the creation of a national ICE forum representing all employees and local arrangements to include non-union employees.

Union insistence on a 'negotiated agreement' under the terms of the ICE regulations led to a lengthy delay in reaching formal agreement. Hence some changes, in particular those providing for non-union employee representation, had not been implemented. Uncertainty remained both as to the operation of election procedures for such representatives and their impact. At workplace level, employee representation continued through the union structure (membership remained at around 80 per cent for groups covered by collective bargaining).

National-level ICE meetings continued regularly and their principal utility consisted of discussing and promoting 'best practice' in HR policy, joint briefings on issues in employment law, and dealing with contentious issues emerging from the UK implementation of corporate HR policy. Effective consultation took place at the European works council, the logical organizational level for consultation over issues of company strategy, in which several members of the national forum were active participants. Matters relating to employment were handled at workplace level. The company's commitment to effective consultation was principally reflected in these activities.

The union provided representation, enjoyed good facilities, and participated in both formal pre-meetings and regular informal liaison between representatives. There were some indications that representation of staff grades was suffering and that representation by and from manual grades was becoming increasingly dominant. The research covered periods of dramatic business growth; there was no opportunity to test the resilience of consultative mechanisms in more turbulent economic times but senior management remained strongly committed to their continuation.

Northern housing association

This charity employs around 160 people providing housing and support services for young offenders. In 2006 it reached a partnership agreement with a trade union which included provisions on information and consultation 'guided by . . . the [ICE] Regulations'. Seeking to combine union recognition with the spirit of the ICE regulations, the agreement is formally based around union recognition supplemented by understandings that the union will ensure that all employees are aware of the activities of the joint consultation and negotiating group (JCNG). The agreement contains a 'reopener' clause that allows investigation of the representative rights of non-union members if membership falls below 40 per cent.

Operating within an increasingly competitive tendering environment, the association has had to take significant costs out of its operation to improve its chances of successful tendering. This has largely been achieved through reducing the numbers of workplaces alongside staff changes and a review of terms and conditions. All have been referred to the quarterly JCNG meetings, attended by the CEO and other senior managers and an employee side whose lead member, the union district officer, has established close links with senior management. Pre-meetings of representatives facilitate a coherent staff side position.

Over two years the JCNG has discussed all aspects of change and has been influential in securing consent to difficult reorganization. Aspects of the terms and conditions review have been modified and the JCNG enjoys widespread support amongst all involved. One successful example was the referral of the important issue of outsourcing out-of-hours cover to a working party of the JCNG for consideration. Monthly team briefings keep all staff informed of developments and although the issue of non-membership remains pertinent it is unlikely to undermine the partnership. The ICE arrangements have developed into a genuine consultation forum and the dominant means of internal information dissemination.

Law firm

The law firm is a regionally based solicitors' practice in southern England. It established a 'voice' forum in 2007. Staff numbers fell from 130 in December 2007 to below 100 in early 2010. Job losses and redundancies were handled through individual or departmental discussions and not discussed directly at voice meetings. After an initial flurry of issues raised by staff representatives—a mix of operational, staff benefits, and housekeeping suggestions and questions about HR policy—the volume of staff-raised agenda items decreased. The frequency of meetings was reduced as a result. In terms of the development of the role of voice, this was offset by staff representatives increasingly raising questions about 'bigger issues'—notably the effects of the recession on the firm's business, the impact of job losses on staff workload and morale, and the prospect for annual pay rises—and by an increase in the number and significance of agenda items tabled by management, particularly changes in HR policy.

Although networking among staff representatives between meetings did not take place, their input at meetings was confident and constructive and occasionally assertive, with pointed questions being asked on some issues. Voice was perceived as valuable by both management and staff representatives interviewed. A number of innovations were introduced by the firm as a result of staff suggestions, and staff views on management's options for Christmas closing arrangements were influential. More generally, staff feedback was reported to the firm's partners. However, notwithstanding the development of the voice process since it was first established, it was used by management primarily for 'communications' purposes. Discussion at 'voice' led on occasion to the modification of management's approach to a particular issue but in general stopped short of formal consultation. Further development of the role of voice was not expected by management in the short term.

Financial processing company

This US-owned multinational is primarily concerned with electronic processing transactions for corporate clients in the finance sector. It has multiple sites in the UK and internationally and the research centred on its main (head office) UK site which employs around 1,800 staff. In 2007, the company was acquired by a private equity group in a compulsory purchase. Other major changes occurring at the site over the period of the research included job losses, mainly as a result of a change in business volume, and management restructuring. One trade union is recognized for collective bargaining although membership was believed to be less than 20 per cent.

The ICE regulations provided an impetus to reforming staff communication and led to the establishment of a communication forum (CF) at the main site in 2005. There are no reserved seats for union members on the CF and there was initial union concern that the forum might undermine collective bargaining arrangements. However, there has been no evidence to suggest this has happened. The forum has met on a regular basis, with special meetings being called on important issues. An independent formal review of the CF took place in 2006 and revealed concerns about the low profile of the forum, its perceived lack of effectiveness, particularly as a forum for consultation, and an overemphasis on minor issues. Since then, the quality of issues discussed has improved and management appears to be more willing to share information and consult.

Discussions have moved away from the traditional mixture of HR and housekeeping items to embrace more meaningful matters such as job losses, management changes, and staff redeployment. There has been greater stability in membership and staff awareness of the CF, although both management and employee representatives would like to see more people actively engaged in the arrangements.

Source: Hall et al. (2010).

The prisoner's dilemma: problem of adversarial non-cooperation in LMEs

The concept of the prisoner's dilemma in game theory is useful for explaining why minimalist design of national information and consultation laws in LMEs encourages tendencies at workplace level towards mutual losses or employer gains, more than mutual gains. When considered in the LME contexts of the UK and RoI, the prisoner's dilemma problem in game theory shows why two parties might not cooperate, even if it initially appears to be mutually beneficial to do so (Leibenstein 1982; Aoki 1984; Freeman and Lazear 1995; Bowles 2006; Marsden and Cañibano 2011). Albert Tucker 'officially' coined the term 'prisoner's dilemma', with the following example of prison sentence outcomes (see Poundstone 1992). Two suspects from a criminal gang are imprisoned on a bank robbery charge. Each prisoner is in solitary confinement so cannot contact the other. The police do not have enough evidence to convict the pair on the principal charge, but plan to sentence both to one year in prison on a lesser charge. However, the police offer each prisoner a deal simultaneously: if s/he testifies against their partner, s/he will go free, but the partner will get ten years in prison on the main charge. But there is a catch. If both prisoners decide to testify against each other, both will receive a five-year sentence. The crux of the theory is whether cooperation and trust between the partners in crime can generate more mutually beneficial win–win outcomes collectively (one-year sentence each). However, if there is mistrust of the other's perceived intentions, then pursuing maximum individual self-interest will prevail, causing both prisoners to betray the other, the result being a lose–lose outcome (five-year sentence each).

Applying the prisoner's dilemma concept to employee–management relations, the combination of decisions by parties as to whether to cooperate or not by sharing power and information can influence perceived outcomes and expected benefits for both parties, in terms of the degree to which their material interests are realized. Management decisions tend to be connected in some way to the desired outcome of maximizing profit, whereas employee decisions are linked to more multifaceted outcomes like pay, working conditions, and better voice.

Leibenstein (1982) applied the prisoner's dilemma concept to cooperative (or non-cooperative) workplace relations, identifying frequent adversarial outcomes in liberal market regimes due to problems of mistrust with regard to dominant choices of employer–employee non-cooperation, at the expense of reducing mutual gains for employees and employers. According to Leibenstein, sharing information and productivity gains would generally seem to be an area of mutual benefit. Yet in reality it often involves a prisoner's dilemma, due to uncertainty about the other party's intentions. That is to say, in LME contexts particularly, either or both individual parties may pursue maximization of their own short-term self-interest rather than choose collective longer-term mutually beneficial options; especially where there are acute power imbalances. For example, in relation to voice, employees may be reluctant to share discretionary knowledge with employers if they perceive that there would be no gain in doing so, or even that to do so might harm their interests. Employee withholding of effort and knowledge can damage productivity because employment contracts are incomplete and indeterminate: employers cannot precisely specify and control all employee contributions (Baldamus 1961). Many employers, meanwhile, are often unlikely to share sufficient power to provide optimum employee voice unless compelled to do so by countervailing power or external compulsion, choosing to preserve managerial prerogative. Leibenstein (1982) observes that a prisoner's dilemma is a zero-sum game (one party's gain equals the other's loss) if the equilibrium falls where all individual players (employers and workers) are worse off than they would be if they cooperate collectively for mutual gains purposes.

Table 11.2 draws on Leibenstein's (1982) prisoner's dilemma payoff matrix, adapting it for this chapter. At this juncture, it is important to remark that the prisoner's dilemma concept cannot exhaustively predict that complex social relations in capitalist work organizations will definitively produce particular (and consistent) choices and outcomes, because there are a multitude of causal contextual variables shaping outcomes. Nevertheless, it offers a useful analytical tool for understanding tendencies towards or away from cooperative mutuality under particular contextual conditions, and provides a benchmark against which real practice can be assessed (Edwards 2003: 22). Accordingly, Table 11.2 is intended to illustrate ideal-type tendencies towards cooperative and non-cooperative outcomes for employers (E) and workers (W), while recognizing that in reality patterns may be mixed and changeable given the indeterminacy of employment contracts and complexities of managing the contradictions of conflict and cooperation in capitalist economies (Edwards 1990, 2012; Spencer 2012). Pay-offs from all four general patterns/ tendencies are shown in the boxes, depicting gains and losses for employers (E) and workers (W).

Box 1: *mutual gains cooperation*: both employers and workers have chosen to cooperate collectively for mutual gains. Employers behave in a 'golden rule' cooperative manner, provide robust employee voice and good pay and employment conditions, and do not pursue profit maximization to its extreme. Employees also behave reciprocally in a 'golden rule' manner, being committed to the firm and willing to release discretionary information to management.

Box 2: *employer adversarialism*: employers choose to pursue their individual utility of cost minimization and/or profit maximization at the expense of workers, who follow the golden rule in the (mistaken) belief management will reciprocate with cooperation. Here employers choose an individualist adversarial approach to maximize power advantage, emphasize effort intensification, provide weak voice, and drive down pay and conditions. Management gains at workers' expense.

Box 3: *worker adversarialism*: workers choose to maximize their interests at the expense of employers who follow the golden rule. Here, workers may see little point in sharing information or cooperating with management. Thus workers gain at management's expense.

Box 4: *mutual losses*: both employers and workers choose to maximize their own separate interests, and neither follow the golden rule of mutual cooperation, in the belief the other side will fail to reciprocate and instead will seek individual gain. This is the prisoner's dilemma zero-sum outcome, because if both parties choose to maximize their own interests, mutual losses often result from reciprocal non-cooperation.

Box 1 in Table 11.2 is the only possible route to Pareto optimal cooperative mutuality. Given it is a zero-sum game no one can be made better off without making the other worse off by moving to boxes 2, 3, or 4. Following Leibenstein (1982: 94), a prisoner's dilemma situation can occur wherever possibilities for adversarial behaviour diminish potential for mutually cooperative outcomes. In LME contexts, minimalist design of national ICE regulations has been insufficient to 'shock' parties into relations of cooperative mutuality, and tendencies towards mutual losses or employer gains continue to prevail. Furthermore, the prisoner's dilemma problem means that in LME contexts ICE arrangements are often too high risk over the long term for management (and employees) to invest in and sustain genuine mutual gains arrangements.

In relation to how outcomes in the four boxes in Table 11.2 are moulded by different institutional contexts, various scholars question the capacity of market-driven economies with voluntarist systems like the UK to nurture and sustain cooperative partnerships in the long run (Dobbins 2010; Wilkinson and Wood 2012). In voluntarist systems, employees are reliant on managerial goodwill to both develop and sustain cooperative arrangements, and this will generally only continue as long as employer interests are

Table 11.2 The Prisoner's Dilemma and Employment Relations Outcomes

	Employer: golden rule	Employer: individual maximization
Worker: golden rule	Box 1 Mutual gains cooperation Win (E) Win (W)	Box 2 Non-cooperation: gains for employer, workers lose Win (E) Lose (W)
Worker: individual maximization	Box 3 Non-cooperation: gains for workers, employers lose Lose (E) Win (W)	Box 4 Non-cooperation: mutual losses for all Lose (E) Lose (W)

Source: adapted from Leibenstein (1982).

met. In comparison, more regulated CMEs like Germany, with stronger legal and institutional regulation, provide mandatory independent employee voice rights and more supportive institutional conditions for encouraging cooperation over long-term time horizons (Streeck 2004; Goergen et al. 2012; McLaughlin 2013). For example, Leibenstein (1982: 96–7) argues that in CMEs (say Germany or Denmark) adversarial prisoner's dilemma tendencies are reduced because the institutional framework 'shocks' parties into cooperating in longer-term productivity coalitions: 'the latent prisoners' dilemma possibilities are held in abeyance by conventions, institutions, and laws ... If the adversarial options are absent, then the mutual choice is the optimal position ... an effective low-cost system of laws which enforces contracts may minimize the inducement to use other types of adversarial behavior.'

However, workplace cooperation in LMEs like the UK is more short term and entails higher risk of uncertainty because it is much easier for parties to exit cooperation in comparatively deregulated labour markets, especially in an era of unstable financialized capitalism (Martínez Lucio and Stuart 2005; Thompson 2013). Streeck (1997: 201) warns that employer defections, even temporarily, from cooperative bargains with employees can lead to mistrust as workers question managements' credibility: 'the mere possibility of defection, as is by definition inherent in any voluntary arrangement, can dilute the positive effects of workplace cooperation'. Clearly, therefore, institutional context matters greatly for distributing gains and losses from information and consultation, and the risks and lifespan associated with cooperation. In LMEs, like the UK and RoI where workplace participation consists of voluntary arrangements influenced by market fluctuations and employer choice (Dobbins 2010), dominant incentives and decision making are often skewed towards adversarial non-cooperative patterns, as depicted by the prisoner's dilemma theory. Given the balance of power in LMEs typically favours employers, boxes 2 or 4 in Table 11.2 will be common outcomes, with box 1 being uncommon and unsustainable.

Conclusion

This chapter has considered the impact of the European Information and Consultation directive, particularly its minimalist national-level transposition in the UK through the ICE Regulations 2004. Existing ICE regulations in the UK are evidently too weak to act as a legal stimulus to enhance employee voice rights or prompt employers to embed lasting cooperative mutuality. Given the minimalist design of the UK regulations, recent literature finds little evidence of diffusion of robust power-sharing ICE practice in UK workplaces in the period after the regulations were implemented (Hall and Purcell 2012; Hall et al. 2013).

Crucially, management would have to allow ICE arrangements to be a breeding ground for organizational pluralism if they are to be genuine attempts at mutuality. Yet this would necessitate major cultural and ideological changes in the prevailing managerial mindset and acceptance that conflict and the contested 'politics of production' are normal features of organizational life given the structural contradictions and uncertainties of capitalism (and as something to be openly addressed on the surface rather than avoided, driven underground, or treated as pathological) (see Bacon and Blyton 2007; Martínez Lucio 2010; Edwards 2012). While it cannot be discounted that some organizations in liberal market economies like the UK, US, Ireland, and Australia can promote and sustain cooperative mutual gains arrangements through best practice information and consultation, such instances are rare under conditions of permissive voluntarism, where employers have few constraints on their unitary authority, and the broader political economy often favours cost competition as the dominant business strategy. Put simply, many employers in LMEs may simply not need or assume they do not need cooperative pluralist mutuality to compete, or view the costs as too high (Godard 2004; Dobbins and Gunnigle 2009).

It can be concluded that when viewed through the analytical lens of the prisoner's dilemma concept in game theory, the minimalist transposition of the ICD in LMEs like the UK and Ireland has meant that the state and employers have redistributed insufficient power to employees and their representatives, thereby limiting potential for collaborative knowledge sharing, employee engagement, and worker–management partnerships. Without sufficient institutional power and security, voice rights will be too weak for employees to have a robust say in workplace governance, and there will often be adversarial mistrust. The resultant effect is possible diminution of the overall quality of, and buy-in to, organizational decision making and a limiting of potential for innovative high value-added productivity coalitions. Therefore, liberalized deregulated economies like the UK with 'flexible' labour markets are less able to resolve the prisoner's dilemma problem pertaining to employee voice, thereby contributing to a productivity deficit and possible mutual 'losses' to all parties, or one-sided employer gains (where there are acute power imbalances). In comparison, in other 'varieties of capitalism', regulatory supported pluralism can 'shock' actors into cooperative mutuality, as exemplified by embedded statutory rights to works councils and codetermination, and/or strong trade unions, in coordinated economies like Germany and 'Nordic' countries. This regulated pluralism may also serve to 'force' employers into high value-added competitive postures, rather than encourage cost competition (Streeck 2004).

A possible (partial) response to the prisoner's dilemma of voice arrangements in voluntarist LMEs could be a review of the directive to provide more robust legislation to compel parties to move to a more equitable power equilibrium. Indeed, this seems to be what the directive originally envisaged, unlike the present 'legally promoted' flexible arrangements, which incentivize employers to construct ICE bodies that fall short of genuine mutual gains collaboration. If there are to be reforms arising from any upcoming review of the ICD, EU legislators might consider incorporating similar rights for ICE representatives as contained in the recently recast European Works Council (EWC) directive designed to encourage more robust processes of representative consultation; especially in member states like the UK and Ireland with relatively new statutory ICE frameworks. The 'recast' EWC directive provides employee representatives of European works councils with rights to paid time off and financial and material resources to conduct their duties, undertake training, call special meetings, hold pre-meetings without management being present, and seek external advice (Hall and Purcell 2011).

But, even robust re-regulation of ICE laws would be insufficient as a stand-alone intervention, because the continued grip of neoliberal financialized capitalism presents a highly unfavourable context for nurturing and sustaining cooperative mutuality at the workplace. This is symptomatic of broader structural factors in LMEs that act as a barrier to cooperative mutuality, not least the nature of product markets and corporate governance (McLaughlin 2013; Thompson 2013). Beyond tinkering with ICE regulations, radical reforms would be required in LMEs to create more favourable conditions for robust industrial democracy to take root; not least by beginning to loosen and correct the destructive ideological hegemony of 'self-regulating markets' (O'Reilly et al. 2011). Given the scale of reform required, the prognosis for embedding stronger employee voice in LMEs like the UK and RoI is pessimistic, a situation even more notable in the USA. Under the prevailing neoliberal climate, few politicians or employers in LMEs appear receptive or able to undertake major reforms advancing democratization of workplace voice; especially when they are depicted or perceived as a radical challenge to managerial authority and power.

▓ NOTES

1. Voluntarism is commonly defined as a system of industrial relations based on voluntary settlements between employers, employees, and their representatives, rather than direct legal regulation and state intervention (Flanders 1970).
2. In many coordinated market economies this cooperative employee participation function is served by generally applicable state-sponsored legally/institutionally

embedded employee voice rights and/or strong trade union representation and coverage.

3. Article 1(2) of the directive states: 'practical arrangements for information and consultation shall be defined and implemented in accordance with national law and industrial relations practices'.

4. Paragraph 7 of the directive states: 'there is a need to strengthen dialogue and promote mutual trust within undertakings in order to improve risk anticipation, make work organisation more flexible and facilitate employee access to training within the undertaking while maintaining security, make employees aware of adaptation needs, increase employees' availability to undertake measures and activities to increase their employability, promote employee involvement in the operation and future of the undertaking and increase its competitiveness'.

▓ REFERENCES

Aoki, M. (1984) *The Co-operative Game Theory of the Firm*. Oxford: Clarendon Press.

Bacon, N. and Blyton, P. (2007) 'Conflict for Mutual Gains'. *Journal of Management Studies*, 44(5), 814–34.

Baldamus, W. (1961) *Efficiency and Effort*. London: Tavistock.

Barnard, C. and Deakin, S. (2000) 'In Search of Coherence: Social Policy, the Single Market and Fundamental Rights'. *Industrial Relations Journal*, 31(4), 311–45.

Barry, M. (2009) 'The Regulatory Framework for HRM'. In A. Wilkinson, N. Bacon, T. Redman, and S. Snell (eds), *The SAGE Handbook of Human Resource Management*. London: Sage.

Bowles, S. (2006) *Microeconomics: Behavior, Institutions, and Evolution*. Princeton: Princeton University Press.

Cullinane, N., Donaghey, J., Dundon, T., Hickland, E., and Dobbins, T. (2013) 'Regulating for Mutual Gains? Non-Union Employee Representation and the Information and Consultation Directive'. *International Journal of Human Resource Management*, 25(6), 810–28.

European Parliament (2002) '2002/14/EC of the European Parliament and of the Council of 11 March 2002 Establishing a General Framework for Informing and Consulting Employees in the European Community'. *Official Journal of the European Communities*, 2380, March, 29–33.

Dobbins, T. (2010) 'The Case for Beneficial Constraints: Why Permissive Voluntarism Impedes Workplace Cooperation in Ireland'. *Economic and Industrial Democracy*, 31(4), 497–519.

Dobbins, T. and Gunnigle, P. (2009) 'Can Voluntary Workplace Partnership Deliver Sustainable Mutual Gains?' *British Journal of Industrial Relations*, 47(3), 546–70.

Dundon, T. and Collings, D. G. (2011) 'Employment Relations in the United Kingdom and Republic of Ireland'. In M. Barry and A. Wilkinson (eds), *Research Handbook of Comparative Employment Relations*. London: Edward Elgar.

Dundon, T., Curran, D., Maloney, M., and Ryan, P. (2006) 'Conceptualising the Dynamics of Employee Voice: Evidence from the Republic of Ireland'. *Industrial Relations Journal*, 37(5), 492–512.

Edwards, P. (1990) 'The Politics of Conflict and Consent: How the Labor Contract Really Works'. *Journal of Economic Behavior and Organization*, 13(1), 41–61.

Edwards, P. (ed.) (2003) *Industrial Relations*, 2nd edn. Oxford: Blackwell.

Edwards, P. (2012) 'Experimental Economics and Workplace Behaviour: Bridges over Troubled Methodological Waters?' *Socio-Economic Review*, 10(2), 293–315.

Flanders, A. (1970) *Management and Unions*. London: Faber and Faber.

Freeman, R. and Lazear, E. (1995) 'An Economic Analysis of Works Councils'. In J. Rogers and W. Streeck (eds), *Works Councils: Consultation, Representation, and Cooperation in Industrial Relations*. Chicago: University of Chicago Press.

Freeman, R., Boxall, P., and Haynes, P. (eds) (2007) *What Workers Say: Employee Voice in the Anglo-American Workplace*. Ithaca, NY: Cornell University Press.

Gallie, D. (2009) 'Institutional Regimes and Employee Influence at Work: A European Comparison'. *Cambridge Journal of Regions Economy and Society*, 2(3), 379–93.

Godard, J. (2004) 'A Critical Assessment of the High-Performance Paradigm'. *British Journal of Industrial Relations*, 42(2), 349–78.

Goergen, M., Brewster, C., Wood, G., and Wilkinson, A. (2012) 'Varieties of Capitalism and Investments in Human Capital'. *Industrial Relations*, 51(S1), 501–27.

Gold, M. (2009) (ed.) *Employment Policy in the European Union: Origins, Themes and Prospects*. Basingstoke: Palgrave Macmillan.

Guest, D. E. and Peccei, R. (2001) 'Partnership at Work: Mutuality and the Balance of Advantage'. *British Journal of Industrial Relations*, 39(2), 207–36.

Hall, M. and Purcell, J. (2011) *Information and Consultation Practice across Europe Five Years after the EU Directive*. Dublin: European Foundation for the Improvement of Living and Working Conditions.

Hall, M. and Purcell, J. (2012) *Consultation at Work: Regulation and Practice*. Oxford: Oxford University Press.

Hall, P. and Soskice, D. (2001) *Varieties of Capitalism: The Institutional Foundations of Comparative Advantage*. Oxford: Oxford University Press.

Hall, M., Hutchinson, S., Purcell, J., Terry, M., and Parker, J. (2010) 'Information and Consultation under the ICE Regulations: Evidence from Longitudinal Case Studies'. London: Department for Business, Innovation and Skills.

Hall, M., Hutchinson, S., Purcell, J., Terry, M., and Parker, J. (2013) 'Promoting Effective Consultation? Assessing the Impact of the ICE Regulations'. *British Journal of Industrial Relations*, 51(2), 355–81.

Hancké, B., Rhodes, M., and Thatcher, M. (2007) *Beyond Varieties of Capitalism: Conflict, Contradictions, and Complementarities in the European Economy*. Oxford: Oxford University Press.

Johnstone, S., Ackers, P., and Wilkinson, A. (2010) 'Better than Nothing? Is Non-Union Partnership a Contradiction in Terms?' *Journal of Industrial Relations*, 52(2), 151–68.

Kochan, T. A. and Osterman, P. (1994) *The Mutual Gains Enterprise*. Harvard, MA: Harvard Business School Press.

Koukiadaki, A. (2010) 'The Establishment and Operation of Information and Consultation of Employees' Arrangements in a Capability-Based Framework'. *Economic and Industrial Democracy*, 31(3), 365–88.

Lavelle, J., Gunnigle, P., and McDonnell A. (2010) 'Patterning Employee Voice in Multinational Companies'. *Human Relations*, 63(3), 395–418.

Leibenstein, H. (1982) 'The Prisoners' Dilemma in the Invisible Hand: An Analysis of Intrafirm Productivity', *American Economic Review*, 72(2), 92–7.

McDonough, T. and Dundon, T. (2010) 'Thatcherism Delayed? The Irish Crisis and the Paradox of Social Partnership'. *Industrial Relations Journal*, 41(6), 544–62.

McKersie, R. B., Sharpe, T., Kochan, T. A., Eaton, A. E., Strauss, G., and Morgenstern, M. (2008) 'Bargaining Theory Meets Interest-Based Negotiations'. *Industrial Relations*, 47(1), 66–96.

McLaughlin, C. (2013) 'The Role of Productivity Coalitions in Building a "High Road" Competitive Strategy: The Case of Denmark and Ireland'. *European Journal of Industrial Relations*, 19(2), 127–43.

Marsden, D. and Cañibano, A. (2011) 'An Economic Perspective on Employee Participation'. In A. Wilkinson, P. J. Gollan, M. Marchington, and D. Lewin (eds), *The Oxford Handbook of Participation in Organizations*. Oxford: Oxford University Press.

Martínez Lucio, M. (2010) 'Labour Process and Marxist Perspectives on Employee Participation'. In A. Wilkinson, P. J. Gollan, M. Marchington, and D. Lewin (eds), *The Oxford Handbook of Participation in Organizations*. Oxford: Oxford University Press.

Martínez Lucio, M. and MacKenzie, R. (2004) 'Unstable Boundaries?' Evaluating the "New Regulation" within Employment Relations'. *Economy and Society*, 33(1), 77–97.

Martínez Lucio, M. and Stuart, M. (2005) 'Partnership and New Industrial Relations in a Risk Society: An Age of Shotgun Weddings and Marriages of Convenience'. *Work, Employment and Society*, 19(4), 797–817.

National Archives (2004) *Information and Consultation of Employees Regulations 2004*. London: HMSO. [Online.] Available at: <http://www.legislation.gov.uk/uksi/2004/3426/contents/made>.

O'Reilly, J., Lain, D., Sheehan, M., Smale, B., and Stuart, M. (2011) 'Managing Uncertainty: The Crisis, Its Consequences and the Global Workforce'. *Work, Employment and Society*, 25(4), 581–95.

Oxenbridge, S. and Brown, W. (2004) 'Achieving a New Equilibrium? The Stability of Cooperative Employer–Union Relationships'. *Industrial Relations Journal*, 35(5), 388–402.

Patmore, G. (2010) 'A Legal Perspective on Employee Participation'. In A. Wilkinson, P. J. Gollan, M. Marchington, and D. Lewin (eds), *The Oxford Handbook of Participation in Organizations*. Oxford: Oxford University Press.

Poundstone, W. (1992) *Prisoners Dillema*. New York: Doubleday.

Sisson, K. (1993) 'In Search of HRM'. *British Journal of Industrial Relations*, 31(2), 201–10.

Spencer, D. (2012) 'Barbarians at the Gate: A Critical Appraisal of Economics on the Impact of the Field and Practice of HRM'. *Human Resource Management Journal*, 23 (4), 346–59.

Streeck, W. (1987) 'The Uncertainties of Management in the Management of Uncertainty'. *Work, Employment and Society*, 1(3), 281–308.

Streeck, W. (1995) 'Neo-Voluntarism: A New European Social Policy Regime?' *European Law Journal*, 1(1), 31–59.

Streeck, W. (1997) 'Beneficial Constraints: On the Economic Limits of Rational Voluntarism'. In J. Hollingsworth, J. Rogers, and R. Boyer (eds), *Contemporary Capitalism: The Embeddedness of Institutions*. Cambridge: Cambridge University Press.

Streeck, W. (2004) 'Educating Capitalists: A Rejoinder to Wright and Tsakalotos'. *Socio-Economic Review*, 2(3), 425–37.

Taylor, P., Baldry, C., Danford, A., and Stewart, P. (2009) 'An Umbrella Full of Holes? Corporate Restructuring, Redundancy and the Effectiveness of ICE Regulations'. *Relations Industrielles*, 64(1), 27–49.

Thompson, P. (2011) 'The Trouble with HRM'. *Human Resource Management Journal*, 21(4), 355–67.

Thompson, P. (2013) 'Financialization and the Workforce: Extending and Applying the Disconnected Capitalism Thesis'. *Work, Employment and Society*, 27(3), 472–88.

van Wanrooy, B., Bewley, H., Bryson, A., Forth, J., Freeth, S., Stokes, L., and Wood, S. (2013) *The 2011 Workplace Employment Relations Study: First Findings*. London: Department for Business, Innovation and Skills.

Wilkinson, A. and Gollan, P. J. (2007) 'The EU Information and Consultation Directive and the Future of Employee Consultation in the UK'. *International Journal of Human Resource Management*, 18(7), 1145–58.

Wilkinson, A. and Wood, G. (2012) 'Institutions and Industrial Relations: The State of the Art'. *Industrial Relations*, 51(s1), 373–88.

Wilkinson, A., Dundon, T., and Marchington, M. (2013) 'Employee Involvement and Voice'. In S. Bach and M. Edwards (eds), *Managing Human Resources*, 5th edn. Oxford: Blackwell.

Wright, P., Dunford, B., and Snell, S. (2001) 'Human Resources and the Resource-Based View of the Firm'. *Journal of Management*, 6, 701–21.

Part 4
Looking Ahead

12 Making voice effective

Imagining trade union responses to an era
of post-industrial democracy

Richard Hyman

Democratization and the labour movement:
a brief history

For most of the past century, it has been common to view democratization as a four-stage process.[1] The first involved the conquest of political (liberal) democracy: the universal right to vote and the freedom to organize electorally and to oppose the incumbent government. In Western Europe at least, the battle for political democracy has been largely won, often at great cost. Though many on the left have at times been sceptical of this achievement— 'if voting changed anything, they would make it illegal'—the experience of fascism and military dictatorship has taught even critics that liberal democracy is necessary, even if insufficient.

The second stage stemmed from the demand that citizenship should not be confined to the right to vote every four or five years, but should have a broader social dimension. Social democracy emphasized the collective character of social and political life, and the mutual responsibility of the individual and collective. The pursuit of rights to collective representation through trade unions and collective bargaining, and for the construction of a 'welfare capitalism' (Esping-Andersen 1990) providing education, health care, pensions, and income support in time of need, was the outcome of a vision of social justice but also reflected awareness that starvation was not a reliable foundation for intelligent democratic participation.

Third, it was thought impossible to be a free citizen in the public sphere but a slave in the workplace. Democracy could not end outside the factory gates: workers were stakeholders in the firm that employed them and must have industrial citizenship rights. Hence the third stage was the demand for industrial democracy: employees should possess an effective voice within enterprise decision making in order to shape the organization of their own work and, not least, to control the ability of the employer to hire and fire.

The fourth stage addressed the question of economic democracy. Workers' representation within workplace decision making was a necessary element in democratization; but decisions affecting day-to-day work arrangements were largely conditioned by prior policies regarding investment, product strategy, and marketing. They were also shaped by the broader macroeconomic context within which the individual enterprise was located; satisfactory democracy within one factory was impossible. The most developed analysis of the case for economic democracy, and of a strategy to achieve this goal, can be found in the ideas developed during the Weimar Republic by Fritz Naphtali (1928), which later proved influential in the German and Austrian trade union movements in the early post-war years.

The 'post-war compromise' between labour and capital, which assumed different forms across Western Europe after 1945, involved uneven advances in all four aspects of democratization. Political democracy was restored in nations that had been subject to fascist dictatorship, even though in some this was not achieved until the 1970s, and the countries of Central and Eastern Europe remained one-party states until after 1989. In some cases, women gained equal electoral rights only after 1945.

Post-war settlements brought considerable advances in the democratization of the social sphere. Keynesian demand management resulted in near-full employment in many—though certainly not all—west European countries. Welfare states were universally expanded, or newly created, though their character differed markedly across countries: some were genuinely egalitarian, others represented a form of 'socialism within one class' in which those in employment in effect insured against the risks of unemployment, ill health, and old age, receiving benefits which matched the original inequality of their incomes. New industrial relations institutions, sometimes graced with the label 'social partnership', were widely established; trade union membership expanded, and in many countries collective agreements covered the majority of the workforce for the first time.

Progress in the third area, democratization within the workplace, was far more uneven. Systems of collective representation through works councils were institutionalized in much of Europe, but in many countries their rights did not extend beyond information and consultation rather than enabling real joint decision making (codetermination). In others, as in France, their main functions covered the organization of social facilities rather than production issues. Even the strongest systems—with Germany the exemplary case—had primary jurisdiction over employment issues arising only after key decisions on investment and product strategy had already been taken. As Briefs (1989), a key trade union figure in works council research, noted: the more strategic the issue for management, the weaker the powers of the councils. Sceptics in some countries—Britain is an obvious example—argued that there was a major risk that employee representatives would share the blame for management decisions that they could not fundamentally influence.

Developments in the broader sphere of economic democracy were particularly uneven and ambiguous. In France, Italy, and Britain, extensive programmes of public ownership were implemented; but though nationalization provided a favourable environment for trade union activity, its bureaucratic character did little to enhance democratic control. Most social democrats soon abandoned, explicitly or implicitly, the idea of comprehensive public ownership. In Germany, another key issue was the demand for parity representation on supervisory boards. The 1952 legislation was a clear defeat for the trade unions, and even the stronger 1976 law did not bring genuine parity, though certainly even a minority voice can help strengthen workers' voice in corporate decision making. In most other countries where board-level representation was enacted, only a symbolic presence was provided.

For Naphtali, socialization of the economy was an essential goal, but it should be achieved, not necessarily and not exclusively through state ownership but through more diverse forms of popular control. In the main, his wide-ranging ideas for measures of democratization between state and company levels were forgotten. One interesting by-product was the strategy developed by Rudolf Meidner in the 1970s for Swedish Trade Union Confederation (LO), involving payment of a share of company profits to wage-earner funds (*Löntagarfonder*).[2] The essence of the policy was to establish *collective* employee ownership of part of the profits of corporate success, in the form of shares held in a fund under trade union control. This, it was envisaged, could provide increasing control over strategic decisions in the dominant private companies. Strenuous opposition from employers, a lack of support from other unions, and the ambivalence of the social democrats meant that the initiative was defeated and disappeared from the political agenda, and not only in Sweden.

The cancer stage of capitalism

Polanyi (1944), writing during the war, interpreted the development of capitalist economies as the outcome of a 'double movement'. The first, in the nineteenth century, involved the imposition of 'free' markets (though the whole idea of free markets is an oxymoron, since all markets are social and political constructs). The damaging social effects of this process, in particular those transforming labour into a 'fictitious commodity' to be hired and fired at will, provoked a counter-movement. Hence the struggles in the twentieth century for social, industrial, and economic democracy, summarized above, represented a countervailing process to impose some constraint on the disruptive social consequences of market liberalism. Markets became 'embedded' in a systematic regulatory web.

Polanyi anticipated a parallel reaction to the excesses of market making at the international level: renewed state regulation of the domestic economy linked to a retreat from 'capitalist internationalism'. What however occurred, wrote Ruggie four decades later, was a new form of international regime, involving a bounded liberalization of external trade, but linked to Keynesian economic management and a partial decommodification of labour at national level. 'The principles of multilateralism and tariff reductions were affirmed, but so were safeguards, exemptions, exceptions, and restrictions—all designed to protect the balance of payments and a variety of domestic social policies' (Ruggie 1982: 381). As Ruggie later summarized it, embedded liberalism involved a social compromise, 'a grand social bargain', which combined 'the efficiency of markets with the values of social community' (Ruggie 2003: 93–4).

We can now see that this post-war social compromise was inherently ambiguous and unstable, for three main reasons. First, it reflected a specific, historically contingent balance of class forces. Second, it assumed different forms cross-nationally, but in all cases involved an accommodation between national labour movements, employers who were primarily national in terms of corporate ownership and production strategies, and governments which were to a large degree autonomous in social and economic policy: an outcome of the bounded character of economic internationalization which Ruggie described. Third, the existence of an alternative socio-economic model to the east—however deformed and repressive—imposed a degree of self-restraint on capitalist aggression.

These three preconditions no longer apply. What has developed in recent decades has been analysed by McMurtry (1998) as the 'cancer stage of capitalism'. Polanyi (1944: 73) described labour, land, and money as 'fictitious commodities' because while they were all subject to market forces, unlike real commodities they were not produced for sale on the market. 'To allow the market mechanism to be the sole director of the fate of human beings and their natural environment, indeed, even of the amount and use of their purchasing power, would result in the demolition of society.' Certainly the post-war compromises imposed firm limits on the commodification of labour, land, and money; but Polanyi's analysis was remarkably prescient. The process which McMurtry describes is the systematic weakening and removal of the social constraints on the destructive dynamic of commodification: a 'carcinogenic mutation' which has released the pathological potential which capitalist economies always contained.

The cancer stage of capitalism is linked as both cause and effect to the erosion of the three preconditions of post-war social compromises. Globalization—of which European economic integration is one important element—has removed the dominant capitalist agglomerations from national control, and has provided an alibi for anti-social policies by governments that insist that there is no alternative to submission to global markets (Weiss 1998). Liberalization of financial markets has spawned an array of exotic fictitious commodities which Polanyi could never have imagined: derivatives, secondary markets, hedge funds, private equity, leveraged buy-outs and credit default swaps, for example. National economies and national labour markets are increasingly *disembedded* from effective social regulation; and the beneficiaries of financialized 'shareholder value' capitalism have little interest in maintaining historic compromises. The balance of class forces has shifted radically.

These trends can be understood, within Polanyi's framework, as a *counter*-counter-movement, a *third* phase involving the deliberate unravelling of the regulatory web constructed in previous decades. The cancer stage of capitalism is objectively, and for many of its drivers deliberately, reactionary. In particular, it rolls back all four dimensions of democratization.

Formally, the institutions of political democracy are intact; indeed their geographical scope has significantly extended with the collapse of the Soviet Union. But form and substance do not always coincide, as Putin's Russia clearly demonstrates. The cancer stage of capitalism mutates the inner workings of the polity. As Crouch has argued, electoral politics has been drained of the capacity to provide popular influence over the most significant dimensions of social life and has become in large measure a stage-managed ritual. 'Behind this spectacle of the electoral game, politics is really shaped in private by interaction between elected governments and elites that overwhelmingly represent business interests' (Crouch 2004: 4).

It is also evident that globalized financial capitalism is one of the principal grave diggers of social democracy. Keynesian macroeconomic management, one of the key foundations of the post-war settlement, presupposed the economic governance capacity of the nation-state; macroeconomic demand management has now been subordinated to the assumed inevitability of national 'competitiveness'. Where significant productive and infrastructural assets were in public hands, in most countries these have now been largely privatized. Trade union membership, as a proportion of the labour force, is almost universally in decline: a trend which Peters (2011) shows can be attributed to the impact of the global financialization of capitalism. In most of Western Europe, collective bargaining coverage remains stable—though this is certainly not true of Britain—but its content has been hollowed out through diverse forms of decentralization and concession bargaining. For two or three decades, the wage share in national income has declined and inequality has increased. Even before the current crisis, government budgets had been squeezed, to an important extent through a competitive reduction in corporation tax in an attempt to avoid capital flight: in consequence, the welfare state has been cut back, transformed increasingly into a minimal safety net.

Even this diminished level of social protection is under threat as part of the current austerity drive, given an explicitly coercive character by the neoliberal rulers of the European Union (EU) and codified through such measures as the Euro-Plus Pact, the Fiscal Compact, and the 'Six Pack'. Indeed, in the current conjuncture the Troika, totally unelected and unaccountable, is able to push through labour market deregulation, bargaining decentralization and cuts in public sector pay regardless of the democratic will in the countries affected (Meardi 2014).

The cancer stage of capitalism likewise undermines the elements of industrial and economic democracy achieved in earlier decades. Codetermination in one company was always precarious; now, the toxic combination of financialization, globalization, and neoliberalism means that primarily enterprise- or establishment-based mechanisms of codetermination are forced to accommodate the externally imposed requirements of intensified global competition. 'The institutions [of employee representation] have not only lost their decommodifying impact on labour, they themselves are gradually commodified' (Holst 2014: 5) as the threat of capital exit can make it imperative to underwrite managerial priorities. Moreover, strategic decision making is increasingly removed from the sphere of codetermination. More seriously still, the very identity of the employer more and more becomes shifting and obscure as companies themselves become treated primarily as commodities to be bought and sold in the interests of share-price maximization; accordingly, 'employers can't keep their side of the bargain' (Thompson 2003). Here, too, the EU governing institutions are helping drive the process. Many German writers have concluded that although formally intact, the machinery of codetermination no longer provides an effective mechanism for asserting and defending workers' interests, giving way to a phase of post-industrial democracy (Streeck 2009; Urban 2011). 'Today, *Mitbestimmung* has become a governing principle for enterprise modernisation, using limited employee participation, information and cooperation to win competitive advantage' (Schumann and Detje 2011: 79).

(How) Can the trend to economic dictatorship be reversed?

Can 'good capitalism' be restored? Since the impact of the crisis in 2008, there has been widespread discussion of the deficiencies in existing systems of corporate governance, particularly as the liberalization of global financial transactions has made 'shareholder value' the overriding corporate goal even in 'coordinated' market economies. With the shock of crisis, some union policy makers have come to recognize that the overriding challenge is to build a movement for greater democratization of the economy and to create new links between different levels of regulation and different issues on the regulatory agenda. But what centre-left trade unionists have often condemned is—in the words of the former ETUC general secretary (Monks 2006)—the 'new, overmighty capitalism' of hedge funds, asset-stripping, financial speculation, and astronomical bonuses. The solution, from this perspective, is to fight to restore the old capitalism: the trade union movement should 'become a champion of good business practices, of decent relations with decent employers while ruthlessly fighting the speculators'. In short, the task is seen as campaigning for a return to 'good capitalism' (Dullien et al. 2009).

Can the genie be forced back into the bottle? Can economic democracy and financialized monopoly capitalism coexist? If the central dynamic of twenty-first century capitalism involves vast concentrations of unaccountable private economic power, the answer is surely no. The solution cannot simply be a technocratic regulatory fix, for the cancer stage of capitalism is linked to a fundamental shift in the relative capacities of capital and labour. Under post-democracy, immense economic resources are easily translated into corresponding political resources, providing a virtual veto on effective regulation; and where new regulations *are* imposed, the rich and powerful possess a battery of weapons to escape their effect (Streeck 2011).

The challenge facing those favouring industrial and economic democracy, and in particular trade unions, is immense. Unions are essentially national organizations, which now have to confront the might of multinational capital. Despite the formal existence of international trade union structures, unions apply their own principle of 'subsidiarity' and are reluctant to delegate authority and resources to their supranational representatives. The EU, once regarded by most trade union movements as a force for social progress, is now dominated by neoliberal fanatics and is driving the demolition of democratic social institutions at national level. Finance capital operates in a time–space continuum that is totally divorced from the terrain on which trade unions engage. How can a *fourth* Polanyian movement be created? As Tawney said almost a century ago (1932: 336), 'onions can be eaten leaf by leaf, but you cannot skin a live tiger paw by paw'. Of course a simple anti-capitalist response is not on the current political agenda. Yet to capture hearts and minds, the labour movement has to commence a campaign against global casino capitalism that is linked to a credible set of alternatives for socially accountable economic life. For the present, what is needed, in Gramsci's terms, is a 'war of position', in order to reshape the terrain of debate and understanding.

While the material forces ranged against a redemocratization of economy and society are immense, the ideological obstacles are no less significant.

Neoliberalism has emerged from the crisis—which surely demonstrated the practical bankruptcy of its recipes—stronger than ever (Crouch 2011), partly because it serves powerful vested interests, but also because of the lack of widespread conviction, even among its opponents, that there is an alternative which is both practical and inspirational. There is a wall in our heads: neoliberalism has become the 'common sense' of our times, positing the inevitability of commodification, competitiveness, private affluence (for some), and public squalor (Galbraith 1952).

A radically different logic is required, of sustainability, solidarity, equity, and dignity. How might this be propagated? In any struggle for renewed democratization of the economy, we have to start from where we are and not from where we would like to be. The ideas of 'free' markets and a consumer society are unquestioned by all but a small minority. But beliefs and understandings are always complex and contradictory. In concrete terms, most people *do* question the current economic system. They are perplexed by a financial dynamic which seems out of control. They are angry that failed bankers can still pay themselves obscene bonuses, that the rich still get richer while the rest of us suffer from cuts in real income and social support, that extremely profitable corporations can exploit tax loopholes and tax havens to avoid paying their share. They are bewildered that hostile takeovers which destroy jobs are not only permitted but are actually encouraged by the European authorities. There is an upswell of popular anger and despair with which trade unions have scarcely begun to connect, though other actors—ATTAC, Occupy, or the Uncut movement—have managed to engage more effectively.

Those of us who seek a renewed movement for democratization must start from this substratum of incomprehension and disconnect. The issue is one of 'framing' the current situation and possible alternatives: showing how immediate experiences fit within the broader picture.[3] In communication, the key issue is less what is *said* than what is *heard*. Everyone possesses a world view, however inchoate, a set of beliefs and assumptions which make sense of a complex social environment and act as selective filters for what is communicated. So, at a time when the banking sector has been rescued by a vast transfer of public funds, democratization of ownership should be a logical corollary; let us make the argument! Pension funds are, in effect, workers' deferred wages; but they have been key actors in the speculative spiral that produced the crisis. Bring them under democratic control! The trade union movement has embraced the demand for a financial transactions tax, but has barely discussed the question of its implementation. Why not use the revenue, not simply to plug the hole in national budgets, but to create investment funds under popular control? The neoliberals preach the need for brutal austerity measures to bring down public debt; let us demand citizens' debt audits to establish which debts are genuine, who is responsible, and thus who should pay the costs!

Much more generally, the economic elites prosper through constructing a web of secrecy to cloak their activities. Knowledge is power, but concealment may mean even greater power. Let us demand democratic transparency so as to subject financialized capitalism to public scrutiny! As Block (2014) insists, we need 'real utopias' directed at the democratization of finance. The task is to develop demands which expose the rottenness at the heart of the cancer stage of capitalism, and at the same time suggest the possibility of an alternative. Whether or not we call this economic democracy, this is the underlying implication.

But economic democracy must be a multi-level process and so must also be built from below. What are the possibilities for economic democratization in the space between state and market? The labour movement has a long tradition of cooperative production and distribution, though in many countries such cooperatives mutated long ago into simple commercial ventures. But smaller-scale, cooperative, economic activity has often been able to provide some counter-power to the commodification of social life, particularly in the global south. In a notable recognition of this role, the Self-Employed Women's Association (SEWA) in India was accepted as a founding member of the International Trade Union Confederation (ITUC).[4] Do such movements offer lessons for trade unions in the developed economies? In the French-speaking world at least, the notion of a 'social economy' has received growing attention on the left (Draperi 2007; Laville 2007). An imaginative response to the cancer stage of capitalism and its crisis ought to draw on such ideas.

Conclusion: what about the unions?

To defend employees at workplace level and no less within the national (and international) political economy requires a confrontation with the dominant policy logic of our age. This implies that unions must turn (or return) to a self-conception as organizations campaigning for rights and engaging in 'contentious politics' (Tarrow 1998): contesting oppression, inequality, and discrimination. It can also imply cooperation, often uneasy, with other social movements that in most countries have never acquired the respectability gained by trade unions. Potentially it redefines unions as outsiders in a terrain where until recently the role of insiders was comforting and rewarding.

The key issues here involve ideas, language, and mobilization. The decline of union organization across Europe in recent years is in part ideological in causation: European unions were able to thrive when the prevailing policy discourse made collective regulation, employment protection, and state welfare provision the commonsense of the times. The ideological counter-revolution of the past three decades has placed trade unions very much on the defensive. They are often seen as representing a vested interest: those who are already relatively secure in the labour market, and have relatively good wages and working conditions; those who are in most cases winners or at least not major losers in the process of economic restructuring. But unions have to convince themselves and others that they are a 'sword of justice' (Flanders 1970), representing the losers as well as the winners and seeking to convert the losers *into* winners. This requires a battle of ideas.

Tilly (2006) has argued that socio-political movements draw on 'repertoires of contention': forms of action that have been developed in the past and provide 'scripts' for the future, but which nevertheless are subject to constant innovation. Such repertoires, he suggests, contain three key elements: 'identity', the assertion that those involved are a group with distinctive interests and the capacity to pursue these vigorously; 'standing', the insistence that their claims and interests deserve to be taken as seriously as those of other more powerful socio-economic groups; and 'programme', an integrated set of demands. All three in his view are mutually supporting. Indeed this is a useful prism through which to regard European trade unions: in their period of greatest strength they could credibly claim to represent a constituency with a strong collective identity, to possess the standing of a recognized actor in societal policy making, and to articulate a programme which reflects the general interest. In more recent times, in most countries, all three claims have been weakened, and the elements in this weakening have been mutually reinforcing. New vocabularies which give meaning to the identity, standing, and programme of trade unionism are part of the key to union survival, renewal, and fight for economic democracy.

The idea of economic democratization offers a vision of popular empowerment which could reinvigorate trade unionism as a social movement and help launch a struggle for a genuinely alternative economy. One in which, at the same time, unions themselves would be more likely to thrive. Indeed the new general secretary of the TUC, Frances O'Grady, has called (2013a) for 'new models of corporate governance that empower all stakeholders, not just shareholders'; and has pointed (O'Grady 2013b: 87–8) to large popular support for worker representation on company boards and to the mobilizing potential of demands for employee voice on company remuneration committees.

To change the world, unions must change themselves. They cannot credibly campaign for the democratization of the economy unless they themselves are patently democratic. Indeed, all unions have their time-honoured procedures of election and decision making, but rarely do these engage more than a tiny minority of enthusiasts. There is no Michelsian 'iron law of oligarchy'; but if union democracy is to be a reality, not mere formality, it is essential to foster the widest possible internal dialogue and debate. By struggling to strengthen and renew their own democratic processes and culture, unions can provide a model and win a legitimacy for a wider campaign for social and economic democracy.

In conclusion, the struggle for the democratization of the economy requires a new, imaginative—indeed utopian—counter-offensive: a persuasive vision of a different and better society and economy, a convincing alternative to the mantra of greed, commodification, competitiveness, and austerity; a set of values which connects with everyday experience at the workplace. Whether this is described as 'good capitalism', post-capitalism, or socialism is of secondary importance. The urgent need is to articulate a more humane, more solidaristic, and more plausible alternative to neoliberalism, finding new ways to express unions' traditional core principles and values and to appeal to a modern generation for whom old slogans have little meaning. And since defending the weak is inescapably a question of power, unions have to help construct a new type of *politics*; in particular, by engaging with campaigning and protest movements that attract the Facebook and Twitter generation in ways which most trade unions have failed to do (even if many have recently begun to make serious efforts in this direction). Do unions dare to abandon old rules and routines in order to create new strategies for industrial and economic democracy?

▓ NOTES

1. For a similar argument, see Marshall (1950). This chapter draws in part on Hyman (2013).
2. For a summary, see Meidner (1978) and Olsen (1992). Meidner took Swedish nationality after escaping from Nazi Germany in 1933.
3. See for example Kelly (1998).
4. SEWA defines itself as both an organization and a movement for women workers on the margins of the formal economy. It has many of the characteristics of a trade union, a non-governmental organization, and a cooperative. See <http://www.sewa.org/About_Us.asp>.

▓ REFERENCES

Block, F. (2014) 'Democratizing Finance'. *Politics and Society*, 42(1), 3–28.
Briefs U. (1989) 'Codetermination in the Federal Republic of Germany: An Appraisal of a Secular Experience'. In G. Széll, P. Blyton, and C. Cornforth (eds), *The State, Trade Unions and Self-Management*, pp. 63–74. Berlin: de Gruyter.
Crouch, C. (2004) *Post-Democracy*. Cambridge: Polity.
Crouch, C. (2011) *The Strange Non-Death of Neoliberalism*. Cambridge: Polity.
Draperi, J.-F. (2007) *Comprendre l'économie sociale. Fondements et enjeux*. Paris: Dunod.

Dullien, S., Herr, H., and Kellermann, C. (2009) *Der gute Kapitalismus... und was sich dafür nach der Krise ändern müsste.* Bielefeld: transcript Verlag.

Esping-Andersen, G. (1990) *The Three Worlds of Welfare Capitalism.* Cambridge: Polity Press.

Flanders, A. (1970) *Management and Unions.* London: Faber.

Galbraith, J. K. (1952) *American Capitalism: The Concept of Countervailing Power.* Boston, MA: Houghton Mifflin.

Holst, H. (2014) '"Commodifying Institutions": Vertical Disintegration and Institutional Change in German Labour Relations'. *Work, Employment and Society,* 28(1), 3–20.

Hyman, R. (2013) 'Demokratisierung der Wirtschaft'. In B. Huber (ed.), *Kurswechsel für ein Gutes Leben. Wege zu einer solidarischen Gesellschaft,* pp. 162–84. Frankfurt: Campus.

Kelly, J. (1998) *Rethinking Industrial Relations: Mobilisation, Collectivism and Long Waves.* London: Routledge.

Laville, J.-L. (ed.) (2007) *L'économie solidaire. Une perspective internationale.* Paris: Hachette.

McMurtry, J. (1998) *The Cancer Stage of Capitalism.* London: Pluto Press.

Marshall, T. H. (1950) *Citizenship and Social Class.* Cambridge: Cambridge University Press.

Meardi, G. (2014) 'Employment Relations under External Pressure: Italian and Spanish Reforms during the Great Recession'. In M. Hauptmeier and M. Vidal (eds), *Comparative Political Economy of Work,* pp. 332–50. Basingstoke: Palgrave Macmillan.

Meidner, R. (1978) *Employee Investment Funds: An Approach to Collective Capital Formation.* London: Allen and Unwin.

Monks, J. (2006) *The Challenge of the New Capitalism,* Bevan Memorial lecture, 14 November. [Online.] Available at: <http://www.etuc.org/a/3052>.

Naphtali, F. (1928) *Wirtschaftsdemokratie. Ihr Wesen, Weg und Ziel.* Berlin: ADGB.

O'Grady, F. (2013a) *From Attlee to Miliband: Can Labour and Unions Face the Future?* Attlee Memorial Lecture, 26 April. [Online.] Available at: <http://www.tuc.org.uk/union-issues/frances-ogradys-atlee-memorial-lecture>.

O'Grady, F. (2013b) 'Interview: Trade Unionism after the Crash'. *Renewal,* 21(2–3), 87–96.

Olsen, G. M. (1992) *The Struggle for Economic Democracy in Sweden.* Aldershot: Avebury.

Peters, J. (2011) 'The Rise of Finance and the Decline of Organised Labour in the Advanced Capitalist Countries'. *New Political Economy,* 16(1), 73–99.

Polanyi, P. (1944) *The Great Transformation.* New York: Rinehart.

Ruggie, J. G. (1982) 'International Regimes, Transactions, and Change: Embedded Liberalism in the Postwar Economic Order'. *International Organization,* 36(2), 379–415.

Ruggie, J. G. (2003) 'Taking Embedded Liberalism Global: The Corporate Connection'. In D. Held and M. Koenig-Archibugi (eds), *Taming Globalization: Frontiers of Governance,* pp. 93–129. Cambridge: Polity.

Schumann, M. and Detje, R. (2011) 'Demokratisierung der Wirtschaft "von unten"'. In H. Meine, M. Schumann, and H.-J. Urban (eds), *Mehr Wirtschaftsdemokratie wagen!*, pp. 68–84. Hamburg: VSA.

Streeck, W. (2009) *Re-Forming Capitalism.* Oxford: Oxford University Press.

Streeck, W. (2011) 'Taking Capitalism Seriously: Towards an Institutionalist Approach to Contemporary Political Economy'. *Socio-Economic Review*, 9(1), 137–67.

Tarrow, S. (1998) *Power in Movement*, 2nd edn. Cambridge: Cambridge University Press.

Tawney, R. H. (1932) 'The Choice before the Labour Party'. *Political Quarterly*, 3(3), 323–45.

Thompson, P. (2003) 'Disconnected Capitalism: Or Why Employers Can't Keep Their Side of the Bargain'. *Work, Employment and Society*, 17(2), 359–78.

Tilly, C. (2006) *Regimes and Repertoires.* Chicago: University of Chicago Press.

Urban, H.-J. (2011) 'Arbeitspolitik unter (Nach-)Krisenbedingungen. Gute Arbeit als Strategie'. *Arbeits- und Industriesoziologische Studien*, 4(1), 48–57.

Weiss, L. (1998) *The Myth of the Powerless State.* Ithaca, NY: Cornell University Press.

13 The future of employee voice in the USA

Predictions from an employment relations model of voice

Bruce E. Kaufman

Introduction

Theory is important in industrial relations (IR) because it helps to identify key determinants of behaviour in employment relationships and the nature of the cause–effect linkages. Among the many behaviours studied in IR, employee voice is particularly prominent and the subject of a large and rapidly growing literature (see Wilkinson et al. 2014). A number of useful conceptual frameworks and models of employee voice have been advanced (for example, Dundon and Gollan 2007; Morrison 2011; Willman et al. 2014). Room for development remains, however, and I devote this chapter to taking voice theory another step. In particular, I frame voice theory in terms of a predictive equation of the sort 'if A then B, given C'. In this equation, A represents the voice dependent variable, B represents causal independent variables, and C represents contingent and contextual variables. The goal of the model is to explain cross-sectional and inter-temporal variation in employee voice; the contribution of theory is to guide the specification of the A, B, and C variables in the model and the nature of the association between them. Since industrial relations is the study of the employment relationship, it makes sense for an IR-oriented theory of voice to approach the subject from this direction, hence the label 'employment relations model' in the chapter title. The model is, in the cross-disciplinary tradition of industrial relations, broadly based but draws principal conceptual inspiration from two sources: Fox's (1966, 1974) IR 'frames of reference' typology and Kaufman and Miller's (2011) economics-based theory of the firm's demand for human resource management (HRM) practices. Heery's chapter in this volume is a nice complement because he too uses the frames of reference typology, although in a somewhat different version and for a different topic. To indicate the model's explanatory insight, I apply it to the case of the United

States and work out a forecast of the broad trends in employee voice to the end of the current decade.

IR frames of reference

An insightful way to think about voice in employment relationships is in the context of the popular IR *frames of reference* schema. The schema's use in both this chapter and Chapter 2 speaks to its fruitfulness. Heery, however, follows more closely the original version with three frames, while this chapter relies more on the revised and expanded version with four frames as developed by Budd and Bhave (2008). They explain that the frames of reference concept originates with Alan Fox, an industrial sociologist affiliated with the British Oxford School of Industrial Relations, in a report prepared for the Donovan Commission (Fox 1966). Fox originally divided industrial relations into two frames, unitarist and pluralist, but later broadened the typology to include a radical frame (1974). Budd and Bhave add a fourth frame, egoist (explained below).

Fox (1966) states that the idea of a frame of reference is 'a familiar one in social science and is obviously basic' (p. 2) but does not give a specific definition. One may say, however, that a frame of reference is analogous to the psychological concept of a gestalt. That is, a frame of reference is a cognitively organized representation and interpretation of external events shaped by an individual's perceptions, experiences, attitudes, and values. Budd and Bhave (2008) give a heuristic definition of a frame of reference as 'how one sees the world' and then, more formally, as 'a theory used to guide and evaluate behaviors, outcomes, and institutions' (p. 92). As the latter statement implies, a frame of reference guides behaviour of individuals and groups, shapes normative evaluations of events and institutions into good/bad and fair/unfair judgements, and influences desired forms of social control through government, institutions, and socio-cultural norms.

The frames of reference idea is used in industrial relations to represent alternative conceptions of the employment relationship. The exact number of frames varies somewhat from author to author but Budd and Bhave (2008) specify four: egoist, unitarist, pluralist, and critical. They display the four frames in a table and list each frame's key characteristics. I have modestly reworked their table so it gives more highlight to employee voice and the different assumptions and implications each frame has for voice. See Table 13.1. The first frame, labelled individualist (Budd and Bhave call it egoist), is associated with the competitive market model of neoclassical labour economics. People are individual 'social atoms', motivated by rational

Table 13.1 Four Frames of Reference

Frame	Organizational Vision	Behaviour Principle	Policy Stance	Voice Form
Individualist	Free market	Competition	Laissez Faire	Open Door/Exit
Unitarist	Harmonious Team	Cooperation	Business Friendly	Bilateral Communication/ Employee Involvement
Pluralist	Competing Interest Groups	Negotiation and Compromise	Institutional Power Balancing and Democratization	Collective Representation: Councils and Unions
Radical	Capitalist Monopoly	Conflict and Struggle	Replace Capitalism	Workers' Control

self-interest and desire for maximum gain, and interact in impersonal markets where competition and the invisible hand convert initial-stage conflict of interests into end-stage harmony through the principle 'all sides gain from trade'. Because markets are highly competitive, firms face considerable pressure to give workers fair terms, conditions, and treatment; also, employment relationships are very fluid and turnover costs are minimal. Internal voice arrangements are not needed because production is relatively simple and if workers feel dissatisfied they can vote with their feet by quitting and looking for a better job elsewhere (Freeman and Medoff 1984; Boeri and Van Ours 2008). The exit option is the main form of 'voice' in this frame.

The unitarist frame is associated with HRM and the use of mutual-gain and commitment HRM practices to establish a harmonious collaboration between managers and workers (Morrison 2011; Avgar and Owens 2014). These firms develop structured internal labour markets (ILMs) and make substantial investments in employee training, above-market wages and benefits, job security, and other such employment practices in order to gain the higher productivity that comes from highly motivated, skilled, and engaged workers. Voice in this frame is largely a constructive and integrative behaviour, takes the form of internal communication and problem solving between individual and small groups of managers and workers, and is aimed at making the firm more efficient so the extra surplus can be shared as higher profit for shareholders and wages and job security for labour.

The pluralist frame is, in the general literature, most closely associated with the industrial relations field (Kochan 1998; Heery et al. 2008). This frame sees employment relationships as having significant but bridgeable conflicts of interest, believes the structure of the employment relationship usually tips power in favour of firms, contends that most firms substantially undersupply employee voice, and advocates that voice features used in the political-electoral realm (for example, independent representation, checks and balances, due process) be brought into the firm as a form of industrial democracy.

Rather than a conception of the employment relationship as a short-term buy–sell arrangement or long-term harmonious partnership model, the IR frame envisions employment relationships as multiple (plural) interest groups brought together as stakeholders in a common enterprise but with a mix of integrative and distributive agendas and power resources. Trade unions and collective bargaining, supplemented with labour law, are favoured as the best way to solve the problems of power imbalance, voice undersupply, and a lack of democratic rights in firms by giving employers and workers an institutional vehicle for working out their differences, resolving disputes, and moving production forward through negotiated compromise and workplace détente.

The radical frame, re-labelled as 'critical' by Budd and Bhave (2008), is associated with a radical-Marxist view of the employment relationship (Hyman 1975; Gall 2003). Conflict of interest is systemic and fundamental since employers' profit drive and the pressure of competition force firms to continually seek lower wages, job deskilling, intensified work speed, and tough discipline which collide with workers' desires for higher wages, satisfying jobs, employment security, and fair and respectful treatment. These conflicts of interest can be stabilized in the short run through trade unions, labour laws, and advanced practices among the minority of progressive employers; over the longer run, however, the tendency toward economic stagnation and intensifying exploitation of labour frays détente and replaces it with capital–labour polarization and mobilization into militant working class unions and political protest movements. In the critical frame, militant class-oriented trade unions and political parties emerge as the vehicles of workers' voices although, in the long run, capitalism is replaced with some form of collective ownership and workers' control of industry. In effect, the end state of the critical frame is a form of socialist unitarism where the workers own and run the companies.

As stated in the introduction, the purpose of this chapter is to lay the conceptual groundwork for an 'if A then B, given C' model of employee voice. The dependent variable (B) is cross-sectional and inter-temporal variation in employee voice, such as across firms, industries, countries, and time periods. The role of theory is to identify important independent (A) and contingent-contextual variables (C) which explain the variation in the dependent variable. The frames of reference model provides a very helpful way to identify appropriate independent and contingent-contextual variables. In a national cross-section of workplaces, for example, we observe different forms and intensities of voice. Each observation is an employment relationship and each employment relationship fits into one of the four categories in Table 13.1. We know that individualist, pluralist, critical, and unitarist employment relationships generate different voice forms and intensities; hence, it logically follows that a central explanatory variable in 'if A then B' is which frame of reference (or combination) best fits each workplace in the data set. If most workplaces have an individualist frame, for example, the pattern of voice will be quite different than if they have a critical frame. The next part of the chapter takes these ideas and develops them further, starting with the dependent variable.

Employment relations model: dependent variable

The dependent variable to be explained and predicted is employee voice. But, both conceptually and empirically, what kind of voice is included and how should it be measured? This question is not of the empty rhetorical kind since voice research in many fields tends to focus on just one frame and, hence, mostly examines one kind of voice. In labour economics, for example, most studies (see, for example, Addison 2005) adopt a pluralist frame and examine collective-conflictive forms of voice (such as union grievances); in organizational behaviour, on the other hand, most studies (for example Morrison 2011) adopt a unitarist frame and examine individual and cooperative forms of voice (such as worker–supervisor communication). In employment relations, this kind of partial approach is ruled out by construction. The reason is because the field is an integrative cross-disciplinary approach which includes *all* types of employment relationships. Hence, our first conclusion is that in an employment relations (ER) model the dependent variable includes *all* kinds and forms of voice.

More structure needs to be given to 'all voice' as the dependent variable, however, or the range of behaviour is so large and amorphous it becomes quite difficult to relate it in a clear-cut way to variation in independent variables across the four frames of reference. The dependent variable, therefore, needs to be distinguished on the basis of the voice phenomenon's most important dimensions. The idea is the same for studies that examine firms' adoption of HRM practices (Kaufman and Miller 2011). The dependent variable in these studies includes all types and forms of human resource practices. Prediction and explanation is much facilitated, however, by distinguishing different categories—such as selection, training, and employee involvement—and intensity of utilization—such as a suggestion box form of involvement versus self-managed work teams.

No consensus exists in the literature on the key dimensions of the voice construct. Different research methodologies could be used to identify voice dimensions (for example, deductive theorizing, meta-analysis of the academic literature) but, given that this chapter seeks to develop an employment relations model of voice, it would seem the most appropriate procedure is to utilize the method favoured by ER researchers. Historically, the favoured method is an empirically grounded 'look and see' approach which develops concepts based on field research, participant–observer techniques, and personal interviews with the actors (Whitfield and Strauss 1998). The study by Wilkinson et al. (2004) is the best example in the literature with regard to using 'look and see' to identify voice dimensions. They conclude from field interviews that managers associate workplace voice with 'consultation', 'communication', and 'say'. They also find that managers tend to define workplace voice along two dimensions. The first is voice *form* (direct versus indirect) and the second is voice *agenda* (shared versus contested).

A follow-up article by Dundon et al. (2004), along with this author's company-level field work (Kaufman 2013a), suggests these two dimensions need to be rounded out with a third. This dimension is voice *influence* and its close synonym *power*, which in turn equate to the idea of muscle. Power means the ability of agent A to induce agent B to change a behaviour, rule, or outcome; the degree of Agent A's power, in turn, is measured by the size (potential or actual) of the shift in Agent B's position (Bowles 2004). Kim et al. (2010) call the power dimension 'substantive' voice and contrast it with 'consultative'. Both dimensions are needed to capture voice as 'say' and 'to be heard and make a difference', per the definitions offered by managers to, respectively, Wilkinson et al. 2004 and Kaufman (2013a).

From an IR perspective, therefore, the three principal dimensions of workplace voice may be specified as *form*, *agenda*, and *influence*. Alternatively, Marchington and Suter (2013) call these same dimensions level, scope, and degree. Each dimension, in turn, varies along a continuum with end points defined by polarities. For example, the three voice dimensions may be represented as (with correlates):

- direct versus indirect (individual, face to face versus collective, representative);
- shared versus contested (integrative, win–win versus distributive, win–lose);
- communication versus influence (suggestion, complaint versus cost–benefit action).

These dimensions of voice yield a matrix with eight permutations. This typology helps define the conceptual nature of employee voice and dimensionalizes it into meaningful categories for theoretical and empirical analysis. Additional insight is provided by going yet another analytical step. In a chapter on conceptualizing employee participation, Wilkinson et al. (2010) present in diagrammatic form an Escalator of Participation (p. 11). It is a forward-sloped line with five steps going from low to high participation.

Figure 13.1 repackages this idea as an Escalator of Voice or, alternatively, Menu of Voice Options. At the low end of breadth, depth, and influence is the

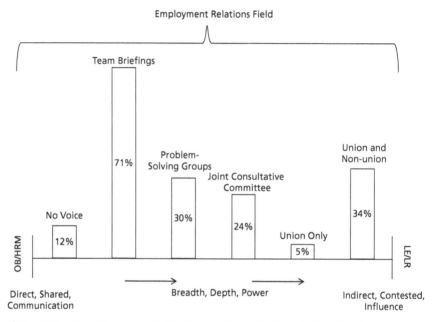

Figure 13.1. Voice Frequency Distribution and Menu Options: United Kingdom
Source: Willman et al. (2009, tables 1 and 3).

triplet: direct, shared, and communication; at the high end is the triplet: indirect, contested, and influence; and positioned between these end points are the remaining six permutations. The exact order is not essential for the model in Figure 13.1. Above the voice continuum is written *Employment Relations Field* to show that it covers *all* forms of voice, indicated by the encompassing bracket. The initials OB/HRM are placed at the low voice end and LE/LR (for Labour Economics/Labour Relations) are placed at the high end of the continuum. This reflects, as a useful generalization, that studies in OB/HRM tend to focus on voice permutations emphasizing individual, integrative, and communication modes typically utilizing small-scale and simple/informal organizational structures (for example, an open-door policy) while studies in LE/LR tend to focus on collective, contested, and power modes often featuring large-scale and complex/formalized structures (for example, an independent labour union). Also shown in Figure 13.1 is a voice frequency distribution displayed above the continuum. It is a plot of data showing the percentage of British workplaces (twenty-five or more people) in 2004 with various voice forms. British data are used because they come from a nationally representative source (the 2004 WERS) and the country's legal system is one of the least restrictive regarding employer–employee choice among voice options (Freeman et al. 2007; Willman et al. 2009).

In this survey only a small minority (12 per cent) of workplaces are reported as no voice, meaning absence of at least one *formal* voice mechanism (informal voice may well still be present). Of the 88 per cent that have a voice mechanism, they sort into three broad categories, with a fourth small residual category 'nature not reported' (2 per cent): non-union only (48 per cent), union and non-union (34 per cent, aka dual channel), and union only (4 per cent). In Figure 13.1, the no voice option is placed at the left-hand end point (least influence), the combined union/non-union voice option is placed at the right-hand end point (having the most forms of voice and thus presumptively the widest and deepest influence), and non-union only and union only occupy positions to the left and right of the middle. If autonomy and use of distributive power tactics are given considerable weight in ordering voice forms, the union only category would move to the end point (again, not important to the model).

Rather than show just the non-union only category, it is modestly disaggregated to show three particular types of voice arrangements. They are: team briefings (71 per cent), problem-solving groups (30 per cent), and joint consultative committees (24 per cent).These three voice forms are selected from a longer list provided by WERS for the non-union only category because they help draw out the visual/descriptive notion of a voice frequency distribution and, also, illustrate the voice escalator idea in terms of ascending from direct and mostly communication forms to indirect and greater influence forms. Note that the bars in Figure 13.1 do not sum to 100 per cent because the percentages for these three items are non-commensurate (*within* frequency for non-union only).

The voice escalator and frequency distribution in Figure 13.1 give a diagrammatic representation of the dependent variable in an employment relations model. Similarly, they call attention to five particular facets of the dependent variable which require explanation: (1) the existence of a continuum of voice types; (2) the shape of the distribution (variance, skewness); (3) the location of particular organizations along the continuum; (4) the major contingency variables that influence an organization's choice of voice form; and (5) reasons for change in the voice distribution across industries, nations, and over time.

INDEPENDENT AND CONTINGENCY VARIABLES

The voice frequency distribution in Figure 13.1 is a specification of the voice dependent variable that is consistent with a broad ER approach to industrial relations. The next step is to identify ER-appropriate independent variables. This step, if it is to be more than ad hoc, requires a model and, in particular, a model of the employment relationship.

A diagrammatic representation of the employment relationship is shown in Figure 13.2. Four key institutions are depicted: the external labour market in panel (a), the firm and internal labour market (including production function at the bottom of the pyramid) in panel (b), an employer, employee and HR/IR representative (the ER intermediary or 'middle man') in panel (c), and the nation state, represented as the 'roof' over the three panels, that sets the rules of the game for the ER. The photo in panel (c) represents what I have earlier claimed to be the birth picture of the early American IR field (Kaufman 2010). It was taken in 1914 when Rockefeller (employer on the right) and King (IR advisor in the middle) travelled to Colorado to meet with employees, such as Archie Dennison on the left, and introduce the new employee representation plan (Gitelman 1988; Rees 2010). Before the plan, the company was located near the zero end of the continuum in Figure 13.1 (no formal and very little informal voice); after its establishment the company moved considerably towards the right-hand side of the continuum—akin in modern terms to the adoption of a fairly advanced company-wide joint consultative committee (JCC; see Pyman 2014).

What independent variable should an ER theory start with to explain the voice frequency distribution? The data in Figure 13.1 reflect voice outcomes across all employment relationships; as observed earlier, therefore, logic says that the four ER frames of reference in Table 13.1 are a central independent variable because they collectively generate the empirical pattern. If 100 per cent of employment relationships are represented by the individualist frame, for example, the frequency distribution degenerates to a single point massed at no voice. Alternatively, if the economy is evenly divided between

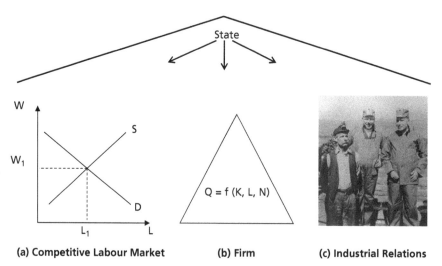

Figure 13.2. The Employment Relationship

the four frames of reference then the frequency distribution is more likely to resemble a horizontal line (uniform distribution).

To make further headway in specifying an explanatory voice model, it is necessary to identify the variables that cause firms to sort into each frame. It is an insightful prediction, for example, to be able to say: if 100 per cent of firms are in the individualist frame, formal voice options = 0 per cent. Even more insight is provided, however, by also explaining *why* all firms locate in this one frame. More generally stated, explanation of the distribution of employee voice types in Figure 13.1 requires explanation of the distribution of firms across frames of reference in Table 13.1. This topic is a major theoretical challenge and not one yet accomplished. The most that can be done here is to take a forward step. Although simple, the model of the employment relationship in Figure 13.2 provides help.

The domain of the economy which is covered by external labour markets (ELMs) in panel (a) versus internal labour markets (ILMs) in panel (b) is surely an important explanatory variable. If ELMs are large and ILMs are small, most worker dissatisfaction is expressed through exit; similarly, managers of small firms with simple production technologies and hire/fire HRM get little profit return from investment in voice structures. Fast-food restaurants are an example. If ILMs in Figure 13.2 are large and ELMs are small, the economy is populated by relatively few mega-corporations, such as General Motors and Microsoft. Many employees have long-tenure jobs and desire internal voice options for both communication and influence, perhaps including collective bargaining. Likewise, substantial breadth and depth of voice options is a paying investment for the companies because they improve organizational coordination, foster stronger loyalty and commitment among employees, and prevent a snowballing of unresolved employee dissatisfaction and complaints. The implication is that places to search for independent variables to explain the distribution of frames of reference are literatures on the firm-market boundary, organizational configurations, HRM architectures, employment relation systems, and transaction costs (Lepak and Snell 2007; Gibbons and Roberts 2012; Grandori 2013; Kaufman 2013b, 2013c). A concrete example is the extent to which work skills are general in nature (ELMs are larger) or firm specific (ILMs are larger).

Another place to look for independent variables is in the structure of ELMs in panel (a) and the structure of firms and ILMs in panel (b). If labour markets, for example, are monopsonistic—say due to few firms and costly worker mobility—employers have a superior bargaining position and can exploit workers by paying below competitive wages and conditions. In this case the competitive demand–supply diagram in panel (a) is replaced with a monopsony diagram (Manning 2003; Kaufman 2010). We can predict, other things equal, that workers have a greater demand for not only voice but voice backed up with muscle, such as possessed by large and powerful trade unions.

Or, assume two firms are of equal employment size but one is decentralized into numerous operating divisions and small plants while the other is centralized into one large bureaucratic organization at a central location. In this case, the pyramid in panel (b) remains the same size but instead of having many sub-pyramids inside (a plethora of small ILMs) it agglomerates into one comprehensive pyramid (one large ILM). A more decentralized organizational structure, other things equal, can be predicted to lead to a smaller-scale and more decentralized voice system (Marsden and Canibaño 2010; Waldman 2013).

Keeping the focus on the market and firm, other determinants of frames of reference can be identified. A key consideration, for example, is the degree to which employer–employee interests are divergent or aligned. A relevant independent variable is corporate governance, such as shareholder versus stakeholder models (Gospel and Pendelton 2010). Another is the profit level of the firm, on the presumption that firms with little profit vigorously cost minimize and have adversarial relations while those with substantial profitability can share rents and gain amicable employee relations (Brown 2008). Yet another relevant contingency variable is the unemployment rate in the economy and extent of boom and bust cycles. High unemployment makes employees reluctant to use individual voice for fear of being easily replaced and, at the same time, more desirous of strong collective voice in order to guard against work intensification and cuts in wages and conditions (Webb and Webb 1897; Gall and Hebdon 2008; Godard 2008). Also, boom and bust cycles make firms less willing to invest in long-term investments in ILMs, specific human capital, and other high performance work practices, thus reducing their demand for formalized voice and involvement systems (Kaufman 2013a). On the other hand, this same condition can expose workers to considerable insecurity and hardship from layoffs and income loss, laying the groundwork for them to look at the employment relationship through a critical frame (Thompson 2003). A final consideration to mention is various worker characteristics, such as skill level, gender, ethnicity, and culture (Wailes and Lansbury 2010). A voice system that fits American cultural values, for example, is typically a poor fit with Asian values (for example, individual versus collective orientation, tolerance for authority and power distance).

The third part of Figure 13.2 is the roof over the market and firm. It represents the nation state. A particular strong point of the industrial relations tradition is its political economy orientation (Hyman 2008). Commons, for example, gave his magnum opus *Institutional Economics* (1934) the subtitle *Its Place in Political Economy* and made 'sovereignty' one of the five core variables. The roof over the market and firm depicts the idea that the nation state through the exercise of sovereignty shapes the socio-economic order by specifying property rights, resource endowments, individual rights, duties and liberties, and the rules of production and exchange (Kaufman 2010,

2013c). The employment relationship, therefore, is politically constructed, starting with the sovereign's decision whether to organize the economy as a private property and for-profit capitalist system or collective property not-for-profit socialist system. The influence of politics extends into a myriad of other ramifications, such as coordinated market versus liberal market economy, macroeconomic management of the economy, extent and generosity of social welfare programmes, and encouragement or suppression of trade unions (Hamann and Kelly 2008; Frege and Godard 2010; Kaufman 2011).

Cross-country variation in the relative presence and strength of alternative frames of reference has an obvious bearing on the characteristics of the voice frequency distribution in Figure 13.1. Not surprisingly, for example, the voice frequency distribution in the USA is more concentrated in the left-hand half of the diagram (7 per cent private sector union density, no works councils, and few JCCs) while that for Sweden is more concentrated in the right-hand half (68 per cent union density, a variety of joint-enterprise-based councils and committees). The voice distribution within a country is also vitally shaped by the legal framework. The legal regime in the UK, for example, imposes few legal restrictions on the form of employee voice and, as a result, has a highly diverse distribution of voice forms (Freeman et al. 2007); the USA, in contrast, has legally banned all forms of non-union employee representation that engage in bilateral dealing with employers over terms and conditions of employment (Kaufman and Taras 2000). A general finding is that workers want more voice opportunity and influence than employers want to provide, leading to what Freeman and Rogers (1999) call a participation–representation gap. Political action to get more voice-friendly laws is one way workers have to reduce the voice gap. However, political action is a two-way street. Freeman et al. (2007) find evidence of sizable participation–representation gaps across six Anglo-American nations. These gaps may indicate that voice undersupply is a structural feature of the capitalist employment relationship, perhaps exacerbated by employers' dominant position in shaping labour law.

Predicting and explaining the future of employee voice: the American case

I have elaborated the 'if A then B – given C' model of employee voice with a description of the dependent employee voice variable, represented by the frequency distribution in Figure 13.1, and various key independent and contingent variables, such as the incidence of the four frames of reference, the determinants of each, and the central role of government rule making. It is useful to put this model to the test by considering a forecast of how the dependent variable—the voice frequency distribution—will change between now and, say, 2020. I hope to save myself too much embarrassment six years from now by noting that this exercise is built on a number of contingencies that could change in ways opposite to my assumptions. Nonetheless, for a field that has a paucity of actionable theory it is a useful exercise to take ER principles and show how they generate a forecast (elaborated in Kaufman 2012b), even if it proves wide of the mark.

The place to begin is with the four frames of reference. The future of employee voice depends, in part, on the compositional shift over the next six years among the four frames. If a greater share of employment relationships fall in the unitarist frame, the forecast for employee voice goes in one direction; if a greater share falls in the critical frame then the forecast goes in a different direction. Also, one has to look within each frame at the intensity of the employment relationship experience; for example, is the sense of unitarism or radicalism weakening or growing among that group of companies and workers?

My forecast for the USA is that the unitarist share shrinks in terms of both share and intensity and the other three frames experience net growth. Shrinkage of unitarism is signalled by visible indicators, such as the erosion of ILMs, less job security, and fewer high performance work systems (HPWS) organizations (Blasi and Kruse 2006; Cappelli 2008). To the degree this forecast is accurate, one can readily infer that unitarist types of employee voice, such as involvement programmes and representational forums, will stagnate and probably shrink. The major exception to this forecast is if the National Labor Relations Act's (NLRA's) company union ban is considerably liberalized so non-union companies can form and operate representational committees and councils. However, the American business community is not exerting visible political pressure for such a move so it seems unlikely—probably because the HPWS-involvement wave passed a decade or more ago, companies successfully operate non-union committees under the NLRA's legal radar, and opening up the NLRA to revision could carry larger costs (stronger protection of the right to organize) than benefits (relaxation of the ban on company unions) (LeRoy 2014).

This not-so-bright forecast puts me at odds with the strategic HRM literature which predicts growth in high performance work systems (Becker and Huselid 2006). However, I regard this literature as naively optimistic and out of touch with the worsening environment for unitarist-based employment relations. I note a caveat to my prediction, however. Companies retrenching from a strong unitarist system (described in Kaufman 2013a) through layoffs and cutbacks may nonetheless implement or continue to utilize employee voice forms as a way to preserve a core of positive employee sentiment, successfully manage the downsizing process, or practise a preventive form of union avoidance.

My pessimistic forecast for *fewer* unitarist organizations in the USA arises from a factor repeatedly cited in the HRM literature as likely to spur *more* unitarism. This factor is the increase in competitive pressure American companies face in global and domestic product markets. The HRM hypothesis is that in the face of greater competition, and the erosion of profit margins it brings, firms react by moving upstream to an HPWS employment system since it yields higher labour productivity (thus lower unit production cost) and is more difficult for competitors to imitate. This scenario is possible but, in my estimation, not probable. Rather, I think industrial relations gets closer to the truth in thinking that intensified competition in product markets, at least past some intermediate point, inevitably leads not to the unitarist frame and HPWS but towards the individualist frame and commodification of labour, the gutting of ILMs, and replacement of positive-sum with zero-sum employment relationships (Kaufman 2010, 2012a).

In Figure 13.2, what I see over the next six years in relative terms is an expanding role of ELMs in panel (a), a shrinking role for ILMs in panel (b), and less close and friendly relations between worker and employer in panel (c). This scenario means movement to a lower performing set of frames of reference and, in Figure 13.1, a change in the voice frequency distribution with less incidence and reduced breadth/depth of non-union voice forms in the left-middle section of the continuum and larger concentration of firms at the left-side no voice end point.

Just as my forecast diverges from that of my HRM colleagues, so too does it diverge in an important respect from my colleagues in labour economics. Assuming competitive pressure continues to intensify across the American economy (from globalization and financialization, for example), the likely scenario is as labour economists predict. That is, labour markets should follow product markets and also become more competitive, with erosion and shrinkage of ILMs and other organizational/HRM practices. The conventional view is that these institutional structures represent 'frictions', 'wedges', and 'imperfections' in the market and thus interfere with competitive demand–supply and cause inefficiency in ELM outcomes (Boeri and Van Ours 2008). In this model, as ELMs expand and ILMs contract in Figure 13.2, the relationship between Dennison the worker and Rockefeller the employer in panel (c) becomes more market mediated, impersonal, and distant, King located between them—representing HRM/IR—is no longer needed with consequent savings in resources and an increase in efficiency, and exit replaces voice in the ER. From a neoclassical perspective, therefore, a condition of 'more competition' is good for all parties to the employment relationship because all sides gain from trade, with a consequent decrease in the need and survival ability of both union and non-union voice forms (Kaufman 2010,

2013c). That is, the former disappear because market forces take over the protection of workers and bankrupt high-cost unionized firms, and the latter disappear because market-coordinated exit is more effective and cheaper than management-coordinated internal voice. The voice frequency distribution, therefore, flattens out and concentrates towards the no voice end of the continuum until, in a state of perfect competition, all firms are one person entities (sole proprietorships, individual contractors), the employment relationship disappears, and the voice frequency distribution is a single point at zero (Kaufman 2010).

This view too is incomplete and misleading. It predicts efficiency and harmony of interests from demand and supply in free labour markets when reality tends towards the opposite. The reason is the foundation idea of industrial relations—firms are not technological production functions and workers are not inanimate commodities and, hence, neither perform well if not buffered from the volatility, insecurity, risk, and opportunism that go with unrestricted competition (Commons 1921; Polanyi 1944; Budd 2004; Kaufman 2010). My forecast for the USA, therefore, is less optimistic than is probably found in labour economics because, from an IR perspective, further intensification in market competition is likely to reduce rather than increase the efficiency of employment relationships; also likely is the corrosion of trust, confidence, equity, and job satisfaction upon which effective and peaceful employment relations are built (Rockefeller 1923; Hicks 1941; Fox 1974). I agree with the prediction of economic theory, therefore, that the short-run consequence of more competition is less organized and formal voice; my diagnosis, however, is that this result is likely associated with a deterioration in job quality and employer–employee relations and sets the stage for a possible backlash. This conclusion is particularly so to the extent that greater market competition is accompanied by a neoliberal-inspired erosion in the safety net provided by protective labour law and social insurance programmes.

Consideration of the unitarist and individualist frames, in conjunction with the maintained assumption of growing competitive conditions in markets, leads to the prediction that both union and nonunion voice forms will likely shrink in frequency, breadth, and influence between now and 2020. However, we have not considered the pluralist and critical frames and key contingencies. Expansion of the individualist free market frame brings with it, albeit perhaps with some lag, an expansion in the pluralist and critical frames. Although free labour markets seem to promise wider choice and more opportunities, or greater 'positive liberty', for many people the experience is actually greater 'negative liberty' from the freedom to experience wage cuts, hours increases, at-will terminations, and repeated job searches (Polanyi 1944; McGovern et al. 2007; Osterman and Shulman 2011). From these experiences with free markets come emotional perceptions, such as insecurity, exploitation, and injustice, that fuel growing employee disenchantment with employers and the capitalism system and the spread of pluralist and radical sentiments (Kelly 1998). Part of my 2020 forecast, therefore, is the shrinking of the unitarist frame, spread of the individualist frame, and resulting shift towards pluralist and critical frames.

Since radical-left sentiments and solutions are unpopular and discouraged in American socio-political life, whatever increase takes place in the critical frame is likely to remain small and mostly latent. I am sceptical, however, that even a significant drift towards the traditional IR pluralist frame will move the ER system towards greater voice for workers. We have seen over two centuries of experience that the default option in American society is individual action, reflected in preference for competitive market solutions, scepticism-to-hostility towards organized labour, and distrust of government regulation and social welfare programmes (Lipset and Katchanovski 2004). Although surveys find anywhere from 30 per cent to 50 per cent of workers express an interest in union representation (Lipset et al. 2004; Freeman et al. 2007), I doubt that deteriorating job market conditions for many American workers will overcome long-standing cultural-political traditions and lead them to take a new look at unions. They will do so, I believe, only in dire circumstances when other solutions appear to be out of reach *and* the employer class and neoliberal market regime are widely seen as the source of the problem. This type of progressive-left tilt in union joining and national labour policy seems highly unlikely, however, even with further economic stagnation and inequality. The political process (the roof in Figure 13.2) is so polarized and dominated by conservative factions, and these factions have so successfully shifted blame to government, progressives, and minorities, that the more likely direction to 2020 is further legal restriction of unions, as recently enacted in several American states. I expect, therefore, that union density and collective bargaining activity will continue to decline to 2020 and, if any accommodation to workers comes from government, it will take the form of strengthened employment law rather than labour law.

Of course, the IR forecaster does well to remember the ignoble fate meted out to another scholar predicting continued union decline. George Barnett, one of the nation's most respected labour economists (Johns Hopkins University), had a model of employee voice in his mind when he told fellow economists in his presidential address to the American Economics Association in December, 1932 (Barnett 1933), 'We may take it probable that trade unionism is likely to be a declining influence in determining the conditions of labour' (p. 6). Unfortunately for Barnett, within six months a wave of strikes and union organizing erupted and then snowballed into the formation of the CIO (Congress of Industrial Organizations) and mass unionization of industry. Barnett erred by not at least qualifying his prediction with 'other things equal' (Kaufman 2001). More fundamentally, however, when Barnett estimated his latent voice regression model he failed to consider the effect of change in two hugely important contingency variables, the Great Depression and the New Deal. The former radicalized workers, the second encouraged them to mobilize into unions, and the combination caused a giant intercept shift in his model and spike in union density. Barnett, naturally, looked foolish and saw a respected career tarnished by what seemed to be a spectacularly ill-informed forecast, although no one at the time—including newly elected Franklin Roosevelt—could see the pro-union direction the New Deal was ultimately to take. (An observer estimated the enactment of the NLRA in 1935 as a 200–1 long shot.) And, in hindsight, perhaps Barnett did not err so badly since—to the forecasting surprise of many IR academics in the 1950s–70s (see symposium summary on 'The Future of Industrial Relations', *Industrial Relations*, Winter 1983)—the pro-union shift variables lost their effect, employers remobilized, and union density began a half-century slide (aka: regression to the mostly non-union mean) that leaves it, for the U.S. private sector, less than when Barnett made his prediction.

My forecast of further union decline to 2020, and overall shrinkage in breadth and depth of workplace voice, is conditioned, therefore, on 'other things equal' and the expectation that the USA does not in the next six years experience some similar 1930s-like bout of labour radicalization and pro-union legal enactment. I assert 'other things equal', however, with some hesitancy because I would not be surprised to see some kind of deeper economic crisis ahead, in part due to factors that precipitated the Great Depression (for example, growing income and wealth inequality). But the timing and probability are unknowable, at least to this amateur forecaster, and it is not at all evident that a crisis would redound to the benefit of unions or, more generally, enhanced employee voice and power. So, I note these contingencies but stick with my 'slow decline' forecast. If, however, for reasons I have missed the American workforce takes to the streets and transforms so-far quiescent voice into what Adam Smith (1776/1937) described as 'animated clamour', I will decamp to find George Barnett so in solace and companionship we can re-read the IR classics to find the key variables and cause–effect relationships we left out of our voice models. Or, perhaps, the problem will be diagnosed as outdated statistical software packages in our cranial computers.

Conclusion

People have been writing about employee voice, and using the term 'voice', for more than two centuries (Kaufman 2014). Most researchers, however, date the first theoretical treatment of voice to Hirschman (1970). Actually, Hirschman only considered voice in the context of dissatisfied consumers so it was another one and a half decades before Freeman and Medoff (1984) applied Hirschman's model to the workplace and employer–employee relations. Since then, numerous writers have contributed additional frameworks and models of employee voice and the literature has spread across all work-related fields. In this chapter, I have sought to promote further integration and the development of employee voice theory with an 'employment relation's' model. This model brings under one theoretical roof all forms and types of employee voice and provides a more analytically structured way to conceptualize the dependent, independent, and contingent–contextual variables for theoretical and empirical voice analysis. A model provides more value added if it helps to explain and predict concrete behaviour in the real world. To indicate the possibilities, the model developed in this chapter is used to forecast the likely trend in employee voice in the USA to the year 2020. Absent economic-political upheaval, the likely trend is erosion and decentralization of organized voice forms.

■ REFERENCES

Addison, J. (2005) 'The Determinants of Firm Performance: Unions, Works Councils, and Employee Involvement/High Performance Work Practices'. *Scottish Journal of Political Economy*, 52: 406–50.

Avgar, A. and Owens, S. (2014) 'Voice in the Mutual Gains Organization'. In A. Wilkinson, J. Donaghey, T. Dundon, and R. Freeman (eds), *The Handbook of Research on Employee Voice*. Northampton: Elgar.

Barnett, G. (1933) 'American Trade Unions and Social Insurance'. *American Economic Review*, 23: 1–15.

Becker, B. and Huselid, M. (2006) 'Strategic Human Resource Management: Where Do We Go from Here?' *Journal of Management*, 32: 898–925.

Blasi, J. and Kruse, D. (2006) 'U.S. High Performance Work Practices at Century's End'. *Industrial Relations*, 45: 457–78.

Boeri, T. and Van Ours, J. (2008) *The Economics of Imperfect Labour Markets*. Princeton: Princeton University Press.

Bowles, S. (2004) *Microeconomics: Behavior, Institutions, and Evolution*. Princeton: Princeton University Press.

Brown, W. (2008) 'The Influence of Product Markets on Industrial Relations'. In P. Blyton, N. Bacon, J. Fiorito, and E. Heery (eds), *The Sage Handbook of Industrial Relations*, pp. 113–28. London: Sage.

Budd, J. (2004) *Employment with a Human Face*. Ithaca, NY: Cornell University Press.

Budd, J. and Bhave, D. (2008) 'Values, Ideologies, and Frames of Reference in Industrial Relations'. In P. Blyton, N. Bacon, J. Fiorito, and E. Heery (eds), *The Sage Handbook of Industrial Relations*, pp. 92–112. London: Sage.

Cappelli, P. (2008) *Employment Relationships: New Models of White-Collar Work*. New York: Cambridge University Press.

Commons, J. (1921) 'Industrial Relations'. In J. Commons (ed.), *Trade Unionism and Labor Problems*, rev. edn, pp. 1–16. New York: Kelly.

Commons, J. (1934) *Institutional Economics: Its Place in Political Economy*. New York: Macmillan.

Dundon, T. and Gollan, P. (2007) 'Re-Conceptualizing Voice in the Non-Union Workplace'. *International Journal of Human Resource Management*, 18: 1182–98.

Dundon, T., Wilkinson, A., Marchington, M., and Ackers, P. (2004) 'The Meanings and Purpose of Employee Voice'. *International Journal of Human Resource Management*, 15: 1149–70.

Fox, A. (1966) *Industrial Sociology and Industrial Relations*. Royal Commission on Trade Unions and Employers' Associations Research Paper 3. London: HMSO.

Fox, A. (1974) *Beyond Contract: Work, Power, and Trust Relations*. London: Faber and Faber.

Freeman, R., Boxall, P., and Haynes, P. (2007) *What Workers Say: Employee Voice in the Anglo-American Workplace*. Ithaca, NY: Cornell University Press.

Freeman, R. and Medoff, J. (1984) *What Do Unions Do?* New York: Basic Books.

Freeman, R. and Rogers, J. (1999) *What Workers Want*. Ithaca, NY: Cornell University Press.

Frege, C. and Godard, J. (2010) 'Cross-National Variation in Representation Rights and Governance at Work'. In A. Wilkinson, P. Gollan, M. Marchington, and D. Lewin (eds), *Oxford Handbook of Participation in Organizations*, pp. 526–51. New York: Oxford University Press.

Gall, G. (2003) 'Marxism and Industrial Relations'. In P. Ackers and A. Wilkinson (eds), *Understanding Work and Employment: Industrial Relations in Transition*, pp. 316–24. Oxford: Oxford University Press.

Gall, G. and Hebdon, R. (2008) 'Conflict at Work'. In P. Blyton, N. Bacon, J. Fiorito, and E. Heery (eds), *The Sage Handbook of Industrial Relations*, pp. 588–605. London: Sage.

Gibbons, R. and Roberts, J. (2012) *Handbook of Organizational Economics*. Princeton: Princeton University Press.

Gitelman, H. (1988) *The Legacy of the Ludlow Massacre: A Chapter in American Industrial Relations*. Philadelphia: University of Pennsylvania Press.

Godard, J. (2008) 'Union Formation'. In P. Blyton, N. Bacon, J. Fiorito, and E. Heery (eds), *The Sage Handbook of Industrial Relations*, pp. 377–405. London: Sage.

Gospel, H. and Pendelton, A. (2010) 'Corporate Governance and Employee Participation'. In A. Wilkinson, P. Gollan, M. Marchington, and D. Lewin (eds), *Oxford Handbook of Participation in Organizations*, pp. 504–25. New York: Oxford University Press.

Grandori, A. (2013) *Handbook of Economic Organization*. Northampton: Elgar.

Hamann, K. and Kelly, J. (2008) 'Varieties of Capitalism and Industrial Relations'. In P. Blyton, N. Bacon, J. Fiorito, and E. Heery (eds), *The Sage Handbook of Industrial Relations*, pp. 129–48. London: Sage.

Heery, E., Bacon, N., Blyton, P., and Fiorito, J. (2008) 'Introduction: The Field of Industrial Relations'. In P. Blyton, N. Bacon, J. Fiorito, and E. Heery (eds), *The Sage Handbook of Industrial Relations*, pp. 1–32. London: Sage.

Hicks, C. (1941) *My Life in Industrial Relations*. New York: Harper.

Hirschman, A. (1970) *Exit, Voice, and Loyalty*. Cambridge, MA: Harvard University Press.

Hyman, R. (1975) *Industrial Relations: A Marxist Introduction*. London: Macmillan.

Hyman, R. (2008) 'The State in Industrial Relations'. In P. Blyton, N. Bacon, J. Fiorito, and E. Heery (eds), *The Sage Handbook of Industrial Relations*, pp. 258–83. London: Sage.

Kaufman, B. (2001) 'The Future of U.S. Private Sector Unionism: Did George Barnett Get It Right after All?' *Journal of Labour Research*, 22: 433–58.

Kaufman, B. (2010) 'The Theoretical Foundations of Industrial Relations and Its Implications for Labour Economics and Human Resource Management'. *Industrial and Labour Relations Review*, 54: 74–108.

Kaufman, B. (2011) 'Comparative Employment Relations: Institutional and Neo-Institutional Theories'. In M. Barry and A. Wilkinson (eds), *Research Handbook of Comparative Employment Relations*, pp. 25–55. Northampton: Elgar.

Kaufman, B. (2012a) 'Strategic Human Resource Management Research in the United States: A Failing Grade after 30 Years?' *Academy of Management Review*, 26: 12–36.

Kaufman, B. (2012b) 'The Future of Employment Relations: Insights from Theory'. In K. Townsend and A. Wilkinson (eds), *Research Handbook on the Future of Work and Employment Relations*, pp. 13–44. Northampton: Elgar.

Kaufman, B. (2013a) 'Keeping the Commitment Model in the Air during Turbulent Times:Employee Involvement at Delta Air Lines'. *Industrial Relations*, 52: 343–77.

Kaufman, B. (2013b) 'The Economic Organization of Employment: Systems in Human Resource Management and Industrial Relations'. In A. Grandori (ed.), *Handbook of Economic Organization*, 289–311. Northampton: Elgar.

Kaufman, B. (2013c) 'The Optimal Level of Market Competition: Neoclassical and New Institutional Conclusions Critiqued and Reformulated'. *Journal of Economic Issues*, 47: 639–72.

Kaufman, B. (2014) 'Employee Voice before Hirschman: Its Early History, Conceptualization, and Practice'. In A. Wilkinson, J. Donnaghey, T. Dundon, and R. Freeman (eds), *The Handbook of Employee Voice*. Northampton: Elgar.

Kaufman, B. and Miller, B. (2011) 'The Firm's Choice of HRM Practices: Economics Meets Strategic Human Resource Management'. *Industrial and Labor Relations Review*, 65: 526–57.

Kaufman, B. and Taras, D. (2000) *Nonunion Employee Representation: History, Contemporary Practice, and Policy*. Armonk, NY: M. E. Sharpe.

Kelly, J. (1998) *Rethinking Industrial Relations: Mobilization, Collectivism, and Long Waves*. London: Routledge.

Kim, J., MacDuffie, J-P., and Pil, F. (2010) 'Employee Voice and Organizational Performance: Team Versus Representative Influence'. *Human Relations*, 63(3): 371–94.

Kochan, T. (1998) 'What Is Distinctive about Industrial Relations Research?' In K. Whitfield and G. Strauss (eds), *Researching the World of Work*, pp. 31–50. Ithaca, NY: Cornell University Press.

Lepak, D. and Snell, S. (2007) 'Employment Subsystems and the "HR Architecture"'. In P. Boxall, J. Purcell, and P. Wright (eds), *Oxford Handbook of Human Resource Management*, pp. 210–30. Oxford: Oxford University Press.

LeRoy, M. (2014) 'What Do NLRB Cases Reveal about Nonunion Employee Representation Groups?' A Typology from Post-*Electomation* Cases'. In P. Gollan, B. Kaufman, D. Taras, and A. Wilkinosn (eds), *Voice and Involvement at Work: Nonunion Employee Representation across Four Countries*. London: Routledge.

Lipset, S. and Katchanovski, I. (2004) 'The Future of Private Sector Unions in the U.S.' In J. Bennett and B. Kaufman (eds), *The Future of Private Sector Unionism in the United States*, pp. 9–27. Armonk, NY: M. E. Sharpe.

Lipset, S., Meltz, N., and Gomez, R. (2004) *The Paradox of American Unionism: Why Americans Like Unions More than Canadians Do but Join Much Less*. Ithaca, NY: Cornell University Press.

McGovern, P., Hill, S., Mills, C., and White, M. (2007) *Market, Class, and Employment*. Oxford: Oxford University Press.

Manning, A. (2003) *Monopsony in Motion*. Princeton: Princeton University Press.

Marchington, M., and Suter, J. (2013) 'Where Informality Really Matters: Patterns of Employee Involvement and Participation (EIP) in a Non-Union Firm'. *Industrial Relations*, 52: 284–313.

Marsden, D. and Canibaño, A. (2010) 'An Economic Perspective on Employee Participation'. In A. Wilkinson, P. Gollan, M. Marchington, and D. Lewin (eds), *Oxford Handbook of Participation in Organizations*, pp. 131–63. New York: Oxford University Press.

Morrison, E. (2011) 'Employee Voice Behavior: Integration and Directions for Future Research'. *Academy of Management Annals*, 5: 373–412.

Osterman, P. and Shulman, B. (2011) *Good Jobs America: Making Work Better for Everyone*. New York: Russell Sage.

Polanyi, K. (1944) *The Great Transformation*. New York: Farrar and Rinehart.

Pyman, A. (2014) 'Joint Consultative Committees'. In A. Wilkinson, J. Donaghey, T. Dundon, and R. Freeman (eds), *The Handbook of Research on Employee Voice*. Northampton: Elgar.

Rees, J. (2010) *Representation and Rebellion: The Rockefeller Plan at the Colorado Fuel and Iron Company 1914–1942*. Boulder: University of Colorado Press.

Rockefeller, J. (1923) *The Personal Relation in Industry*. New York: Boni and Liverwright.

Smith, A. (1776/1937) *An Inquiry into the Nature and Causes of the Wealth of Nations*. New York: Random House.

Thompson, P. (2003) 'Disconnected Capitalism: Or Why Employers Can't Keep Their Side of the Bargain'. *Work, Employment and Society*, 17: 359–78.

Wailes, N. and Lansbury, R. (2010) 'International and Comparative Perspectives on Employee Participation'. In A. Wilkinson, P. Gollan, M. Marchington, and D. Lewin (eds), *Oxford Handbook of Participation in Organizations*, pp. 570–89. Oxford: Oxford University Press.

Waldman, M. (2013) 'Theory and Evidence in Internal Labour Markets'. In R. Gibbons and J. Roberts (eds), *The Handbook of Organizational Economics*, 520–71. Princeton: Princeton University Press.

Webb, S. and Webb, B. (1897) *Industrial Democracy*. London: Longmans, Green.

Whitfield, K. and Strauss, G. (1998) *Researching the World of Work: Strategies and Methods in Studying Industrial Relations*. Ithaca, NY: Cornell University Press.

Wilkinson, A., Dundon, T., Marchington, M., and Ackers, P. (2004) 'Changing Patterns of Employee Voice: Case Studies from the UK and Republic of Ireland', *The Journal of Industrial Relations*, 46(3), 298–322.

Wilkinson, A., Gollan, P., Marchington, M., and Lewin, D. (2010) 'Conceptualizing Employee Participation in Organizations'. In A. Wilkinson, P. Gollan, M. Marchington, and D. Lewin (eds), *Oxford Handbook of Participation in Organizations*, pp. 3–25. Oxford: Oxford University Press.

Wilkinson, A., Donaghey, J., Dundon, T., and Freeman, R. (2014) *The Handbook of Research on Employee Voice*. Northampton: Elgar.

Willman, P., Gomez, R., and Bryson, A. (2009) 'Voice at the Workplace: Where Do We Find It, Why Is It There and Where Is It Going?' In W. Brown, A. Bryson, J. Forth, and K. Whitfield (eds), *The Evolution of the Modern Workplace*, pp. 97–119. Cambridge: Cambridge University Press.

Willman, P., Bryson, A., Gomez, R., and Kretschmer, T. (2014) 'Employee Voice and the Transaction Cost Economics Approach.' In A. Wilkinson, J. Donaghey, T. Dundon, and R. Freeman (eds), *The Handbook of Research on Employee Voice*. Northampton: Elgar.

■ INDEX